The Works of Edmund Spenser

A Variorum Edition

INDEX

TO THE POETRY

LONDON: OXFORD UNIVERSITY PRESS

THE WORKS

OF

EDMUND SPENSER

A Variorum Edition

Volume 9

EDITED BY

EDWIN GREENLAW

CHARLES GROSVENOR OSGOOD

FREDERICK MORGAN PADELFORD

RAY HEFFNER

Baltimore

THE JOHNS HOPKINS PRESS

INDEX

TO THE POETRY

COMPILED BY

CHARLES GROSVENOR OSGOOD

Baltimore

THE JOHNS HOPKINS PRESS

PREFATORY NOTE

Now index-learning turns no student pale
Yet holds the eel of science by the tail.

So Pope in his day might sneer. But his eel has since grown to a Leviathan, a Midgarth serpent, and indexes, however akin to Dullness, are indispensable. Nor is the making of an index so dull as might seem. It is, in fact, a work of imagination and memory. At every entry the compiler must stretch his imagination to include every reason, however curious, which a reader might have for consulting that entry. He must also remember not only the satisfactions he has enjoyed in a good index, but the exasperating frustrations he has suffered from a bad one. There are rules for index-making, of course, but rules that leave plenty of room for the maker's discretion. However mechanical the process, it may both amuse and entertain.

The names of the most frequent commentators I have omitted. If the index fails at any point, the Concordance, or C. H. Whitman's *Subject-Index*, or Sawtelle's or Lotspeich's studies of Spenser's mythology may pick up the trail.

An index to a single author is a simple task. An index to a hundred or two different commentators, in perverse disagreement on titles, names, terms, editions, texts, spelling, and often scant or careless in their references, is another matter. The attempt to reconcile these myriad differences and bring them into some sort of conformity has greatly delayed the compilation of this index. I can only hope that the reader's satisfactions may be many, and his exasperations—some are inevitable—may be very few.

To my friend, Dr. James Whaler, I am immeasurably indebted for help in reading the proof, and to the J. H. Furst Company for their skilful care and patience in producing this book.

C. G. O.

Princeton, January 15, 1957

CORRIGENDA

(except obvious misprints)

VOLUME 1

Page 184, line 13 up: *for* Meta *read* Mela
"   196, "   9 up: *for* 5. 812 *read* 812
"   205, "   18 down: *for* Langland *read* Langham
"   237, "   26 down: *for* 4-5 *read* xlv. 4-5
"   259, "   9 down: *for* 19 *read* 9
"   278, "   8 up: *delete* 5
"   306, "   20 up: *for* 482 *read* 422
"   311, "   4 down: *for* 2. 1. 1-4 *read* 2. 1-4
"   364, "   12 down: *for* hear *read* heart
"   390, "   7 up: *for* Montjoy *read* Mountjoy
"   497, "   17 down: *for* couchant *read* couching
"   509, "   20 down: *for* 1. 1 *read* 1. 11
"   510, "   17 down: *for* canto *read* book
"   551, "   19 up: *for* 8 vols *read* 9 vols

VOLUME 2

Page 216, line 10 down: *for* heavenly Love . . . 63 *read* Beauty . . . 253-4
"   231, "   20 down: *for* 4. 16 *read* 4. 10
"   234, "   19 up: *for* 43 *read* 42
"   247, "   6 down: *for* 1. 11 *read* 1. 10
"   253, "   10 down: *for* 4. 37 *read* 3. 37
"   291: *transfer note on* xxiv. 7 *to* xxiii, *page* 290
"   378, "   16 up: *for* 20 *read* 21
"   416, lines 13, 14, 15, 16 up: *rearrange in order* 16, 13, 15, 14
"   419, line   1 up: *for* 7. 17 *read* 7. 7
"   428, "   15 up: *for* Guyon *read* Red Cross Knight

VOLUME 3

Page 242, line   4 down: *delete line*
"   245, "   13 down: *for* out *read* our
"   331, "   4 down: *delete* 2.
"   362, "   5 down: *for* censors *read* censers

VOLUME 4

Page   50, stanza 21:   *for* Paliumord *read* Palimord
"   185, line 22 down: *for* 28 *read* 27
"   200, "   7 up: *for* metaphysical *read* metaphorical
"   201, "   7 down: *for* *Virgil's Gnat* 12 *read* *Visions of Bellay* 157-8
"   213, "   8 up: *delete* and 9. 1
"   213, "   6 up: *for* stanza *read* canto
"   278, "   17 up: *for* 8. 3 *read* 3
"   329, "   16 up: *for* 13. 50 *read* 14. 50

VOLUME 5

Page 166, line 11 up:	*for* 49 *read* 42
" 185, " 18 down:	*for* 1.(2 *read* 1.32
" 194, " 14 up:	*for* Herebus *read* Heberus
" 231, " 6 up:	*for* 701 *read* 601

VOLUME 6

Page 195, line 13 up: *for* R. Carew *read* G. Carew
" 267, " 21 down: *for* 517 *read* 654
" 303, " 11 down: *for* 23-20 *read* 27-30
" 409, lines 2, 3 down: *for* 457 ff., 173 ff., and 572 ff. *read* 2.457 ff., 3.173 ff., and 5.572 ff.

VOLUME 7

Page 27, line 11 down: *for* down *read* downe
" 27, " 5 up: *for* figuratively *read* figuratiuely
" 43, " 14 down: *for* himself *read* himselfe
" 57, " 10 up: *for* pupil *read* pupill
" 57, " 2 up: *for* That *read* The
" 75, " 7 up: *for* is supremacie *read* in supremacie
" 106, " 9 down: *for* have *read* haue
" 112, " 5 down: *for* might *read* night
" 115, " 69:   *for* Todestool *read* Todestoole
" 125, " 7 up: *for* Lyon *read* Lyon,
" 197, " 86:   *for* and *read* with
" 321, " 2 down: *for* 13 *read* B
" 337, " 14 down: *for* terebrinth *read* terebinth
" 341, " 9 down: *for* 839 *read* 5.839
" 353, " 14 up: *for* complaint of *read* complaint against Rome shading into the English complaint of
" 382, " 17 up: *for* refuses *read* enforces
" 382, " 16 up: *for* above *read* below
" 473, " 14 down: *for* 1693 *read* 1593
" 551, " 4 up: *for* 726 *read* 5.726
" 579, " 21 down: *for* 6 *read* 5
" 696, " 13 down: *for* Carl F. *read* Carl H

VOLUME 8

Page 285, line 8 down: *for* 423 *read* 323
" 663, " 9 up: *for* 1696 *read* 1596
" 741, " 18 up: *for* 234 *read* 254

INDEX

The references designate volume and page in the eight volumes of the Variorum containing the poetry thus disposed:

Volume 1: Faerie Queene, Book I
Volume 2: Faerie Queene, Book II
Volume 3: Faerie Queene, Book III
Volume 4: Faerie Queene, Book IV

Volume 5: Faerie Queene, Book V
Volume 6: Faerie Queene, Books VI-VII
Volume 7: Minor Poems, Part I
Volume 8: Minor Poems, Part II

Aaron, 7. 332-3; 8. 358-60
Abaster, 5. 213
Abbott, Edwin A., 7. 305
Abel, 7. 331-3
Abessa, 1. 461, 465, 467, 499; 6. 209
Abib, 7. 244
Abiogenesis, 1. 184-7; 3. 250-1, 342, 348; 6. 403, 409-10
Ablutions, 1. 287
Absalom, 4. 223
Abstemius, 8. 592
Abus, 2. 309
Académie Française, 7. 625
Accademia della Crusca, 7. 625
Acceleration, 1. 207
" Accepit omen," 5. 218
Accession Day, 2. 203; 5. 185; 8. 503
Acclamatio, 7. 247, 391, 444
Achates, 2. 219
" ache," 7. 340-1
Achefleur, 6. 368-9
Achelous, 3. 242
Acheron (beast), 1. 402-3
Acheron (river), 4. 196
Achilles, 1. 211, 246, 322, 511; 2. 218-9; 3. 218, 240; 4. 316; 5. 198, 200, 269; 6. 202; 7. 393, 509, 518-9, 642; 8. 301-2, 345, 472
Achilles Tatius, 6. 233-4, 372, 376, 379, 430-1; 8. 402
Acidale (brook), 8. 483
Acidale, Mount, 2. 372; 4. 194; 6. 247, 252, 285, 346; 8. 477
Acis, 4. 269
Acontius, 2. 264-6
Acrasia, 1. 346, 356; 2. 183-5, 192, 194, 234, 348-9, 351-2, 372-4, 376, 379, 383, 391-4, 402-3, 406, 410-2, 417-9, 426, 437, 462; 3. 363, 365; 6. 250; 7. 521; 8. 397; and Acratia: 2. 443-4; is Earthly Venus: 2.

430-1; a Celtic *fée*: 2. 447; is Incontinence: 2. 437; 3. 324
Acrates, 1. 230; 2. 231, 232, 404
Act of Supremacy, 1. 472
Actaeon, 3. 253, 392, 395; 6. 283, 285, 289-90, 409, 425-6, 430-2; 8. 396
Action, 1. 224
Active Life, 1. 224, 288-9, 415, 417, 513; 2. 423, 430; 3. 246, 327; 6. 358
Adagia Scotica, 7. 305
Adam, 1. 290, 301; 2. 429-31; 3. 256
Adamant, 2. 353, 355-6
Adams, T., 8. 479
Adare, 5. 174; 7. 475
Adders, 1. 183
Addison, Joseph, 5. 172; 7. 406, 617; 8. 371
Adicia, 5. 225-6, 232, 288, 314; 6. 194
Adjectives, 7. 272; 8. 530
Admetus, 3. 295
Adonio, 5. 169
Adonis, 1. 245; 3. 255, 260-1, 344, 346-7, 351-2, 393-4; 6. 398, 429; 7. 440, 486, 499, 505-7; 8. 396, 470. *See* Garden of Adonis
Adoxography, 8. 547-8
Adrastea, 3. 269
Adrastus, 3. 276
Adriatic Sea, 2. 254
Adventure, 1. 391-5, 399-401; 5. 243
Aeacidae, 6. 253
Aegina, 3. 397
Aegis, 1. 253-4; 5. 228
Aelfric, 1. 379
Aelian (Claudius Aelianus), 1. 184; 2. 360-3, 378; 6. 204; 7. 336
Aemonia, 7. 491
Aemylia, 4. 205, 208, 213, 323
Aeneas, 1. 340-1, 345, 357-8, 511; 2. 210, 219, 307, 351; 3. 281-2; 4. 223; 5. 226-7, 259; 6. 376; 7. 509, 519

1

Aeneas Silvius, 5. 199
Aengus ' Mac ind Oc ', 6. 426
Aeolian harp, 8. 308
Aeolus, 4. 214-5
Aeschines, 1. 270; 4. 172
Aeschylus, 3. 332; 6. 299; 7. 335-6, 440; 8. 396; *Agamemnon*: 5. 216, 249; *Eumenides*: 5. 217; 7. 285; fragment: 5. 255; *Prometheus Bound*: 1. 278; 3. 242; 4. 182; 6. 212; 7. 514; *Seven against Thebes*: 2. 230; 3. 264
Aesculapius, 1. 363; 3. 242-3; 6. 211
Aesop, 5. 189; 7. 260-2, 304, 356, 379, 599; 8. 405-7, 572, 578, 591-2, 610
Aetiologia, 7. 444
Aetion, 7. 448, 464, 472-4
Aetna, 1. 295, 304; 2. 292
Affectionate Shepherd, 7. 285-7
Agamede, 3. 246
Agamemnon, 1. 322, 341, 345, 511; 5. 200, 269; 8. 395, 510
Aganippe, 7. 281
Aganippus, 2. 315, 318
Agape, 4. 181, 283
Agave, 5. 231
Agdistes, 2. 351, 374-6; 6. 398
Age, 7. 255-9, 593-4
Agenor, 4. 246
Ages, 2. 299
The Ages of Sin, 1. 183
" aghast." *See* Amazement
Aglaia, 6. 251, 253
Agrippa, Cornelius, 3. 322, 338; 7. 561
Agrippa, Menenius, 4. 174
Aided Duinn, 6. 427
Aikin, J., 8. 371, 628
Ailill Aulom, 6. 426
Ailred, St., 4. 328
Aine, 6. 426
Air, 7. 263
Ajax, 1. 241; 6. 202, 207; 8. 344-5
Alabaster, William, 7. 448, 463, 469-70; 8. 319-20
Aladine, 6. 199, 324, 326-7, 334
Alain de Lille, 1. 448; 2. 374-5, 425; 3. 394; 5. 215; 6. 401, 403, 407, 413, 422-3, 428, 449; *Anticlaudianus*: 7. 285; *De Planctu Naturae*: 1. 418; 2. 433, 436-8; 6. 297, 396-8; and *F. Q.* 2: 2. 436-8; and *F. Q.* 4: 4. 333-4; and *F. Q.* 7: 6. 293-7; met. 1, pr. 1: 2. 437-8; pr. 1: 2. 433; 6. 293; pr. 2: 2. 437; 7. 283; pr. 3, 4: 6. 296; pr. 3: 1. 446; 2. 338, 437-8; 4. 227; 6. 293-4; met. 4: 4. 228; 6. 296; met. 5: 4. 217; pr. 6: 2. 377; pr. 8: 8. 473, 492; *Liber in Distinctionibus*: 1. 446; *Liber Parabolorum*: 7. 360

Alain li Gros, 6. 369
Alamanni, Luigi, 2. 205; 6. 187, 430-1; 7. 408; 8. 369
Alba Longa, 3. 281-2
Albanact, 2. 309; 4. 261
Albania, 2. 309, 315, 317; 4. 261
Albertus Magnus, 1. 355
Albion, 2. 304-8; 4. 246
Albion, Knight, 2. 434
Albricus, 6. 281
Albright, E. M., 3. 342; 4. 314-6; 5. 320-1, 236; 6. 401-4, 439-44, 447-8; 7. 310, 511, 550; 8. 331, 717
Alcestis, 2. 195; 7. 518-9; 8. 343
Alciati, Andreas, 2. 226-7; 5. 266; 7. 262, 289; 8. 405, 407-8, 456, 625-6
Alcibiades, 4. 164-5
Alcina, 1. 202, 204-5, 213, 262; 2. 183, 217, 394, 439, 441-3; 3. 253, 371; 4. 167, 317
Alcinous, 2. 242, 381. *See* Garden of Alcinous
Alcmena, 1. 265; 3. 253, 293-4; 8. 299, 310, 377, 484, 714
Alcon, 7. 464, 468
Alcuin, 2. 424, 426
Alcyon, 7. 431, 434, 437-9, 466-7, 501
Alcyone, 1. 382-4; 7. 434, 438-9
Alden, R. M., 8. 570
Aldine. *See* Aladine
Aldus, 2. 460; 6. 328
Aleman, Mateo, 7. 238
Alençon, Francis, Duke of, 1. 452; 2. 206, 219; 5. 185, 307; 7. 605; 8. 543-4, 567-8, 571, 578; is the Ape: 7. 603; 8. 574, 578-9; is Braggadochio: 2. 207, 219, 401-2; 3. 380; 5. 302; is Cymochles: 2. 404; is " frog ": 8. 571; is snake: 8. 543; is witch's son: 3. 379. *See also* Henry III of France
Alexander of Alexandria, 1. 309-10
Alexander the Great, 1. 238, 444; 4. 168, 278; 5. 191, 220; 6. 293; 7. 372, 392-3, 642; 8. 287, 300, 302, 328, 591-2
Alexandrian, 8. 395, 402, 544, 547-8
Alexandrine, 2. 389-90, 508; 3. 244, 292; 4. 225; 7. 395, 397, 400, 412, 641; 8. 415, 423, 643, 715, 719
Alexis, 7. 448, 463, 597
Alford, B. H., 3. 247
Alfred, King, 1. 483
Algrind, 7. 292-3, 296, 300, 323-4, 354, 582, 601. *See also* Grindal
Alichius, Andreas, 3. 206
Alienations, 8. 361-2
" alipedus," 6. 277; 8. 310
" all," 2. 195
Allectus, 2. 330

Allegations against the Surmised Title, 5. 320

Allegoria, 7. 246, 504; 8. 676

Allegory, 1. 181, 201-4, 207, 211, 213-4, 240, 312, 314-6, 323-4, 326-7, 338-40, 363-72; 2. 250, 438; 7. 682; Aristotelian: 2. 427; Catholic, 6. 208-9; and character: 3. 383-4; 8. 666; and Chivalry: 1. 416, 418; courtly: 7. 447; Elizabethans loved it: 1. 492; in Emblems: 8. 304, 625; in Established Church: 6. 209-10; in *F. Q.* 1-3: 3. 365; in *F. Q.* 1-2: 1. 345; in *F. Q.* 1: 1. 422-95; in *F. Q.* 5: 5. 225-8, 285-6, 299-335; historical: 1. 211, 244, 246, 251, 256, 264, 268, 275, 296, 308, 343-4, 349, 390; 3. 310-1, 377-80; 4. 205-6; 5. 211, 247-55; Italian: 1. 333, 335-7, 345, 366; limitations: 8. 666; of love: 1. 405-6; 3. 261, 357-9, 375-6, 391; 8. 475; in masques and pageants: 1. 473-82, 491, 494; 3. 353-9; medieval: 2. 437; 8. 511; moral: 1. 213, 217, 240, 244, 247, 256, 263-4, 270-1, 326-30, 336-7, 343, 349, 378, 396, 491; 2. 256; 5. 286; 8. 622; moral-historical preeminent in *F. Q.*: 1. 425; moral and political blended: 2. 339, 345; in mythology: 5. 234; 8. 402; Neoplatonic: 1. 358; and personification: 2. 412-3; allegorical persons: 2. 257; Platonic: 1. 341, 346; in Plutarch and Spenser: 5. 215; propriety of Spenser's: 1. 363-72; 8. 363; Protestant: 6. 208-9; in the Renaissance: 1. 341-2, 431; in romance, Italian and Spanish 6. 372; romantic fiction, mixed with: 1. 367; 2. 427-8; scholastic: 2. 427; shifting: 5. 310-11; spiritual: 1. 254, 263-4, 295, 301-2, 308, 309, 367-8, 422-48; and the "Vision": 8. 304. *See also* Ancients; Ariosto; *Faerie Queene*, Spenser, Edmund; Tasso; Virgil

Allen. Bog. of, 1. 188; 2. 282, 285

Allen, Francis, 7. 458

Allen, Hill of, 6. 425

Allen, P., 8. 319, 369, 375, 605

Allen, William, 7. 360

Alley, William, 7. 608

All for Money, 2. 433-4

Alliteration, 1. 194, 255, 281; 2. 221, 246, 304, 309, 367, 385; 4. 208; 5. 205; 6. 225; 7. 239, 245, 335, 360, 361, 365, 380, 385, 412, 483, 578, 618, 641, 647; 8. 332, 337, 415, 538; with asyndeton: 6. 309

Allo, 4. 266-7; 7. 455-6

Alluvion, 5. 194-5

Alma, 1. 346-7, 367; 2. 183, 185, 284, 286, 406, 416, 426, 427-8, 478. *See* Castle, House of Alma

Alma Mater, 4. 259

Almanacs, 7. 633-4

Alpheus, 4. 248; 6. 290, 409, 425; 7. 454

Altercatio, 6. 292-3

Althorpe, 7. 477; 8. 310-1, 501

Alton, 7. 475

Altrocchi, Rudolph, 8. 430

Alva, Duke of, 5. 247, 252-4; is Geryoneo: 5. 249; is Sansloy: 1. 449, 458-60; is seneschal: 5. 302

Amadas, Philip, 2. 185

Amadis, 5. 169

Amadis of Gaul, 1. 488; 2. 275; 3. 295, 360-2, 365; 6. 378-9

Amalteo, Giambattista, 7. 590

Amalthea, 6. 307

Amaranth, 3. 259; 8. 348-9

Amaryllis, 7. 471-2, 477. *See also* Spencer, Alice

Amavia, 2. 184, 194, 204, 402, 410, 427, 460

Amazement, 1. 268; 4. 175; 6. 193, 216, 237; 7. 478; 8. 304, 403, 421

Amazons, 2. 185, 219; 3. 331-2, 336; 4. 205, 248; 5. 196-200, 221

Ambassadors, 5. 226

Ambition, 1. 341; 2. 252, 286, 408, 414, 425-6, 427-9, 461; 5. 262; 7. 324, 352; 8. 576-7

Ambrose, 2. 332, 423-6

Ambrosia, 7. 403, 416; 8. 433, 512

America, 2. 185; 5. 248

American Antiquarian Society, 7. 708

Ametheus, 5. 213

Amictus, 1. 218

Amidas, 5. 195, 273, 278, 289, 296, 304

Amis and Amiloun, 1. 346; 4. 294, 303-4, 322-4

Amity, Masque of, 4. 315-6

Ammianus Marcellinus, 3. 250; 5. 225

Amoretta, 1. 441; 2. 348; 3. 256, 261-2, 303-4, 310-3, 316, 318, 320, 326, 329, 333, 353-6, 359, 362, 366; 4. 165, 173, 208, 215-6, 235, 283-4, 286-7; 6. 205, 230; 7. 519, 661; 8. 396, 446; character: 3. 381-6, 389-90; 4. 320-1; is Elizabeth Throckmorton: 4. 206-7; is Marquess of Northampton: 3. 378; is Mary Queen of Scots: 3. 249; her story: 4. 305

Amoretti, 4. 306, 314-5; 7. 436, 451, 501, 509; 8. 393, 404, 416-54, 459, 544, 615; most beautiful sonnet: 8. 442; biographical significance: 8. 629-38, 651; chronology: 8. 421-2, 428, 431, 439-41, 443, 445, 447-8, 450-2, 623-4, 636; and *Colin Clouts Come Home*: 8. 635, 638; commendatory sonnets: 8. 417-8, 632; composition: 8. 421-2, 631-8, 642; criticism: 8. 431, 628-

31, 637-8; date: 8. 631-8; and *Doleful Lay of Clorinda*: 7. 501-2, 504-5; Elizabeth, addressed to: 8. 631-2; and *Epithalamion*: 8. 629-30, 633-8, 646, 651, 655, 674; and *F. Q.*: 8. 629-31, 635, 637; form: 8. 629; and *Hell of Lovers*: 8. 519; humor in: 8. 518; and the *Hymnes*: 7. 656-8, 660, 665, 674; " lady of the sonnets ": 7. 536; 8. 419-21, 428, 434, 436, 445, 473, 629, 632-7; in manuscript: 8. 431; metre: 8. 629, 631, 643-4; and *Muiopotmos*: 8. 600; Platonism in: 7. 665; 8. 421-2, 424, 427, 434-5, 446-8, 450, 453-4; and *Prothalamion*: 8. 674; publication: 8. 417; punctuation: 7. 501-2; 8. 426; rhetoric: 7. 504; 8. 421, 644; run-over lines: 8. 644; as sequence: 8. 630, 632-4, 637-8: set to music: 8. 643; sources: 7. 671; 8. 638-43; style: 8. 440, 643-4; text criticism: 8. 426, 687, 697-704, 719-20; Dedication: 8. 417; 1: 8. 419-20; 2, 5, 6: 8. 473; 2: 6. 222; 3, 7, 9, 12, 26, 41: 8. 637; 3, 8, 15, 21, 35, 61, 72, 79, 87: 7. 665; 3, 8, 9, 55, 79: 8. 440, 450; 3: 8. 434, 473, 498; 4: 4. 221; 6. 296; 7. 660; 8. 634; 5, 11-2, 20, 36, 50, 52, 57, 62-3, 86: 5. 284; 8. 422; 5, 6, 19, 70: 6. 214; 5, 6, 51: 7. 517; 5, 6, 26: 8. 436; 6: 8. 630; 8, 84: 6. 214; 8. 507; 8: 8. 639; 9: 8. 425, 438; 10, 45: 8. 643; 11, 12, 14, 52, 57, 69: 8. 423; 12: 8. 432; 13, 25, 31, 38, 41, 47, 49, 55, 57: 8. 424; 14: 4. 169, 234; 8. 632, 638; 15, 76-7: 8. 442; 15, 64, 76: 8. 449, 519; 15: 2. 384, 8. 424, 473-4, 639; 16, 19, 21-2, 26, 46, 51, 68, 70: 8. 422; 16, 75: 8. 423; 17: 4. 195; 8. 472; 18: 8. 633; 19: 8. 445, 466; 21: 8. 478, 639; 22, 27, 35, 45, 78-9, 88: 8. 439-40, 642; 22: 8. 443, 450, 477; 23: 8. 445; 25, 31, 38, 41, 47, 49, 55, 57: 8. 424; 25: 7. 660; 8. 462; 26, 51, 63, 69: 8. 428; 26: 2. 383; 4. 216; 27-9, 36, 48-9: 8. 423; 27: 7. 528; 8. 436, 444; 28, 37, 48, 50, 71, 75: 8. 435; 28: 8. 638; 30: 8. 638; 32, 60, 80: 6. 219; 32, 55: 5. 255; 33: 8. 451, 520, 632; 34, 56, 59: 5. 181; 8. 441; 34: 3. 379; 6. 434; 8. 638; 35, 45, 78: 8. 454; 35: 7. 365; 8. 452, 473; 37: 8. 451; 38, 43, 50, 53, 56: 8. 600; 38: 4. 249; 8. 434; 39-40: 8. 638; 39: 4. 165; 8. 299, 499; 40: 2. 215; 41, 43: 8. 433; 42: 7. 660; 8. 424; 43, 56, 67, 72-3, 76-7, 81, 84: 8. 640-1; 43; 8. 421, 467; 44: 4. 169; 8. 421; 45: 8. 442, 465, 638-9; 46: 8. 633, 648; 47, 48: 8. 435, 437, 638; 48: 7. 505; 50: 4. 278; 52: 8. 485, 633; 54: 3. 355; 8. 506; 55: 4. 234; 8. 423; 56: 8. 431; 57:

7. 481; 58: 6. 192; 8. 330; 59: 8. 439; 60-76: 8. 642-3; 61, 72, 79, 88: 8. 427; 61: 6. 349; 7. 482; 8. 428, 442, 450, 633, 639; 62: 8. 629, 634, 638; 63: 8. 638; 64, 76-7: 8. 424, 441, 474-5, 632; 65: 4. 311; 8. 445; 66: 8. 434, 633; 67: 8. 630, 635; 68: 8. 427, 639; 69, 75: 8. 429; 69: 7. 482; 8. 478, 494;70: 4. 203; 8. 426; 71: 8. 605, 610, 636; 72: 7. 679; 8. 447, 640; 73, 78, 83: 8. 638; 73: 8. 433; 74: 8. 468, 629, 632-3, 638; 75: 8. 442, 648; 79: 6. 257; 8. 439, 640; 80: 3. 300; 4. 314; 6. 185, 434; 8. 431, 632; 81: 2. 214; 7. 536; 82: 8. 453; 83: 7. 536; 8. 432, 631; 84: 7. 506; 8. 476; 85-9: 8. 462, 637; 85: 2. 253; 7. 534; 8. 452, 641; 86: 5. 207; 8. 638; 88: 8. 435, 637-40; 89: 8. 322

Amoretti and Epithalamion, 1595, 8. 697-705, 718, 735

Amphialus, 3. 393

Amphidamas, 2. 265

Amphion, 8. 388

Amphisa, 3. 249

Amphitrite, 4. 242, 316

Amyas, 4. 205, 286, 299

Amyntas, 3. 259; is Ferdinando Stanley, Lord Strange: 3. 260, 306; 7. 468; is Henry Lord Compton and Monteagle: 3. 259-60; is Sidney?: 7. 471; is Thomas Watson: 3. 260

Amyot, Jacques, 8. 302, 314, 328

Anabaptists, 5. 175-6, 181, 278, 289, 293-4, 336-45; 8. 352.

Anachronism, 2. 341; 3. 209

Anacoluthon, 5. 229

Anacreon, 1. 192, 296; 7. 266, 567; 8. 445, 455-8, 463, 474

[*Anacreontics*] (Spenser's), 2. 273; 8. 455-8, 704, 729; authenticity: 8. 455; text variants: 8. 704; title: 8. 455

Anadiplosis, 6. 189; 7. 618; 8. 530, 595

Anagnostes, 2. 301

Anagogy, 6. 278

Anamnestes, 2. 299-301, 466

Anaphora, 6. 189; 7. 246, 444, 474, 618; 8. 342, 347, 384, 404, 469, 484, 595, 644

Anaxius, 1. 451

Ancestry, 6. 255, 329-30, 334, 337-8, 345. *See also* Breeding, Nobility

Anchises, 3. 231, 281

Anchor, 1. 284-6

Ancients, 1. 366, 370-1, 421; 5. 152. *See also* Classical, Antique World

Ancren Riwle, 1. 412-3; 2. 456

Andalo de Negro, 7. 243-4; 8. 387

Anders, H. R. D., 8. 541

Anderson, Ruth L., 2. 340, 462-4, 468
André, Bernard, 1. 484
Andreas, 1. 487-8
Andreas Capellanus, *De Amore* (ed. Trojel,
 1892): 6. 231; p. 10: 4. 223; pp. 92-3:
 3. 353; p. 99: 2. 371; p. 100: 2. 382;
 p. 106: 4. 202, 214; 6. 256; pp. 271 ff.:
 6. 292; p. 311: 5. 207; 6. 244
Andreini, Giambattista, 7. 552, 657
Andrews, Lancelot, 7. 331; 8. 361
Andrews, Mark E., 5. 195
Andromache, 1. 305, 496
Andromeda, 1. 208, 498; 8. 309
Andromedes, 3. 333
Angela, 3. 236-7
Angelica, 1. 246, 248-9, 419; 3. 201, 205,
 246, 269-70, 315, 333, 368-9, 371, 373-4
Angels, 1. 389; 2. 270-2, 475; 3. 234; 6.
 258; 7. 673-4; 8. 279, 331, 477-8, 493,
 633; Hierarchy or Nine Orders: 1. 310;
 2. 476-7; 7. 540-1, 553-4; 8. 331, 493
Anger, 2. 189, 195, 197, 200, 225, 227,
 230, 293, 414-6, 418, 425, 427, 461, 468,
 471; 3. 301 (Ire). *See also* Wrath
Angles, 3. 236
Angling, 4. 211, 255, 257; 7. 330; 8. 463-4
Anglo-Saxon, 7. 322, 349; metre: 7. 275,
 292
Animal-fable. *See* Fable
Animals, 2. 359-64; 8. 405; symbolic: 1.
 407-13; 3. 364; 8. 571-2, 585-93
Animation, 1. 239
Animus, 1. 446
Anjou, Duke of. *See* Alençon, Henry III of
 France.
Anne, Countess of Warwick. *See* Russell,
 Anne
Annius Viterbiensis, 6. 274
Annotation, 7. 650
Annual Feast, 1. 313, 322, 324-5, 334-5, 350;
 2. 202
Annus Magnus. *See* Platonic Great Year
Ant, 7. 379-80; 8. 408
Ant and the Nightingale, The, 1. 200; 5. 253-4
Antaeus, 2. 347; 4. 319
Antanaclusis, 6. 189
Antanactasis, 8. 377
Anthems, 8. 477
Anthologies. *See* Greek, Latin
Anthypophora. *See* Subjectio
Antichrist, 1. 439, 471, 473
Anticlimax, 3. 277; 8. 446
Antigenidas, 7. 392
Antigone, 5. 258
Antimetabole, 7. 246, 444; 8. 530
Antioch, 1. 291
Antiochus, 4. 167

Antipater, 6. 252
Anti-platonism, 8. 446, 454
Antiquarianism, 1. 484; 2. 407; 4. 179, 260;
 5. 321; 6. 423; 8. 672
Antique World, 1. 305. *See also* Ancients
"Antiquitas mundi . . . ," 5. 155
Antistrophe, 7. 247, 444; 8. 285-6, 595
Antithesis, 7. 246, 444; 8. 331, 595, 644
Antoninus Liberalis, 1. 235; 3. 301-2, 330,
 332-3
Antonius Musa Brasavolus, 5. 219
Antonomasia, 8. 676
Antony, Marc, 5. 224
Antwerp, 5. 252-3
Anvil, 5. 201
Aon, 4. 246
Ape, 2. 341; 3. 280; 5. 236; 7. 266, 603;
 8. 349, 355, 363, 371, 561, 564, 570-1,
 574, 577-80, 586-9, 606
Apelles, 3. 309; 4. 194; 7. 567; 8. 390
Aphrodite, 3. 253; 7. 399, 497, 499; 8. 468;
 Ourania: 4. 216; 8. 330; Pandemos: 2.
 199. *See also* Venus
Apocrypha, 6. 241; 7. 563-4, 662; "Wisdom
 Books": 8. 536; 2 Esdras: 4: 5. 175, 180;
 9. 10: 8. 285; 14. 10: 4. 211; Tobit:
 8. 3: 4. 208; Book of Wisdom: 2. 287;
 7. 560; 1. 4-7: 7. 517, 548, 561, 565;
 2. 4: 8. 286; 3. 11: 8. 314; 6. 12-9: 7.
 566, 569; 6. 20-1: 7. 548, 567; 7-8: 7.
 567; 8. 330; 7. 8-9: 7. 570; 7. 10-1, 14:
 7. 548; 7. 25-9: 7. 555, 565-6; 8. 330;
 8. 1-4: 7. 564-6; 8. 5: 8. 315; 8. 16-8: 7.
 569-70; 8. 21: 7. 568; 9. 4, 10: 7. 558,
 565; 9. 15: 2. 289; 8. 447; 11. 20: 5. 177;
 13. 2-3: 7. 551; 17. 18: 2. 211; Ecclesi-
 asticus: 7. 560; 8. 330; 6. 20-9: 8. 331;
 13. 1: 7. 300; 24. 3-7: 7. 565-6; 24. 8: 8.
 489; 24.7: 7. 548; 26. 29: 8. 303; 42. 15-
 chap. 43: 7. 556; Baruch: 7. 560; 3. 15:
 7. 548, 567; 4. 2: 7. 570; 1 Maccabees:
 1: 1. 238; 1. 7-8: 4. 168; 9. 39: 8. 469;
 2 Maccabees: 5. 15: 5. 163; 13. 2: 5. 226
Apollo, 1. 296, 371; 2. 304, 366, 379; 3.
 268, 295, 394-6; 4. 204; 6. 194, 282, 293,
 423, 426; 7. 319; 8. 332, 334, 400, 481,
 541
Apollodorus, *Library*: Book 1: 4. 274; 2. 4:
 3. 297; 2. 6: 4. 243; 4. 1: 2. 357; 4. 5:
 2. 204; 6. 1-4: 3. 279; 5. 219; 7. 10:
 6. 243; 9. 1: 3. 293; 9. 26: 5. 166; 9. 28:
 2. 272-3; Book 2: 5. 162; 1. 1; 4. 3;
 7. 2: 4. 245-6; 4. 3: 8. 377; 4. 8: 3. 293;
 5. 2: 6. 270; 5. 10: 5. 250; 6. 2-4: 5. 198;
 7. 7: 5. 203; Book 3: 1. 1: 3. 293; 8. 401;
 4. 1: 2. 298; 4. 3: 4. 244; 5. 2; 5. 162; 5.
 5: 3. 294; 9. 2: 2. 265; 10. 7: 8. 498; 12.

4: 1. 304; 12. 6: 4. 245; 13. 5: 6. 254,
299; 15. 2: 6. 243; Schol. on Apollonius
Rhodius: 5. 250
Apollonius Rhodius, *Argonautica*: 2. 351,
373; 3. 336; 4. 169; 5. 298; 7. 440; Book
1: schol. on: 117: 4. 245; 492 ff.: 4. 174;
schol. on 554: 3. 296; 570 ff.: 7. 460;
740-1: 8. 388; 1092-1150: 5. 215; 6. 278-
9, 398; 1226: 8. 465; 1239: 6. 307; 1310:
4. 243; Book 2: 3. 296; 88: 4. 189; 985:
5. 198; 1236: 3. 296; 1241: 3. 297; Book
3: 1212: 1. 233; 1364: 2. 346; Book 4:
57-8: 8. 490; 469: 3. 239; 789 ff.: 8. 346;
813: 6. 307; 1143-4: 8. 463; 1196: 8.
462, 464; 1479: 2. 259; 1640-8: 5. 165-6;
Book 5: 864-5: 2. 365
Apollyon, 1. 377
Apostles, 8. 279
Apostrophe, 1. 256; 3. 271, 288; 5. 259,
262; 7. 246-7, 504; 8. 530
Apotheosis, 6. 237; 7. 506
Apperson, G. L., 2. 206; 8. 352, 362
Appetites, 2. 458-60, 469; 5. 287; 6. 447-8
Apples, 2. 445-6; 7. 317; 8. 449
Apuleius, 7. 506; *De Deo Socratis*: 2. 376;
De Dogmate Platonis: 8. 493; *De Magia*:
5. 162; *De Mundo*: 5. 161; .*Meta-
morphoses*: 2. 392; 3. 261; 5. 216; 6. 413;
7. 273, 521; 8. 396-7
Aquarius, 6. 308
Aquila, 8. 309
Aquilant, 2. 346
Ara, 8. 310
Arabian Nights, 2. 354-5
Arabs, 3. 216; 7. 671
Arachne, 3. 291-2, 396-7; 8. 396, 400-1, 403,
597-600, 604, 606
Aragnoll, 8. 400-1, 404, 597, 605-7, 609
Aratus, 1. 230; 5. 164
Arber, Agnes, 7. 287
Arber, Edward, 7. 472
Arbor, 3. 259; 6. 296
Arcadia, 1. 242
Arcadian Romance, 7. 591
Arcalaus, 3. 362
Arcana Naturae, 1. 232
Archaism, 2. 247; 3. 234; 4. 178-80, 238;
5. 202; 6. 188; 7. 236-9, 253, 290, 330,
413, 453, 571-3, 575-6, 595, 614-30, 682;
8. 351, 373, 410, 467, 473, 542, 595, 610,
618
Archangels, 1. 310; 7. 553
Archers, Society of, 1. 485, 489
Archigald, 2. 322-3
Archimago, 1. 309, 311-2, 323, 399, 419;
2. 187, 207, 211, 276, 406; 3. 327; 6. 384;
8. 516-7; is Gardiner: 1. 458, 461, 464-5;

is not historical: 1. 466; is Hypocrisy:
1. 422, 426, 432, 451; is Lord Burleigh:
1. 449, 451; 2. 401-2; is Papacy and
Catholicism: 1. 440, 454, 456, 466; 2. 402-
4; 3. 380; 6. 384; is Pole: 1. 458; role
in *F. Q.* 2: 1. 454; 2. 428; is Satan: 1. 455;
2. 429
Architecture, 2. 379; 4. 219, 229; 5. 217-8,
224, 237; 8. 288, 382
Arcite, 7. 517
Arden of Feversham, 5. 234; 6 .200
Arden(ne), Forest of, 7. 495
Ardenne, Fountain of, 1. 331
Areopagus, 7. 488, 644; 8. 534, 538
Arethusa, 2. 196; 6. 290, 409, 425, 430;
7. 454
Aretino, Pietro, 7. 252; 8. 516-7
Argante, 2. 372; 3. 266, 313, 319-20, 327;
6. 437
Argenia, 1. 291
Argo, 8. 308, 339, 346
Argonauts, 4. 169
Argus, 7. 382, 392
Ariadne, 6. 247, 251; 8. 482
Arianism, 7. 539
Arimanius, 3. 244
Ariodante, 2. 441
Arion, 2. 342; 4. 249-50
Ariosto, Ludovico, 1. 197, 209, 314-20, 324,
327, 330-7, 360-1, 366, 378, 411, 510;
2. 274, 390, 435; 3. 367-76; 4. 235; 5.
186, 191, 311; 6. 214, 227, 243, 257, 269;
7. 495, 679; 8. 532, 637; Spenser, compared with: 1. 316, 319, 335-7, 366-7,
373-8; 2. 221, 438-43; 3. 201-2, 213, 227;
3. 273-4, 367-76, 386; 4. 189, 192, 328;
5. 156, 221; 6. 313-4, 444, 446; Spenser
hopes to "overgoe": 1. 330, 332, 335,
361, 366; Spenser prefers A. to Tasso:
1. 316-7, 332-3, 337
    Cinque Canti: 4. 167; Comedies: 8.
516-8
    Orlando Furioso: 2. 206-7, 329; 4. 174;
5. 273; 8. 319; abrupt transition: 1. 248;
allegory in: 1. 333, 335-7, 345, 366, 493,
513; 2. 228, 438-43; 3. 317, 371-6; 5.
348-9; 6. 313; cantos, beginnings of: 1.
206; conclusions: 3. 272; 4. 182, 192;
5. 193, 206, 223, 232, 268; 6. 198; episodic: 1. 349; *F. Q.*, less important source
of than the romances: 1. 351; in *F. Q.*
3, 4, more used: 3. 375; historical: 1. 359;
another *Iliad*: 1. 419; 3. 367; purpose:
1. 336, 512; romances the groundwork of
O. F.: 1. 367; serious?: 1. 366, 378, 419;
3. 367-76; 5. 221; Spenser's handling: 1.
413; 3. 214, 314-5; Spenser's conception

of: 1. 332-7, 378, 418-21, 513; style: 1. 376; transitions: 1. 248; 2. 197, 339; 4. 188, 192, 196, 203, 239; 5. 163, 194, 217, 232, 258; 6. 220; *see also Faerie Queene*, transitions; Cantos 1-2: 1. 246-7; Canto 1: 3. 368; possible source of *F. Q.* 1. 6. 34 ff.: 1. 419; 1: 173, 209; 2: 6. 185; 21-3: 1. 336; 3. 205, 315, 368; 33-5: 3. 205, 262, 315; 40: 3. 219; 53: 6. 265; 58: 2. 391; 59, 72: 1. 248-9; 60 ff.: 3. 203, 314; 72 ff.: 2. 207; 74-5: 5. 191; 77-81: 3. 268; Canto 2: 1: 3. 367; 3: 3. 268; 5: 6. 258; 8. 4-8: 1. 227; 12-13: 1. 188; 32-3: 3. 370; 34 ff.: 3. 288-9; 50: 6. 232; 55-6: 1. 251, 253, 254; Canto 3: 2. 301-2; 1: 2. 303; 10: 3. 224; 17-48: 3. 227; 45-6: 2. 228; 57: 6. 255; Canto 4: 4: 3. 206; 17: 1. 227; 18: 3. 303; 22: 6. 290; 27: 1. 211; 60 ff.: 2. 228-30; 72: 3. 272; Canto 5: 4: 3. 272; 18: 3. 219; 88: 1. 226; 89: 1. 211; Cantos 6, 7, 8, 10: 2. 439-43; Canto 6: 5: 5. 194; 18: 6. 217; 19-22: 3. 253; 26 ff.: 1. 202-4; 2. 394; 59: 1. 213; 2. 284; 60-6: 2. 339-41; 74: 4. 223; 78-9: 253; Canto 7: 1. 205; 1: 2. 185-6; 2-5: 3. 253; 10: 6. 255; 11: 2. 212, 214; 4. 201; 5. 189; 14: 2. 217; 21 ff.: 3. 213; 23: 1. 226; 28: 2. 392; 57: 1. 246; 71-3: 1. 204, 262-3; Canto 8: 14 ff.: 2. 394; 17: 3. 204; 29-50: 3. 333; 31, 68: 3. 269; 44 ff.: 3. 270, 333-4; 54: 3. 270; 66: 4. 165; 71: 2. 353; Canto 9: 17: 5. 247; 29: 6. 217; 67: 5. 235; 77: 2. 347; 91: 1. 249; Canto 10: 8. 309; 39-40: 2. 381; 40: 1. 299; 61-3: 3. 253; 64: 1. 282; 96: 5. 189; 98-9: 2. 296; 105: 5. 261; 6. 259; 107-10: 5. 228; 109; 5. 188; Canto 11: 1. 295; 1: 2. 440; 3. 287; 4. 202; 6: 6. 217; 20: 1. 241; 22: 2. 341; 23: 1. 249; 34-43: 1. 374-6; 42: 6. 230; 47: 2. 277; 65: 7. 497; 67: 6. 234; 71: 4. 195; Cantos 12, 13: 4. 323; 6. 371, 374, 379; Canto 12: 1. 197-8; 30-1: 2. 210; 59: 2. 276; 6. 228; 89 ff.: 4. 205; 91 ff.: 6. 257, 371; 94: 2. 215; Canto 13: 4-14: 4. 205; 26-8: 1. 239; 35: 5. 235; Canto 14: 30-1: 3.218; 38 ff.: 3. 268; 40: 1. 211; 43: 2. 207, 210; 78 ff.: 6. 313-4; 99: 3. 297; 8. 488; 102: 1. 193-4, 195; 108: 3. 204 ; 109: 1. 188; Canto 15: 12: 5. 181; 13: 1. 268; 14: 1. 257; 44, 56: 2. 393; 5. 235; 67 ff.: 2. 346; Canto 16: 3: 4. 173; Canto 17: 11: 4. 185; 30: 4. 203; 33: 4. 205; 35 ff.: 3. 286-7; 82: 5. 183; 86-113: 5. 186-7; 88-90: 4. 190; 90, 110: 5. 192; Canto 18: 11: 6. 217; 19: 2. 277; 6. 207; 34: 1.

365; 35: 6. 259; 93: 5. 192; 118: 3. 204; Canto 19: 22: 3. 246; 29: 3. 247; 57: 5. 196, 198; 84: 2. 275; Canto 20: 1, 2: 3. 237-8, 331-2; 57: 5. 197; 104-5: 6. 216; 106-29: 4. 188-9; 110: 6. 200; 134-42: 4. 173; Canto 21: 1: 1. 285; 16: 4. 183; 53: 2. 199; Canto 22: 1: 3. 273; 12 ff.: 2. 207; 23: 3. 303; 31-6: 3. 370; 48: 6. 216; 53: 6. 216-7; 76-9: 6. 216; 81-2: 1. 254; 84-6: 1. 259; 85-7: 5. 228; Canto 23: 10: 3. 210; 15: 3. 204, 237; 33 ff.: 2. 207; 67: 4. 278; 82: 3. 269; Canto 24: 58-9: 2. 207, 210; 62: 6. 226; 96: 1. 297; 105-6: 2. 234-5; 114: 4. 313; Canto 25: 12: 5. 181; 17: 3. 243; 78: 2. 210; Canto 26: 28: 4. 166; 31: 1. 263; 39: 3. 224; 70 ff.: 4. 215; 111: 3. 264; 132: 1. 210; 4. 191; Canto 27: 31-6: 4. 202; 39 ff.: 4. 195; 103-7: 4. 196; 133: 4. 175; Canto 28: 3. 267; 1-2: 3. 273-4; 62-3: 3. 213; Canto 29: 5. 345; 26-7: 3. 272; 4. 212; 35: 5. 169; 61: 5. 228; Canto 30: 3. 370; 11: 2. 243; 51: 4. 185; 58: 5. 164; 60: 1. 299; 76-81, 84 ff.: 3. 370; 4. 203; 5. 207; Canto 31: 1: 4. 199; 33: 6. 199; 67: 5. 172; 86: 1. 255; Canto 32: 3. 204; 10: 3. 370; 5. 507; 14, 28: 5. 209; 63-80: 3. 272, 276; 79-80: 3. 210, 278; 4. 167, 200; 5. 202; 7. 497; 83: 6. 201; 100: 4. 173; 108: 4. 278; 5. 264; Canto 33: 3. 292; 9: 1. 265; 3. 226; 84: 1. 297; 5. 199; 92 ff.: 2. 207; 96: 6. 232; Canto 34: 11-43: 6. 221, 224; 49-51: 3. 253; 53: 3. 201; 88: 4. 182; Canto 35: 38: 5. 213; Canto 36: 3. 371; 5. 221; 1: 6. 198, 216; 37-8: 2. 190; Canto 37: 42: 6. 189; 77: 1. 299; 78: 4. 212; Canto 38: 33: 3. 226; Canto 39: 14: 2. 342; 26: 3. 226; 52: 6. 207; 54: 6. 230; Canto 40: 31: 2. 342; 3. 265; Cantos 41, 42: 2. 279; Canto 41: 52-6: 1. 289; 57: 1. 189; 60 ff.: 3. 371; 95-6: 2. 276; Canto 42: 53-64: 2. 261; 91: 2. 382; Canto 43: 3. 372; 63: 3. 232; 66: 5. 169; 76: 4. 185; 98: 1. 204; 168: 4. 191; Canto 45: 21: 3. 269; 39: 6. 232; 72: 4. 215; 73: 4. 183; 80: 4. 200; 112: 1. 299; Canto 46: 1: 1. 311; 118: 1. 200; 131: 3. 266; 140: 3. 245; 4. 212; 5. 172

Sonnets: 8. 441; *Suppositi*: 8. 319. *See also* Harrington, Sir John
Aristaenetus, 2. 217, 265
Aristaeus, 3. 239-40
Aristocracy, 5. 293-4; 6. 337-8, 340
Aristophanes, 7. 532; *Acharnians*: 2. 254; *Birds*: 7. 481; *Clouds*: 6. 225; *Ecclesiazusae*: 2. 217; *Frogs*: 1. 238, 243; 2. 254,

268, 318; 8. 388;*Knights*: 7. 381; *Lysis-trata*: 2. 217; 3. 253; *Peace*: 3. 253; 8. 471, 652; *Plutus*: 2. 224, 253; 4. 182, 247; 5. 220

Aristotle, 1. 360-1; 2. 192, 251, 253, 279, 295, 459, 483; 4. 235, 284; 5. 228; 6. 348, 401, 406, 422; 7. 324, 381, 387, 428, 550, 553, 562, 671; 8. 352-3; doctor of Catholics: 6. 209; doctrine of the Mean: 2. 348, 412-26; 3. 319-20; gentleman, idea of: 6. 334-5; Italian interpreters: 1. 343; Nature, conception of: 6. 281; psychology: 2. 365; Spenser departs from: 4. 282; Spenser's knowledge of: 2. 419; 3. 319-21; 4. 291; State, theory of: 8. 303; *De Anima*: 2. 462, 468; 3. 258; *De Generatione Animalium*: 1. 187; 2. 468; 6. 403; *De Partibus Animalium*: 2. 468; *Historia Animalium*: 2. 292, 361, 369; 8. 406; *Metaphysics*: 7. 481; *Nicomachean Ethics*: 1. 251, 327-30, 333-4, 337, 353-7, 431-3, 495; 2. 194, 351, 414-26, 470; commentators on: 1. 354-6, 361; 2. 424; *F. Q.* based on: 1. 340-3; *F. Q.* not based on: 1. 327-30; 2. 197, 294; 5. 285; and the Fathers: 2. 424; in the Middle Ages: 2. 423-4; Book 2: 1: 2. 230; 3: 2. 240; 5: 2. 197; 6-9: 5. 180; 6: 2. 200-1; 8. 476; 7, 8: 4. 305; 5. 267; 7: 1. 328, 354; 2. 294, 419; 8: 2. 198; Book 3: 4: 2. 417; 9 ff.: 1. 328; 10: 1. 219; 2. 210, 417; 5. 187; 11: 2. 419; 13: 2. 418; 15: 2. 420; Books 4, 8, 9: 4. 282; Book 4: 1. 328; 2: 6. 335; 3: 3. 321; 7-9: 1. 445; 2. 418, 421; 8: 2. 241; 9: 2. 294, 421; 11: 2. 189; 12-4: 6. 335-6; 12: 6. 325-7; 15: 2. 418; Book 5: 5. 281-2, 287-90; 2, 9: 5. 281; 2: 1. 328; 3: 5. 175; 4-6: 5. 293; 5, 7: 5. 288; 11: 5. 285; 14: 5. 295; Book 7: 2. 420; 6. 392; 1-11: 2. 418, 1: 2. 418; 5: 2. 415; 6, 7: 3. 320; 7: 2. 419; 15: 8. 397; Book 8: 1: 4. 226, 288, 297, 303, 328; 3: 4. 303; 5: 4. 304, 329; 8: 4. 213; 9: 5-281; 12: 1. 341; Book 9: 1: 4. 213; 6: 4. 313; 8: 4. 181; *Physics*: 3. 260; *Politics*: 1. 340-1, 495; 2. 406; 3. 320-1; 5. 281, 336; 6. 392, 403; 7. 391-2; *Rhetoric*: 3. 321

Ark of the Covenant, 8. 308

Arlo, 1. 507; 3. 247; 4. 271; 6. 235, 273, 282-9, 425, 439-40; 7. 462, 495

Armada, 1. 298, 454, 457, 470, 484, 490; 3. 247; 5. 227-30, 246, 316, 333; 7. 434; 8. 281, 536-7, 540, 602, 607

Armeddan, 5. 186

Armida, 1. 228, 331; 2. 183, 238, 372, 381,

398, 428, 435, 447; 3. 258, 303; 4. 193; 5. 224; and Phaedria: 2. 445

Armor, 1. 176, 251, 313, 390, 425; 2. 207, 209-10, 234, 273, 275-6, 329, 393; 3. 290, 370-1; 5. 191-2, 200, 203, 222, 226-7, 231; hanging of: 6. 210

Armoric, 5. 248

Armour, George W., 6. 458; 8. 681

Armoy, 6. 425; 7. 455

Armulla, 4. 271; 6. 287, 425; 7. 455

Arnaut Daniel, 7. 347

Arnobius, 2. 374-5; 6. 398; 7. 273

Arnold, Matthew, 1. 489; 7. 397, 408; 8. 674

Arnus, 6. 439

Arran, 1. 214

Arras, 1. 214; 3. 392-9

Arrian, Flavius, 2. 271, 285, 374; 4. 176; 7. 393

Arrow, 3. 245, 295; 7. 480

Arsace, 1. 214

Art, 8. 397

Artegall, 1. 359-60, 378, 432, 485; 2. 280, 372; 3. 310-5, 363, 369-71, 381, 383, 387, 389, 391; 4. 201; 5. 192, 238, 259, 270-98, 337; 6. 304, 342, 345, 7. 661; 8. 353; allegorical identity variable: 5. 286; equals Arthur: 3. 228; and Britomart: 3. 325; 4. 285, 303-4; 5. 161, 293, 297, 310, 348-9; 8. 503; career: 5. 269, 297-8; character: 5. 273-5, 285, 297-8; crocodile, imaged in: 5. 220, 295; education: 5. 163, 166-7; ancestor of Elizabeth: 2. 449, 453-5; 3. 228, 369; and Envy: 5. 265-7, 285; is Essex: 5. 260, 286, 326, 331; in *F. Q.* 6: 6. 319, 356; not a fairy: 1. 253; 2. 449, 453-5; 5. 161; son of Gorlois: 2. 453; 3. 228; is Lord Grey: 3. 317-8, 369; 5. 161, 163, 172-3, 244, 264, 271, 298, 300, 303, 310, 313; 6. 318, 437; hero of *F. Q.*: 3. 369; imperfect: 2. 427; 5. 297-8; 6. 320; and Ireland: 3. 380; 5. 173; 6. 435; and Justice: 5. 285, 288-9, 298, 310; 6. 384; is primitive Manhood: 4. 301; is merciful: 5. 264; and Mercilla: 5. 243-4; mere name: 1. 378; name: 3. 228; 5. 160-1, 300; and Radigund: 5. 302, 349; 6. 437; reflects international relations of Elizabeth's time and accession of Tudors: 2. 455; Round Table, knight of: 3. 228; and women: 5. 196, 201-2; 6. 280

Artemis. *See* Diana

Arthur, son of Henry VII, 2. 335

Arthur, Prince, 1. 311-3, 321-7, 337, 360, 378, 424-4, 500-1, 510; 2. 183-4, 186, 187, 274, 279, 301, 339, 341-7, 352; 3. 310, 312-3, 317, 319, 324-5, 368-9, 371,

374, 375; 5. 192, 238, 282; 6. 210; 7. 388;
is animus, voluntas, fortitudo: 1. 446;
apotheosis of all virtues: 1. 432; is "Arthur of Britain": 1. 485-95; in *Arthur of
Little Britain*: 3. 362-4; in Avalon: 3. 235;
and Belge: 5. 247-55; date: 3. 236; defender of Mary Stuart: 3. 322; dragon,
fight with: 1. 395, 399; is Earl of Essex:
1. 449, 452-3; is Elferon: 2. 453; Elizabeth's ancestor: 2. 449, 453-5; is England:
5. 315; 8. 503; is English chivalry: 3. 380;
5. 306; in *F.Q.* 1 and 2: 1. 495; 2. 452;
in *F.Q.* 4: 4. 289, 296, 300, 319-20; in
F.Q. 5: 5. 285, 293; in *F.Q.* 6: 6. 202,
229, 231-2, 322, 326, 328, 333, 349;
faery origin and nurture: 1. 264-6; 2. 335-
6; Faery Queen, lover of: 1. 416; 6. 427;
feast of: 2. 203; is Heavenly Grace: 1.
438, 441, 466, 501; 2. 418; 3. 323; 5.
279; helmet: 1. 252; hero of *F.Q.*: 1. 315,
317-8, 321-3, 332, 334, 350, 359; 2. 186-7;
3. 369; histories of: 2. 329 (*see also History of Prince Arthur*); is Justice: 5. 290;
King: 1. 301-3, 482-90, 493-5; 2. 326;
6. 366; is Leicester: 1. 343, 345, 346,
451, 452, 458, 460, 465; 2. 303, 403;
3.263, 379; 5. 271-2, 300-1, 310, 316;
lineage: 1. 438; 3. 227-8; love story: 1.
267-8; Maleger, fight with: 2. 338-48,
418, 442; 4. 319; and Mercilla: 5. 243-4;
mere name: 1. 378; one of the Nine
Worthies: 3. 338-9; power of England,
represents: 1. 424, 453; 2, 434, 452; and
Rinaldo: 3. 205; is Sidney: 5. 299-300;
and the Soldan: 5. 226-8; Spenser loses
interest in: 4. 286; Spenser projected poem
on: 1. 323; Tudor line, represents: 1. 352,
450, 455, 482-95; 2. 407, 453-5; unde-
veloped: 1. 311, 317, 349, 362; is Will:
1. 446-7
Arthur of Little Britain, 1. 291; 2. 188; 3.
362-4; greatest single influence in *F.Q.*:
3. 363
"artistic diminutive," 2. 244
Arundel, Earls of. *See* Howard
Arviragus, 1. 176; 2. 324-7
Ascalaphus, 4. 196
Ascension Day, 8. 633
Ascham, Roger, 1. 488; 6. 343; 7. 372, 587,
608, 621-2, 626, 643; 8. 313, 538, 591;
The Schoolmaster: 1. 340; 2. 409; 6. 211-
2, 337-8; 7. 237-8, 262, 289, 363, 623;
8. 361; *Toxophilus*: 3. 210
"A Scholar's Love," 6. 443
Asclepiodate, 2. 330-1
Ashdown Forest, 7. 330
Ashes, 6. 218

Ashley, I., 8. 508
Aspdene, John, 7. 306
Asphodel, 7. 443
Ass, 1. 243, 399, 400, 411; 8. 351, 371, 562,
577; symbol of humility: 1. 433
Assaracus, 2. 307
Assembly of Gods, 1. 272, 410, 412-3; 2. 287,
433
Assembly of Ladies. *See* Chaucer (pseudo)
Assonance, 2. 367, 385; 6. 200, 242; 7. 256;
8. 715
Assumption, Feast of, 7. 346
The Assumption, 1. 192
Assyria, 8. 287
Astarolle, 1. 513
Asterie, 3. 294; 8. 396-7, 597, 599, 606
Astolfo, 1. 202, 204-5, 257; 2. 393; 3. 237
Aston, Sir Edward, 8. 417
Aston, Frances, 8. 417-8
Astonishment. *See* Amazement
Astraea, 5. 158, 163-4, 166-7, 292, 298; 6.
305; 8. 331, 350
Astraeus, 4. 244
Astrology, 3. 206, 220, 248-9; 7. 528, 533;
8. 493
Astronomy, 5. 157, 177-8; 6. 310-1, 414,
423-4; 7. 539, 551, 613; 8. 329, 350
Astrophel, 6. 351, 355; 7. 443, 453, 463,
474, 490, 492, 497, 499; 8. 307-8. *See*
Sidney, Sir Philip
Astrophel, 3. 259-60; 7. 487, 501, 503-4;
8. 284, 396, 459, 522, 526, 528; and *Colin
Clouts*: 7. 492; composition: 7. 484-6;
and *Daphnaida*: 7. 484, 486; date: 7. 483-
6; 8. 296; metre: 7. 484, 487; and *Mother
Hubberds Tale*: 7. 495; and *Muiopotmos*:
8. 604; publication: 7. 492; and *Ruines of
Time*: 7. 484, 486-8; 8. 295; and *S.C.
November*: 7. 399; sources: 7. 486-7; and
Teares of the Muses: 7. 484-5; text: 7. 712,
722; title: 7. 490; *Dedication*: 7. 490,
492; 1-6: 7. 483; 8. 320, 459; 20: 8. 320;
21-2: 6. 188; 28: 3. 355; 8. 316, 320;
31-48: 6. 351; 8. 296; 34: 8. 472; 35-41:
7. 494; 53-66, 147-62: 7. 494; 72-8: 6.
354; 175 ff.: 6. 355; 211: 6. 351; 213-6:
7. 500
Astyanax, 2. 298
Asyndeton, 6. 309; 8. 595
Atalanta, 2. 264; 8. 448-9
Ate, 2. 233, 266; 4. 167, 169, 173, 189, 196,
281, 283, 297, 299, 305; 5. 322-4; and
Mutability: 4. 310; 6. 278, 449. *See also*
House of Ate
Athanasius, 7. 559-60
Athelstane, 2. 334
Athenaeum, 8. 614

Athenaeus, 5. 165; 8. 510
Athenagoras, 2. 297
Athletics, 6. 354, 358
Athos, Mt., 8. 335
Atin, 2. 184, 230, 383
Atlante, 1. 251, 253-4, 331; 3. 303, 372-3; 6. 290
Atlas, 2. 264-5; 7. 308; 8. 483
Atmosphere, 1. 223
Atoms, 3. 340, 342-4, 347
Atossa, 1. 214
Atropos, 7. 416, 512
Attis, 2. 375
" atween," 8. 473
Aube, 8. 466
Auberon, 1. 254, 292-3
Aubrey, John, 3. 217; 7. 312, 475, 651-2, 654
Aubrian, 4. 264-5
August, 5. 165; 6. 305
Augustan poets, 8. 331
Augustine, St., Archbishop of Canterbury, 1. 453-4
Augustine, St., Bishop of Hippo, 1. 282; 2. 426; 6. 314, 398; 7. 672, 674, 676; 8. 329; De Civitate Dei: 1. 446; 7. 554; 8. 493; De Quantitate Animae: 7. 675; Enarratio on Ps. 146: 8. 493
Augustus Caesar, 2. 324; 5. 220; 7. 597; 8. 537
Aulus Gellius, 2. 297; 4. 244; 7. 239
Aurelius, 2. 334
Aurora, 1. 198, 304; 2. 211; 8. 466, 471
Ausonius, 1. 514; 8. 541; Cento Nuptialis: 8. 462; Eclogues 2. 15-23: 3. 242; Epigrams 33: 2. 226; Technopaegnion 13. 9: 2. 223; (pseudo) De Rosis Nascentibus 23-50: 2. 390-1
Austria, 1. 459
Autumn, 6. 306
Auxesis, 7. 552; 8. 677
Avantance, 1. 406
Avarice, 1. 410-3; 2. 252-3, 257-8, 269, 425-6, 439, 461; 3. 253, 372; 6. 269
Avernus, 2. 354
Avicenna, 7. 562, 671
Avon (river), 4. 255
Avonbeg, 4. 271-2
Avonmore, 4. 266
A. W. (in Davison's Poetical Rhapsody 1. 63 ff.): 7. 489, 594
Awbeg, 4. 268; 6. 429; 7. 453-6; 8. 464
Awdeley, John, 7. 409; 8. 355, 591
Awniduff, 4. 266-7
Axiochus: 1. 280; 4. 172; 6. 202, 246; 7. 723; 8. 286, 315
Aydelotte, Frank, 8. 355
Aye, 3. 332

Ayenbite of Inwyt, 1. 301, 412
Aylmer, John, 3. 337-8; 6. 272; 7. 243, 261, 296, 299, 325-6, 606-7; 8. 575, 577. See also Morrell
Ayres, H. M., 4. 322-4
Azores, 3. 308

Babel. See Tower of Babel
Babington Plot, 5. 245, 322, 324
Baby, 6. 203-4
Babylon, 2. 288-9; 8. 280, 305, 380
Bacchus, 1. 363; 2. 193, 271, 382; 3. 296-7, 394, 397; 5. 162, 168, 169, 231; 7. 389; 8. 328, 482
Bacon, Anthony, 8. 666
Bacon, Francis, 1. 486; 2. 287; 4. 291, 293; 5. 177, 296; 6. 383; 7. 514; Advancement of Learning: 6. 277; 8. 436; Apology: 6. 362; Essays: 2. 382; 3. 206; 4. 218; 5. 184; 6. 298; 7. 434; 8. 374; History of Henry VII: 6. 310; Wisdom of the Ancients: 7. 434
Bacon, Lady, 2. 295
Bacon, Nicholas, 7. 359
Bacon, Roger, 1. 354-5; 3. 216, 224
Badius, Jodocus, 7. 289, 328-9, 331, 337, 382, 390, 392, 650
" baffle," 5. 193
Bagpipes, 6. 234, 250
Bagwell, Richard, 5. 236, 263
Baiardo, 1. 297; 2. 342; 5. 191
Báine, 6. 426
Bait, 4. 211; 5. 206; 7. 481; 8. 446-7
Baker, Carlos, 7. 481; 8. 395
Baker, Philip, 7. 296
Baldwin, C. S., 8. 658
Bale, John, 1. 471, 483-4, 488; 5. 340; 6. 227, 267
Balisarda, 2. 275; 5. 191
" balk," 7. 358
Ball, John (agitator), 8. 352
Ball, John (editor), 7. 310; 8. 566, 632
Ball, L. F., 2. 432-4
Ballads, 1. 181, 390; 3. 275, 308; 4. 192, 200; 5. 326-7; 6. 190; 7. 277, 636-9
Ballyhoura Hills, 3. 246, 278; 6. 284, 425-6; 7. 453-6
Ballyvonare, 8. 464
Balsam, 8. 399
Banba, 3. 334; 5. 312
Bancroft, Richard, 7. 261
Bancroft, Thomas, 7. 473
Bandello, Matteo, 2. 228
Bandon, 4. 270, 272
Bangor, 3. 233
Bankis of Helicone, 7. 341
Banks, T., 7. 494, 655

Bann (river). 4. 265-7
Banosius, 6. 354
Banquet, 8. 449
Baptism, 1. 300-3, 455
Baptista Fulgosus, 2. 363
Barbarism, 8. 532, 534, 539-41
Barbosa, Duarte, 6. 226
Barbour, John, 7. 620
Barclay, Alexander, 7. 240, 264, 582, 586,
590; *Eclogues*: 7. 239, 249, 257-8, 297,
332, 372-3, 593-4, 632; 8. 321, 324, 591;
Life of St. George: 1. 380-1; *Ship of
Fools*: 7. 594; 8. 595
Bards, 1. 225
Baret, John, 2. 341
Barlowe, Arthur, 2. 185
Barnabas, St., 8. 476, 479, 633, 648
Barnes, Barnabe, 2. 253; 8. 514
Barnfield, Richard, 2. 261; 7. 273, 410, 466,
472-3, 594; 8. 475
Barons, 5. 169
Baroque, 8. 380
Baroway, I., 6. 234; 8. 424-5, 441, 448-9,
489, 519
Barrow (river), 4. 269; 6. 424
Barry, 3. 224-5
Bartholomaeus Anglicus, 2. 458, 480; 8. 398;
De Rerum Proprietatibus: 3. 206, 237; 5.
206; 8. 294, 407, 421, 437
Basciante, 8. 366
Basil, 8. 399
Baskervill, Charles, 7. 489, 643; 8. 466, 539,
575
Basse, William, 7. 324, 594
Bassianus, 2. 330
Bateson, F., 8. 361
Bath, 2. 314; 4. 255; 8. 447
" bathed in bliss," 1. 196
Bathsheba, 4. 223
Bathurst, Theodore, 7. 259, 270, 300, 422,
610, 692, 715, 717-8
Batman uppon Bartholome, 1. 185; 2. 344,
462-3, 465-6, 469; 4. 227; 5. 206
Battle of the Books, 1. 485-90; 5. 320-1
Baudoin, J., 2. 227
Baxter, Nathaniel, 8. 284
Bayne, Ronald, 2. 256
Beadsmen, 2. 194
Beall, C. B., 8. 430
Bear, 1. 263, 413; 6. 259, 269, 381; 7. 343;
8.581; and babe: 6. 203; Great: 8. 308,
431; is Persia: 8. 287; and ragged staff:
7. 384, 392; 8. 304, 306
Bear-baiting, 2. 346
" bear the bell," 4. 190
Beard, 2. 392; 6. 189-90, 365-7
Beast-fable. *See* Fable

" beastlihead," 7. 305
Beast-Man, 1. 244-5; 2. 394-5; 7. 545
Beasts, 2. 394-5; 3. 327; 6. 259, 300
Beast with seven heads, 1. 471; 8. 279, 287
Beatific Vision, 7. 564, 569
Beatrice (Dante's), 1. 305, 358, 496; 3. 245;
4. 321; 6. 250; 7. 654
Beatrice (Shakespeare's), 1. 284; 4. 284
Beaumains. *See* Gareth
Beaumont and Fletcher; *Bonduca*: 7. 271;
King and No King: 5. 193; *Wife for a
Month*: 3. 301
Beaumont, Francis, 1. 190; 4. 240
Beaumont, Joseph, 1. 273
Beauty, 2. 270; 3. 223, 390; Absolute: 7.
552-3, 560-1; angelic: 7. 506, 570; 8.
440; earthly: 1. 501; 2. 429; 4. 211; 7.
294, 569-70, 657, 661-76, 680; 8. 440,
450; emanation from God: 4. 211, 307;
6. 237, 347; 7. 523-5, 657; 8. 440, 450,
639-40; friendship, source of: 4. 293;
gradation: 7. 556; 8. 450; Heavenly: 1.
501-5; 2. 429; 4. 211, 419; 7. 388, 515,
538, 546-50, 553-70, 661-76, 678; 8. 420-
1, 446, 450, 498, 639-40; of Holiness:
1. 238; ideal: 6. 250; 7. 524, 677; 8.454;
intellectual: 7. 677, 679; 8. 454; and Love:
7. 514-5, 525-6, 539; 8. 639-40; physical:
7. 525-8; of soul and body: 7. 529-31;
8. 424, 428, 639-40; spiritual: 7. 525-7;
8. 450, 473; true and false: 4. 306-7; 5.
187-90; and Truth: 2. 272; worship of:
3. 386-7. *See also* Castle of Beauty
Beaver, 8. 372
Bebhionn, 3. 278
" Be bold," 3. 298; 6. 276
à Becket, Thomas, 2. 293
Becon, Thomas, 6. 210
Bede, 1. 486; 2. 450-1
Bedell, William, 7. 470, 594
Bedford, Earls of. *See* Russell, Edward,
Francis
Bedingfield, Thomas, 5. 237
Beelzebub, 1. 192
Beer, M., 5. 345
Bees, 5. 199; 8. 456-8
Beethoven, Ludwig von, 8. 645
Beggars. *See* Vagabonds
Behanna, 6. 287-90, 424-6, 429
Bel Merodach, 1. 238
Bel-accueil, 1. 405
Belach Febrat, 7. 455
Belden, H. M., 3. 219, 269-70; 5. 189-90;
6. 441-2
Belgarde Castle, 6. 262, 349, 374
Belge, 5. 247-55, 299-301, 317, 329
Belinus, 2. 321, 323

Bell, Idris, 2. 512

Bell Pucell, La, 1. 407

Bellamour, 6. 260-4, 349, 374; is Edward, Lord Roos: 6. 263; is Henry Hastings: 6. 353

Belleau, Remy, 8. 455, 463, 465, 474, 481, 488, 652

Belleforest, François de, 2. 228

Belleze del Furioso di M. L. Ariosto, 2. 228

Bello, Francesco, 5. 264

Bellona, 3. 279, 425-6; 4. 166; 6. 274, 278, 281, 392, 449; 7. 394; 8. 414

Bells, 8. 479; on bridles: 1. 200; 8. 362

Belphoebe, 1. 378, 497, 502; 2. 183, 205, 211-20, 222, 256, 348, 426; 3. 310, 313, 315, 317-8, 320, 325-6, 333, 366, 373-5; 4. 235, 284; 5. 200; 6. 343, 437; 8. 396, 474; and Angelica: 3. 374-5; and Britomart: 4. 320; character: 3. 381-4, 387, 389-90; and Diana Bentivoglio: 3. 338; is Elizabeth: 1. 449; 2. 211, 402, 409; 3. 246-9, 310, 375, 389; 4. 206-7, 287, 319; 6. 186; is Heavenly Venus: 4. 319; name and nativity: 3. 249; and Timias: 2. 218; 3. 312, 315, 319, 325-6, 389; 4. 205, 286-7, 300

Belus, 4. 246

Belvoir Castle, 6. 262, 349-50

Bembists, 8. 641

Bembo, Pietro, 2. 429; 3. 318; 6. 292; 7. 371, 388, 621, 663, 668, 670-1, 674; 8. 334-5, 337, 341, 343, 440-1, 454, 517, 642; *Asolani*: 7. 482, 662; *Rime*: 7. 442-3; text of *Virgil*: 8. 545-6, 548-9

"Benevolo," 6. 448

Benivieni, Girolamo, 6. 390; 7. 661, 670, 674; *Ammonitione*: 7. 550, 680; *Canzona dello Amor Celeste o Divino*: 7. 509-12, 514, 524, 528-30, 540, 549, 557, 567, 650, 662, 666-7, 671-2, 676-7, 680

Bensley, Edward, 1. 201-2; 7. 426

Bentham, James, 8. 361

Bentivoglio, Diana, 3. 338

Bentley, Richard, 5. 241; 7. 541; 8. 314

Beowulf, 4. 333; 8. 460

Berecynthia, 6. 301

Bergomas, Jacob, 2. 312

Berli, H., 8. 540

Bernard of Chartres, 1. 513; 6. 428

Bernard of Clairvaux, 2. 287; 7. 672, 674; 8. 286-7

Bernard of Ventadorn, 5. 210

Berners, Lord, 2. 336

Berni, Francesco, 1. 366; *Orlando Innamorato*: 1. 206; 1. 1. 43: 3. 204; 1. 2. 4: 4. 173; 1. 2. 20: 3. 204; 1. 3. 72: 1. 211; 1. 4. 97: 3. 266; 1. 5. 19: 4. 173; 1. 5. 22:

3. 222; 1. 5. 75: 5. 257; 1. 14. 38: 3. 246; 1. 22. 11: 4. 203; 1. 24. 22, 27: 1. 257; 1. 25. 3: 5. 157; 1. 25. 19: 2. 254; 1. 30. 2-3: 4. 234; 1. 36. 3: 3. 274; 1.37. 36: 3. 291; 1. 43. 56: 3. 277; 2. 4. 3: 3. 212; 2. 7. 70: 2. 276; 2. 16. 57: 2. 276; 2. 17. 13: 2. 275; 2. 20. 20: 5. 255

Bernon, 8. 486

Berosus, 6. 274

Bersmannus, 8. 485

Bestiaries, 1. 228, 289

Betrothal, 8. 491, 505, 664-6; Una and the Red Cross Knight: 1. 308; 5. 169

Bevis of Hampton, 1. 183, 207, 301, 398; 2. 189-90, 192, 217, 235, 348; 3. 210, 274; 5. 192; 6. 227; 7. 383; possible source of *F. Q.* 1: 1. 393, 395-6, 398, 404

Beza, Theodore, 8. 359

Bhattacherje, Mohinimohan, 5. 287-92; 7. 370, 381, 513, 516, 526-7, 531, 533, 537, 552, 562, 671, 673, 678; 8. 421, 427, 435, 450, 641

Bibiena, Bernardo, 8. 516-7

Bible, 1. 303, 471, 473; 2. 269; 5. 338; 6. 198, 281; 7. 541-2, 564, 662; 8. 329, 357-8, 536, 564, 592, 720; Bishops': 7. 541-2; 8. 307, 360; Cranmer's: 7. 541; 8. 360; in *F. Q.* 2: 2. 436; Geneva: 7. 541-2, 544-5, 557, 566; 8. 279, 305, 360, 412; Great: 7. 541; 8. 280; King James: 7. 557; Platonism, mingled with: 7. 541-2; versified: 8. 519-20; versions used by Spenser: 4. 210; 7. 321, 541-2, 557; Wycliffe version: 8. 504; Genesis: 3. 343, 346; 6. 401, 403; 7. 511; 8. 330; 1. 2-6: 2. 298; 7. 512, 560; 1. 22: 3. 257; 1. 26-7: 5. 253; 7. 542; 2. 7: 2. 289; 7. 542; 2. 9: 1. 300; 2. 11-4: 1. 255; 3: 7. 542; 3. 19: 8. 286; 3. 23: 7. 311; 4: 7. 332; 6. 3: 6. 280; 6. 4: 6. 274; 7. 11: 2. 339; 4. 183; 8. 352; 8. 9: 4. 210; 10. 9: 4. 168; 10. 20: 1. 290; 11. 1-9: 2. 289; 8. 305; 18. 23: 7. 441; 18. 27: 8. 443; 20. 6: 5. 221; 22. 16: 6. 280; 24. 15, 45: 1. 207; 28. 12: 1. 291; 32. 10: 7. 438; 41. 15: 5. 221; 46: 7. 333; 49. 9: 3. 229; Exodus: 1. 1-4: 7. 337; 3. 2 ff.: 7. 333; 10. 21: 6. 257; 12-13. 1-4: 7. 244; 14. 21-3: 1. 286, 291; 19. 2: 7. 329; 20. 1-17: 2. 276; 5. 338-9, 341, 345; 20. 5: 2. 276; 23. 15: 7. 244; 24: 1. 291; 24. 18: 1. 291; 25-40: 7. 548; 25. 5: 8. 308; 25. 18-20; 7. 554; 25. 21-2; 30. 6; 33. 8-19: 5. 247; 28: 8. 359; 30. 34: 7. 479; 32. 1-4; 33. 11; 34. 35: 7. 333; 33. 20: 7. 548, 556; 34. 18: 7. 244; Leviticus: 8: 8. 359; 9. 7, 15: 8. 360; 13. 7: 7. 462; 16. 2:

5. 247; 18. 21: 5. 257; 18. 28: 7. 239;
19. 1: 1. 433; 21. 5: 5. 217; 23. 34:
7. 244; 26. 36: 2. 211; Numbers: 1. 38:
7. 329; 7. 89: 5. 247; 17. 8: 8. 358;
29: 7. 244; Deuteronomy: 5. 6-21: 2.
276; 5. 338-9, 341, 345; 7. 13: 8. 492;
9. 21: 5. 174; 10. 9: 7. 302; 12. 23:
2. 247; 14: 8. 486; 16: 7. 244; 18. 1:
7. 301; 28. 26: 1. 232; 32. 15: 2. 255;
32. 42: 1. 247, 256; 34: 1. 291; Joshua:
10. 12: 1. 286; 10. 24: 2. 236; 6. 219;
Judges: 4: 3. 331; 4. 21: 3. 238; 5. 12:
8. 444; 7: 1. 286; 9. 33: 5. 224; 9. 53:
6. 215; 16. 17, 19: 5. 224, 370; 1 Samuel:
2. 6, 7: 5. 178-9; 2. 8: 7. 517, 550; 2.
22, 29: 1. 208; 3. 19: 1. 196; 13. 6: 6.
259; 16. 23: 4. 174; 17. 4 ff.: 8. 306;
17. 44, 46: 1. 232; 2. 274; 18. 3; 20. 11;
23. 18: 4. 223; 18. 6: 5. 258; 21. 9:
5. 227; 24. 14: 2. 209; 25. 3, 8, 9: 3.
275; 25. 37: 1. 250; 28: 8. 486; 31. 10:
5. 227; 2 Samuel: 1. 21: 5. 261; 3. 35:
6. 191; 9. 8: 2. 209; 10. 4: 6. 189; 12.
1-9: 7. 360; 15. 6: 6. 188; 16. 5-13: 5.
268; 16. 9: 2. 209; 17. 8: 6. 259; 22. 11:
3. 287; 1 Kings: 3. 16-27: 5. 168; 5: 4.
225; 6. 28: 7. 548; 7. 50: 7. 478; 10. 21:
2. 290; 11. 11: 8. 377, 19. 11, 12: 3.
301; 21. 10: 5. 239; 2 Kings: 5. 14:
1. 302; 6. 16, 17: 2. 271; 7. 2: 4. 183;
8. 352; 20. 10: 1. 286; 23. 10: 5. 257;
1 Chronicles: 28. 2: 7. 548; 28. 9: 7. 558;
2 Chronicles: 9. 8: 5. 214; 20. 6: 5. 179;
Ezra: 7. 14: 1. 214, 217; Esther: 1. 14:
1. 214, 217; Job: 6. 396; 7. 441, 560; 1.
21: 5. 179; 7. 1: 2. 271; 9. 25: 6, 7: 7.
445; 9. 33: 2. 276; 10. 11: 3. 257; 14. 2:
5. 178; 14. 7-10: 7. 408; 19. 24: 1. 262;
21. 18: 5. 261; 26. 10-1: 7. 548, 550;
28. 15-9: 7. 570; 28. 23-5: 5. 177, 180;
30. 19: 8. 493; 31. 38-40: 7. 425; 35. 1-5:
5. 261; 36. 7: 5. 179; 38. 4: 8. 383; 38.
17: 4. 183; 39. 10: 2. 236; 41. 11: 5. 179;
41. 15: 1. 297; 41. 18: 2. 359; 41. 32: 2.
357; 42. 2: 5. 179; Psalms: 8. 477; Penitential: 8. 520; 1. 4: 5. 261; 5. 9: 8. 359;
6. 6: 3. 218; 7. 16: 6. 194; 7. 312; 8. 6: 2.
236; 9. 8: 7. 557; 9. 13: 4. 183; 9. 16:
6. 194; 10. 18: 1. 290; 15. 11: 5. 179;
16. 10: 3. 257; 19. 2: 7. 556; 19. 5:
1. 224; 8. 472; 22. 12: 7. 359; 22. 21:
1. 240; 23. 1: 7. 299; 24. 4, 7: 7. 542;
8. 337, 476; 26. 6: 2. 268; 27. 4: 8. 331;
31. 14: 1. 262; 36. 7: 7. 509; 39. 11:
2. 200; 42. 3: 7. 444; 42. 10: 1. 207;
45. 2: 7. 566; 45. 6: 7. 548, 557; 51. 2:
1. 287; 52. 8: 7. 285; 56. 8: 6. 232;

56. 13: 5. 196; 57. 1: 5. 220; 57. 6: 6.
194; 65. 13: 2. 246; 68. 2: 7. 479; 69.
31: 1. 258; 73. 7: 1. 219; 74. 13: 5. 179;
75. 6: 5. 339; 75. 7: 5. 179; 75. 8: 5.
167; 78. 39: 6. 280; 80. 1: 7. 299; 80.
35: 6. 194; 82. 1, 6: 5. 160; 89. 14:
5. 217; 90. 5-6: 3. 281; 90. 17: 7. 548-9;
91. 12: 8. 464; 94. 3: 3. 290; 95. 4:
8. 383; 97. 2: 5. 217; 99. 5: 7. 548;
100. 5: 4. 170; 103. 1: 8. 388; 103. 5:
1. 302-3; 103. 14-6: 5. 178; 7. 445; 104.
1- 7: 7. 548; 104. 26: 8. 407; 106. 37-8:
5. 257; 107. 10: 8. 313; 107. 18: 4. 183;
109. 24: 7. 250; 110. 3: 3. 249; 113. 7:
7. 517; 114. 3: 2. 354; 118. 19: 8. 476;
119. 103: 8. 322; 119. 176: 6. 216; 127.
3: 8. 492; 128. 3: 7. 285; 129. 7: 6. 305;
131: 8. 576; 132. 11: 8. 492; 136. 9: 6.
276; 140. 3: 5. 267; 140. 9: 5. 225;
141. 3: 2. 291; 144. 3: 2. 271; 145. 9:
1. 280, 288; 4. 170, 277; 147. 4: 8. 493;
Proverbs: 7. 560; 1. 9: 8. 330; 2. 6: 7.
548-9; 3. 13-6: 6. 241; 8. 315; 4. 9:
8. 330; 4. 23: 2. 456; 5. 3: 1. 278; 7. 17:
1. 182; 8. 15-6: 5. 179, 214, 339; 8. 17:
7. 569; 8. 18-21: 6. 241; 7. 548, 567;
8. 27: 7. 560; 8. 30: 7. 564; 9. 1: 2. 183;
4. 260; 9. 5: 7. 570; 9. 10: 7. 565; 10.
12: 7. 263; 15. 1: 2. 247; 15. 18: 2.
273; 7. 263; 16. 14: 4. 210; 16. 24: 7.
478; 17. 12: 6. 259; 20. 27: 6. 199; 23.
32: 1. 183; 24. 3-4: 6. 241; 25. 22: 7.
359; 26. 21: 2. 273; 26. 27: 6. 194;
28. 25: 7. 263; 30: 7. 303; 30. 13: 1.
215; Ecclesiastes: 3. 306-9; 7. 417, 441;
8. 519, 536; 1. 2: 8. 279, 428; 1. 7: 6.
186; 1. 14: 8. 307; 2. 11-4: 8. 307, 313;
3. 20: 8. 493; 7. 26: 3. 214; 11. 3: 1.
288; 12: 2. 286, 290; 3. 209; Song of
Songs: 1. 182; 6. 233-5; 7. 563; 8. 309,
449, 473, 519; 2. 1: 2. 214; 2. 10-3: 8.
445; 2. 14: 8. 460; 4-7: 8. 474; 4. 4-5:
6. 234; 8. 475; 4. 7: 1. 308; 2. 213; 7.
281; 4. 10-6: 8. 441-2, 448-9; 4. 11: 1.
278; 2. 215; 7. 478; 5. 2: 8. 460; 5. 10-6:
8. 424-5; 5. 10: 2. 214; 5. 14: 6. 233; 8.
449; 5. 15: 2. 217; 6. 9: 8. 460; 6. 10: 8.
489; 7. 3-8: 8. 448-9; 7. 4: 6. 233; 7. 7:
2. 217; 8. 2: 1. 225; *see also Canticum
Canticorum*; Isaiah: 1. 16: 1. 287; 2. 19-
21: 6. 259; 2. 22: 8. 298; 6. 2: 7. 548;
6. 3: 5. 241; 9. 2: 7. 446; 11. 1: 3. 227;
8. 358; 11. 6: 7. 304; 11. 16: 4. 211;
13. 10: 1. 239; 16. 5: 5. 247; 21. 9: 1.
304; 24. 18: 8. 352; 34. 4: 8. 481; 35.
10: 7. 541; 40. 6-8: 5. 178; 40. 11:
7. 299; 40. 12: 5. 177; 41. 15-6: 5. 261;

49. 23: 1. 178; 51. 17: 5. 167; 53. 3: 7. 542; 53. 6: 6. 216; 54. 13: 8. 358; 64. 11: 8. 324; 65. 25: 7. 304; Jeremiah: 2. 13: 1. 205; 5. 6: 7. 360; 5. 8: 2. 255; 8. 2: 8. 481; 9. 1: 8. 314; 10. 13: 4. 215; 15. 18: 7. 456; 19. 13: 8. 481; 23. 5: 5. 160; 31. 34: 8. 358; 32. 35: 5. 257; 46. 10: 1. 247; 50. 17: 6. 216; 51. 17: 2. 192; Lamentations: 1: 8. 285; 1. 1: 5. 250; Ezekiel: 8. 405; 1: 7. 548; 1. 20: 2. 242; 10. 3-5: 8. 478; 28. 13-6: 7. 337; 30. 2: 2. 247; 34. 2 ff.: 7. 299; 34. 14: 7. 329; 37. 1: 2. 259; 40. 2: 1. 291; 44. 17, 20: 5. 217; 48: 8. 389; Daniel: 6. 188; 2. 31-3: 8. 305; 3: 1. 237-8; 3. 13-5: 8. 305; 4. 27: 8. 380; 4. 35: 5. 179; 6. 27: 1. 208; 7. 3-7: 1. 250; 8. 287; Hosea: 2. 15: 5. 205; 13. 8: 2. 277: 14. 7: 1. 226; Joel: 2. 10: 1. 239; 2. 13: 6. 258; Micah: 5. 8: 7. 304; Habakkuk: 1. 13: 7. 547; Zechariah: 2. 1-2: 8. 389; 13. 10: 7. 542; Malachi: 3. 10: 4. 183; 8. 352; Matthew: 1. 17: 2. 299; 1. 23: 7. 542; 2. 1-2: 7. 542; 2. 14: 1. 243; 3. 10: 7. 261; 4. 8-9: 2. 254; 4. 23: 7. 542; 5. 7: 6. 192; 5. 14-6: 7. 548-9; 5.45: 5. 160; 6. 24: 2. 254; 6. 28: 2. 246; 7. 527; 7. 5: 6. 192; 7. 13: 4. 168; 7. 14: 1. 283; 7. 15: 7. 302, 360, 363; 7. 24-7: 1. 213; 8. 305; 8. 20: 5. 252; 9. 15: 1. 310; 9. 20: 7. 462; 10. 16: 7. 360; 12. 40: 2. 269; 15. 11: 2. 268; 16. 18: 7. 413; 16. 28: 5. 194; 17. 1-8: 6. 296; 19. 6: 7. 533; 20. 15: 5. 179; 20. 19: 2. 268; 20. 22-3: 5. 167; 20. 28: 7. 358; 21: 1. 243; 7. 329; 21. 8: 1. 307; 21. 21: 1. 286; 22. 13: 2. 237; 22. 21: 5. 339; 22. 37-9: 7. 544; 22. 37: 7. 542; 23. 35: 7. 332; 23. 37: 2. 273; 24. 3: 7. 329; 24. 29: 1. 239; 5. 156; 24. 33: 5. 210; 24. 43: 3. 276; 25. 33: 7. 336; 25. 34-40: 7. 545; 25. 46: 6. 236; 26. 26: 7. 542; 26. 34, 69-75: 5. 210; 26. 36: 7. 329; 26. 39: 5. 167; 26. 41: 1. 281; 2. 192; 7. 365; 27. 1-38: 7. 542; 27. 24: 2. 268; 27. 34: 182; 27. 39: 7. 543; Mark: 4. 28: 8. 390; 6. 37: 2. 268; 8. 8: 7. 720; 8. 36: 2. 256; 9. 6: 6. 296; 14. 30, 68-72: 5. 210; 15. 11: 2. 268; 15. 23: 1. 182; Luke: 1. 52: 5. 179; 1. 78: 7. 544; 1. 79: 7. 446; 8. 313; 2. 10: 6. 307; 2. 35: 1. 280; 7. 442; 3. 7: 6. 259; 3. 9: 7. 261; 6. 36: 7. 545; 10. 34: 1. 228; 11. 34: 6. 198; 12. 24: 6. 300; 15. 1-7: 7. 360; 16. 13: 2. 254; 18. 7: 1. 261; 19. 36: 1. 307; 22. 45: 6. 233; 22. 60-1: 5. 210; John: 7. 540; 1. 3:

7. 481; 1. 4: 8. 423; 1. 9: 7. 548; 1. 14: 2. 325; 7. 543; 1. 18: 8. 325; 1. 29: 7. 544; 3. 14: 1. 285; 3. 19: 3. 244; 3. 31: 2. 347; 4. 7: 1. 207; 4. 10: 1. 205, 300; 4. 14: 1. 300; 5. 14: 2. 230; 6. 26-58: 8. 358; 6. 35; 13. 34; 15. 17: 7. 545; 8. 32-6: 8. 314; 8. 52: 5. 194; 9. 7: 1. 302; 10: 7. 360; 10. 11: 7. 299; 10. 12: 7. 298; 10. 18: 7. 542; 10. 34: 5. 339; 12. 31: 2. 254; 13. 34: 7. 545; 13. 38: 5. 210; 14. 2: 8. 493; 14. 3: 1. 291; 15. 9, 12: 7. 542, 674: 8. 444; 19. 24: 7. 542; 19. 34: 1. 285; Acts: 5. 338; 1. 18: 1. 188; 2. 30: 8. 492; 3. 14; 5. 30; 7. 52; 10. 39: 7. 544; 3. 15: 8. 443; 7. 30: 1. 291; 12. 10: 2. 259; 17. 30: 8. 322; 21. 16, 17: 7. 299; 26. 13: 6. 296; 27. 41: 1. 216; Romans: 1. 19-20: 7. 556, 674; 1. 21: 1. 208; 5. 10: 7. 542; 6. 9: 8. 444; 6. 12: 2. 339; 8. 314; 6. 19: 2. 192, 339; 6. 23; 7. 23: 7. 543; 7. 21: 1. 257; 7. 23-4: 2. 339; 8: 2. 192; 8. 1, 3, 6: 1. 281; 8. 1: 7. 544; 8. 3: 7. 543; 8. 21: 7. 544; 9. 22: 8. 314; 10. 18: 1. 257; 11. 33: 5. 180; 12. 1: 8. 296; 12. 20: 7. 359; 13. 1-5: 5. 179, 339; 14. 10: 7. 299; 14. 17: 7. 559; 1 Corinthians: 2. 6: 2. 254; 6. 20: 7. 543; 7. 5: 6. 214; 10. 3: 8. 358; 10. 12: 5. 206; 8. 439; 11. 16: 7. 303; 13: 1. 287; 13. 12: 6. 185, 296; 7. 555; 15. 3: 7. 542; 15. 20: 8. 443; 15. 22: 2. 325; 15. 25: 2. 236; 15. 31: 7. 413, 445; 15. 39: 3. 257; 15. 42, 53-4: 7. 531; 15. 47: 2. 347; 15. 51: 6. 313; 15. 55-7: 8. 444; 2 Corinthians: 1. 9: 8. 439; 3. 18: 6. 296; 7. 519, 542; 5. 1: 2. 269, 289; 8. 493; 6. 9: 7. 445; 6. 14: 7. 304; 6. 17: 8. 560; 7. 3: 7. 445; 8. 9: 7. 542; 9. 8: 1. 288; 10. 4: 2. 271; 10. 5: 7. 544; 12. 2-4: 7. 674; 12. 3: 7. 569; Galatians: 3. 15: 1. 291; 3. 20: 3. 246; 5. 1: 8. 360; 5. 13-4: 7. 544; 5. 26: 7. 303; Ephesians: 1. 11-5: 7. 302; 1. 18: 1. 286; 1. 21: 1. 310; 2. 3: 8. 314; 2. 8-9: 1. 283; 4. 4: 1. 286; 4. 8: 8. 444; 4. 18: 1. 208, 260; 5. 18: 2. 415; 5. 25-7: 7. 544; 6. 11-7: 1. 176, 416, 418, 425-6; 5. 261; 8. 322; 6. 11-2: 1. 313; 6. 16: 1. 254, 281; Philippians: 1. 21: 7. 445; 2. 7: 7. 543; 3. 8: 7. 570; 4. 7: 1. 240; Colossians: 1. 16: 1. 310; 2. 14: 1. 281; 3. 24: 7. 302; 1 Thessalonians: 5. 14: 1. 281; 2 Thessalonians: 2. 13: 1. 281; 1 Timothy: 1. 19: 2. 356; 4. 1: 8. 322; 6. 10: 2. 251, 254; 2 Timothy: 2. 9: 2. 295; 4. 17: 1. 240; Titus: 3. 1: 5. 339; 3. 3-7: 5.

544; Hebrews: 1. 3: 7. 544; 1. 14: 2. 271; 2. 8: 2. 236; 5. 1: 8. 360; 6. 19: 1. 286; 9. 4: 8. 358; 9. 5: 7. 548; 10. 23: 1. 285; 11. 1: 1. 285; 11. 3: 7. 555; 11. 21: 7. 438; 12. 24: 7. 332; 13. 17: 5. 339; 13. 20: 7. 288, 299; James: 1. 10-11: 5. 178; 1. 27: 1. 288; 2. 3: 8. 355; 2. 13: 6. 192; 2. 19: 5. 262; 4. 14: 8. 286; 5. 4: 6. 315; 1 Peter: 1. 16: 1. 433; 1. 19: 1. 291; 7. 542, 544; 1. 24: 5. 178; 8. 439; 2. 5: 1. 283; 2. 11: 2. 341; 2. 13-4: 5. 179, 339; 2. 25: 7. 299, 329, 358; 8. 358; 3. 10: 6. 212; 3. 19: 1. 234; 5. 4: 1. 287; 3. 259; 7. 299; 2 Peter: 1. 5: 1. 184; 2. 4: 7. 541; 2. 14: 3. 210; 2. 19: 8. 314; 2. 22: 1. 219; 2. 395; 7. 545; 3. 16: 1. 286; 1 John: 1. 8: 8. 330; 3. 3: 1. 286; 4. 7: 8. 326; 4. 16: 7. 674; 4. 19: 7. 544; 8. 444; 5. 6: 1. 285; Jude: 2. 237; 7. 241-2; Revelation: 1. 370; 6. 188; 7. 241; influence in *F. Q.* 1: 1. 256, 368, 370; 8. 279-80; 1. 5: 444; 1. 18: 1. 177; 2. 7: 1. 301; 3. 12: 1. 291; 3. 16: 7. 239; 4-22: 7. 557; 4. 5: 7. 548; 5. 1: 1. 286; 5. 9: 7. 542; 6. 9-10: 1. 261, 368; 6. 15-7: 6. 259; 7. 548; 7. 9-14: 5. 241; 7. 442, 548, 554; 8. 444, 477; 7. 17: 8. 250; 8. 3-5: 7. 478, 548; 8. 13: 2. 234; 9. 7: 1. 183; 11. 2: 1. 256; 12: 1. 249, 470-1; 12. 3-9: 1. 176, 250, 256, 368; 7. 541, 557; 13: 6. 269; 8. 279; 13. 1-2: 1. 263, 471; 8. 287; 14. 8: 1. 304; 2. 192; 15. 3: 5. 241; 16. 13: 1. 184; 16. 18: 7. 548; 17: 1. 200, 249, 258, 263, 281, 368, 470-1; 2. 190, 192, 261; 8. 279-80, 412; 18. 1-2: 8. 279; 18. 7: 1. 250; 19. 1: 8. 478; 19. 6-7: 1. 308, 310; 7. 548; 19. 9: 7. 442; 19. 11-20: 2. 183; 8. 279; 20. 2-8: 1. 309; 2. 183, 187; 4. 208; 20. 14: 7. 542; 21: 1. 291, 368; 8. 279-80, 309, 413; 22. 1-16: 1. 205, 300-1, 369; 2. 395; 7. 544, 552; 8. 279-80, 309. *See also* Apocrypha; New Testament; Old Testament; Ten Commandments

"bidding base," 3. 288; 7. 379. *See also* Prisoner's base

Bidpai, 8. 585, 592

Bien Avise, Mal Avise, 2. 433

"bigger notes," 6. 291; 7. 384

Bingham, Richard, 5. 173

Bion, 7. 266-73, 397, 593, 595; 8. 307, 657; Idyll 1: 7. 268, 399, 486-7, 491, 499, 505, 590; 8. 381; 7-9: 3. 208; 7. 496; 16: 7. 496; 29 ff.: 7. 249, 497; 40-9: 7. 496; 53: 3. 242; 60-1: 7. 495; 66: 7. 440; Idyll 4: 7. 268; Idyll 9: 8. 481

Birch, Thomas, 5. 299, 331-2; 6. 271; 7. 326, 575; 8. 291, 303, 431, 511, 559, 666

Birds, 1. 412; 2. 274; 6. 300; 8. 279, 343, 406-7, 442, 466

Birthmark, 6. 263-4

Bisaltis, 3. 296

Bishop, Cortlandt F., 8. 681

Bishop of Ross. *See* Leslie, John

Bishops, 7. 302, 304, 324, 331, 352, 354, 356, 358, 363

Bitter sweet, 4. 216-7; 7. 272-3, 491, 507

Bitumen, 2. 288-9

Black brow, 3. 240

Black Knight, 1. 394-5

Black Pinnace, 8. 308

Blackfriars Theatre, 8. 316

Blackmore, Richard, 1. 314, 493; 2. 450; 3. 228

Blackwater, 4. 266-8; 6. 286; 7. 454-6

Blackwood's Magazine. See Wilson, John

Bladh, 4. 269-70

Bladud, 2. 314-5

Blake, William, 7. 637; 8. 335, 443, 471-2, 481, 659

Blandamour, 3. 374; 4. 170-1, 173, 188, 284, 299, 330; 5. 322, 324; is Earl of Norfolk: 5. 187; is Earl of Northumberland: 3. 378; 4. 171; 5. 245, 299, 301

Blandford, 4. 256

Blandina, 6. 200-1, 216, 327-8, 348

Blank verse. *See* Verse

Blaskets, 2. 349-50

Blasphemy, 4. 212; 5. 239

Blatant Beast, 1. 364, 367, 417; 2. 252; 3. 327; 5. 284-5, 297, 307, 315, 319; 6. 188, 209, 236, 277, 318-9, 327, 356-7, 382-8; character: 6. 341-2; is Malice, Malevolence, Envy, Despite, Contentiousness, Detraction, Deceit: 6. 326-7; is the mob: 6. 384; name: 5. 267; 6. 271; origin: 6. 212-3, 268-9, 382-8; is Puritans: 1. 481; 6. 267, 364, 382-3, 386-8; 7. 582; is Scandal: 6. 203, 205-6, 265, 267, 269, 327, 363; is Slander: 6 323-4, 341-2, 356, 363,383-6

"blatter," 5. 267; 6. 271

Blaze, St., 7. 328

"blear," 7. 327

Blenerhasset, Thomas, 7. 280, 465

Blenheim, 6. 298

"bless," 1. 200

Blessednes of Brytaine, 1. 266

Blind Devotion, 1. 208

Bliocadran, 6. 369-70

Blod, 6. 425

Blomius, 6. 424-5

"Blood will tell." *See* Ancestry, Breeding

"bloody," 1. 210; 2. 197

Blount, Christopher, 6. 364
Blount, Edward, 8. 320
" blubbered," 3. 270-1
Boadicea, 2. 327-30; 3. 236, 334, 339; 8. 288-9
Boaistnau, Pierre, 8. 627
Boar, 1. 412; 3. 261; 8. 571, 605
Boate, Gerard, 4. 270
Boatwright, Evelyn, 1. 313
Boccaccio, Giovanni, 1. 483; 3. 394; 4. 244-5, 274; 7. 240, 378, 589, 596, 621, 661; *Ameto*: 1. 195; 6. 372; 7. 240, 323, 344-5, 406, 591, 631; 8. 474, 516; *Amorosa Fiammetta*: 2. 297, 392; 3. 218, 270; 5. 204; 7. 318; *Amorosa Visione*: 3. 292; 5. 204; *Bucolicum Carmen*: 7. 598; *Decameron*: 1. 349; 4. 224; 8. 350, 586, 589; *De Casibus Illustrium Virorum*: 1. 237; *De Montibus*: 7. 308, 337; *Eclogues*: 7. 632; 1: 7. 249, 269, 332, 345, 365, 385; 2: 7. 251, 310; 3: 7. 249, 365; 4: 7. 251, 365; 5: 7. 270, 385; 6: 7. 342, 345; 7: 7. 249; 9: 7. 365; 10, 14, 15: 7. 672; 13: 7. 270, 345, 347; 14: 7. 413; 441-2; 15: 7. 249, 310, 318; 16: 7. 318; *Filocolo*, 1. 203; 6. 292; *Filocopo*, 5. 204; *Genealogia Deorum*: Book 1: 1: 1. 191: 2. 231-2; 5. 234; 2: 3. 257; 7. 512; 3: 2. 232; 4. 169; 5: 4. 182; 6. 281; 10: 2. 253; 8. 301; 13: 2. 347; 4. 319; 14: 2. 267; 18: 5. 266; 20: 5. 212; 8. 345; 21: 1. 231; 5. 251; Book 2: 2: 6. 278; Book 3: 2: 6. 301; 4, 13, 14: 4. 196; 6: 2. 200; 14: 4. 239; 16: 2. 232; 22: 2. 273; 3. 254; 4. 193; 7. 480; 8. 327; Book 4: 1: 8. 384; 3: 8. 470; 4: 6. 308-9; 9: 3. 220; 16: 3. 266; 6. 276; 7. 329; 31: 7. 308; 35: 7. 274; 47: 4. 193; 61: 7. 273, 289-90; 68: 5. 219; Book 5: 22: 3. 261; 25: 3. 212; 5. 232; 7. 389; 35: 6. 247, 252, 254; 7. 289; 47: 7. 290; 48: 3. 426; 7. 394; Book 6: 4: 6. 308; 6: 2. 342; 22: 3. 280; 7. 333; 55-73: 3. 282; Book 7: 9: 3. 270; 20: 2. 365-6; 36: 3. 243; 41: 3. 339; Book 8: 1: 3. 297; 2: 7. 244; 4: 8. 339; 5: 5. 212-3; 6: 2. 251-2, 257-8; 8: 6. 307; Book 9: 1: 5. 190; 6. 301; 8. 491; 2: 6. 308; 8. 492; 35: 3. 339; Book 10: 12: 2. 308; 4. 246; 27: 8. 301-2, 309; 61: 2. 258; Book 11: 1: 8. 298, 493; 2: 1. 512, 514; 8. 313, 324; 4: 4. 228; 5: 1. 174; Book 12: 52: 3. 240; 7. 274; 65: 2. 375; Book 13: 1: 2. 308; 3. 294; 4. 169, 246; 5. 169, 204, 228; 8. 299, 484; 17: 1. 243; 26: 2. 273; 68: 3. 293; 71: 1. 238; Book 15: 6: 7. 244; *Ninfale Fiesolano*: 6. 430;

Teseide: 1. 1: 7. 281; 7: 2. 285, 391; 3. 211; 4. 226, 228-9, 232; 9: 5. 264; 11: 1. 181
Bocchus, 8. 348
Bodenham, John, 7. 339
Bodin, Jean, 1. 483; 3. 321; 5. 155, 177, 204, 296-7
Bodinus, 1. 204
Bodleian Library, 1. 517, 519; 4. 354; 6. 458, 472; 7. 696, 708, 719; 8. 282, 680-2, 697-9, 706, 709, 721
Body, Allegory of, 2. 436-8, 472-85. *See also* Castle of the Body
Boece, Hector, 1. 483
Boethius, Anicius Manlius, Severinus, 3. 321; 6. 400, 416-9, 421-2; 7. 537; *De Consolatione Philosophiae*: 6. 393, 396; 7. 674; 8. 315; 1, met. 5: 5. 178; 2. 1, pr. 1: 1. 289; 2. 4: 8. 325; 2. 5: 2. 255; 2, met. 8: 1. 264; 2. 261; 4. 227; 7. 481; 3, pr. 1: 7. 341; 3, met. 2: 1. 264; 4. 215; 6. 417-8, 422; 3, met. 9: 6. 295, 299; 4, pr. 6: 6. 417, 422; 4, met. 6: 5. 178; 6. 417; 4. 7. 1: 6. 282; 5, pr. 6: 3. 350-1; *De Musica*: 7. 392
Boetus, 8. 336
Böhme, T., 7. 525
Boiardo, 1. 248, 331, 359, 360, 378; 2. 275; 3. 272, 369-70; 6. 214, 220; and *F. Q.* 2: 2. 444; Spenser, compared with: 2. 283; 3. 202; Spenser ignorant of: 3. 369-70; *Orlando Innamorato*: 4. 174; 5. 186; Book 1: 2. 35: 5. 187; 3. 2-6: 1. 299; 3. 9: 6. 201; 3. 69: 6. 255; 4. 44: 5. 232; 4. 65: 3. 243; 4. 66: 1. 195; 6: 2. 393; 6. 74: 1. 195; 8. 1-14: 3. 208; 8. 11: 2. 214; 5. 189; 11. 9: 4. 190; 11. 11: 4. 185; 13. 17: 6. 217; 14. 29: 5. 235; 17. 63: 1. 226; 19. 45-52: 1. 248; 21. 31: 1. 304; 23. 12-3: 1. 241; 24. 50-1: 1. 299; 26. 28-32: 1. 299; 30: 1. 510; Book 2: 2. 230; 1. 35-6: 2. 220-1: 3. 5: 6. 217; 4. 18: 3. 264; 7. 4: 6. 217; 7. 6: 1. 226; 9. 3 ff.: 2. 229; 9. 49-53: 2. 240-1; 12-13: 1. 191, 204; 12. 3: 5. 180; 15. 43-8: 6. 245; 17. 11: 5. 232; 17. 19: 5. 181; 18. 34: 6. 233; 19. 16: 2. 283; 20. 49: 1. 226; 20. 60: 5. 183; 24. 56: 3. 264; 26. 53: 2. 283; 27. 25-33: 6. 260-2; 29, 30: 6. 185; 30. 8: 5. 261; 6. 259; Book 3: 3. 218; 1: 3. 291; 2. 3-9: 4. 218; 2. 28: 6. 197; 2. 46: 2. 282; 2. 48 ff.: 2. 346; 2. 49-52: 1. 299; 3. 24 ff.: 3. 263; 3. 44: 5. 228; 4. 21: 6. 217; 4-5. 33: 3. 370; 5. 35-7: 1. 246; 6. 30: 6. 217; 7. 10-6: 1. 182; 7. 39: 3.

312; 7. 45: 1. 304; 8. 14: 5. 261; 8. 38: 2. 235

"bold, bad man," 1. 190

Boldness, 1. 257

Boleyn, Anne, 1. 461, 466; 8. 497; is Syrinx: 7. 274-5, 281

Bolingbroke, Henry St. John, 5. 306

Bolton, Edmund, 2. 205-6, 329; 6. 359; 7. 615, 681-2

Bonaventura, 4. 260; 7. 564, 672, 674

Bonduca. See Boadicea

Bonefas, 1. 398

Bonfires, 8. 480

Bonner, Edmund, 1. 460

Book of Common Prayer, 1. 472, 544; 5. 243; 6. 228, 241; 8. 357, 443

Booke of Death, 7. 409

Boor, 6. 191

"boot," 8. 306

Bootes, 1. 197; 5. 191

Boozing-can, 1. 411-2

Borage, 7. 498

Boreas, 5. 262

Borghesi, Peter, 8. 629

Borland, Lois, 8. 644

Borlase, William, 2. 323

"borrow," 7. 303

"bosom," 8. 325

Boston Public Library, 7. 709; 8. 681; 722

Boswell, Alexander, 7. 642

Boswell, J., 7. 469

Bosworth, William, 5. 164

Botticelli, Sandro, 1. 224; 2. 217, 366; 3. 395; 6. 254; 7. 267, 282; 8. 661

Botting, R. B., 7. 276-7, 296, 327, 449, 613-4

Bouchart, Alain, 2. 452

Bouchier, Jonathan, 3. 425

Boughner, D. C., 2. 464-6

Bourchier, John, Lord Berners, 2. 188

"bower," 8. 337

"bower and hall," 6. 242

Bower of Bliss, 1. 238, 396; 2. 184-5, 348, 350-2, 370-4, 382, 402, 410-2, 417, 426, 428-31, 462; 3. 273; 6. 254; 8. 390; and Celtic lore: 2. 446-8; and Eden: 2. 430-1; from Homer?: 2. 43-6

Bowes, Robert, 5. 244

Box, diamond, 1. 471-2

Box (plant), 8. 348

Boxley, 7. 328

The Boy and the Mantle, 4. 192

Boyle, Alexander (Elizabeth's brother), 8. 651-2

Boyle, Elizabeth, 5. 207, 283-4; 6. 219-20, 250, 252, 254, 349, 353; 7. 482, 602, 679; 8. 419-20, 424, 434, 440-1, 448, 452-4,

463, 473-4, 476, 494, 501, 651, 635-8, 647-52; and Rosalind: 7. 654

Boyle, Richard, Earl of Cork, 7. 452, 482; 8. 463, 648-9, 652

Boyle, Stephen (Elizabeth's father), 8. 651

Boyne (river), 4. 265-6

Bracidas, 5. 195, 273, 278, 289, 296, 304

Brackbawn, 6. 286-90

Bradamante, 1. 211, 249, 336, 360, 378; 2. 439; and Britomart: 3. 202, 272, 289, 332, 334, 369-73; 5. 213, 221, 348-9

Bradner, L., 7. 328

Braggadochio, 1. 347; 2. 183, 205-13, 219, 222, 231, 234, 411, 421, 425-6; 3. 268-9, 285-6, 313-15, 317, 319, 328, 374; 5. 273, 278, 280, 285, 288, 296, 304; is Alençon: 2. 207, 219, 401-2; 3. 246, 380; and Martano: 5. 192

Brain-pan, 6. 215

Brand, burning, 1. 412

Brand, John, 1. 243; 7. 297

Brandimarte, 5. 172; 6. 260-1

Brandon, Samuel, 6. 437-8

"bransles," 3. 284

Brantôme, Pierre de Bourdeilles, Seigneur de, 5. 247

Brasidas, 5. 195

Brass, 8. 395

Brathwaite, Richard, 8. 369

"brazen," 4. 261; 5. 165, 298; 6. 239; 7. 556; 8. 314, 404

Breeding, 6. 194, 255, 258-9, 338, 345. See also Ancestry; Nobility; Obscure origin

Bregog, 4. 268-9, 271; 6. 424-6, 429, 441; 7. 448, 454-7; 8. 529

Brendan, Saint, 2. 349, 355-6, 358, 381, 447-8

Brennus, 2. 321

Brent (river), 4. 254

Brerewood, Edward, 2. 424

Breton, Nicholas, 3. 307; 7. 466, 469, 675; 8. 283, 375, 516; Forte of Fancie: 1. 406; 2. 285-6; 4. 226, 229; A Straunge Dream: 1. 405

Breviary, 1. 412-3; 8. 485

Breviary of Britayne, 1. 266

Brian, 4. 191; 6. 187

Briana, 6. 187, 190-1, 317, 324, 326-8, 333

Briar, 6. 209; 7. 253-5, 260-6, 294; 8. 577; is Aylmer: 7. 261; is Burleigh: 7. 254; is Church of England: 7. 603

Bribery, 5. 347

Bridegroom, 1. 224-5

Bridge, 5. 169-70, 172, 213, 345-7; 8. 306

Bridges, Robert, 4. 243

Bridgewater, Earl of. See Egerton, John

Bridgewater Manuscripts, 4. 226; 7. 466, 470; 8. 520

Brie, Friedrich, 2. 213
Brigadore, 2. 440; 3. 203
Brigandine, 8. 396
Brigands. *See* Thieves
Briggs, H. E., 8. 445
Briggs, W. D., 3. 218
Bright, Timothy, 1. 275-6
Brigliadore, 2. 342, 440; 5. 191
Brinkelow, Henry, 8. 591
Bristol, 4. 255
Britain, 2. 324-5, 330-2; 3. 215; 8. 672;
    Matter of: 1. 359, 482-90, 493, 495
British Critic: 8. 632
British Museum, 1. 517-9, 521; 3. 235, 428;
    4. 354; 6. 458; 7. 696, 708, 719; 8. 501,
    680-1, 687, 697, 706-7, 709
Britomart, 1. 339, 346, 359-60, 378, 425,
    432, 497; 2. 348-9, 372, 396; 3. 278,
    283, 288, 300, 311, 313-6, 320, 324-5,
    328-9, 353, 355-6, 359-61, 363-4, 367-73;
    4. 173-4, 276, 283-6; 5. 273; 6. 230, 306,
    319; 7. 509, 519, 661, 665; 8. 315; and
    Amoret: 4. 319-21; and Artegall: 4. 285-6,
    294, 301, 317-9; 5. 207-9, 220, 348-9;
    8. 503; and Belphoebe: 4. 320; and Brada-
    mante: 3. 202, 272, 276, 278, 314-5, 332,
    334, 369-73, 386-8; 4. 166; 5. 207, 213,
    221; Britain's might, embodies: 3. 334;
    5. 310; character: 3. 202, 381-3, 387-91;
    4. 285-6; 5. 207, 273-4, 284; is chastity:
    3. 273, 289, 320, 334; 5. 348; crisis in
    her story: 4. 285; is Elizabeth: 2. 303,
    454; 3. 203, 310, 320, 379-80; 4. 319;
    5. 211, 221, 305-6, 316; 6. 186; is Eliza-
    beth's ancestress: 2. 449, 453-4; 3. 369;
    and Fiammetta: 3. 218; Friendship, high
    type of: 4. 294; and Galahad: 3. 204;
    hair: 4. 285; is ideal love: 4. 317-21; is
    Isis: 5. 295; jealous: 5. 208; is Justice:
    5. 214; and Malecasta: 4. 319; and Mari-
    nell: 4. 318; name: 3. 219; noblest poetry,
    inspires: 4. 285; origin: 3. 330-9; piety:
    5. 213-4; and Radigund: 5. 214, 221-3,
    316; realistic: 3. 214; 4. 285-6; Renais-
    sance perfect lady: 3. 324; and Rinaldo:
    3. 288-9; romantic: 3. 237; and Scuda-
    mour: 4. 320; her son, Conan: 3. 228;
    her spear: 3. 204, 237; story incomplete:
    3. 365; and Talus: 5. 279; and Timias:
    4. 319-20; is Womanhood on defence: 4.
    301
Britomartis, 3. 330, 334, 339
Britons, 8. 289
Brittain, F. W., 8. 361
Brittany, 3. 215, 235; 5. 248-9
Broadsides, 7. 277
Broadus, E. K., 1. 392-3

Brockwell, 2. 396; 3. 232
Bromley, 7. 327-8, 404, 610, 613-4
Brontes, 4. 244
Brook, Ralph, 8. 292
Brooke, Christopher, 7. 375, 594
Brooke, Tucker, 1. 215; 5. 195; 6. 230
Brooke, William, Lord Cobham, 7. 353
Brotanek, Rudolph, 2. 308; 8. 287, 315, 384,
    406
Broukhusius, Janus, 1. 184; 2. 326; 3. 297
Browne, Sir Thomas, 2. 355, 484; 6. 424;
    7. 238, 514; 8. 463
Browne, William, 2. 377; 6. 430; 7. 255,
    375, 398, 585; *Britannia's Pastorals*: 1.
    173, 283; 2. 271; 3. 303; 4. 275-6; 6. 200,
    359; 7. 311; 8. 500; *Inner Temple Masque*:
    2. 367; *Shepheards Pipe*: 7. 352, 369, 594;
    Visions: 7. 491; 8. 405
Browning, Elizabeth Barrett, 1. 414-5; 7. 516
Browning, Robert, 7. 293; 8. 409
Bruce, J. D., 3. 252
Bruin, 6. 334, 350
Brunehaut, 1. 292
Brunello, 5. 186
Brunetto Latini, 1. 398, 407
Brunner, K., 7. 616
Bruno, Giordano, 3. 340, 348-9; 6. 389, 401,
    403, 405, 419; 7. 664-5, 671, 676; *De gl'
    Heroici Furori*: 3. 343; 6. 391, 406; 7.
    515-6, 519-20, 527-30, 532-5, 555-6, 662,
    670; *Spaccio de la Bestia Trionfante*: 3.
    343; 6. 390-1, 393, 400, 406; 8. 376;
    Trattato della Causa: 6. 389-90
Brusantino, Vincenzo, 6. 228
Brut, 2. 306, 452. *See also* Layamon, Wace
Brut Tysilio, 2. 302, 312; 3. 228, 232-3
Brutus, ancestor of Britain, 1. 196, 482-4;
    2. 307-9, 320; 3. 234, 272, 282-3; 5. 220
Brutus II (Greenshield), 2. 312-3, 396
Bryce, Thomas, 6. 222
Brydges, Egerton, 7. 466-8, 477; 8. 708
Bryskett, Lodowick, 4. 314; 6. 440; 7. 457,
    486-7, 490, 495-7, 500, 507; 8. 430, 528;
    and Spenser: 7. 457; *Discourse of Civill
    Life*: 1. 329-30, 341-2, 354-6; 2. 230,
    397-8, 409; 4. 292-3; 6. 402; 7. 457; 8.
    529; *Mourning Muse of Thestylis*: 7. 457,
    486, 494, 500, 507, 594
Buchanan, Dorothy, 5. 209-10
Buchanan, George, 1. 483; 5. 320; 7. 304,
    590; 8. 325; *Desiderium Ptolomei*: 8. 486;
    Epigrams: 4. 279; 8. 383; *Fratres Fra-
    terrimi*: 8. 386; *Jephtha*: 7. 363; *Rerum
    Scoticarum Historia*: 2. 450
Buck, P. M., 1. 458-60; 2. 402; 3. 251, 287,
    299, 379-80; 7. 250-1, 314, 350, 383, 402;
    8. 373, 401, 510, 512-5, 517, 571, 687

Buckhurst, Lord. *See* Sackville, Thomas.
Buckingham, Duke of. *See* Villiers
"build the song," 8. 388
Bullen, Anne, 7. 281, 476
Bullinger, Henry, 5. 338, 341; 6. 210
Bulls, 1. 246; 2. 277; 6. 218, 226-7, 230; 8. 406
Bunduca. *See* Boadicea
Bunyan, John, 1. 377; 6. 208; compared with Spenser: 1. 377, 424, 441; 2. 256, 286, 339; 6. 318; *Holy War*: 2. 456; *Pilgrim's Progress*: 1. 272, 276, 290-1, 431; 2. 253
Buonamici, Buonamico?, 8. 382
Buoni, Tommaso, 8. 450
Burbon, 5. 259-61, 263, 264, 280, 299, 326, 329-31; 6. 361
Burial of the Dead, 2. 194, 346
Burke, C. B., 8. 297, 518
Burke, Edmund, 1. 175; 2. 221
Burleigh, Lord. *See* Cecil, William Lord Burleigh
Burlesque, 5. 183
Burley, Walter, 1. 356
Burmann, Pieter, 2. 379; 3. 294, 296; 4. 194
"burn—freeze," 5. 255
Burne-Jones, Sir Edward, 3. 389
Burnley, 7. 250, 269, 297, 306, 313
Burns, Robert, 7. 319, 576; 8. 598
Burton, Robert, 2. 481; 6. 214; 7. 514; 8. 445; *Anatomy of Melancholy*: 2. 459-63; 3. 273; Part 1: 2. 460-2; Part 2: 2. 460; 3. 284; 8. 368; Part 3: 1. 266-7; 4. 234; 5. 224; 6. 313; 8. 472; Part 4: 1. 271
Bush, Douglas, 2. 365, 435-6; 5. 264; 6. 249, 314, 447-9; 7. 248-9, 268, 283, 288, 598; 8. 401
Busirane, 1. 318, 346, 441; 3. 287-90, 292, 300-3, 320, 326, 354-8, 362, 365, 372-3, 388-9; 8. 446; is Lord Burleigh: 3. 380. *See also* House of Busirane
Busiris, 2. 190; 3. 287
"busy care," 6. 290
Butler, Samuel, 2. 198; *Hudibras*: 3. 217; 5. 157, 159, 224; 8. 470
Butler, Thomas, Earl of Ormonde, 3. 380; 5. 259; 7. 475-6
Butterfly, 8. 396, 400-1
Buttevant, 4. 268; 6. 283; 7. 454
Buyssens, E., 8. 715
Bynneman, Henry, 8. 273, 622, 623, 626-7, 735-6
Byron, George Gordon, 8. 409

Cabbala, 7. 558-9, 561-3, 565-8
Cabbalists, 7. 558-9, 563, 567, 671
Cacophony. *See* Dissonance
Cacosyntheton, 8. 595

Cacus, 4. 203; 5. 162, 234
Cadence, 6. 312; 7. 502, 505-6; 8. 338-40, 380, 402, 409, 412, 433, 446, 468, 497, 616, 618. *See also* Metre; Music; Sound; Verse
Cadiz, 5. 334-5; 8. 503-4, 663-4
Cadmus, 2. 298
Cador, 2. 253; 3. 228-9
Caduceus, 4. 186-7; 8. 377
Cadwalader, 1. 483, 488, 490; 2. 449, 453; 3. 234
Cadwallin, 3. 233
Caecily, 2. 319
Caelia, 1. 405-6
Caelite, 3. 246
Caer. *See* "Cair"
Cahir, 6. 283; 7. 454
Cain, 6. 447
"Cair," 2. 313-4
Cairleon, 2. 313
Cair-Merdin, 1. 265
Caius and Gonville College, Cambridge, 7. 646
Caius, John, 1. 483; 4. 259-60
Cajetan, Jacopo, 1. 355
Calais, 1. 483
Calcagnini, Caelius, 5. 219
Calderhead, I. G., 7. 237
Caleb, 1. 294
Calendar, 6. 302-3, 312; 7. 242-4, 253, 630-4
Calendar of Salisbury MSS, 8. 579
Calepine, 6. 201-3, 205, 215, 233, 235-6, 317, 322, 325-7, 334, 348, 377; is the Earl of Southampton: 6. 363
Calepine, Ambrogio (lexicographer), 7. 273; 8. 326, 541
Caliburn, 2. 275; 5. 191
Calidore, 1. 340, 346, 432, 485; 5. 156-7, 275, 284, 313; 6. 187-91, 200, 242, 255, 259-60, 317-35, 346; 7. 278; and Aeneas, Rinaldo, Ruggiero, Ulysses: 6. 244; character: 6. 321-5, 327-8, 330-3, 338-40, 342-4, 348, 360-1, 364; dubbed: 6. 193; is Essex: 6. 351-4, 357-64; and the Graces: 6. 245; and Guyon: 6. 191; and Hercules: 6. 270; and the pastoral tradition: 6. 373-81; is Sidney: 6. 187, 252, 267, 318, 349-51, 354-7; is Spenser: 6. 318
Caligorant, 2. 393; 5. 235
Callimachus, *Hymns*, 2. 196, 216, 261; 3. 330, 333; 4. 245; 6. 312
Calliope, 1. 406, 506-15; 6. 439; 8. 311-2, 327-8, 532, 536-8, 540, 602. *See also* Muse, Spenser's
Callisto, 6. 283, 409
Callot, Jaques, 1. 366

Calpurnius, 7. 249, 251, 266, 345, 385, 571, 590, 596, 632
Calumny, 6. 188-9, 350, 383
Calvin, John, 1. 472; 6. 269; 7. 545, 567-9, 662, 676, 678; *Institutes*: 1. 432-3; 7. 539, 541, 545, 554-5, 568-9, 667
Calvinism, 1. 275, 432-3, 438-9, 448; 2. 345; 5.342-3; 7. 543, 545, 567, 602, 608-9, 666, 668-9, 673, 676, 678, 680; 8. 279
Calvinists, 1. 273, 275; 7. 292; 8. 612
Calypso, 1. 208; 2. 348, 380
Cam, 4. 258
Camalodunum, 2. 328
Cambel, 1. 432; 3. 391; 4. 176-8, 188, 282-4, 286, 295, 300, 328; 5. 182
Camber, 2. 309, 317
Cambina, 4. 281, 283, 295, 328
Cambria, 2. 309, 315, 317
Cambridge, 2. 424; 4. 253, 258-60; 5. 328; 6. 310, 439, 443; 7. 252, 262, 289, 293, 312-4, 352, 361, 391, 402, 415, 420, 423, 457, 468, 589, 602, 611-2, 614, 620, 646, 650, 653, 657-8, 662, 664-70; 8. 282, 310, 418, 565; humanists: 7. 621-2
Cambridge University Library, 1. 413; 8. 321
Camden, William, 1. 349, 483; 2. 295, 302, 304, 306, 307, 325, 327-8, 332, 407, 451; 5. 179, 269; 6. 385, 387; 7. 653; 8. 291-2, 504, 672; Spenser praises: 8. 291-2, 525-7, 529
  Annals or *History of Elizabeth*: 1. 474; 3. 264; 7. 359, 403; 8. 291; following references cited by dates, 1558: 1. 474; 2. 295; 1563, 1564: 5. 320; 1567: 2. 400; 1568: 3. 264; 1571: 5. 320; 1573: 6. 383; 1577: 5. 301; 1579: 7. 304; 8. 567-8; 1580: 5. 301; 1588: 5. 227; 1593: 5. 330; 1594: 6. 364; 1595: 4. 211, 249; 1598: 5. 325, 333; 7. 457; 8. 291, 501
  Bridale of the Isis and Tame (in *Britannia*, Oxfordshire, Holland's translation, pp. 373, 384-8): 4. 240, 272; 8. 292, 515, 672-3; *Britannia*: 1. 350-1, 484; 2. 186, 450, 452; 4. 240-1, 251; 7. 456; 8. 526-7; (references to Latin ed. of 1590 by page) 1: 2. 304; 37-42: 2. 327-8; 115: 2. 306; 129: 2. 307; 173: 4. 253; 184-5: 4. 254; 227: 4. 257; 281: 4. 253, 313: 4. 254; 317, 326: 8. 290; 328: 4. 254; 344-5: 4. 253; 355: 8. 289; 374: 4. 257; 384: 4. 258-9; 409-11: 8. 288-90; 423-4: 4. 259; 436: 4. 260; 516: 3. 225; 595, 776: 4. 262; 643: 4. 261; (following reff. to Philemon Holland's translation of *Britannia*, 1610, by page): 82: 4. 257; 84: 4. 252; 184-5: 4. 254; 196, 233-9: 4. 255; 245-6: 4. 256; *Surrey*: 2. 382;

255: 4. 254; 296: 4. 256-7; 323-6: 8. 290; 374, 451, 476: 4. 257; 384: 4. 252; 385: 4. 272; 410-2: 8. 289-90; 451: 4. 257; 461: 8. 300; 489: 4. 253; 533: 4. 259; 547: 4. 260; 602-4, 669, 753-4: 4. 263; 643: 3. 225; 646, 799: 4. 261; 649: 3. 225; 646, 673, 696-7, 701, 730, 776, 799: 4. 261-2; 662: 3. 226; 806: 3. 233; *Reges, Reginae, Nobiles, etc.* (ed. 1606) p. 70: 8. 501; *Remains*: 2. 190; 6. 359; 7. 238; 8. 370
Camel, 1. 412
Camelodunum, 8. 289
Camerarius, 8. 406
Camilla, 3. 331-2, 336-7
Camoens, Luisvaz de, 2. 214, 357, 384; 3. 216; 8. 520
Camoge, 7. 455
Camomile, 8. 399
Campbell, George Douglas, 6. 215
Campbell, Lily, 2. 468; 8. 330
Campbell, Thomas, 7. 290, 576
Campion, Edmund, 5. 320; 7. 360; 8. 737
Campion, Thomas, 4. 260, 315-6; 5. 327; 8. 475
Campus Martius, 4. 194
Canace, 3. 249; 4. 176-8; 7. 517
"Cancred carle," 3. 275
Candida, 7. 477
Candidus, 7. 324, 327, 329, 351, 354, 368, 373-6, 380, 382, 385-6, 389
Canterbury, 7. 343, 652
Canticum Canticorum, 7. 563; 8. 270, 283, 474; in Spenser's other works: 8. 519. *See also* Bible, Song of Songs
Canutus, 2. 307-8
Canzone, 8. 646, 654-8, 661, 674-5
Capella, Galeazzo Flavio, 3. 322
Capellanus. *See* Andreas Capellanus
Capriano, Francesco, 1. 348, 513
Capricorn, 6. 307
Carados, 3. 236
Carausius, 2. 330
Cardano, Girolamo, 2. 236
Care, 1. 367; 2. 257; 3. 301; 4. 196-8, 276, 281, 287. *See also* House of Care
Careticus, 3. 231
Carew MSS, 5. 174, 263, 304; 7. 457
Carew, Richard, 2. 307, 450; 6. 195; 7. 238, 461
Carey, Edward, 7. 354
Carey, Sir George, Lord Hunsdon, 3. 260; 7. 457, 476; 8. 392-4, 507
Carey, Henry, Lord Hunsdon, 1. 449; 2. 402-3; 3. 260, 308; 5. 227; 7. 476; 8. 374, 392, 532
Carey, Lady. *See* Spencer, Elizabeth

Carey, Robert, 5. 184
Carlisle, Earl of. *See* Harclay
Carlyle, Thomas, 8. 586
Carmarthen, 3. 224-5
Carmelianus, Peter, 1. 484
Carmina Illustrium Poetarum Italorum, 8. 381-2
"Carpe diem." *See* "Gather ye rosebuds"
Carpenter, F. I., 8. 356, 405, 418, 516, 590, 626
Carrigeen, 6. 287-9
Carrignagloor, 6. 287
Cartari. Vincenzo, 6. 412
Cartwright, Thomas, 5. 157, 338; 6. 386; 7. 254, 295, 301-2, 304, 325, 334, 352-3, 364, 602, 607; 8. 357, 591
Casady, Edwin, 8. 432, 440-2, 445-7, 642
Case, Robert H., 8. 485, 494, 660, 670-1, 735
Caspian Sea, 2. 254
Cassibellaun, 2. 323-4
Cassiopeia, 1. 208; 8. 309
Castalia, 8. 301-2, 313, 324, 334, 541
Castalio, 7. 596
Castellani, Tomaso, 8. 459
Castelvetro, Lodovico, 1. 349-50, 513
Castiglione, Baldassare, 3. 322, 325; 6. 187, 386, 399; 7. 371, 388, 492; 8. 363, 374, 591, 641; and Spenser's idea of Courtesy: 6. 328-33, 337-40, 342; 8. 365-8; *Alcon*: 7. 408; *Il Cortegiano*: 1. 224, 440; 3. 317, 337; 4. 163; 6. 292, 328-33, 338; 7. 663, 670; *The Courtier* (Hoby's translation, cited by page in the *Everyman* edition): 1. 340; 32-3: 6. 330; 33-81: 6. 338-9; 40, 42: 6. 331-2; 8. 366; 41: 2. 224; 42: 6. 332; 8. 365; 68-9: 8. 313; 70-1: 8. 328, 368; 75: 8. 367; 90: 8. 367; 97-8: 6. 339; 106: 8. 368; 111: 6. 339-40; 115: 8. 364; 119: 4. 329; 120: 4. 162, 289, 332; 129: 6. 340; 133: 8. 366; 166-7: 8. 366; 176: 8. 365; 185-256 (Bk. 3): 7. 662; 195, 198: 3. 338; 234: 7. 518-9; 242, 311-2: 7. 517; 246-7: 7. 536; 247, 305, 311, 317: 7. 516, 535; 8. 439; 257-324 (Bk. 4): 2. 429; 3. 317-8; 4. 306; 7. 662, 667-8, 671, 677-8, 680-1; 8. 453-4, 642; 269-70: 2. 422-3; 276-7: 7. 463, 659; 301-6: 8. 440; 302-22: 8. 642; 302, 304, 306, 313: 7. 515; 303: 8. 642; 304-5, 309: 7. 525-6; 304, 310-2: 5. 188; 305: 6. 333; 306: 3. 318; 308: 7. 482; 309: 7. 549; 310-1: 7. 529, 531; 312-3: 7. 534; 312: 7. 509; 313, 317: 6. 332-3; 313-4: 7. 536; 8. 433; 313: 6. 332-3; 7. 532; 8. 642; 314-6: 8. 441; 316-9: 8. 642; 317: 6. 333; 7. 534, 678-9, 681; 8. 427, 442, 454; 318, 321: 7. 512; 8. 446;

321: 4. 313; 7. 569-70; *Eclogue*: 8. 477, 490; *Sonnet*: 8. 382
Castle, 1. 290-1; 2. 434, 469, 485; 3. 284; 5. 170; 8. 374. *See also* Chateau Merveil
Castle enchanted, 1. 347
Castle Joyous, 3. 208, 324, 366, 393-4; 5. 237; 6. 193
Castle Mortal, 1. 400
Castle of Alma, 1. 367; 2. 434, 456-7, 466, 480-5; 8. 475
Castle of Beauty, 3. 355
Castle of the Body, 2. 456-7
Castle of Chastity, 1. 267
Castle of Copper, 1. 400
Castle of Fortune, 1. 405
Castle of Grace, 1. 407
Castle of the Holy Grail, 1. 400; 3. 361-2
Castle of Inwyt, 2. 286
Castle of Love, 3. 357
Castle of Love, 2. 286, 456
Castle of Maidens, 2. 287
Castle of Medina, 2. 411
Castle of Perseverance, 1. 405; 2. 433-4
Castle of the Strand, 3. 380
Castle of Venus, 1. 407
Castle of Virtue, 2. 287
Castle Perilous, 3. 365
Castor, 5. 186; and Pollux: 5. 158; 6. 304; 8. 299, 505, 667
Castriot. *See* Scanderbeg
Catachresis, 1. 258
Catalogue, 1. 179-81; 4. 243; 7. 285-7; 8. 398, 424, 474-5, 596-7
Catechism, 1. 302
Catherine of Arragon: 1. 461
Catherine de' Medici, 5. 198, 297
Catherine, St., 7. 329
Catholic. *See* Roman Catholic
Cats, 6. 269
Catullus, 3. 301; 6. 398; 8. 462, 662; 3: 4. 232; 7: 3. 297; 5. 166; 8. 488; 8, 36, 52, 57: 3. 290; 34: 8. 491; 61: 1. 196; 4. 238; 8. 458, 460-1, 469, 471, 473, 476, 479, 482, 488, 490, 500, 652-4; 62: 2. 390; 3. 247; 8. 478, 480-1, 483, 652-3; 64: 1. 259; 2. 357; 6. 254, 299; 8. 401, 461-2, 483, 493, 499, 597, 652; 68: 4. 231; 68a: 6. 310; 7. 480; 86: 7. 527
Caulier, Achille, 1. 405-7; 3. 211; 4. 221, 229-30, 237; 6. 221-2
"cause removed," 6. 214
Cavalcanti, Guido, 7. 666-7, 677
Cave, 5. 234, 254; 7. 525; 8. 331
Cavendish, Thomas, 5. 248
Caxton, William, 1. 347, 349, 488; 2. 305, 309, 311, 313-18, 320, 322, 326, 330, 331, 452; 3. 208; *Chronicles of England*: ch.

3: 2. 309; ch. 5: 2. 309; ch. 7: 2. 311; ch. 9: 2. 313; ch. 14: 2. 318; ch. 20: 2. 320; ch. 40: 2. 326, 330-1; *Description of England*: 3. 237; *Destruction of Troy*: 5. 196-7; *Eneydos*: 3. 281; 8. 714; *Godfrey of Boloyne*: 3. 286; *Lives of Saints*: 1. 380, 389; 7. 634; Preface to Malory's *Morte Darthur*: 1. 347; *Mirror of the World*: 8. 595; *Morale Proverbes of Crystyne*: 7. 235; *Recuyell of the Histories of Troy*: 2. 219; *Renard the Fox*: 8. 562, 586-9

Cayet, Pierre, 5. 326

Cazza, Agostino, 8. 429-30

Cebes, 1. 279, 287, 289; 2. 380; 3. 256, 345; 4. 228; 6. 256

Cecil, Anne, 3. 380; 8. 605

Cecil, Sir Robert, 5. 307; 8. 373, 574, 579-80, 583-4, 606-7, 686, 712

Cecil, Sir Thomas, 6. 263

Cecil, William (son of Sir Thomas), 6. 263

Cecil, William, Lord Burleigh, 1. 483; 2. 404-6; 5. 233, 283, 307-9, 319, 333-4; 6. 362, 383, 385; 7. 261, 298-9, 326, 335, 360, 435, 603-4, 606; 8. 528, 536-7, 584, 602-7, 686; is the Ape: 8. 571; is Archimago: 1. 449, 451-2; 2. 401-2; is big Bull of Basan: 7. 359; is the Briar: 7. 254; is Busirane: 3. 380; character: 8. 579-81; and Essex: 8. 570, 574, 579-80, 599, 605-7; is the Fox: 7. 293, 304, 603; 8. 293-4, 573, 576-9, 591, 604, 606-7; and James VI: 8. 579; is Kingdom's Care: 5. 245; and Leicester: 8. 510, 521, 571, 573, 579, 602, 607; is leviathan: 8. 571; is lion: 8. 604, 606; and the Earl of Oxford: 8. 605; and Raleigh: 8. 570, 574; is the serpent: 8. 544; and Sidney: 8. 603; and Spenser: 3. 303-4, 428; 4. 163; 5. 301, 309; 6. 271-2; 7. 335, 448, 478, 522, 606; 8. 302-3, 319, 356, 370-5, 409, 510-11, 518, 521, 524, 533, 536, 559-61, 570, 572, 575, 582-3, 603-6, 663-4, 712; is spider: 8. 602-7; is " spirit ": 8. 571

Cecil House, 8. 605-6

Cecil MSS, 5. 334; 6. 362

Cecilia, 1. 305, 496

Cedar, 8. 407-8

" Celer," 8. 406

Celestial City, 1. 290-1

Celibacy, 3. 319-20

Celsus, 1. 236

Celtic, motives in *F. Q.* 2: 2. 435, 444-9; 4. 204; Otherworld: 1. 352

Censorinus, 2. 284, 297

Centaurs, 4. 168-9; 6. 251

Cephissus, 1. 302

Cerberus, 1. 303; 2. 253; 6. 188, 341, 388; 8. 341

Ceres, 7. 445; 8. 339

Cervantes, Saavedra, Miguel de, 1. 196; 3. 217, 286; 5. 191, 210; 6. 189, 193

Cestus, 4. 192-3, 321. *See also* Florimel " chaffred," 7. 355

Chain, 1. 233, 264; 2. 252, 261, 436; 4. 170; 6. 277; 7. 513-4; 8. 363

Chalcidius, 1. 446

Challenge, 5. 185-6, 191, 257, 263

Chalmers, G., 8. 317, 320, 631

Chaloner, Thomas, 7. 237, 264, 467-8, 642

Chamard, Henri, 8. 277, 380-91, 410-13, 613

Chambers, David, 2. 330, 333, 453

Chambers, E. K., 3. 305; 5. 186, 237-8; 7. 282, 421, 447, 585; 8. 317

Chambers, Robert, 1. 243

Champernowne, Frances, 7. 434

Champneys, B., 8. 659

Change, 6. 390-5, 397, 400, 404-5, 410, 415-7, 420, 429, 437; 8. 400, 439, 522, 525. *See also* Mutability; Vicissitude

Change of Heart, 1. 287

Changeling, 1. 292

Chaos, 1. 230-2; 2. 232; 3. 257, 349; 4. 181-2; 6. 279, 404, 405, 415, 440; 7. 511-2; 8. 387

Chapin Library, 1. 519; 7. 709, 723; 8. 680-1

Chapman, George, 1. 378, 489, 492, 513; 2. 222-3; 7. 464; 8. 376, 507; *De Guiana*: 4. 249; *Georgicks*: 2. 222; Homer, translation of: 3. 306; 8. 491, 496; Musaeus, translation of: 4. 217, 237; *Parcarum Epith.*: 8. 493

Character, 3. 383-4

Chariclea, 6. 377

Charillis, 7. 476-7; 8. 635

Chariot, 1. 214; 2. 414; 5. 226-30

Charis, 2. 273

Charissa, 1. 284-5, 406-7, 430, 432; 3. 399; 7. 509

Chariteo, sonneteer, 8. 433

Charity, 1. 284-5, 287, 407, 424, 504; 7. 305

Charlemagne, 1. 257, 359; 3. 236; 5. 192; 8. 329; is Orgoglio: 1. 449

Charles, Archduke of Austria, 3. 380

Charles the Bold, 5. 250-1, 317

Charles V, Emperor, 1. 454; 5. 251, 317-8

Charles IX (of France), 2. 404

Charles's Wain, 8. 329

Charleville, 6. 283

" charm," 5. 235; 8. 322

Charon, 2. 357; 8. 301

Charron, Pierre, 2. 340, 464-5

Chartier, Alain, 4. 221; 6. 222-4; 8. 566

Charybdis, 2. 183, 348, 351, 354-5; 8. 341, 346

Charyllis. *See* Spencer, Anne

Chase. *See* Hunting

Chastity, 1. 243, 267, 329, 339; 2. 295, 426; 3. 266, 273, 287, 289, 310-3, 316, 318-28, 330, 333, 339, 353-5, 363, 370-3, 376, 378-9, 386-91; 4. 192, 207, 320; 5. 348-9; girdle of: 5. 190; Love, contest with: 3. 354-5; relation to other virtues: 3. 323; 4. 301; a Renaissance virtue: 1. 345. *See also* Castle of, Tower of

Chateau Merveil, 3. 361, 365

Chatsworth Library, 7. 712; 8. 706

Chatterton, Thomas, 7. 629, 637; 8. 623

Chaucer, Geoffrey, 1. 188-9, 256, 362; 2. 433; 3. 292, 394; 6. 189, 200, 253, 280, 290, 365, 422-3, 449, 475; 7. 253-5, 337, 362, 396, 422, 449, 572-3, 577-8, 583-7, 603, 609, 630, 661, 681; 8. 308, 383, 388, 492, 531, 644; canon: 7. 604; as love poet: 7. 320, 517, 604; metres: 7. 593, 634-40; portraiture: 3. 392; Spenser, compared with: 1. 307; 2. 235; 3. 221, 273; 7. 236, 339; 8. 560-3, 566, 593, 608-10; Spenser, influence upon: 4. 176-8; 6. 293-6; 7. 260, 291, 585, 592, 595, 604, 615-20, 622, 626; 8. 562, 564, 567, 572-4, 608-10; and Spenser: 1. 307; 2. 235; 3. 221, 273; 4. 176-80; 5. 209, 294; 6. 198, 238; 7. 255, 308-9, 311, 319-20, 516-7, 597, 599, 604, 615-20, 622, 626, 634-40; 8. 511, 518, 547, 559, 564, 593, 601, 678; is Tityrus: 7. 253, 260, 319-20, 452; *Anelida and Arcite*: 3. 425; 4. 180; 7. 281; *Balade of Gentilesse*: 6. 336-7, 340; *Boece*: 6. 393, 417-8; 7. 263, 330; 8. 325; *Book of the Duchess*: 1. 189, 193, 195; 2. 238; 4. 209; 6. 255, 298; 7. 430-3, 438-42, 444-6, 640; *Canon Yeoman's Tale*: 3. 280; *Canterbury Tales*: 3. 274; 4. 170-1; 7. 637-8; 8. 350, 560, 586; *Clerk's Tale*: 3. 267; 4. 175; 6. 213; 8. 357, 442, 598; *Complaint of Mars*: 3. 297; 7. 320; *Complaint of Venus*: 3. 297; 7. 321; *Complaint unto Pite*: 7. 517; *complaints*: 7. 320; *Cook's Tale*: 7. 635; *Former Age*: 5. 160; *Franklin's Prologue and Tale*: 3. 207; 6. 213, 307; 7. 331; *House of Fame*: 1. 415, 514; 3. 216; 7. 598, 640; 8. 308; 69: 1. 193; 120: 1. 291; 130: 3. 292; 220: 2. 243; 521-2: 6. 185; 7. 281; 535: 6. 217; 737: 7. 413; 934: 5. 229; 1113-1200: 1. 213; 1184-7: 3. 208; 4. 229; 1223-6: 6. 236-7; 7. 258; 1247-9: 5. 183; 1293-1304: 2. 373; 1307: 3. 256; 1311: 2. 461; 1345-6: 4. 229; 1520-5: 5. 199;

1559 ff.: 8. 314; 1573-1688: 2. 253; 1573-7: 3. 223-4; 1678: 8. 314; 1982-4: 6. 187; *Knight's Tale*: 1. 223; 4. 191, 213; 5. 170; 6. 378; 7. 663; 1: 3. 250; 4. 176; 886-7: 4. 199; 902: 3. 241; 972, 1068: 2. 189; 1010: 7. 265; 1098: 3. 279-80; 1156-9: 6. 254-5; 1165: 4. 200; 1251-4: 6. 241; 1275: 1. 227; 1303-33: 7. 320; 1351-1412: 5. 214; 1363-1402: 4. 234, 278; 1364: 6. 218; 1466: 3. 250; 1491: 8. 466; 1542-73: 7. 320; 1592-3: 2. 300; 1623-6: 5. 263; 1658-60: 1. 248; 1759: 1. 216; 1768: 5. 222; 1761: 6. 219; 1918-66: 4. 217; 1918-54: 3. 292; 1930: 2. 295; 1936-7: 6. 248; 1936: 3. 254; 1941: 1. 283; 4. 217; 1962: 4. 232; 1963: 3. 298; 7. 481; 1967-2050: 4. 168; 1997-2012: 1. 223; 2003: 2. 258; 3. 213; 7. 303; 2013: 7. 356; 2023: 1. 174; 2097: 1. 223; 2158: 8. 464; 2198: 6. 213; 2220: 4. 175; 2223: 3. 254; 2265-9: 4. 238; 2273: 1. 223; 2273: 1. 208; 2430-6: 4. 238; 2443: 3. 297; 2461-3: 2. 300; 2551-2: 5. 186; 2604, 2648-9: 4. 191; 2641-2: 5. 186; 2687: 4. 190; 2745: 3. 226; 2987-92: 1. 264; 2. 261; 7. 537; 2990 ff.: 4. 227; *Legend of Good Women*: Pr. 69: 7. 321; 130 (118) ff.: 4. 235; 236: 3. 298; 296, 1159: 7. 495; 422-3: 7. 346, 405; 637: 2. 341; 3. 281; 851: 6. 201; 1110: 1. 226; 3. 210-11; 1377: 2. 374; 2146-81: 6. 253-4; 2318-22: 1. 241; 2334, 2695: 7. 356; 2395: 6. 199; *Manciple's Tale*: 2. 243; *Man of Law's Tale*: 1. 228, 307; 3. 243; 5. 183; 7. 355; *Merchant's Tale*: 2. 243; 3. 273; 6. 219; 8. 312; *Miller's Tale*: 3. 280, 303; 7. 306; 8. 400; *Monk's Prologue*: 6. 199; *Monk's Tale*: 1. 237; 6. 213; 7. 265, 272, 641; 8. 394; *Nun's Priest's Tale*: 1. 200; 2. 230; 6. 258; 7. 303, 592; 8. 608-10; *Pardoner's Tale*: 4. 183; 8. 358; *Parlement of Foules*: 1. 213; 3. 345; 6. 293-6, 378, 413, 422; 7. 432; 120-2: 1. 406; 2. 373; 176-82: 1. 180; 183-96: 4. 222; 185: 2. 371; 204-7: 2. 377-8; 211: 3. 298; 218-27: 3. 299; 230-1: 3. 208; 4. 229; 239-45: 4. 226; 267-73: 2. 392; 267: 2. 285; 284-94: 3. 292; 298-318: 6. 293-6; 298: 6. 255; 316-82: 6. 396-7, 478; 323-4: 6. 245; 330-65: 8. 466; 330-1: 1. 289; 343: 2. 369; 355: 8. 460; 361: 8. 486; 517-8: 7. 263; 596-7: 6. 217; *Parson's Tale*: 1. 218, 220, 271, 413; 4. 212; 5. 177, 294; 6. 259; *Physician's Tale*: 3. 201; 6. 296; 7. 360; *Prioress's Prologue*: 3. 280; *Prologue to the Canterbury Tales*: 3. 392; 7. 604, 634-5, 638; 8. 595;

8: 8. 356; 11: 4. 236; 62-3: 2. 274; 79-95: 8. 365; 165 ff.: 8. 357; 179: 8. 371; 188: 7. 298; 193-4: 3. 218; 5. 300; 200-2: 1. 218; 205: 3. 222; 209: 8. 351; 236: 4. 213; 269-70: 7. 536; 319: 8. 369; 351: 1. 231; 381: 8. 399; 494: 6. 213; 523: 7. 263; 8. 356; 529-41: 8. 355; 613: 8. 355; 712: 7. 479; 721, 788, 828: 3. 275; 751-2: 5. 238-9; *Reve's Tale*: 2. 247; 6. 306; 7. 258-9, 327, 616; *Romaunt of the Rose*: 2. 285, 374; 3. 299, 301-2; 4. 320; 7. 480, 640; 8. 349, 511; 54, 102: 7. 297; 65-6: 7. 394; 135-9: 2. 373; 147-55: 1. 223; 4. 226; 181: 1. 221; 248-50: 1. 222; 528-32: 4. 220; 531-644: 1. 406; 576: 1. 302; 665: 8. 466; 680: 2. 365; 745 ff.: 4. 237; 888-91: 6. 309; 918: 3. 298; 939-48: 3. 295; 1020-1: 3. 277; 1079: 7. 297; 1218: 3. 278; 1352-1438: 4. 222; 1605-14: 2. 382; 1723-9: 3. 279; 1778: 3. 279; 2009-12: 4. 202; 2135-8: 6. 231; 2231-3: 6. 270; 2295-6: 4. 217; 2301-3: 4. 217; 2325-8: 4. 233; 2445-6: 7. 251; 2467-71: 5. 206; 2631-2: 5. 210; 2825: 3. 211; 3011 ff.: 3. 211; 3015 ff.: 4. 221; 3726 ff.: 4. 239; 3912: 7. 327; 4350: 2. 210; 4750: 4. 185; 4761: 7. 272; 4778: 1. 231; 4812: 2. 261; 5001-4: 4. 183; 5709: 7. 321; 5795-6: 7. 341; 7307: 7. 303; *Second Nun's Prologue* and *Tale*: 1. 218; 3. 212, 215; *Shipman's Tale*: 7. 300-1; *Sir Thopas*: 1. 267-8; 2. 208, 276, 336; 3. 266-7, 275, 425; 4. 170, 190, 199; 6. 196, 225-6; 7. 265, 267, 274; 8. 399, 466, 602, 608-10; *see also* Topas, Sir; *Squire's Tale*: 1. 307-9; 2. 242; 3. 216; 4. 176-8, 190, 194, 311; 5. 164, 183, 199; 6. 219, 260; 7. 303, 320, 333, 479; *Tale of Melibee*: 7. 305; *To Rosemounde*: 8. 465|; *Troilus and Crisseyde*: 7. 517; 8. 308; Book 1: 6: 7. 438; 218 ff.: 4. 277; 240: 3. 303; 316: 8. 351; 348: 7. 303; 637-44: 3. 274; 663-5: 3. 295; 809: 7. 236; 837: 5. 205; 947-50: 3. 212; Book 2: 1-7: 1. 311; 65-6: 3. 241; 151: 7. 236; 344-7: 2. 247; 584-5: 6. 251; 687: 3. 243; 764-70: 4. 173; 824: 2. 189; 963: 7. 303; 1380-4: 1. 259; 7. 262; 1681: 7. 479; Book 3: 1-14: 4. 233; 198: 4. 190; 250-2: 4. 313; 787: 4. 182; 1046: 5. 168; 1427: 7. 478; 8. 484; 1625-8: 8. 325; 1744: 2. 261; 1750: 1. 264; 1751 ff.: 4. 227; 1776-8: 4. 164; 1796: 8. 351; Book 4: 197-201: 6. 241; 501-4: 2. 191; 539: 7. 330; 627: 7. 265; 763: 2. 247; Book 5: 531: 7. 305; 774: 5. 206; 839-40: 7. 341; 1786-92: 4. 180; 7. 235, 427; *Wife of Bath's Prologue*: 1. 267; 7. 306, 330, 346; 8. 477; *Wife of Bath's Tale*: 2. 220; 6. 198, 229, 337; 7. 361, 719

Chaucer (pseudo), 7. 320; *Assembly of Ladies*: 5. 240; *Complaint of the Blacke Knight*: 1. 180, 182; *Court of Love*: see s. v.; *Flower and Leaf*: 4. 175; *History of Beryn*: 3. 285; 7. 635; *La Belle Dame sans Merci*: 6. 224; 7. 365; *Lamentation of Marie Magdaleine*: 3. 244, 269; *Physician's Prologue*: 3. 280; *Plowman's Tale*: 7. 263, 284, 290, 297-8, 334-5, 337, 341, 427-8, 604, 609, 634-5; 8. 356; *Remedy of Love*: 7. 272, 325, 328, 438

Chaucer's Dream, 2. 373
Chauntecleer, 8. 609
Checklaton, 6. 225-6
" checkmate," 7. 422
Cheerfulness, 3. 385; 4. 237
Cheke, Sir John, 4. 179; 5. 342-3; 7. 237, 363, 621-3, 626; 8. 353
Cherubim, 1. 310; 7. 553-4; 8. 478
Cherwell, 4. 252
Cherwellon, 7. 315
Chess, 7. 439
Chester, Robert, 1. 181; 2. 364
Chettle, Henry, 2. 281; 7. 464, 594; 8. 294
Chevalier aux Deux Epées, 6. 366
Chevalier Berinus, 2. 355
" chevisaunce," 7. 287, 301
Chevy Chase, 7. 489
Chiaroscuro, 1. 183, 232, 306; 2. 258; 6. 234, 258
Chiasmus, 6. 189
" Child," 5. 255; 6. 196
" childing," 6. 265
Children of Paul's, 8. 318
Chimaera, 6. 188, 341, 388
Chinard, Gilbert, 6. 202
Chinon of England, 1. 488
Chiron, 1. 246; 3. 296-7; 6. 307
Chivalry, 1. 247, 324, 327, 488, 493, 502; 2. 221, 224, 234, 250, 273, 351, 415: 3. 368, 387; 4. 192, 226, 294; 5. 192-3, 196; 6. 187, 344-5; 7. 480, 515; and allegory: 1. 416, 418; 3. 317; books of: 1. 320; 3. 298; and Courtesy: 6. 344-5, 358; feasts: 1. 309, 324-5; 5. 243; flower of: 8. 504; *Order of*: 2. 415; parting gifts: 1. 268; and pastoral: 7. 495; and Platonism: 7. 519; and romance: 1. 332; 2. 224; Spenser's and Ariosto's: 1. 332, 336; Spenser's and Malory's: 2. 415. *See also* Tower of
Chloe, 6. 377
Chloris, 7. 284, 289-90

Chrestien de Troyes, 1. 251, 347, 488-9; 6. 365-71

Christ Church, Cork, 8. 470, 649-50

Christian, 1. 377; blending with classical: 1. 266, 273, 295, 363, 439; 2. 403; ethics: 1. 333; 2. 365, 414, 425-6; gentleman: 1. 432-7; graces: 1. 287; idea of life as moral warfare: 1. 433; imagery: 1. 254; virtues: 1. 288, 439-40

Christian, in *Pilgrim's Progress*, 1. 290, 424

Christianity, 1. 246, 275, 361, 437, 500; 6. 344; 7. 254; 8. 329, 413; England, introduction into: 1. 453; mingled with paganism: 1. 363, 439; 6. 398, 403; 7. 551, 562, 591, 601; mingled with Platonism: 2. 416; 6. 403, 423, 7. 537, 539, 559, 657-9

Christians, 1. 240, 243, 438-40

Christocentric, 7. 537, 544, 546-7, 673-6

Christ's College, Cambridge, 7. 646

Christs Kirk on the Green, 6. 193

Chronicle History, 2. 449-55; 4. 246; 5. 306

Chroniclers, 1. 225; 2. 187, 302-34, 406, 408, 449-55; 5. 194

Chronographia, 7. 246; 8. 495

Chronology, 1. 256; of Spenser's Works: 4. 312, 315-7

Chronos, 6. 308

Chrysaor, 4. 245; 5. 163-5, 191, 264-5, 298, 301, 312

Chrysogone, 3. 249-51, 326

Church, 1. 310, 390, 437; 8. 579; corruption: 1. 208; feasts: 7. 634; High: 7. 303-8; 8. 359, 565; orthodox: 1. 450; Reformed: 1. 178; Una, Sancta, Catholica, Apostolica: 1. 308. *See also* England; Roman Catholic

Church, Ralph, 8. 513

Church, R. W., 1. 424; 7. 236, 314, 424, 579, 601; 8. 512, 518, 561, 629, 645

Churchyard, Thomas, 1. 266, 483; 4. 313; 7. 353, 464, 469; 8. 610

Churl, 3. 262-3

The Churle and the Byrde, 7. 320

Churton, Edward, 8. 451

Chylde, Machabyas, 8. 472, 651

Cicero, Marcus Tullius, 1. 300; 3. 321; 4. 194; 7. 387, 615, 621, 647; 8. 329; Spenser's thought most formed by: 1. 361-2; 2. 425; *Academica*: 1. 225; *Brutus*: 7. 239, 264; *Against Catiline*: 8. 529; *De Amicitia*: 4. 291, 294, 296, 304, 313, 327-9, 332; 7. 441; *De Divinatione*: 1. 294; 2. 252; 4. 182, 197; 5. 218; 6. 185; 7. 426; *De Finibus*: 1. 361-2; 2. 233-4; 4. 164, 225; 5. 214, 256; 8. 315; *De Legibus*: 1. 286; *De Natura Deorum*: 1. 361; Book 1: 28: 7. 238; 34. 93: 4. 164; 40: 8. 492;

Book 2: 5: 3. 205; 14: 1. 288; 18: 2. 479; 20: 8. 440; 23: 1. 285; 26: 2. 254; 35: 7. 460; 47: 1. 208; 54 ff.: 2. 290; 56: 2. 288, 297; Book 3: 14: 3. 250; 15: 5. 214; 8. 328-9; 17: 1. 230; 2. 233, 257; 3. 244; 21: 6. 312; 7. 319; 22: 3. 243; 44: 4. 181; 51: 5. 190; *De Officiis*: 1. 361-2; 2. 423-4; 4. 291; Book 1: 4: 6. 336; 8. 330; 5: 5. 214; 10: 5. 297; 6. 205; 12: 3. 285; 13: 5. 297; 17: 4. 328; 23: 3. 291; 43: 2. 188; 153: 8. 331; Book 2: 2: 8. 331; 5: 8. 476; Book 3: 10: 4. 225; 21: 5. 263; 8. 372; *De Oratore*: 2. 244; 4. 164; 7. 236-7; *De Re Publica*: 4. 198; 8. 493; *De Senectute*: 1. 278, 280; *Letters to Atticus*: 2. 301; *Letters to his Brother Quintus*: 7. 394; *Letters to his Friends*: 5. 235; *Orator*: 1. 207; 7. 237, 264; *Post Reditum in Senatu*: 7. 322; *Pro Archia*: 7. 376, 381, 393; 8. 302; *Pro Cluentio*: 2. 187; *Somnium Scipionis: see De Re Publica; Tusculan Disputations*: Book 1: 9: 3. 250; 10: 2. 297; 16: 2. 354; 24, 40: 2. 263; 41: 8. 297; 46: 1. 280; Book 2: 8. 315; 23: 5. 252; Book 3: 5: 1. 122; 2. 227; 9: 4. 200; 11: 2. 233; 26: 6. 244; Book 4: 8: 1. 270; 9: 1. 122; 15: 2. 233; 25: 7. 441; Book 5: 35: 7. 307; 8. 510; 63: 4. 225

Cimbri, 1. 258

Cimmerians, 1. 258; 8. 322-3

Cinthio. *See* Giraldi

Circe, 2. 183, 192, 194, 339, 366, 370, 373, 377, 381, 394, 462; 3. 246; 7. 426; allegorized: 2. 365, 436

Circle, 2. 473-84

Circumcision, 7. 248

City, 1. 290-1

Clapham, David, 3. 338

Claribell, 6. 260-4, 353

Clarice, 2. 213, 219

Clarin, 5. 293

Clarinda, 5. 205

Clarion, 2. 198; 8. 396, 400-1, 597, 608-9; is the Earl of Oxford: 8. 605; is Essex: 8. 606; is Leicester: 8. 607; is Raleigh: 8. 601; is Sidney: 8. 604; is Spenser: 8. 601-3, 605; is Youth: 8. 599-600

Claris of Laris, 3. 365

Clark, C. W., 7. 708

Clark, Mrs. E. H., 8. 605

Clark Memorial Library, 8. 681

Clarke, Charles C., 2. 360

Clarke, Samuel, 1. 276

Classical: and Christian blending: 1. 266, 273, 295, 363, 404, 439; 2. 403; Gothic,

contrasted with: 1. 324-7, 337; with medieval: 4. 228-9; 8. 562; metres: 7. 349; names: 7. 316; security: 1. 306. *See also* Pagore

Classics, Spenser's debt to: 1. 421; 2. 205, 435-6; 4. 228, 303

Claude Lorraine, 1. 306

Claudian, 3. 301; 5. 312; 6. 423, 428; 8. 308; *De Bello Gildonico*: 1. 230; 5. 261; *De Bello Gothico*: 2. 210; 3. 269; *Epithalamium de Nuptiis Honorii*: 8. 482, 652; Pr.: 8. 460; 5: 1. 236; 14-5: 8. 480; 29-95: 3. 258; 49 ff.: 2. 377, 381; 4. 228; 56-9: 2. 373; 3. 256, 258, 345; 60 ff., 83, 93-6: 3. 256; 4. 222; 72-3: 4. 232; 85-91: 4. 229; 99-101: 5. 242; 6. 248; 122-3: 8. 465; 144-70: 8. 463; 188: 6. 297; 188: 6. 297; 190-281: 8. 499; 191-3: 8. 485; 202-3: 8. 468; 208-10: 1. 310; 8. 476, 478, 482; 265-71: 8. 474; *Fescennine Verses*: 4. 238; 8. 471, 473; *On the Consuls Probinus and Olybrius*: 3. 211; 4. 252; 6. 297; *On the Consulship of Manlius Theodorus* 1: 5. 256; *On Stilicho's Consulship*: 3. 339; 5. 171; 6. 413; 7. 386; *On the Third Consulship of Honorius*: 3. 247; *In Rufinum*: 1. 174; 2. 252-4, 257; 3. 244; 4. 223; 6. 423; *De Raptu Proserpinae*: 2. 445; Pr.: 1. 311; Book 1: 48 ff.: 4. 182; 271-4: 2. 296; Book 2: 71-2: 6. 297; 97: 3. 298; 101-4: 6. 245; 107-11: 1. 180; 128 ff., 290 ff.: 3. 258; 287-94: 2. 264; 290: 2. 268; 328-60: 8. 485; 363: 6. 308; *Shorter Poems*: 22: 8. 426; 25: 4. 238; 8. 460, 499; 30: 6. 297; 31: 8. 459, 462; 51: 5. 219

Claudius, 2. 325

Cleanness, 1. 416

Clee, 4. 257-8

Cleland, James, 6. 343

Clemens, Mrs. Samuel, 8. 509

Clement of Alexandria, 5. 256; 7. 674

Clement VI, Pope, 7. 359

Cleodolinda, 1. 498

Cleopatra, 1. 444; 5. 224

Cleopolis, 1. 282, 290, 291, 514; 2. 334-5; 8. 662

Clergy, Anglican: 7. 600-2, 606-9; 8. 357-62; Reformed: 1. 471: 8. 279. *See also* Church; Roman Catholic

Clerke, William, 8. 539

Cleveland, John, 6. 382

Cliach, 6. 282

Clifford, Ann, 7. 314, 471

Clifford, George, Earl of Cumberland, 1. 449; 3. 307

Cliffs, 3. 287

Climax, 8. 390, 677

Clinton, Edward, Earl of Lincoln, 7. 435

Clinton, Elizabeth, 7. 435

Clio, 1. 363, 371, 506-15; 4. 241; 6. 439; 7. 399; 8. 313, 327, 329, 532, 534-5, 539-40. *See also* Muse, Spenser's

Clitheroe, 7. 653

Cliton, 8. 486

Clitophon and Leucippe. *See* Achilles Tatius

Clíu, 6. 426

Cloisters, 6. 298

Clopinel, Jean, 6. 336

Clorinda, 3. 332; 5. 200; 6. 351; 7. 474, 499, 500, 503

Clotho, 4. 182; 7. 416, 512

Cloud, 1. 228

Cnoc Aine, 6. 426

Cobham, Lord. *See* Brooke, William

Cock, 1. 412; 4. 196

Cock, Grace, 7. 362

Cockatrice, 8. 436

Cockburn, John, 1. 223

Cocytus, 2. 266-7

Codet, Gyles, 2. 452

Coeffeteau, Nicolas, 2. 463

Coelia, 1. 424, 430, 432, 499

Coffers, 1. 411

Coined words, 6. 275; 7. 618-9, 628-30, 649; 8. 371, 675. *See also* Diction, Vocabulary

Coins, 1. 390

Colchester, 2. 328, 330

"cold," 1. 198

Coleridge, Henry N., 8. 660

Coleridge, Samuel Taylor, 1. 206-7; 2. 301, 389; 3. 383, 386; 4. 198; 7. 359, 378, 390, 489, 578, 615; 8. 377, 478, 630-1, 660; *Christabel*: 7. 398, 635, 637, 639; *Lectures*: 1. 206-7; 2. 301, 389

Colewort, 8. 399

Colin, 7. 395-6, 400, 406, 643

Colin Clout, 1. 511; 5. 308; 6. 236, 245, 252, 254, 318, 327-8, 339, 345, 353, 374; 7. 247, 275-6, 280, 309, 316, 338, 342, 347, 349, 369, 373-5, 388-9, 395-6, 447-8, 452, 467, 469, 501-2, 579, 584-5, 588, 590, 595, 613-4, 630-4, 641, 648, 653; 8. 294, 517

Colin Clout, Mrs., 8. 650

Colin Clouts Come Home Again, 1. 348; 3. 366, 379; 5. 156, 309; 6. 244, 320, 377, 402, 448; 7. 247, 340, 366, 375, 377, 387, 594-5, 603, 611, 620, 656, 660; 8. 284, 527, 535, 633; and *Amoretti*: 8. 635, 638; and *Astrophel*: 7. 492; criticism: 7. 447-9; and *Daphnaida*: 7. 449; date:

6. 442; 7. 436-7, 450-1, 470-1; and *Doleful Lay of Clorinda*: 7. 501-2; editions: 7. 708-9; and the *Hymnes*: 7. 449, 656, 660-1, 665; metre: 7. 276, 447, 449-50; and *Mother Hubberds Tale*: 7. 447-8; 8. 364, 560, 575, 585, 593-4; and *Muiopotmos*: 8. 598, 601; and *October*: 7. 481, 665; punctuation: 7. 501-2; revision: 7. 451, 471, 477; and *Shepheardes Calender*: 7. 447-9, 451, 482; style: 7. 448-9; and *Teares of the Muses*: 7. 454; text: 7. 479, 708-11, 721-2; variants: 7. 409-11; *Dedication*: 7. 450-1; 8. 575; 1-200: 7. 625; 1-9: 5. 235; 6. 237; 3, 771-4: 6. 236; 8: 8. 473, 22-31: 7. 583; 8. 321; 37, 50: 7. 468; 56-9: 6. 284; 66: 5. 308; 92-155: 4. 173, 269; 5. 308; 6. 252, 289, 424-7, 441-2; 8. 529; 100-55: 8. 463; 173-6, 252-5: 3. 377; 180-93: 6. 252; 197: 8. 402; 212-23: 8. 408, 624; 233-53: 8. 540; 262-3: 5. 308; 274-5: 3. 287; 308-19: 8. 535; 326-51: 6. 221; 7. 531; 337-9: 8. 463; 351: 8. 472, 475; 368-455: 8. 333, 532, 534-5, 539-40; 384-5: 7. 501; 400 ff.: 8. 320; 424-43: 7. 450; 432-41: 3. 259; 448-51: 7. 487; 450-1, 487: 6. 351; 459-583: 7. 284; 464-83: 8. 650; 480, 895: 6. 265; 482-3: 8. 460; 486-91: 8. 283; 509-16: 3. 378; 537-41: 8. 501; 540-64: 8. 350; 563: 8. 472, 475; 596-615: 8. 473, 519; 605: 8. 472; 613: 2. 476; 614-5: 8. 472, 475; 635-6: 6. 247; 648-728: 8. 369; 651-786: 6. 343; 688-770: 6. 305, 337; 690, 727: 5. 283; 735-8: 7. 403; 760-77: 7. 661; 762-3: 4. 256; 768 ff.: 6. 310; 771-94: 7. 538; 8. 325; 782: 2. 231; 799-883: 3. 342; 6. 401; 7. 511; 801-2: 6. 412; 827-30: 7. 389; 835-94: 7. 661, 665; 841-52: 4. 309; 841: 1. 232; 863-82: 7. 514; 903-51: 8. 459; 919-24: 7. 288; 927-51: 6. 252; 7. 651-2, 655; 947-50: 6. 222; 953-6: 7. 390

Collen, 2. 446

Collier, J. P., 5. 245; 8. 575, 708

Collina Clouta, 7. 651

Collins, Arthur, 6. 233; 8. 292

Collins, J. B., 7. 524, 534, 539, 544, 550, 554, 564, 673-6

Collins, William, 1. 199; 2. 369; 8. 674

Colne (river), 4. 254

Colne (town), 7. 250

Colon, 7. 501-2

Colon, Ferdinand, 2. 356

Color, 1. 219; 2. 216, 352, 379; 4. 210; 6. 433, 450-1; 7. 263, 282; 8. 396

Colossus at Rhodes, 8. 306

Columba, 2. 381

Columbell, 3. 267

Columbus, Christopher, 2. 356

Columella, Lucius Junius Moderatus, 1. 512

Colvile, George, 6. 418; 7. 674

Combat, 5. 201, 221, 263

Comedy, 8. 437

Comets, 3. 206-7

Comfort, Sir, 1. 407

Comic Relief, 1. 306

Commendatory Sonnets, 8. 505-9; bibliography: 8. 736, 738-45; text criticism: 8. 687, 707-9, 723; 1: 7. 311, 325, 462, 478, 588; 8. 506, 643; 2: 8. 506-7, 708, 723, 736; 3: 8. 422, 507, 708, 736; 4: 8. 507-9, 708, 736

Commendatory Verses, 3. 305, 427-8; 7. 487, 489; 8. 328

Commentators, 1. 171; 2. 181, 450-1; 3. 199

Common Sense, 1. 178, 238; 2. 458, 463-4, 468, 481

Commons, 1. 424

Communion, 1. 302, 455, 472; 7. 544-5, 676

Communism, 4. 332; 5. 155, 175-6, 294, 336-41; 8. 353

Compar. *See* Parison

Complaint, 1. 383; 3. 290, 325; 4. 277; 5. 209-10; 6. 257; 7. 245, 320, 440-1, 503-4, 591, 593; 8. 459, 541, 719

Complaint of the Blacke Knight. See Chaucer (pseudo)

Complaints, 6. 392, 440; 7. 377, 432, 436, 445; 8. 279, 281-416, 400, 581; bibliography: 8. 735, 737-45; "calling in": 8. 592-5, 686; composition: 8. 282-3, 393; date: 8. 281-2, 316, 679; manuscripts: 8. 687-8; metres: 7. 431; publication: 7. 438; 8. 281-3, 613-5, 679, 686; text, notes on: 8. 711-8; variant readings: 8. 678-97; Printer's Epistle: 8. 270, 281-2, 511, 602

Compliment, 6. 251-2; 7. 284, 287-8

Composers. *See* English

Compost, 7. 633

Compound words, 6. 433, 438, 445-7, 450-1; 8. 476-7

Compton, Henry Lord, 3. 259-60; 7. 476; 8. 349-50

Conan, 2. 449; 3. 228-30; 7. 456

Concatenatio, 1. 215; 5. 164, 195; 6. 204, 207, 219, 230, 271; 7. 512; 8. 333, 404

Conceit, 5. 208

"concent." 8. 714, 720

Concord, 4. 226-7, 282-4, 287-8, 297-9, 307-12, 324-7; 6. 278, 323, 427; 7. 285; Concord-Discord antithesis: 4. 309-12, 324-7; 6. 427-8, 449; and Venus: 4. 334

Concupiscence, 2. 461, 468; 6. 212

Condla, 2. 448

Conduplicatio. *See* Ploce
Confession, 1. 283, 287, 407
Confusion, 1. 268
Coningsby, Thomas, 5. 326
Conn, 2. 350
Constable, Henry, 3. 309; 5. 189; 7. 295, 339, 346, 464, 594; 8. 634
Constance, 1. 305, 496
Constancy, "Legend" of. *See Faerie Queene*, Book 7
Constans, 2. 332
Constantine, Roman Emperor, 1. 199, 450; 2. 331-2; 8. 413
Constantine, King of Britain, 3. 228-9
Constantinople, 8. 365
Constantius, 2. 331
Consuls, 8. 386
Contaminatio, 8. 305, 311
Contareno, Gasper, 8. 507-8, 709, 736
"conteck," 7. 303
Conte du Graal, 6. 367-71
Contemplation, 1. 288-91, 357, 406-7, 504; 2. 278; 6. 208; Heavenly: 1. 424; Mount of: 1. 406, 430, 503-4
Contemplative life, 1. 288-9, 348, 357-8, 415, 417, 513; 2. 423, 430; 3. 246; 6. 358-9
"contemptus mundi," 7. 674, 676
Continence, 2. 294-5, 414-23, 426; 3. 322-3, 329, 354; in Ariosto and Spenser: 2. 439-41; Temperance contrasted with: 2. 420, 426
Contrast, 1. 175, 227, 238, 255, 288, 311-2; 4. 299-300, 302, 309-12; 6. 190, 205, 334, 348; 7. 263, 349, 367, 408, 429; 8. 404. *See also Faerie Queene*, Contrast
Contrition, 1. 287; Dame Contrition: 1. 407
"contrive," 2. 299
Convention, 7. 245, 248, 417, 429, 438, 441, 483, 588
Conventualism, 6. 208-9
Conway (river), 4. 263
Cook, Albert S., 1. 174, 177, 193; 3. 330-2; 5. 158, 226; 7. 283, 285, 299, 377; 8. 719-20
Coolatinny, 6. 287-9
Cooper, C. H. and T., 7. 646
Cooper, Lane, 1. 181
Cooper, Thomas, 1. 185; 2. 452; 3. 265; 7. 273, 302, 326; 8. 328, 541
Cope, Joan (mother of Elizabeth Boyle), 8. 651
Cope, Stephen, 8. 651
Cope, William, 8. 651
Copernicus, 5. 177-8; 6. 401
Copland, Robert, 8. 591
Copland, William, 2. 188
Corbenic, 3. 361-2, 364-5

Corbett, J. S., 5. 334
Corceca, 1. 260, 431
Corculum, 8. 436
Cordelia, 1. 269, 272, 496; 2. 315-8
Corflambo, 4. 276, 286
Coridon, 3. 263; 5. 208; 6. 255-6, 258-60, 323, 327, 331, 333-4, 339-40, 344, 349, 373-4, 381; 7. 246, 317, 448, 464-6
Corineus, 2. 307-8; 3. 236; 7. 461
Corinna, 7. 252, 654
Cork, 4. 270; 7. 456, 458, 461-2; 8. 463, 647-50
Cornelius Agrippa, 3. 216
Cornelius Nepos, 2. 301
Cornell University Library, 8. 681
Cornish, F. W., 5. 186, 199
Cornwall, 2. 317; 7. 459, 461-2
Coronis, 1. 237; 3. 295
Corpus Christi College, 7. 343
Correggio, Antonio Allegri, 3. 393, 395
Correlativi, 1. 300
Corrozet, Giles, 2. 226
Corruption, 8. 358, 361-2, 373-5
Corser, T., 7. 469
Corybantes, 1. 242
Corydon. *See* Coridon
Coshma, 7. 475
Cosmogony, 1. 232
Cosmography, 1. 194
Costume, 3. 209; 6. 224-6
Cotswolds, 7. 651-3
Coulin, 2. 308
Coulter, C. C., 7. 273, 289
Council of Trent, 1. 201
Councillors, 1. 341, 406, 410
Couper, Robert, 8. 343
Courage, 1. 328, 341; 2. 417-8
Court, 1. 215; 3. 252; 6. 186-7, 238, 329-33; 7. 370, 375, 448, 478, 594, 611, 629; 8. 587-8; of Elizabeth: 1. 485, 491, 515; 2. 262; 5. 156; 6. 242-3, 330, 362; 7. 326, 451, 480; 8. 363-5, 503, 560-1, 563, 565-6, 579; poets: 8. 333; school of courtesy: 3. 327; 6. 187, 343, 358
Court of Cupid, 6. 222-4, 292-3
Court of Cupid, 2. 397, 399; 3. 299-300; 6. 222-4; 7. 241; 8. 511, 513
Court of Cupid (Spenser's), 6. 223, 325; 8. 513
Court of Love, 1. 214, 418; 2. 279, 293, 349, 352, 371, 374, 378, 382, 391; 3. 208, 210, 256, 262, 290, 292, 299-300, 318; 4. 209, 216, 220-3, 225-34, 237-8, 278; 5. 240, 242-3; 6. 221-4, 231-2, 292-3; 7. 626; 8. 513, 518
Court of Love, possible source of *F. Q.*: 1. 406-7; 2. 285; 3. 353.9, 353-9; 6. 222;

52-4: 4. 203; 74-5: 4. 229; 76-82: 3. 208; 4. 229; 129-30: 3. 299; 158-60: 1. 406; 231-8: 3. 292; 246: 1. 286; 295 ff.: 1. 407; 316-9: 5. 210; 351-4: 4. 202; 365-71: 6. 256; 505-6: 3. 299; 519: 6. 231; 570-4: 4. 232; 591-7: 4. 233; 883-5: 5. 206; 1024-1316: 3. 301; 1058-61: 1. 220; 1198: 2. 297; 1254-60: 1. 406; 1255-5: 1. 222; 1300: 7. 272; 1316: 3. 295; 7. 481

Court of Nature, 6. 292-3, 391, 393, 400, 428

Court of Venus, 5. 242-3; 6. 248

Court of Venus, 5. 242-3; 6. 222

Court of Venus Moralized, 6. 222

Court of Virtue, 6. 222

Courtenay, Edward, 1. 463-5

Courtesy, 1. 231, 264, 329, 336, 340, 342, 407, 416; 3. 319, 322, 327, 385; 4. 237; 6. 199, 247, 260, 379; in Aristotle: 6. 325-7, 334-5, 346-7; Chivalry the source of: 6. 344-5, 358; derived from Court: 3. 327; 6. 187, 343, 358; false: 6. 216; includes honesty and tact: 6. 335-6; Italian writers on: 3. 322-3; 6. 328-34, 340, 345; in lowly life: 6. 342-3, 345-7; and lying: 6. 199, 205, 218, 340-1; matter of the heart: 6. 342-3; and Plato: 6. 346; the poetry of conduct: 6. 347; a Renaissance virtue: 1. 345; 2. 403; 6. 334; and the romances: 6. 365, 379; self-interest in: 6. 344; Sir Courtesy: 1. 407; Spenser's idea of: 6. 320-48; theme of whole *F. Q.*: 6. 334; a virtue: 6. 191, 342

Courtesy Books, 3. 322; 6. 337-44, 358

" courtesy man," 8. 355

Courthope, W. J., 1. 374-8; 2. 221, 246; 3. 215-6, 234, 386; 5. 180, 200; 7. 582-3

Courtier, 5. 191; 6. 255-6, 328-33, 358, 364; " brave " 8. 349, 563, 570; Elizabeth's: 8. 363

Courtly Love. *See* Love

Courtly tradition, 7. 277

Le Court Mantel, 4. 192

Coustard de Massi, 3. 204; 5. 193

Coventry pageants, 1. 390

Covetousness, 2. 258, 461

Covington, F. F., 4. 185, 264

Cowardice, 5. 192

Cowley, Abraham, 8. 622

Cowper, William, 1. 181, 370; 8. 467

Cox, Richard, 6. 386; 8. 361

Coyll, 2. 326, 330-1

Cozens Manuscript, 8. 515-6, 678, 687-8

Crane (river), 4. 272

Crane, Clara W., 4. 210

Cranmer, Thomas, 1. 461, 469-70; 7. 271

Crashaw, Richard, 2. 220; 6. 302; 7. 552

" craven," 6. 215

Crawford, Charles, 1. 250

Crawley, Alfred, 8. 469

Creation, 7. 513, 524, 538-40, 541-3

" creature," 8. 474

Creighton, Louise, 3. 305

Creighton, Mandell, 5. 252

Cressida, 4. 223; 6. 293

Crete, 1. 242

Creusa, 2. 372, 374

Crime, 4. 204-5

Crimea, 1. 258

Criseyde, 7. 517

Critias, 2. 263; 4. 164-5

Criticism, 1. 336; 5. 285-7; contemporary, Spenser's debt to: 1. 361; Eighteenth Century: 1. 319-20; Elizabethan: 1. 348; inadequate: 5. 286-7; Italian: 1. 348-51; Renaissance: 7. 393

Critics, 1. 180-1, 321, 344; 2. 287; 7. 259; 8. 518; disagree about *F. Q.*: 1. 331; 6. 389; fashions among concerning Spenser: 4. 290

Crocodile, 5. 214-6, 218, 220, 295; 8. 372

Croesus, 1. 444; 4. 167

Croke, Sir John, 8. 520

Crompton, Richard, 5. 245

Cromwell, Thomas, 1. 467-9

Croom, 7. 475

Cross, 2. 331; 5. 225

Cross, T. P., 7. 507

Crowd, 8. 470

Crowley, Robert, 5. 176, 294; 8. 591

" crown with cups," 1. 209

Crudor, 6. 190, 324, 326-8, 333

Cruelty, 5. 295-6

" crumenall," 7. 359

Cteatus, 4. 245

Cuckoo, 2. 295

Cuddie, 7. 259, 294, 334, 338, 345, 347, 349, 368, 370, 373-6, 382, 384-6, 388-9, 448, 454, 501, 579, 585, 589, 631, 641; 8. 319

Cudworth, Ralph, 1. 232; 7. 481

Cuffe, Hugh, 8. 417

Culpeper, Nicholas, 8. 398

Culpepper, Thomas, 7. 573

Cumberland, Earl of. *See* Clifford, George

Cumin, 8. 398

Cumming, W. P., 1. 186; 6. 276, 280, 283, 300, 302-6, 310, 313, 408-10

Cundah, 2. 318-9

Cunning, Sir, 1. 407

Cunningham, Allan, 7. 576

Cunningham, Peter, 8. 647

Cup, 1. 249, 285, 471; 2. 377, 381

Cupid, 1. 363, 371, 374, 405; 2. 271-3, 379,

383; 3. 251-2, 256, 292, 297-303, 351, 353-60, 365, 392, 397; 4. 165, 205, 217, 277; 7. 267-74, 448, 480, 509, 662, 679; 8. 308, 396-7, 402, 456-8, 482, 487-8, 640, 652; altar: 4. 229-31; 7. 521; arrows: 3. 295; 6. 255; clothes: 6. 309-10; Court of: 6. 222-4, 292-3; Masque of: 2. 353-66; 4. 234; 7. 510; 8. 625; presiding deity: 6. 222; and Psyche: 3. 261; 8. 396-7, 488; Spenser's: 4. 203; 7. 480, 560; and Spring: 6. 304

Curse, 5. 225
Cursor Mundi, 1. 275
Curtius, Quintus, 1. 214
Cybele, 4. 253-4; 6. 191, 279, 301, 398-9; 7. 445-6
Cycle, 3. 257; 6. 390, 397, 416-7; 7. 256
Cyclops, 5. 169; 7. 246
Cycnus, 8. 307-9
Cycones, 8. 346
Cydippe, 2. 264-6
Cyllatus, 2. 342
Cymbeline. See Kimbeline
Cymochles, 1. 230; 2. 231-2, 234, 241, 274, 402, 404, 427, 471; is Alençon: 2. 404
Cymodoce, 3. 240; 4. 276-7
Cymoent, 3. 240-1, 243, 325; 4. 276-7; 7. 504
Cynosure, 8. 431-2
Cynthia, 2. 454; 6. 276, 310, 437, 439; 7. 447, 453, 458, 463; 8. 466, 488-90
Cyrene, 3. 240, 242
Cyrus, 1. 214, 344; 4. 248; 6. 204
Cytheron, 3. 254; 6. 248-9

Dacia, 3. 231
Dacians, 2. 332
Dacier, André, 6. 306
d'Acquaria, Lorenzo, 8. 462
" daedale," 3. 201
Daemon, 8. 389
Dagger, 1. 411
Dalinda, 2. 230
Dalliance, 1. 407
Dametas, 2. 213; 6. 381; 7. 595
Damon, 2. 383; 4. 223, 225, 284, 303, 329; 7. 589. See also Edwards, Richard
Damon and Pythias, 2. 242; 4. 329
"Dan," 8. 308
Danae, 3. 253, 393, 397
Danao, 2. 306
Danaus, 1. 235
Dance, 1. 240-1; 3. 356-9; 4. 165-6; 6. 254; 7. 442; 8. 324, 365, 470; of Death: 2. 277; 6. 298; 7. 409; of nymphs and Graces: 6. 244-5, 249-52, 254, 339; 7. 284

Danes, 3. 235; 4. 226
Danger, 1. 366; 3. 253, 302; 4. 217, 220-2, 225, 276, 298; 5. 317
Daniel, Rose, 6. 220; 7. 321, 652
Daniel, Samuel, 6. 220; 7. 463, 471, 652, 654; 8. 284, 299, 507, 536, 540, 628; Cleopatra: 7. 450, 470; 8. 539, 637, 708; Complaint of Rosamond: 7. 450, 470; Defence of Rhyme: 7. 388; Delia: 2. 390; 7. 471, 615; 8. 539, 634; Eclogues: 7. 276; Tethys's Festival: 4. 240
Daniello, Bernardo, 1. 348, 513
Danius, 2. 321-2
Dante Alighieri, 1. 356, 358, 433, 513; 2. 203; 343; 5. 251; 6. 396, 399; 7. 553, 578, 586-7, 674-6; 8. 516, 599 Canzone: 7. 479; 8. 656-7; Convivio: 7. 553; 8. 493, 656
    Divina Commedia. Inferno: 1. 434; 1: 4. 168; 1. 22-7: 1. 239; 2. 53-117: 7. 444; 2. 127-9: 4. 278-9; 5. 264; 3: 3. 298; 3. 1-9: 1. 271; 7. 543; 4. 1 ff.: 4. 175; 5. 28-30: 1. 299; 5. 121-3: 8. 325; 6. 13: 1. 195; 6. 17: 1. 208; 6. 25-7: 1. 234-5; 7. 82: 3. 292; 7. 85-120: 7. 543; 7. 100-30: 1. 271; 7. 109: 2. 267; 8: 2. 257; 8. 31: 2. 248; 9. 64: 4. 215; 13: 1. 202, 271; 13. 4-6: 2. 262; 13. 10: 2. 258; 15. 19: 2. 259; 16. 1: 5. 199; 17. 1-12: 1. 182, 183, 205; 20. 10-5: 1. 260; 22. 24: 6. 217; 22. 128: 5. 181; 24. 47-51: 2. 220; 26. 45: 1. 216; 34. 45: 1. 184; Purgatorio: 1. 1-3: 1. 311; 1. 52-63: 7. 444; 1. 118: 2. 353; 2. 10-51: 8. 413; 2. 124: 3. 243; 6. 236; 5. 14: 2. 277; 9. 28: 6. 217; 10. 30-96: 3. 292; 12. 88-90: 8. 505; 15. 118 ff.: 4. 175; 16: 2. 422; 19. 19-24: 2. 367; 19. 64-7: 1. 297; 19. 118-23: 2. 269; 23. 22-4: 1. 261; 29. 104; 31. 70 ff.: 4. 183; 32. 100-5: 7. 444; 32. 109: 6. 217; Paradiso: 7. 550, 552, 564; 1. 1-3: 7. 556; 1. 12: 3. 238; 1. 46: 1. 289; 1. 61: 5. 188; 2. 1-7: 1. 311; 13. 136-8: 4. 192; 18. 34: 6. 217; 22. 100-5: 7. 444; 25. 118-20: 6. 244; 28: 1. 310; 7. 540, 553; 28. 76-9: 7. 554; 29, 30: 6. 250; 30. 25-7: 6. 244; 30. 64-6: 6. 251; 31. 1: 5. 199; 31. 70-93: 4. 163; 33. 1-3, 19-21: 7. 565; 33. 13-8: 7. 568; 33. 145: 7. 680
    Sonnets: 7. 250
Danube, 8. 306
Daphnaida, 6. 406; 7. 246, 340, 403, 501, 503; 8. 393, 459, 645; and Astrophel: 7. 484, 486; and Colin Clouts: 7. 449; composition: 7. 430; 8. 530; criticism: 7. 429-33; date: 7. 432, 435-8; and Doleful

Lay of Clorinda: 7. 501, 503, 505; editions: 7. 706; metre: 7. 430-1, 433; publication: 7. 706; rhetoric: 7. 441, 444, 503; and *Ruines of Time*: 8. 295, 645; source: 7. 430-1; text: 7. 706-8, 721; title: 7. 433; variants: 7. 707-8; *Dedication*: 8. 622; 11: 6. 477; 8. 459; 16: 4. 182; 22-42: 8. 495; 22-5: 8. 480; 67: 7. 355; 86, 403: 7. 627; 165: 6. 305; 211-7; 7. 506; 323-43: 8. 312, 485; 386-8: 7. 505; 435: 8. 498; 475: 7. 415-6; 487-90: 8. 295

Daphne, 2. 196, 378-9; 3. 295, 395; 7. 433, 465; 8. 429

Daphnis, 6. 262; 7. 249, 338-9, 400, 433, 496, 589

Daphnis and Chloe. See Longus

Darbishire, Helen, 7. 330, 415, 613

Darcie, Abraham, 8. 293

Darent, 4. 254-5

Dares Phrygius, 2. 218

Darius, 4. 186; 7. 393

Darnley, Henry Stuart, 2. 402; 5. 246

Dart (river), 4. 255

Darwin, Erasmus, 7. 282

Dative Case, 7. 305, 316

d'Aubigny, Agrippa, 7. 588

d'Auvergne, Martial, 6. 292

D'Avenant, William, 6. 300; 7. 615

David, 1. 414; 2. 258; 4. 174, 303; 5. 227, 268; 8. 306, 333

David, Johann, 2. 226

Davies, Sir John, 7. 464; 8. 281; *Discovery of the True Causes*: 6. 385; *Nosce Teipsum*: 1. 301; 2. 463, 465-6, 481; *Orchestra*: 4. 324; 7. 318

Davies, John of Hereford, 7. 585, 594; 8. 284; *Commendatory Poems*: 4. 350; *Humours Heaven on Earth*: 2. 464; *Muses Sacrifice*: 8. 520; *Mirum in Modum*: 2. 463, 465; *Wit's Pilgrimage*: 8. 437

Davies, Richard, 7. 296, 354

Davison, Francis, 4. 260, 315-6; 5. 236; 7. 258, 280, 324, 405, 489, 500, 502, 594; 8. 320, 520, 709-10, 723, 737

Davison, William, 4. 316; 5. 320-1; 8. 607

Day, 6. 302, 308, 420

Day, Angel, 8. 507, 708

Day, John, 8. 626-7

"dead . . . living," 1. 177; 7. 445; 8. 294, 530

Dead Sea, 2. 248

Dean, 7. 315

Death, 1. 407, 410, 417-8; 2. 195, 257, 259, 361; 3. 230; 6. 302, 309, 313, 420, 440; 7. 381, 408, 440; 8. 286, 599-600; Death's door: 4. 183; Death for inactivity or sorrow: 8. 321. *See also* Dance, of Death

De Baif, Lazare, 7. 340, 410, 596-7; 8. 438, 455-8, 634, 657; *Eclogues*: 7. 342, 496; *Marmot*: 7. 345; *Passetems*: 7. 273

Debat, 1. 247; 7. 255

Debate, 6. 292; 7. 255, 324, 603-4

Debon, 2. 307-8

Debora, 3. 238, 331

De Buttet, Marc-Claude, 8. 461-2, 464, 469-71, 473, 478, 481, 488-9, 493-4, 653-4

Decay. *See* Degeneration

Deceit, 1. 311; 6. 207

de Chambrun, Clara L., 6. 220

Declaration of the True Causes of the Great Troubles, 8. 579-81

De Condé, Jean, 4. 237; 8. 466

Decorum, 1. 231, 262, 305, 317, 365-6; 2. 273, 425; 4. 172, 174, 201; 5. 203; 6. 259, 429; 7. 256, 259, 294, 370, 451, 571, 576, 579, 599, 625-6, 631, 660; 8. 320, 564, 677

Dedannans, 4. 269

Dedicatory Sonnets, 1. 343, 492-3; 3. 306-9, 428-9; 7. 471; 8. 419, 459; and *Teares of the Muses*: 8. 539-40; text: 3. 428-9; 1, 3, 4, 5: 3. 307; 2: 5. 309; 8. 303, 419, 559, 574, 576, 582; 3, 5, 6, 9, 13: 1. 449; 3: 8. 319, 576, 582-3; 6, 12, 16: 8. 350; 6, 9, 11, 13: 3. 308; 6, 7: 6. 185; 6: 1. 296, 452; 2. 400-1; 5. 260, 325, 329, 331, 335; 6. 353, 356, 359, 434; 8. 503; 7, 8: 7. 475; 7: 5. 259; 7. 476; 8. 316, 510; 8, 11, 13, 15: 8. 328; 8: 3. 355; 4. 277; 8. 494, 540; 9, 10, 16: 8. 393; 9: 2. 402-3; 7. 476; 8. 393; 10: 8, 393, 510; 11: 7. 465, 473; 12: 6. 291; 8. 302; 13: 8. 418, 510; 14-17: 3. 309; 14: 7. 458; 15: 6. 351, 353-4; 7. 487, 489, 499; 8. 295; 16: 6. 237; 7. 476-7; 8. 393, 599-600, 634-5; 17: 4. 194, 216

Dee (river), 1. 266; 4. 240, 263; 6. 246

Dee, John, 1. 483; 5. 177-8; 7. 243

Deer, 6. 425-7

Defender of the Faith, 1. 207, 208, 211, 430, 466

Degeneration, 2. 254; 4. 311; 5. 154-6; 6. 275, 303, 396, 404, 413, 415, 423-4, 437, 441, 444; 7. 542; 8. 380

Degore, Sir, 1. 260

De Guileville, Guillaume, 1. 414; 2. 434; 3. 208; 6. 209; 7. 563-4, 627

de Heere, Lucas, 8. 626

Deianira, 1. 299; 5. 203

De Institutione Ordinis Periscelidis, 3. 265

Dekker, Thomas, 1. 479-82; 4. 240; 5. 346

DeLacy, Hugh, 3. 206-7, 220, 248; 6. 310; 8. 400

De la Noue, François, 4. 324

De la Perrière, William, 2. 226
De la Taille, Jean, 6. 238
De la Torre, Francisco, 8. 451
Delattre, Floris, 2. 335
Delay, 4. 220-1, 276
Delectable Mountains, 1. 290-1, 424
De l'Hôpital, Michel, 4. 324; 5. 214, 264
Delia, 7. 471
Delicacy, 1. 262
Delight, 3. 301; 6. 214; 7. 506; 8. 317
the "Delight," 2. 358
Delitiae cc. Italorum Poetarum, 8. 382
Della Casa, Giovanni, 6. 342
Delle Rime . . . nella Lingua Thoscana, 8. 382
Deloney, Thomas, 7. 346
Delos, 2. 244, 356
De Magny, Oliver, 8. 456
Demeter, 5. 217; 7. 446
Demiurge, 7. 524
Democracy, 5. 175-81, 290, 293, 304, 341-4; 6. 337-8, 340
Democritus, 6. 282
Demogorgon, 1. 190-1; 2. 232; 4. 182; 5. 234
Demophoon, 8. 338-9
DeMoss, William F., 1. 340-3; 2. 419; 3. 275, 319-21; 4. 296-8; 5. 281-2; 6. 325-7, 392-3, 436-7; 7. 324, 381; 8. 352-3, 397
De Musarum Inventis, 1. 514; 7. 288, 415; 8. 312 (full text), 328-9, 331, 541
Den, 5. 234
Denham, Sir John, 8. 496
Denis, St., 1. 205
Denkinger, E. M., 8. 604
Dennis, John, 7. 574
Deois, 3. 294
De Phillide et Flora, 3. 256; 6. 222, 292
De Pontoux, Claude, 8. 435, 441, 639
Deptford, 8. 671
Derby, Earl of. *See* Stanley, Ferdinando
De Rebus Gestis Britanniae, 1. 482
Derham, William, 2. 319
Dering, Edward, 7. 608
Der Kittel, 1. 406-7; 4. 229; 6. 248
Derrick, John, 6. 239
De Sainte-Palaye, Jean Baptiste de la Curne, 2. 224; 6. 196
Des Autels, Guillaume, 8. 529
Deschamps, Eustace, 4. 223, 231-2
Description, 1. 180-1, 188-9, 192-4, 250, 268-9, 274-5, 277, 298, 316, 413; 2. 211-3, 238, 244, 254, 256, 258-9, 287, 338, 371; 3. 241; 6. 313; coldly elaborate, indiscriminately minute: 2. 386
Desdemona, 1. 206, 496
Desire, 1. 365; 3. 301, 358

Desmond, Earl of. *See* FitzGerald, Gerald
Desmond, Sir James, 5. 314
Desmond, Sir John, 5. 313-4
Desmond War, 7. 360, 454
Despair, 1. 259, 266, 269-80, 305, 312, 429-30, 438, 498; 2. 256, 318, 352; 3. 301, 365, 4. 287; 5. 243, 275; is England's despair: 1. 459, 465, 472
Despencer, House of, 8. 501-2
Despériers, Bonaventure, 8. 445
Despight, 1. 230; 2. 232, 404; 4. 222; 6. 207, 222
Despondency, 1. 287
Desportes, Philippe, 8. 299, 434-5, 438, 441, 634, 639; and Spenser: 8. 639-42; *Amours*: 8. 436; *Cléonice*: 8. 430, 440, 444, 514, 640-1; *Diane*: 8. 424, 427, 435, 443, 639, 641; *Hippolyte*: 8. 425, 434, 450, 640-1
Despotism, 2. 249-50
Destruction of Troy, 6. 290
Detail, 1. 241
Detraction, 1. 417; 5. 266-7, 283, 285, 292, 307, 319; 6. 207, 345, 384; 7. 450. *See also* Slander
Deus ex machina, 1. 311; 4. 186; 8. 569
De Venus la Deesse d'Amor, 1. 406; 4. 220, 229, 278; 6. 222
de Vere, Aubrey, 1. 212, 270, 281-2, 496-8; 2. 197, 211-2, 249, 371; 3. 382; 6. 390; 8. 654
De Vere, Edward, Earl of Oxford, 1. 449; 2. 246; 3. 307; 7. 464; 8. 319, 375, 536, 577; is the Ape: 8. 569; is the boar: 8. 571; and Burleigh: 8. 603-5; is Clarion: 8. 605; is Paridell: 3. 380; is Phedon: 2. 402; is Sansfoy, Sansjoy, Sansloy: 1. 449; and Sidney: 8. 313, 317, 569, 599, 603-4; and Spenser: 3. 307; 8. 319, 320; is Willy: 8. 319
Devereux, 8. 504, 648
Devereux, Penelope, 3. 392; 6. 355, 373; 7. 350, 399, 476, 484, 490-5; 8. 397, 604. *See also* Stella
Devereux, Robert, second Earl of Essex, 1. 296, 481; 2. 188, 295; 5. 185, 260, 263, 307; 7. 434; 8. 363, 394, 502-4, 531, 580, 708; is Artegall: 5. 260, 326, 331; is Arthur: 1. 449, 452-3; and Burleigh: 8. 375, 574, 579, 599, 605-7; is Calidore: 6. 351-4, 357-64; character: 6. 357-64; and Elizabeth: 3. 308; 5. 329-31, 333-5; 6. 206, 362; 7. 492; 8. 489, 495, 503, 563, 576; in *F. Q.* 5: 5. 325-35; in France: 5. 326-34; is Guyon: 1. 491-2; 2. 190, 278, 297, 400-1; 3. 203-4; is the Kid: 7. 293; and literature: 8. 504, 507; and Raleigh: 6. 205-6; 7. 457-8; 8. 599, 601,

603; and Robert Cecil: 8. 373, 574; is
Scudamour: 3. 380; and Spenser: 3. 308;
5. 309, 324-35; 6. 205-6, 355-6, 360; 7.
485, 488, 492-3, 497, 600; 8. 495, 502-3,
576, 606, 661, 663-4; *Apology*: 6. 359
Devereux, Walter, first Earl of Essex, 5. 233;
8. 567, 606
Devereux, W. B., 5. 185, 263, 326; 6. 206,
352, 363; 8. 606
Devereux Papers, 8. 606
" devices," 5. 184
Devil, 1. 416. *See also* Satan
Devonshire, 7. 435, 461
D'Ewes, Simonds, 5. 323-4
Dew of Sleep, 1. 190
de Worde, Wynkyn, 7. 409
Dialect, 7. 360, 614-30, 649; Midland: 7.
361; northern: 3. 422-3; 7. 312, 331, 355,
357, 364, 573, 581, 616-8, 620, 622;
rustic: 7. 594-5; southern: 7. 361; Welsh:
7. 354. *See also* " Doric " dialect
Dialectic, 7. 552-3
Dialysis. *See* Divisio
Diana, 1. 236-7, 507, 515; 2. 193, 196, 204,
211-3, 216; 3. 246, 252-3, 319-20, 330,
332, 377-8, 389, 395; 6. 275, 288-90, 306,
425-6, 429-31, 437; 7. 281, 460; 8. 472,
490; in painting: 3. 392; 7. 458; temple
at Ephesus: 8. 306
Diana. See Montemayor
" Diapase," 2. 479-80, 484-5
Diaz de Bivar, Roderick, 5. 192
Dickens, Charles, 5. 305
Dictators, 8. 386
Diction, 1. 206; 7. 614-30; 8. 549; altera-
tions: 7. 624; innovations: 7. 622-3, 628-9;
importations: 7. 238, 623-4, 628, 630, 647.
See also Coined Words; Compound Words;
Vocabulary
Dido (*Aeneid*), 2. 195, 218; 3. 281-2, 387;
4. 223; 5. 205-6; 6. 293, 376, 378; 8. 472
Dido (*S. C. November*), 7. 396, 399, 400-4,
406, 601
" die of war," 2. 236
Digby, Kenelm, 2. 438, 472-8
Digges, Thomas, 5. 178; 8. 391
Diggon, 7. 468, 603, 643
Diggon Davy, 7. 352-4, 356-8, 603
Dilation, 6. 417
Dill, 8. 399
Dillingham, William, 7. 610
Dindrane, 1. 399
Dindshenchas, 6. 426; 7. 455-6
Dingley, 7. 315
Dinley, Rose, 7. 653
Dio Cassius, 2. 327-8; 8. 306
Dio Chrysostom, 7. 392-3; 8. 548

Dioclesian, 2. 306
Diodorus Siculus. *Library of History*: Book
1: 7: 1. 185-6; 11, 14, 17: 5. 215-7; 16:
4. 186; 25: 5. 218; 28: 4. 246; Book 2:
1: 2. 289; 4: 2. 448; 38: 5. 162; 45: 5.
197-9; Book 3: 53: 5. 199; Book 4: 5.
162; 2: 6. 270; 7: 8. 329; 21: 5. 219;
36: 1. 300; 59. 5: 6. 279; 67: 3. 296;
4. 214; 71: 6. 211; 72: 4. 246; Book 5:
24: 4. 246; 71: 5. 219; 76: 3. 339; Book
17: 7: 7. 336; 17: 7. 322; Book 22: 10.
4: 4. 225
Diogenes, 1. 279
Diogenes Laertius, 1. 222, 288; 3. 283; 4.
226; 8. 371
Diomedes, 5. 228, 269
Dionysius the Areopagite. *See* Pseudo-
Dionysius
Dionysius Cato, 2. 226
Dionysius Periegetes, 7. 415
Diotima, 7. 372, 678
Dirce, 2. 366
" dire dropsie," 1. 220
Dirge, 7. 638; 8. 359. *See also* Elegy
Dis, 2. 257-8
Disciples, 7. 332-3
Discord, 1. 364; 2. 200, 227, 231-2, 237,
266, 408; 4. 169, 195, 283, 294-6, 307-11,
324-7; 6. 323; Discord-Concord antithesis:
4. 309-12, 324-7; 6. 427-8, 449; 7. 238.
See also Eris
Discretion, 1. 416
Disdain, 1. 417; 2. 261; 6. 191, 224-6, 328,
347-8, 350; 7. 652; 8. 364
Disguise, 4. 208-9; 5. 223
Disillusion, 1. 444; 3. 300, 327; 6. 319; 8.
281, 369. *See also* Pessimism; Spenser,
Edmund
Disney, Walt, 7. 380
Disorder, 6. 419, 423
Disport, 1. 407
Disputatio inter Cor et Oculum, 3. 290
Disraeli, Isaac, 2. 386
Dissemblance, 1. 339, 365
" Dissemble," 3. 277
Dissonance, 8. 338, 340
Distributio, 7. 444; 8. 452, 469, 474, 484,
658, 676-7
Distrust, 3. 301
Disyllables, 8. 352, 373
" divine," 7. 441
Divine Idea, 3. 245-6
Divine Right, 5. 160, 236-7
Divisio, 8. 425, 644
Doctrine, Dame, 1. 405. *See also* Tower of
Doctrine
Dodoens, Rembert, 8. 398-9

Dodona, 8. 339

Dog Star, 1. 209

Dogs, 1. 194, 209, 233; 2. 200, 341; 3. 207; 4. 197; 5. 232; 6. 226-7; 7. 351, 356, 361-2

Dolce, Lodovico, 1. 355

Dolcio, L., 8. 466

Doleful Lay of Clorinda, 7. 247, 485; and *Amoretti*: 7. 501-2, 504-5; authorship: 7. 500-7; 8. 284; and *Colin Clouts*: 7. 501-2; and *Daphnaida*: 7. 501, 503, 505; date: 7. 501; metre: 7. 501; punctuation: 7. 501-2; rhetoric: 7. 503-5; and *Ruines of Time*: 7. 500-1, 503; 8. 296; and *Shepheardes Calender*: 7. 501, 503; style: 7. 500, 502-3; and *Teares of the Muses*: 7. 501-2; text and variants: 7. 712; 64-5: 2. 476

Dolistone, 6. 260

Dolon, 1. 277; 5. 172, 211-2, 285, 288, 293, 297, 314, 316, 348; 8. 345-6

Dolphin, 2. 359, 362

Domenichi, Lorenzo, 3. 322

Domesticity, 1. 305

Dominations, 1. 310; 7. 553

Donatus, 2. 326

Doneraile, 7. 454

Donhage, 5. 319

Doni, Antonio Francesco, 2. 456; 7. 335-6; 8. 585-6, 589, 591

Donne, John, 6. 424; 7. 324, 415, 470, 552; 8. 281, 636, 658-9

Don Quixote, 2. 208, 342; 6. 189, 193, 212, 216

Don Quixote, 2. 242, 275

Donwallo, 2. 396

Dony, 5. 169

Doocarrig, 6. 287

Door, 2. 373; 5. 205

Doralice, 3. 268

Dorastus and Fawnia. See Greene, Richard, *Pandosto*

Dorat, Jean, 8. 460

Dorchester, 8. 672

Dordoni, Traiano, 8. 474

"Doric" dialect, 7. 573, 575, 581, 595-6, 615, 617

Dorke, Walter, 4. 224-5

Dorset, 7. 439

Dort, 5. 319

Doubt, 1. 365; 3. 253; 4. 217, 220-1, 225, 276

Douce, Francis, 7. 409

Doucepere, 3. 285-6

Douglas, Gawin, 3. 303; 6. 337; 7. 620; *King Hart*: 2. 286; *Palice of Honour*: 1. 406-7; 4. 223, 229; 6. 248; *Virgil*: 1. 188, 340; 3. 238; 4. 211; 7. 344, 616; 8. 312

Doune (river), 4. 273

Dove, 1. 412-3; 4. 210-11, 232, 286-7; 7. 463

Dove, John, 7. 300, 642-3

Dowden, Edward, 1. 206, 310, 498-500; 2. 212, 348, 415-6, 458-9, 480-1; 3. 383-6; 4. 288-9; 7. 366-7, 579-80

Downe (river), 4. 258

Dragon, 1. 250, 252, 259, 296, 364, 368-9, 371, 374, 376-7, 389-90, 393, 395-6, 401-4, 416-7, 425, 508; 2. 183; 5. 170, 220, 250; 7. 557; 8. 407; is Antichrist: 1. 466; is Church of Rome: 1. 466; is priesthood: 8. 279; is Satan: 1. 455; 7. 557; Spenser's best described in romance: 1. 377, 401-4; Welsh: 1. 483, 490

Dragontina, 3. 303

Drake, Sir Francis, 2. 358; 5. 226, 248-9, 307-8, 333-4; 8. 536, 540

Drama, Elizabethan: 1. 271; 8. 316-21, 517-8, 532; in Spenser: 2. 224-5; 8. 516-8. *See also* Spenser, drama; dramatic power; Theatre

Drant, Thomas, 7. 300, 367; 8. 422, 519

Draper, J. W., 1. 348-51; 2. 204-5, 229, 231, 243, 343; 3. 202, 249; 4. 276; 5. 167, 196; 6. 201, 238, 265; 7. 620, 629; 8. 637

Drawing, 1. 219

Drayton, Michael, 1. 488; 4. 353-4; 7. 369, 464, 472-4, 581, 585, 596, 654; 8. 299, 540, 637, 688; his copy of Spenser's *Works*, 1611 (?): 2. 507, 510-3; 4. 350, 353-5; 5. 366-74; 6. 470-4, 476, 478-9; 7. 721; 8. 688, 716; and Spenser compared: 7. 581; 8. 628, 630-1, 634, 639; imitates Spenser: 4. 240; 7. 330; 8. 673; praises Spenser: 7. 642; 8. 400; *Ballad of Dowsabell*: 8. 602; *Barons' Wars*: 3. 395; *Endymion and Phoebe*: 7. 473; *Epistle of Rosamond*: 4. 214; *Harmony of the Church*: 7. 473; *Heroical Epistles*: 3. 216; 7. 473; 8. 355; *Idea*: 8. 435, 514, 628, 630-1, 634, 637, 639; *Man in the Moone*: 7. 540; 8. 490; *Matilda*: 3. 248; 7. 473; metrical versions of the Psalms: 5. 309; *Muses Elysium*: 4. 199; 7. 302; 8. 328; *Nimphidia*: 8. 598, 602; *Owl*: 2. 369; *Pastorals* (Hebel's edition of Drayton, 2. 523-66): 2: 7. 262; 3. 7. 279, 287, 387; 8. 496; 4: 7. 332; 8: 7. 469; 9: 6. 193; 7. 312, 347, 651-3; *Polyolbion* (vol. 4 in Hebel's ed.): *Upon a Frontispiece*: 3. 203; 1: 1. 225; 2. 307; 4. 199; 7. 461; 3: 1. 258; 4: 1. 477; 2. 275; 3. 224; 6. 190, 366; 5: 3. 226; 7. 316; 8: 2. 322; 10: 1. 265-6; 2. 196; 11: 4. 239-40;

12: 2. 193; 14: 5. 158; 15: 4. 240; 7. 287;
16: 2. 320; 8. 285; 18: 4. 240, 272; 7.
330; 20: 4. 243; 24: 2. 280; 4. 259; 26:
6. 193. *See also* Selden, John; *Shepheards
Garland*: 7. 255, 472, 594; 1: 7. 246;
2: 7. 253, 278; 3, 6, 9: 7. 473; 3: 7. 247,
286-7, 380; 8. 287, 291, 496, 673; 4: 7.
318, 399, 414; 6: 8. 451; 8: 7. 251, 259,
346, 356, 419; 8. 399; *Third Nimphall*:
7. 379
Dread, 2. 257
Dream motif, 1. 418; 7. 432
Dreames, 2. 397; 3. 299-300; 7. 241, 416,
613, 646, 648; 8. 273, 280, 404-5, 414,
511-2, 514-5, 624-5; and *Ruines of Time*:
8. 512, 526-8; and *Vision* poems: 8. 511-2,
613
Dreams, 1. 181, 195, 197, 426; 4. 198; 5.
221; 8. 377; awaking from: 4. 175; Gates
of: 1. 193-5
Dress, 1. 215
Dromedary, 8. 571
Drowes, 4. 268, 271
" drown," 8. 410
Druids, 7. 265
Drummond, William, 1. 481; 6. 277, 382;
7. 389, 463, 541, 553; 8. 420, 628
Drury Lane Theatre, 7. 426
Dryden, Erasmus, 6. 220-1; 7. 652, 654; 8.
651
Dryden, John, 1. 208, 344; 3. 218; 5. 212,
309; 6. 220; 7. 383, 421, 576, 599, 617,
625, 627, 652, 654; 8. 317, 319, 331, 524,
560, 564-6, 594, 651, 674; Arthur, meditated story of: 1. 359; his copy of Spenser's
Works, 1679: 2. 508-12; 4. 350-5; 5. 367-
70, 372; 6. 472, 475, 477; 8. 688,
716; Spenser, imitates: 4. 234; *Alexander's
Feast*: 7. 392; *Cymon and Iphigenia*: 2.
211; *Dedication of the Aeneis*: 7. 615;
Dedication of the Pastorals: 7. 573; *Essay
on Satire*: 1. 315, 449, 492; 7. 552, 618;
The Hind and the Panther: 2. 344; 6. 382;
8. 578; *Indian Emperor*: 7. 460; Preface
to *Sylvae*: 7. 573; *Religio Laici*: 6. 276;
The Rival Ladies: 5. 181; *Satires*: 8. 563;
Song for St. Cecilia's Day: 2. 289, 485
Dryden, John (poet's great-grandfather), 6.
220; 8. 651
Duanaire Finn, 6. 425-7
Du Bartas, Guillaume Salluste, 6. 401, 423-4;
7. 623; 8. 281, 391, 398; *Sepmaines*: 8.
378-9, 391; *Première Semaine*: 2. 286,
288, 291-3, 297-8; 7. 264; 8. 329-30, 391;
Second Week: 7. 281, 414; *Uranie*: 8.
326, 329-30, 379, 391. *See also* Sylvester,
Joshua

Dubbing, 5. 203; 6. 196
Du Bellay, Joachim, 4. 179, 253; 7. 340, 372,
384, 393, 523, 595-6, 615, 623; 8. 291,
299, 398, 409-14, 435, 530, 535-6, 538,
549, 618; *Antiquitez de Rome*: 7. 416;
8. 378-91, 522-3, 525, 529, 617, 620,
625; *Contre les Envieux Poetes*: 8. 657;
*Deffence et Illustration de la Langue Fran-
caise*: 7. 239, 622, 624; 8. 298, 302, 327,
332, 379, 391, 537-8; *Discours au Roy*:
8. 298, 314; *Du Premier Jour de l'An*:
8. 421; *Epithalame . . . Prince Philibert
et Madame Marguerite*: 8. 465, 483, 487-8,
653-4; *Imitation de l'Ode Latine de Dorat
sur la Mort de la Roine de Navarre*: 8. 657;
La Musagnoeomachie: 8. 322; *L'Olive*: 8.
426, 438, 474; *Le Poete Courtisan*: 8. 327,
368; *Regrets*: 7. 443, 478; *Romae Des-
criptio*: 8. 382; *Songe*: 4. 167; 8. 277-80,
284-5, 306-7, 409-14, 512, 522-3, 529,
611-27; *Tumulus Romae Veteris*: 8. 381
Dubitatio, 7. 504
du Bos, Abbé, 1. 368-9
Dudley, Ambrose, Earl of Warwick, 5. 182,
185; 7. 435, 437, 442, 474; 8. 294, 304,
306, 459
Dudley, Catherine, Countess of Huntington,
6. 353; 7. 474; 8. 295
Dudley crest, 7. 384, 392; 8. 304, 306, 308,
567
Dudley family, 4. 251; 7. 395, 402-3; 8.
294-5, 306, 326, 522-8
Dudley, Margaret, Countess of Cumberland,
7. 474
Dudley, Mary, 8. 295
Dudley, Robert, Earl of Leicester, 1. 251,
264, 268, 285, 335, 344-5, 441, 452; 2.
207, 345, 408; 5. 227, 239, 251, 320, 335;
6. 272, 356, 383-4; 7. 289, 298, 354, 367,
370, 435, 448, 606, 642, 649; 8. 284,
292-4, 304, 308, 418, 495, 502, 532, 572;
is Arthur: 1. 343, 345, 441, 451-2, 458-60,
465, 485; 2. 303, 403; 3. 379; 5. 244, 246,
271-2, 300-1, 310, 316; 7. 382; is the
bear: 8. 571, 576; is the beast: 8. 363;
and Burleigh: 8. 375, 510, 521, 571, 573,
579, 602, 607; character: 8. 578, 607; is
Clarion: 8. 607; is Cupid: 8. 606; and
Elizabeth: 8. 304, 371, 489, 567-8, 571-2,
576, 606; is the fox: 8. 576; lamented:
8. 522, 524-8; is the lion: 5. 242; 8. 567,
571; is Lobbin: 7. 395-6, 402-4, 479; 8.
320; marriage: 8. 567-8; in the Netherlands: 5. 251-2, 256, 319; patron of the
arts: 3. 392, 395; politics: 5. 333; and
Spenser: 2. 186; 5. 307, 309-11, 325; 7.
235, 291, 293, 489, 586, 600, 605, 610-11,

613-4, 642; 8. 292-3, 371, 374, 396, 459, 495, 502-3, 510-11, 521, 543-4, 559, 563, 565, 567, 570, 573-6, 602, 607, 642, 661, 663-4

Duello, 1. 223

Duels, 1. 223, 226; 4. 183

Duessa, 1. 255, 305, 308, 398-9, 428, 437, 443-4, 459, 498; 2. 428, 443; 3. 302, 365; 5. 187, 233, 285, 291; 6. 278, 449; 7. 363; 8. 364; her beast: 1. 254, 368-9; is Falsehood: 1. 422-4, 435; is Mary Queen of Scots: 1. 459-60, 465-6, 481, 492; 5. 244-7, 273, 286, 296, 317, 321-4; is Mary Tudor: 1. 441, 459-60, 462, 465-6, 470; 5. 286; is Popery: 1. 440; is Roman Church: 1. 426, 450, 452, 455, 465; stripped: 1. 248, 311, 429; 2. 190; is Dekker's *Whore of Babylon*: 1. 481. *See also* Fidessa

Dugdale, William, 7. 403

Dulcippa, 4. 181

Dumaeus, A., 7. 415, 426; 8. 312, 316, 334, 336-7, 342, 345, 347, 548-58

Dumarin, 3. 240

Dumb-show. *See* Pantomime

Dumps, 8. 422, 436-7

Dunbar, William, 2. 391; 7. 620; 8. 466

" dunghill," 6. 217; 8. 326

Dunloe, 6. 190

Dunster, Charles, 7. 547

Dunwallo, 2. 320

Duodo, Pietro, 6. 358

Dürer, Albrecht, 1. 294-5, 310; 2. 366

Durham House, 8. 374

Durinda, 2. 275; 5. 191-2

Durindana, 2. 207, 275-6; 5. 191

Dust, 6. 217; 7. 517; 8. 382, 447

" Dust out of the," 7. 517; 8. 382

Dutch, 8. 364

Du Tyard, Pontus, 8. 424, 432, 435, 441, 639

Dwarf, 1. 393, 424; is Common Sense: 1. 435; is inadequate holiness: 1. 431; is Humility in *F. Q.* 1: 1. 428; is Prudence in *F. Q.* 1: 1. 425, 428, 434

Dyce, Alexander, 1. 253; 5. 185

Dyer, Sir Edward, 3. 307; 7. 367, 464, 466, 490; 8. 418, 514, 536

Dyer, John, 8. 380

Dying Pelican, 7. 241, 393; 8. 270, 283, 515-6

Dymmok, John, 5. 263

Dynevor, 3. 224-5

Eagle, 1. 263, 289, 302-3; 2. 341; 3. 234; 7. 335, 557, 564; 8. 407. *See* Aquila

Earth, 2. 347; 5. 178; 6. 279; man of: 1. 290-4; mother of: 3. 397

Earthly Beauty. *See* Beauty, earthly

Earthly Love. *See* Love, earthly

Earthly Paradise, 1. 255; 2. 395; 3. 253, 258, 345; 6. 202; 7. 336-7

Easter, 8. 443-5

Easterlings, 2. 332

Easton, 7. 315

East Smithfield, 7. 419

" eat the heart," 8. 371

Ebony, 1. 174

Ebranck, 2. 311-2

Eccles, Mark, 8. 651

Ecclesiastes (Spenser's version), 5. 175; 8. 270, 283, 519, 536

Echidna, 1. 182; 5. 250, 257; 6. 188, 212-3, 270, 341, 388

Echo, 2. 295

Eclipsis, 7. 247; 8. 530

Ecliptic, 5. 158

" Eclogue," 7. 242, 589

Ecphonesis. *See* Exclamatio

Ector, Sir, 1. 264, 399

Eden, 1. 255, 300, 312; 3. 345; 8. 596; king and queen of: 1. 295

Eden (river), 4. 261

Eden, Richard, 4. 204, 248

Edgar, 1. 482; 2. 334; 7. 365

Edinburgh University Library, 8. 682, 697-8

Editors of Spenser, 1. 171, 209, 506

Edmer, 8. 288

Edmund, St., 8. 300, 306

Education, 1. 340, 417; 2. 409; 3. 338

Edward, Black Prince, 1. 247

Edward I, 2. 307; 3. 236

Edward II, 1. 309; 8. 502

Edward III, 1. 256, 293; 2. 203; 4. 200, 259; 5. 240-1

Edward IV, 1. 389-90; 6. 262

Edward V, 2. 281

Edward VI, 1. 211, 390, 441, 457, 464; 2. 335, 338, 407; 5. 337, 341-2; 8. 359

Edward, Lord Roos, Earl of Rutland, 6. 353

Edwards, Richard, 4. 225, 328-9; 7. 318

Edwards, Thomas, 3. 307; 7. 472, 474

Edwin, Jonathan, 3. 403; 7. 707; 8. 737

Effin, 8. 362

Egerton, John, Earl of Bridgewater, 7. 471

Egerton, Thomas, Viscount Brackley, 7. 471; 8. 310, 571

Egfrid, 1. 482

Eglantine, 1. 202, 205; 2. 383; 7. 467

Egyptians, 3. 257; 7. 529; 8. 352

Eichelberger, Captain, U. S. N., 8. 490

Eighteenth Century, 1. 237

Eirene, 5. 243-4

E. K., 6. 431-2; 7. 273, 278, 291, 399, 403, 415-8, 421, 426, 436, 580, 584, 586-7, 589, 593-4, 596-7, 599, 602-3, 611-2, 617-

8, 622, 625, 645-50; characterized: 7. 650; a composite of Spenser and another: 7. 648-50; is Harvey in part: 7. 650; is Spenser: 7. 242, 278-9, 288, 307, 416, 599, 645-50; is other than Spenser: 1. 509; 7. 645-50

Eldol, 2. 334

Eldorado, 3. 240; 4. 248-9

Eldred, 8. 287-90

Election, 1. 275; 7. 676

Elegy, 7. 395-401, 429-32, 483-6, 503, 594; 8. 522-3, 525, 530. *See also* Dirge

Elements, 1. 195; 2. 474, 479, 483; 3. 344; 5. 177-8; 6. 390, 394, 402, 407, 409-10, 414, 439, 441, 447, 449; 7. 263, 481, 514-5, 527, 529, 550

Elene, 1. 392

Elephant, 1. 416; 8. 408

Eleusinian Mysteries, 2. 269

Eleutherillida, 5. 240

" elf," 7. 322

Elfant, Elfar, Elficleos, Elfiline, Elfinan, Elfine, Elfinel, Elfinor, 2. 334-6, 453

Elferon, 1. 480; 2. 334

Elfin, 1. 292; 2. 334

Elidure, 2. 322-3

Eliot, T. S., 8. 497

Elisa, 7. 402, 404

Elissa, 2. 197, 201-2, 411, 417, 425-6; 7. 404

" Elizabeth," 8. 631, 633-5, 638

Elizabeth I, 1. 173-4, 196, 244, 251, 256, 263, 266, 291, 296, 305, 317, 323, 334, 340, 344-5, 438, 449-53, 458-9, 463-6, 472-80, 482-5, 490-5, 512; 2. 190, 201, 214, 335-6, 371, 400, 409; 3. 201; 4. 314, 324; 5. 198, 227; 7. 448, 452, 459, 462, 465; 8. 525; against abbeys: 6. 268; and Alençon: 1. 452; 2. 206, 219; 3. 380; 5. 185, 307; 7. 605; 8. 543-4, 567-8, 571, 578, 604; is Amoretta: 3. 377-8; *Amoretti*, addressed in: 8. 631-2; appearance: 2. 384-5; 7. 282; arms: 5. 240-1; is Belphoebe: 1. 449; 2. 211, 454; 3. 246, 310, 375, 377-8, 389; 4. 206-7; 5. 310; Boethius, translation of: 6. 418; 7. 537, 674; bride of England: 8. 503; is Britomart: 2. 303, 454; 3. 203, 310, 320, 326, 379-80; 5. 211, 221, 305, 310; 8. 503; character: 2. 295; 5. 239, 318; and the Church: 7. 602; claim to the throne: 2. 408; corresponds to Virgil's Augustus and Ariosto's Hippolito: 3. 310; Court of: 5. 237-8, 240, 343; 7. 292, 370, 480; 8. 363, 572, 601; and Courtesy: 6. 186, 343; is Cynthia: 2. 454; 7. 447, 458-9; 8. 503; is Dido: 7. 404; dress: 4. 226; is the eagle: 7. 335; at Elvetham: 6. 304, 309; her enemies: 6.

383; England, speaks for: 2. 412; 8. 333; entertainments: 3. 355, 358; 7. 284-5; and Essex: 3. 308; 5. 329-31, 333-5; 8. 503, 598, 664; is Europa: 8. 607; in *F. Q.* 3: 3. 379-80; in *F. Q.* 5: 5. 299; is false Florimell: 3. 380; the great *fée*: 2. 455; and flattery: 8. 333, 451; is Gloriana: 1. 449-50; 2. 336-7, 453-5; 4. 319; 5. 197, 310; 8. 503; is the goat: 7. 304; godmother: 7. 403; heaven fights for her: 3. 247; and Henry IV of France: 5. 260-1, 329-30; impersonations: 5. 310; and Ireland: 5. 233, 259, 303-10, 331-2; 6. 440, 444; at Kenilworth: 7. 283, 289; and Leicester: 2. 407; 5. 244, 310-7, 367; 7. 383, 403; 8. 304, 371, 543-4, 567-8, 606; life set forth in *F. Q.* 1: 1. 482; is the lion: 8. 363, 573; Margaret of Navarre's poem, translates: 7. 674; and Mary Stuart: 5. 225, 244-7, 249, 276, 301, 303-7, 316-7; is Mercilla: 1. 449; 2. 454; 5. 225-6, 244-7, 296, 299, 305-6, 310; is Minerva: 8. 604, 607; mirror of virtues: 6. 186; and monopolies: 5. 170-1; in the Netherlands: 5. 249, 251-2, 256, 316-7, 319; one of the Nine Women Worthies: 3. 339; and the Earl of Oxford: 8. 605; and patronage: 7. 356; 8. 333; peaceful reign: 1. 490; 2. 211, 440; 5. 241; 7. 277, 285; 8. 403; and Philip II: 5. 211, 226, 303, 305, 307; plots against: 5. 201, 211; 6. 383; and poetry: 7. 459, 463; 8. 333; policy: 2. 406; 5. 303-10, 325-6; 7. 588; her porter: 5. 238; and Puritanism: 7. 291; is Radigùnd?: 5. 202; and Raleigh: 2. 185; 3. 326; 4. 205-7, 249; 5. 248; 7. 450-1, 458; 8. 601; and scandal: 6. 383-4; the sea, rules: 8. 403, 599, 607; in *Shepheards Calender*: 6. 254; 7. 263, 275-89; and Sidney: 8. 604, 606; in Sidney's *Arcadia*: 3. 377-8; and Spain: 5. 248; and Spenser: 2. 186, 280; 3. 311; 4. 201; 5. 156, 160, 204, 214, 223, 276, 321-2; 6. 186, 7. 254, 281, 288, 313, 370, 441, 597, 606; 8. 319, 357, 371, 451, 459, 488-9, 495, 501, 521, 571-2, 629, 665, 669; spies: 5. 211; statutes: 8. 356; succession: 5. 320-1; 6. 299; 8. 525, 528-9, 579; suitors: 3. 326; is Syrinx: 2. 384; 7. 282; is Tanaquill: 2. 453-4; 3. 337; Tudor descent: 1. 352; 2. 408, 453-5; 3. 325, 339; is Una: 1. 441, 463, 473; is Venus: 8. 397, 604, 606-7; verses by: 2. 407-8; is Verulam: 8. 529

Elizabethan, 1. 196, 344, 352, 357, 488-90; 2. 294; adventurous: 2. 254; 5. 345; allegory: 8. 402; architecture: 4. 213, 219; armor: 5. 222; astrology: 3. 249; author-

ship less personal: 7. 645; Chastity vs. Love: 3. 354; comedy: 8. 316-21; education: 2. 409; England: *see* England; English: 7. 618-9, 628; 8. 347; ethics: 8. 476; games and pastimes: 3. 288; 5. 224; 7. 379; 8. 350-1, 357, 366; hidden meaning, fond of: 1. 492; 2. 208; 8. 503; Ireland, soldiers in: 4. 265; Ireland, view of: 5. 265; literature: 8. 321, 531-40; magnificence, love of: 8. 374, 502; manners: 3. 212; moral truth, search for: 4. 333; 7. 579; music: 8. 367; navigation: 1. 338; philosophy: 3. 347, 351; poetry: 7. 583, 617; prosperity: 8. 533; psychology: 2. 458-66; restless: 1. 305; revolutionary age: 5. 155; witches, belief in: 3. 262; women, idea of: 3. 317-8

Elizabethan Club, 7. 709; 8. 680-1, 706-7

Ellipsis, 1. 236-7

Ellis, Alexander John, 7. 423

Ellis, Robert, 7. 426

Elmes, Henry, 8. 508

Elmore. *See* Aylmer

Elocution, 7. 241

Elphin, 7. 585

Elton, Oliver, 1. 209-10; 4. 240; 6. 390-1, 434; 7. 390, 594, 664; 8. 293, 297, 497

Elves, 2. 334-6

Elviden, Edmund, 5. 183

Elyot, Thomas, 5. 343; 6. 342; 7. 238, 621, 623-4; 8. 374; *Castle of Helthe*: 1. 278; 8. 398-9; *Defence of Good Women*: 3. 337-8; *The Governour*: 1. 340; 2. 294-5; 4. 304, 332; 5. 306, 342; 6. 337-8; 1. 18: 2. 224; 2. 3-5: 5. 293-4; 6. 194, 337-8; 2. 12: 4. 224; 2. 122-4: 4. 313, 328-9; 2. 163: 4. 328; 3. 3: 5. 293-4

Elysian Fields, 3. 258; 4. 222

Emblems, 1. 219, 271, 284; 2. 226-7; 3. 358; 7. 633; 8. 278, 304-10, 378, 405-8, 525, 624-7; and poetry: 8. 625; restored: 7. 425-6; and *Vision* poems: 8. 624-7

Embroidery, 8. 605-7

Emerson, F. W., 4. 178

Emerson, O. F., 8. 334-49, 391, 393, 545, 598-9, 714

Emerson, Ralph Waldo, 7. 530; 8. 596, 599

Emiline, 3. 236; 6. 369

Empedocles, 3. 340, 342-3, 347, 349; 4. 226, 313; 6. 389, 401-3, 407-10; 7. 511

Emperors, 1. 199, 359

Empress of India, 1. 457

" emprise," 7. 365

Empyrean, 7. 553

The Enchanted Cup, 4. 192

Enchantment, 1. 393; 2. 275

Enderbury, P., 6. 190

" endless," 6. 188

Endurance, 1. 289

Endymion, 7. 329, 337; 8. 490

Enfance, 1. 292-4

" engine," 5. 213

England, 5. 247; Church of: 1. 450-1, 454-5, 472-3; 5. 339; 6. 386; 7. 262, 292-6, 298-304, 325, 351-4, 357-9, 601-9; 8. 357-62, 374, 561, 563, 565, 592; Elizabethan: 1. 344, 352; 2. 260, 403; 6. 314; 7. 586; is Fairyland: 1. 344; 2. 202; 3. 215; in Ireland: 5. 233, 236, 259, 265; language: 8. 535; is lion: 8. 579; praise of: 2. 406; on the sea: 7. 461, 467; sobriety: 5. 192

England's Helicon, 7. 280, 319, 339, 346, 585

England's Parnassus, 2. 261, 510

English, composers: 7. 276; idiom: 7. 270; language: 7. 614-30; 8. 535; reality: 7. 592; tradition: 7. 268, 277, 346

The English Poet, 7. 241-2, 368, 370, 372, 376-8, 421, 586, 647; 8. 332, 514; and *Teares of the Muses*: 8. 514

Enias, 6. 217-8, 327, 340

Enjambement. *See* Run-over Lines

Ennius, 1. 357; 2. 353; 4. 180; 7. 393; 8. 372

Enricius Cordus, 7. 249

Ensigns, 3. 235

Entertainments, 3. 355-9; 6. 310

Enthusiasmus, 7. 366, 376, 389, 391; 8. 641

Enueg, 7. 444

Enumeratio. *See* Expeditio

Envy, 1. 406, 410-3, 417; 2. 227, 461; 4. 231, 326; 5. 266-7, 280, 283, 285, 292, 307, 319; 6. 326, 345, 384; 7. 235, 519; 8. 403, 453, 459

Epanalepsis, 8. 595

Epanodos, 7. 444; 8. 530

Epanorthosis, 6. 189, 285; 7. 247, 251

Epic, 5. 222; 7. 382-3, 390; 8. 394-5, 404, 517; animal: 8. 586; of Britain: 5. 311; classical: 1. 513; didactic: 1. 348-9; in *F. Q.*: 2. 435-6; 6. 439; historical basis: 1. 349; history its body, allegory its soul: 1. 513; Irish: 6. 218; Italian: 1. 493, 513; 2. 283; mock: 8. 394, 487, 518; poetry: 1. 325, 332, 334, 359; 2. 257; Renaissance: 1. 493; 5. 306; Roman: 1. 359; romance, distinguished from: 1. 359; tradition: 1. 335, 337

Epicureans, 6. 282, 441

Epicurus, 6. 401, 406

Epigram, 8. 594

Epigrams (in *A Theatre for Worldlings*), 8. 273-7, 410, 414-6, 512, 595, 611-27; authenticity: 8. 273-4, 611-24; variants:

8. 678; 4. 6-7: 6. 247. *See also Vision poems*

Epigrams. See [*Anacreontics*]

Epimone, 1. 304; 8. 658

Epinogrus, 4. 165

Epiphonema, 7. 394; 8. 530, 644

Episcopacy, 7. 265, 607-8

Epithalamion, 2. 477; 3. 303, 306; 4. 314-5; 5. 284; 7. 451, 487, 608, 641; 8. 295, 455, 458-94, 533, 593; and *Amoretti*: 8. 629-30, 633-8, 646, 651, 655, 674; composition: 8. 451, 471; criticism: 8. 295, 533, 645-7, 654-7; date: 8. 650; and *F.Q.* 1, 4: 8. 471, 630, 650; finest of its kind: 8. 645-6; folklore and convention, blends: 8. 652; and *Hymnes*: 8. 674; idyllic: 8. 655; influence: 8. 658-9; masque and pageant in: 8. 646-7; metre: 8. 646, 654-8; Platonism in: 7. 665; 8. 473; poetry and life, unites: 8. 647; and *Prothalamion*: 8. 657-62, 670, 674-6; publication: 8. 417; refrain: 8. 647, 652-3, 657-8; rhetoric: 8. 658; and *Ruines of Time*: 8. 295; and *S. C. April*: 7. 274, 280; 8. 657; and *S. C. November*: 8. 657; sources: 8. 652-4; structure: 8. 647, 655; style: 8. 644-7, 654-8; text criticism: 8. 493-4, 655, 687, 697-9, 704-5, 720-1; themes: 8. 653; 18: 6. 235, 299; 8. 426, 494, 497, 647; 26-9: 3. 355; 30, 34: 6. 186; 32-3: 8. 428, 453; 37: 8. 312; 39: 8. 448, 648; 45-7: 8. 499; 68: 6. 299; 88-9: 8. 499; 96-109: 6. 251; 99: 8. 449; 103-8: 8. 344, 448; 129-39: 6. 235; 140: 1. 196; 141: 5. 201; 148-66: 7. 281; 8. 423, 648; 149-90: 8. 636; 154-8: 2. 384; 8. 497, 499; 167-203: 8. 424, 519; 167-80: 8. 647; 185-203: 4. 195; 7. 665; 8. 438, 452, 655; 208: 8. 428; 227: 7. 263; 234: 8. 424; 243-4: 8. 444; 266-7: 8. 633-4; 269-70: 8. 655; 301: 7. 506; 302-4: 8. 401; 310: 6. 247; 317-8: 8. 428; 321: 1. 231; 326-33: 7. 583; 328-9: 6. 270; 8. 548; 334-52: 8. 436; 372-5: 8. 344, 519; 424-5: 8. 655; 427-33: 8. 494, 635, 650; 429: 8. 453

Epithalamion Thamesis, 2. 303, 396-7, 399; 4. 239-42, 250, 273; 6. 442; 7. 330; 8. 292, 509-11, 515, 670-1

Epithalamium, 1. 310; 5. 184; 8. 652-3, 659

Epithet, 1. 225, 258; 2. 359, 360; 4. 245, 255, 264, 268, 274-5; 5. 193, 258, 262; 8. 596, 644; compound: 8. 398

Epitheton, 8. 676

Ἐπιθυμητικόν, 2. 411-2

Epizeuxis, 1. 214-5; 8. 372

Epyllia, 8. 547-8

Equality, 5. 175-81

Equinox, 5. 157

Equity, 5. 195, 215, 218, 295-6; 6. 379

Erasmus, 1. 340, 486; 4. 172; 5. 235; 6. 265, 384; 7. 252, 301, 307, 596; 8. 532, 591; *Colloquies*: 8. 316, 540-1; *New Testament*: 8. 357

Erato, 7. 284; 8. 312, 532

Eratosthenes, 6. 307-8

Erbe, Theodor, 2. 308

Erebus, 1. 230-1; 2. 232-3, 257, 259

Eridanus, 6. 308

Erifila, 3. 253

Erigone, 3. 296

Erinnyes, 2. 200; 4. 199

Eris, 2. 232, 266. *See also* Discord

Erminia, 5. 205; 6. 219, 242, 375

Ernst von Baiern, 2. 355

Eros, 8. 468

Erotema. *See* Interrogatio

" Errant damzell," 3. 207, 214

Error, 1. 231, 311, 364, 372, 414, 422, 425-6, 473-4; 3. 365; 5. 257; 6. 213; 8. 540; battle with is advance of New Learning: 1. 466; her brood the Catholic infiltration: 1. 479; is error of doctrine: 1. 442; is heresies: 1. 450, 455; is Lutheranism: 1. 466; is misunderstanding: 1. 456; is Pelagianism: 1. 453; her vomit the pamphlets of Henry VIII's reign: 1. 458

Erskine, John, 4. 289-96; 7. 245, 280, 345, 397, 430, 486, 500, 506, 583; 8. 424, 427-8, 443, 522, 629, 655, 661

E. S., *De Rebus Gestis Britanniae*: 1. 482

Escapism, 1. 305, 335; 6. 275, 319-20; 8. 405

Esclarmonde, 1. 290, 291; 3. 228-9

Esperance, 1. 407

Espoir, 1. 407

Esquiline, 8. 381

Essex, Countess of. *See* Knollys, Letitia

Essex, Earls of. *See* Devereux

Essex House, 8. 495, 500, 502-3, 567, 571, 648, 663-6, 673

Este, 1. 336, 512

Estienne, Henri, 7. 623; 8. 455

Estrild, 2. 310

Eteocles, 5. 257-8

Eternity, 1. 230; 2. 231-2

Ethelfleda, 3. 339

Ethics, 2. 470-1; 8. 329

Eton, 8. 671

Etymology, 1. 245, 249, 264; 2. 229, 305, 335; 4. 214, 245, 256, 268-9, 271, 275-6; 5. 186, 195, 212; 6. 187, 243, 247, 307, 424; 7. 242, 322, 336, 461, 630; 8. 333, 491

Eucharist. *See* Communion

Eudaimonia, 3. 261

Euhemerism, 5. 163, 216; 7. 308; 8. 329
Eumelos, 8. 470
Eumenides, 2. 200
Eumnestes, 2. 297, 300-1
Eunomie, 5. 243-4
Euphemus, 4. 245
Euphrates, 4. 247
Euphrosyne, 6. 251, 253
Euphues, 4. 223
Euricius Cordus, 7. 423
Euripides, 7. 338; *Alcestis*: 1. 237; 2. 195; 8. 343; *Bacchae*: 5. 232; 6. 232; Frag. 132 (ed. Nauck): 3. 298; *Hecuba*: 5. 232; 6. 211, 309; 7. 415; *Helen*: 2. 365; 3. 270; 5. 187, 190; *Hippolytus*: 1. 174, 236; 3. 219, 298; 7. 444; *Ion*: 1. 229, 231; 3. 279; 6. 308; *Iphigenia in Tauris*: 1. 287; 4. 304; *Medea*: 1. 302; 2. 227, 374; 3. 221; 5. 206; *Orestes*: 3. 244; 4. 224, 304; 8. 394; *Phaethon*: 1. 229; *Phoenissae*: 1. 308; 5. 263; 8. 372, 461; *Suppliants*: 5. 170; 8. 388; *Trojan Women*: 8. 652
Europa, 3. 293, 391; 5. 158; 8. 401-2, 497, 597
Eurydice, 7. 381, 392, 445-6; 8. 299, 344
Eurynome, 6. 251, 253
Eusebius, 7. 307
Eustathius, 1. 184; 2. 364; 4. 237, 247; 5. 166; 7. 274
Euterpe, 8. 312, 318, 540
Evander, 6. 199
Evans, Sebastian, 6. 311, 365, 389, 433
Eve, 2. 431; 3. 384, 387
Evelyn, John, 7. 498
Evensong, 8. 479
Everyman, 1. 283, 287; 7. 303, 305
Evesham, Vale of, 7. 653
" E. W.," 8. 312, 398
Excalibur, 1. 251
Excess, 1. 305; 2. 350, 376, 415; 3. 355; 8. 497
Exclamatio, 7. 246-7; 8. 469
Exempla, 1. 346-7; 2. 427; 5. 292; 8. 591
Exeter conspiracy, 1. 464-5
Expansiveness, 1. 224
Expeditio, 7. 504; 8. 372, 384, 404, 423, 438, 549, 644, 677
Expiation, 1. 210-11
Explicator, 8. 666
Expositio, 7. 504
Extortion, 5. 336, 340, 347
Extravagance, 1. 294-5, 297, 314-5
Eyes, 1. 220, 411; 2. 214, 290, 298; 3. 279; 7. 481, 515-6, 535-6, 559; 8. 422-3, 467, 483-4

Fable, 7. 253-5, 258-66, 293-5, 304, 324, 335-6, 352, 356, 360, 362, 380, 583, 591, 594, 599, 601, 603-4, 606, 632; 8. 294, 351, 355, 371-2, 375, 405-8, 564; beast-fable: 7. 304; 8. 559, 564, 571, 573, 576-8, 580, 585-94, 610
Fabliau, 3. 221, 273
Fabri, G., 8. 481
Fabricius, Johann A., 2. 365
Fabyan, Robert, 2. 302, 452
Fading flower and leaf, 5. 178, 257
Faerie Queene, 7. 375, 383, 611; 8. 538, 580-1, 669, 679; absurdities mixed with beautiful and sublime: 1. 366; action: 1. 321, 333-4, 359; 4. 281; may be greatly admired without accepting its ideas: 1. 442; allegorical method: 1. 339-40, 351, 353, 406, 457; 5. 209, 211-2, 310-11; allegory best in Book 7: 6. 273; allegory, bond of many materials: 2. 251; allegory confined to Book 1: 1. 454; allegory " continued?": 1. 492, 494; allegory contrasted with Bunyan's: 1. 441; allegory not the chief interest in *F. Q.*: 5. 276; allegory elegant and learned: 5. 250; allegory fades as poem proceeds: 2. 409; 3. 315-7; 6. 348; allegory, faults of: 1. 366-6, 366-72, 440-2; 2. 286; 5. 250; allegory general not minute: 1. 494; allegory on a grand scale: 2. 250; historical allegory: 5. 223; allegory meaningless sometimes: 1. 367; allegory mixed: 1. 353, 367, 406-7; moral allegory: 3. 272-3; moral-historical allegory preeminent in *F. Q.*: 1. 425, 513; moral-historical allegory confused: 1. 441; allegory praised: 4. 276; allegory sustained only in Books 1 and 2: 1. 345; allegory, two types of: 1. 339; allegory vague and loose: 5. 250-1; *F. Q.* and *Amoretti*: 8. 629-31, 635, 637; and *Amoretti* 1: 8. 419-20; ancient models, disregards: 1. 314-5, 366; anticipation: 4. 165; antiquarian: 6. 184; and Apocalypse: 1. 256; 8. 279-80; Arguments: 1. 212-3; Ariosto, vies with: 1. 330, 332-3, 335, 361, 366; aristocratic: 1. 340; 5. 275; Aristotle, based on: 1. 340-3; Aristotle, not based on: 1. 327-30; 2. 197; Aristotle, not a systematic translation of: 1. 495; art: 2. 409; Arthur, return of, its organizing principle: 1. 493, 495; Arthurian romance, debt to: 1. 346-7, 349, 351; 3. 363; most beautiful passage: 2. 270, 365, 371; 3. 218, 302; beauty and barbarism, mixture of: 1. 315; beauty, secret of its enduring life: 2. 270; beginning, middle, and end: 1. 321, 331, 334-5; bibliography: 1. 516-7, 551-6; 2. 515-7; 3. 431-2; 4. 357; 5. 375; 6. 505-6; Books

projected: 1. 296, 317-9, 333-4, 343, 357; 2. 280, 467; 5. 310-11; 6. 205, 356, 419; Cantos, first stanzas of, 1. 197, 206; 2. 270-1; 5. 155, 194; Catholic doctrine mingled with paganism: 2. 270; characters: 1. 245, 311, 339-40, 346, 378; 2. 210-11; chief interest is humanity, idealism, art: 5. 276; circulation in MS: 1. 224, 252, 270, 298; 2. 230; classic precedent: 1. 325-6, 332-3, 337; classic unity: 1. 331, 334; coarse sometimes: 1. 184, 221, 263, 364; combines antiquarianism, national feeling, and political intention: 1. 493; combines England and Celtic Otherworld: 1. 352; combines medieval romance with mythology: 2. 270; comparison and contrast: 4. 302; composite: 1. 348, 350, 362, 483, 495; composition: 1. 275, 329, 330, 333-5, 346, 351, 357, 359, 412, 413, 420, 507; 2. 302-3, 315, 396-9; 3. 300, 314; 5. 282, 331, 333; 6. 377, 448; 8. 450-1; conclusion of Books: 4. 309; conclusion of cantos: 3. 272; 4. 182, 192; 5. 193, 206, 223, 232, 268; 6. 198, 201; consistent: 1. 322-3; contemporary costume: 3. 209; contrast: 3. 281, 384; 4. 299-300, 302 (see also Contrast); courtesy book, the noblest: 2. 466; dates of various Books: 5. 282; description superior to design: 1. 316; design: 3. 237; 5. 261; "disposition": 1. 360; distinguished from other Renaissance expositions of gentleman: 1. 439-40; dramatic: 8. 437; most dramatic episode: 3. 328; dullest part: 2. 197, 301; early editions: 1. 516-27; effect: 1. 378; eight books of eight cantos each: 6. 419, 449-50; Elizabeth, celebrates: 1. 474; 2. 454; Elizabeth and religion, allegory of: 1. 476; and Emblems: 8. 625-6; English, chivalric, Italian, modern: 2. 380; epic: 1. 325-6, 332-3, 338, 343-5, 347, 360-1, 493, 512-3; 2. 186; 6. 255, 439; epic and romance combined: 1. 360; episodes: 1. 331-2, 338; 4. 301-2; 6. 346; escape: 1. 305, 335; 6. 275, 319; faeries not distinguished from mortals: 1. 316; all fairy-land: 1. 373; form: 1. 314-27; formless: 1. 314-5; future, epic of: 1. 343-5; genesis in Spenser's imagination: 1. 332; Gothic: 1. 324, 331-2; 2. 366; Gothic architecture, like: 1. 315, 324, 331, 4. 281; hero: 1. 251, 317-8, 331-2, 334; heroes: 1. 318-9, 432; 2. 350, 427-8; heroine: 1. 334; 3. 369; highest reach: 3. 387; historical basis: 1. 321, 326, 334, 343-4, 359, 485, 488; historical identification of persons recent: 1. 492; historical matter distinguished from epic: 1. 509-10; historical

in parts: 1. 506; history, conceived as: 1. 512-3; Homer, compared with: 1. 316, 321-2, 337; 2. 301, 366-7, 436; 3. 310; 5. 269; 6. 273; humanity: 2. 409; and the Hymnes: 7. 656-60, 665; idealism: 1. 335, 339-40; 5. 276; ideas: 6. 184; improbable and chimerical: 1. 314-5; incomplete: 1. 360; 2. 467; 3. 269; 6. 374; incomplete lines: 3. 242; inconsistent, 1. 297, 303, 454; 5. 190, 209, 264; indelicate: 1. 221; in medias res: 1. 334, 337, 350-1, 360; 2. 202; insertions: 6. 439-40, 442, 448; interruptions: 4. 188; invention: 1. 363-6; 2. 250; Jonson, clearer than: 7. 617; knights either faery or British: 1. 353; language: 1. 206; 2. 304; 4. 178-80; 6. 213; 7. 572-3, 619-20, 627-30 (see also Vocabulary); learning, enriched with: 1. 330-1; 5. 225; and Legendes: 8. 513; lives for ever: 5. 176; loose ends: 3. 304; "lost" Books: 6. 273; 8. 306, 431, 520; "lost works," contains: 8. 511, 513; lowest point: 5. 232; masques in: 3. 354-9; medieval?: 1. 359; mixes divine with profane: 1. 368-70; moral with sensuous, combines: 2. 380; moral purpose: 1. 327, 330-1, 357-8; moralities, comparable with: 1. 431, 446; 2. 432; its Muse: 1. 506-15 (see also Spenser's Muse); narrative poem: 1. 326-7; a national epic, nearest approach to: 2. 186; nature, truth to: 1. 180-1, 443; 7. 275, 282; 8. 398; opposites, virtues shown by: 4. 296; Orlando Furioso, compared: see Ariosto, Spenser, compared; oversights: 1. 248, 303, 454; 2. 190, 209-10 (see Spenser, nods); paganism in a Christian people, form in a northern imagination: 2. 380; partakes of fable, mystery, and allegory: 6. 350; a patriotic poem: 2. 186; "perfect" parts: 4. 210; permanent position in English poetry: 1. 332; physiology: 2. 468-71; plan and conduct: 1. 314-62; 2. 467; 3. 237; 5. 292; 6. 317-48; plan artificial: 1. 360; original plan: 6. 419; Platonism in: 7. 665; plot and underplots: 1. 322-3, 337; popularity: 7. 605, 644; presentation copy?: 8. 419-20; probability: 1. 323; prophetic: 1. 343-4; psychology: 2. 458-9; publication: 1. 252, 270, 298, 483; 2. 315, 399; 3. 322, 385; 4. 314-6; 6. 440, 480; 7. 451, 643-4; 8. 528, 671, 685-6; punctuation: 6. 480-503; purpose: 1. 336-7, 340-1, 343-4, 493, 509, 512-3; rambling: 1. 338; range: 6. 184; rapidity: 1. 175, 197, 207, 272-3, 425; 2. 324; realism: 1. 188, 194, 207, 245, 249, 275, 335, 339-40, 373, 377; 3. 328;

solid reality to contemporaries: 2. 186; more religious than *Paradise Lost*: 6. 428; Renaissance epic: 1. 493; revisions: 4. 302; ridiculous at times: 1. 366; romance: 1. 338; 6. 255 (*see also* Romances); romance motifs in Books 1-3: 1. 346; *Romance of the Rose*, descended from: 1. 378; romances, closer to than to Aristotle: 1. 320; most romantic part: 3. 385; and *Ruines of Rome*: 8. 379, 388; scope: 6. 184; secret history of 16th century England key to its allegory: 1. 491; set pieces: 1. 211-2, 331; 2. 256; and *Shepheardes Calender*: 7. 574, 579, 581-2; shifting, yet coherent: 2. 249; simplicity: 1. 321; Spenser's life and experience, charged with: 1. 335; 5. 276; story not chief interest: 5. 275-6; structure: 1. 344-5; stubborn material: 1. 333; style and vocabulary: 7. 614-30; stylistic change: 6. 495; sublimity: 1. 175, 250, 257, 296, 330; 2. 260; 3. 244; 6. 449; suggestion: 1. 305; surprise: 1. 308-9; suspense: 1. 272, 294, 295-6, 320, 321, 322, 350, 430; 2. 320; 3. 269, 272; 4. 174; a great tapestry: 6. 440; and *Teares of the Muses*: 8. 533; text: 1. 516-49; 2. 388, 486-513; 3. 403-27; 4. 340-55; 5. 229, 248, 356-73; 6. 458-79; 8. 582; time reckoning: 5. 208-9; title: 1. 322; transitions like Ariosto's: 1. 248; 2. 197, 339; 4. 188, 192, 196, 203, 239; 5. 163, 194, 217, 232, 258; 6. 220; true to life: 1. 245; 2. 210-1, 295; 6. 274; twelve books: 1. 357, 360-1; 2. 280; 6. 434; twelve books of *Aeneid* and twelve paladins chief determinant of plan: 1. 360; two movements, composed of: 2. 280; two worlds fused in: 1. 339; uncertainty, ends in: 6. 393; unfinished: 1. 205, 351; 3. 218; 4. 287; 6. 350, 374, 429; 8. 430-1; uniformity, lacks: 1. 315, 317-8, 320-1; unity: 1. 309, 324-7, 331, 333-5, 344-5, 349, 359; 2. 186-7, 202, 278; 5. 269; unnatural: 1. 262; unwritten Books: 2. 280; 4. 287; 5. 186, 311; 6. 450 (*see also* Books projected); variety: 1. 323-4, 331, 338-9, 349; 6. 184; *View of Ireland*, contradicts: 5. 315; Virgil, compared with: *see* Virgil; and *Visions of the World's Vanity*: 8. 625; vivid: 5. 210; its women: 3. 381-91; yearning for fuller life: 1. 335;

Dedication: 8. 459

Books 1-3: 3. 365; 8. 598, 602, 613

Books 1 and 2: constructed like a Morality: 6. 209; most systematic and careful of the six: 2. 184

Book 1: more allegorical than Book 2; allegory of *F. Q.* confined to Book 1: 1. 454; historical allegory explained: 1. 449-95; moral-historical allegory confused: 1. 425; moral-historical allegory preeminent: 1. 441; allegory moral and spiritual, explained: 1. 422-48, 501-5; allegory, sources of: 1. 431-3; bibliography: 1. 551-6; Aristotle's *Ethics*, debt to: 1. 431; 2. 197; Arthurian romance and morality mixed: 1. 345, 347, 431; autobiographical element: 1. 442, 444; bibliography: 1. 516-7, 551-6; Book 2, connection with, comparison and contrast: 2. 183-4, 186-7, 197, 404-6, 410, 412, 416, 432, 467-71; Christian discipline and Platonic idealism mixed: 1. 501; Church of England represented: 1. 450, 454-5; circumstantial: 1. 311; compared with other Books: 3. 311; compared with tragedy: 1. 311; complete: 1. 318; conclusion of cantos: 6. 198; "Defender of Faith," allegory of: 1. 425-31, 455-7; Elizabeth's part in Reformation, a history of: 1. 475-6, 494; Elizabeth's reign of peace in religion and politics: 1. 490, 494; English Christian the hero: 2. 412; and *Epithalamion*: 8. 650; Fair Unknown, a sixth version of: 1. 394; history of Church represented: 1. 449; and Landini's interpretation of Virgil: 1. 357; reign of Henry VIII not its subject: 1. 494; reigns of Henry VIII and Mary Tudor: 1. 460-5, 490; more intellectual and spiritual than moral: 2. 197; and Morality plays: 2. 432; pageants, modeled on: 1. 473-82, 493-4; 3. 287; a pilgrim's progress: 1. 431; punctuation: 1. 525-7; Reformation shadowed forth in: 1. 449, 453-4, 466-73, 491; religion the subject: 1. 482; mixes romance with Book of Revelation: 1. 368-70; romances, follows scheme of: 1. 431; romantic indefiniteness: 1. 175-8; most serious of the *F. Q.*: 1. 440; sources: 1. 379-421; Ruskin's analysis of: 1. 422-4; spelling: 1. 521-5; text: 1. 516-49; theology: 1. 432; vocabulary: 7. 614-30; variants: 1. 527-43; variations: 3. 287; Proem: 6. 481-2; 8. 328, 459; 1: 1. 326; 6. 437; 2: 1. 506, 511-2, 514; 2. 303; 4: 2. 304; 6. 186; 8. 452; Canto 1: explained: 1. 433-4; 1-5: 6. 481-2; 1: 1. 391; 7. 625; 8. 404; 8: 8. 398; 11: 2. 186; 12: 1. 391; 14: 1. 306; 2. 259; 19: 1. 211; 20: 1. 221, 364; 8. 487; 21: 8. 406, 470; 23: 8. 598; 32: 8. 342; 37: 1. 230; 6. 293-4; 38: 5. 261; 39: 8. 402, 484; 41: 5. 199; 8. 340, 485; 45: 2. 347; 5. 187; 8. 470; 47-9: 7. 273; 48: 8. 471; Canto 2: explained: 1. 435;

1: 2. 203; 5: 6. 199; 7: 1. 304; 8. 466;
13: 8. 279; 17: 2. 290; 24: 2. 189; 25:
1. 453; 30-44: 2. 197; 32: 2. 346; 33:
5. 262; 38: 5. 176; 44-5: 1. 215; Canto 3:
explained: 1. 435-6; 4, 5: 1. 502; 5: 8.
314; 6: 1. 501; 8: 8. 460; 9: 1. 503; 16:
2. 203; 30: 6. 197; 8. 462; 33: 1. 230;
35: 6. 201; Canto 4: 1. 451; explained:
1. 436; 2: 1. 393; 4-5: 8. 305; 4: 4. 228-9;
7: 6. 191; 8-14: 1. 405; 11: 6. 293-4;
14-5: 6. 305; 8. 364; 16: 7. 491; 8. 469,
472; 18-36: 1. 364, 371; 22: 1. 374; 27:
5. 176; 30: 2. 227; 4. 231; 31: 3. 288;
35: 2. 285; 36: 2. 259; 38: 1. 230; Canto
5: 1. 451, 459; 4. 167; explained: 1. 436;
2: 2. 204; 3. 236; 6: 2. 205; 10: 2. 237;
13: 1. 227, 462; 16: 5. 201; 18: 8. 406;
20: 2. 231, 285; 22: 1. 191, 230; 30:
8. 486; 33: 2. 237; 34-5: 2. 269; 8. 341,
544; 39: 6. 258; 40-3: 1. 363; 44: 8. 480;
45: 1. 268; 46: 6. 191; 48: 8. 305; Canto
6: explained: 1. 436-7; 1: 5. 181; 6-19:
1. 363; 8: 1. 370-1; 13: 4. 229; 8. 464;
14: 8. 460; 15: 4. 253; 16: 4. 165; 17:
1. 503; 23: 8. 492; 31: 1. 501; 34 ff.: 1.
419; 47-8: 1. 463; Canto 7: explained:
1. 437-8, 459; parallels in *Marriage of
Wit and Wisdom*: 1. 446-7; 1-14: 1. 446-
7, 450; 2: 1. 437; 3: 8. 466; 4: 8. 402;
5: 8. 465; 7: 2. 231; 8: 8. 507; 10: 6.
191; 16: 1. 368; 8. 279; 22: 4. 182; 29:
2. 187; 30: 1. 453; 31: 2. 275; 32: 1.
224, 270, 374; 2. 399; 7. 474; 8. 472;
33-5: 4. 221; 43: 1. 224; 4. 247; 44: 1.
451-2; Canto 8: explained: 1. 438, 451;
1: 1. 501; 3: 2. 283; 11: 1. 224; 2. 399;
8. 460; 24: 1. 366; 25: 1. 368; 26: 8.
475, 504; 29: 4. 208; 31: 1. 366; 35:
1. 214; 36: 1. 368; 40-2: 4. 208; 42: 1.
444; 5. 222; 43: 6. 207; 46: 2. 190;
47: 1. 205, 221; 50: 8. 342; Canto 9:
explained: 1. 438; is prose: 2. 286; 3: 8.
438; 13: 8. 474; 15: 1. 452; 31: 1. 268;
36: 2. 285; 38: 2. 256; 42: 2. 275-6; 45:
5. 176; 47: 2. 192; 51: 1. 497; 52: 1.
444; 6. 197; Canto 10: explained: 1. 439;
and *F. Q.* 2. 9: 2. 467; 1: 1. 447; 2. 192;
3-46: 1. 406; 3: 1. 405; 6: 1. 406; 28:
1. 497, 499; 30: 7. 509; 42: 8. 482; 46-
54: 1. 368, 370; 52: 1. 503; 53: 1. 368;
8. 279; 58: 1. 504, 514; 65: 1. 453; 67:
1. 504; Canto 11: 1. 396, 431, 439; 5.
258; 7. 324; 4, 8: 1. 403; 5-7: 1. 508,
514; 5: 1. 363, 371, 509; 8. 328; 7: 1.
323; 6. 205; 8-54: 1. 377; 9: 8. 407;
20-1, 50-1: 1. 215; 22-37: 1. 364, 371;
29: 1. 403-4; 2. 196; 8. 279; 30: 1. 393,
404; 2. 196; 47: 6. 295; 49: 1. 231; 6.
308; 51: 8. 466; 54: 1. 259; 63: 1. 504;
Canto 12: 1. 393; is excess and denoue-
ment: 1. 305; explained: 1. 439; 2: 8.
481; 6: 1. 224; 8. 451; 7: 8. 465; 8: 8.
473; 18: 1. 296, 323; 21-2: 8. 467, 472,
504; 22-3: 1. 437-8; 8. 279; 23-4: 1.
215; 23: 1. 504-5; 28: 1. 243, 457, 460;
36: 2. 183; 37: 8. 402, 461, 477; 38: 8.
461, 478; 39: 1. 389; 8. 493; 40: 1.
505; 4. 201; 41: 1. 391-2; 2. 186; 42:
8. 315, 451

Book 2: allegory: 2. 183-4, 350-1, 365,
400-13, 466; combines Aristotle with
Plato: 2. 406, 427, 459; Aristotelian virtues, covers almost the whole ground of:
2. 197; bibliography: 2. 515-7; and Boiardo: 2. 444; Book 1, connection with,
comparison, and contrast: 2. 183-4, 197,
404-6, 410, 412, 416, 432, 467-71; other
Books of *F. Q.* compared with: 3. 311,
387; Celtic motives in: 2. 435, 444-9; and
the Classics: 2. 435-6; date and composition: 2. 396-9; English gentleman the hero:
2. 412; explained: 6. 399; and Landini's
interpretation of Virgil: 1. 357-8; for
melodious diction and beautiful description, alone in English Literature: 2. 183;
and the Morality plays: 2: 432-3; and
Paradise Lost: 2. 428-31; and *Paradise Regained*: 2. 429-30; paradoxical union of
resistance to evil and divine Providence:
1. 358; has no plot: 2. 184; sources: 2.
435-55; story of moral development: 2.
184, 278-9, 432-4; structure: 2. 427, 459,
467-71; and Tasso: 2. 444; text, critical
notes on: 2. 507-513; in two parts: 2. 411-
2, 428, 459; variant readings: 2. 486-506;
unity, lacks: 2. 184; Proem: 1. 449; 2.
185; 7. 448; 1-4: 6. 311; 2-5: 6. 493-4;
4: 2. 400; 6. 186, 349; Cantos 1-6: episodic: 2. 427; Canto 1: 1: 2. 183; 2: 5.
181; 3-5: 2. 428; 5. 176; 5-54: 2. 417;
5-6: 2. 414; 14, 18, 56: 6. 197; 18: 7.
263; 20: 5. 254; 28: 2. 236; 32: 8. 493;
34: 2. 420; 41: 2. 296; 55: 2. 415; 6. 231,
301; 59: 3. 230; Canto 2: 2. 398; 1-12:
6. 204; 1: 1. 309; 6: 6. 295; 7: 8. 402;
10: 8. 494; 11: 2. 400; 12-46: 8. 518;
13: 2. 441; 17-8: 2. 417; 19: 2. 461;
21: 2. 205; 24: 5. 181; 30: 2. 185; 31:
2. 441; 36: 2. 231; 42: 2. 400; 46: 1.
363; 49: 1. 220; Canto 3: 2. 411; Argument: 1. 212; 1: 226; 10: 6. 192; 11 ff.:
2. 428; 20: 8. 460; 21-3: 7. 288; 24: 2.
290; 8. 452, 519; 25: 2. 399; 6. 186; 7.
322; 8. 514; 31: 8. 472; 36: 3. 264; 38:

2. 253; 39-40: 2. 231; 8. 407; 41-2: 2. 256, 412; Canto 4: 2. 411; 2: 2. 420; 5. 191; 12: 1. 366; 22: 8. 462; 30-2: 2. 461; 34: 2. 430; 35: 1. 252; 2. 471; 38: 2. 205; 41: 1. 230; 8. 447; 44: 2. 285; Cantos 5-8: 2. 398; Canto 5: 1: 1. 358; 2. 459; 6: 2. 205; 15: 6. 192; 24: 2. 460; 29: 2. 369; 8. 397; 31: 8. 466; Canto 6: 2. 231, 411; 1: 2. 425; 8. 314; 3: 7. 491; 8: 8. 314; 11 ff.: 8. 450; 12-4: 2. 371; 15: 6. 295; 16: 8. 482; 18-26: 7. 506; 24: 8. 466; 25: 2. 231; 27: 2. 231; 47: 2. 428; 49: 2. 247; Canto 7: 2. 461; 3, 39: 5. 341; 6. 309; 5: 7. 263; 16-7: 5. 155; 23: 8. 487; 36: 2. 446; 37: 4. 175; 42: 1. 232; 44: 6. 191; 8. 279; 47: 6. 305; 50: 2. 184; 8. 363; 52: 2. 248; 54: 2. 446; 8. 449; 57-60: 8. 418; 59-62: 1. 363; 65: 2. 469; Canto 8: 1: 1. 251, 358; 2: 6. 185; 5: 1. 203; 8. 407; 6: 1. 363, 371; 17, 52: 1. 211; 21: 1. 251; 23: 1. 201; 24: 2. 2. 188, 307; 43: 2. 236; 46: 2. 247; 55: 2. 217; 56: 6. 192; Cantos 9-11 unconnected with rest of Book: 2. 278; Canto 9: 2. 443, 456-7, 459, 467-71; 5. 215; in bad taste?: 2. 467; becalmed, ingenious, absurd: 2. 279; corresponds to F. Q. 1. 10: 2. 467; ethics, physiology, and psychology: 2. 470-1; important in structure of Book 2: 2. 467; 3: 8. 371, 475; 10-33: 8. 475; 16: 1. 258; 2. 398-9; 19: 8. 472; 20-31: 1. 367; 2. 197-8; 21: 8. 305; 22: 2. 472-85; 28: 2. 481; 34: 2. 272; 40-1: 2. 418; 45: 4. 228; 47 ff.: 2. 463; 50 ff.: 3. 292; 5. 199; 52: 3. 297; 58: 2. 466; Cantos 10, 11, summarized: 2. 437; Canto 10: 1. 493; 2. 301; 8. 513; one of the dullest in F. Q.: 2. 302-3; 1-2: 8. 451-2; 5: 6. 309; 9, 13, 41, 47, 48: 2. 397; 9: 3. 282; 14: 4. 262; 24: 7. 263; 25: 2. 198; 8. 649-50; 26: 4. 259; 35: 5. 263; 49: 2. 301; 56: 2. 373; 69: 2. 186; 75-6: 2. 186-8; Canto 11: presents theme of Book 2 in epitome: 2. 471; 2: 8. 473; 3: 4. 183; 8. 352; 8: 8. 459; 20: 1. 199; 2. 235; 23: 2. 227; Canto 12: 1. 396; 2. 185, 231, 379, 421-2, 429-30; 8. 315; allegory: 2. 421-6; fails imaginatively: 2. 351; an *omnium gatherum*: 2. 435; most striking part of F. Q.: 2. 352, 370-1; and Tasso 2. 444; and Trissino 2. 443-4; unrivalled in . . . any language: 2. 389; 6: 8. 341, 346; 12: 7. 263; 23: 6. 295; 8. 385; 26: 8. 386; 29: 2. 460; 31: 1. 363; 33: 2. 244; 8. 311; 36: 8. 486-7; 38: 2. 420; 39: 1. 258; 42 ff.: 8. 449; 46, 48, 50: 6. 295; 8. 397,

442; 47-9: 8. 492; 53: 1. 215; 56: 2. 415; 8. 497; 58: 2. 461; 8. 450; 59: 8. 397; 65: 8. 468, 504; 66: 8. 475; 70: 2. 239, 244; 4. 181; 7. 311; 8. 311; 71: 6. 247; 8. 466; 72-80: 7. 506; 74: 8. 499; 75: 8. 445; 77: 2. 259; 81-2: 8. 404; 87: 8. 324

Book 3: 3. 318-9; allegory more complex: 3. 317; allegory historical: 3. 310-1, 377-80; Ariosto, most indebted to: 3. 315, 367-71; bibliography: 3. 431-2; other Books of F. Q. compared: 1. 346, 360; 3. 311, 315-7, 321, 365-6; 4. 287-8; complementary to Book 2: 1. 346; conclusion of Cantos: 6. 198; confused: 1. 344; episodic: 3. 312; explained: 3. 323-9; 6. 399; mirror of Spenser's world: 3. 319; philosophy of love, contains: 3. 365; plan and conduct: 3. 310-29; sources and analogues indexed: 3. 400-2; structure: 3. 201, 311, 313, 317, 321-9; text, critical notes: 3. 422-7; text, variants: 3. 403-21; two endings: 3. 300, 303-4, 385; 4. 215-6, 290, 302; Proem: 1. 449; 4: 7. 506; 8. 321; 5: 2. 454; 4. 319; 6. 186; Canto 1: 3. 368; Argument: 1. 213; 4 ff.: 3. 314; 13: 1. 336; 6. 192; 17: 1. 199; 22: 4. 202; 32: 4. 229; 34-9: 3. 393-4; 7. 497; 34: 1. 214; 3. 292; 36: 2. 290; 39: 2. 231; 40: 8. 466; 42: 1. 226; 43: 3. 278; 45: 2. 349; 48: 2. 231; 49: 4. 223; 51: 1. 363; 8. 478; 54: 5. 235; Canto 2: 1: 3. 331; 16-7: 1. 215; 18-21: 8. 434; 24: 2. 187; 25: 5. 300; 39, 52: 4. 278; 6. 212, 222; 40-1: 3. 320; 4. 205; 44: 8. 349; 45: 8. 432; Canto 3: 1. 493; and *Aeneid* 6: 3. 310; uneven: 2. 397; 1-2: 3. 367; 4. 164; 8. 476; 2: 7. 505; 3: 2. 253; 4: 1. 296, 506, 513-4; 2. 186; 8. 470, 657; 5, 17, 18: 4. 278; 8: 8. 311; 15: 2. 307; 17: 1. 451; 20: 1. 304; 8. 466; 22: 6. 186; 26: 2. 282; 3. 369; 28: 3. 371; 8. 474 33: 2. 359; 36: 2. 318; 53: 1. 199; 54: 2. 328; Canto 4: 3. 237; 1: 3. 331; 6: 6. 222; 9: 8. 315; 12-39: 7. 503-4; 12: 4. 164; 14: 2. 205; 19 ff.: 4. 276; 23: 5. 225; 26: 6. 222; 37: 6. 231; 39; 2. 217; 46: 3. 315; 51: 8. 481; 54: 4. 233; 55: 2. 232; 4. 277; Canto 5: 1: 7. 661; 5: 6. 437; 27-55: 3. 319; 35: 2. 220; 39-40: 8. 305, 450; 43, 48: 4. 278; 44: 8. 449; 52: 2. 476; 4. 212; 6. 185; Canto 6: 5. 215; 1-29: 6. 187, 343, 437; 8. 396; 2: 2. 477; 4-10: 4. 276; 4, 51-2: 3. 379; 6-9: 8. 470; 7-50: 3. 340-52; 8: 8. 406; 9: 1. 187; 11-25: 7. 272; 13-5: 4. 234; 16: 8. 465; 19: 6. 237;

20: 2. 272; 21-2: 3. 319; 24: 2. 247; 7. 506; 26: 2. 217; 29: 6. 248; 8. 450; 29-54: 8. 305; 30, 44: 6. 295; 31: 8. 468; 32: 2. 477; 6. 437; 42: 1. 207; 43-51: 7. 521; 8. 442; 44: 4. 215; 45: 8. 349, 548; 47: 6. 416; 49: 2. 293; 50: 5. 216; 8. 396; 53: 3. 250; Canto 7: 6-7: 3. 311; 17: 6. 244; 26: 4. 205; 35: 2. 248; 41: 4. 183; 48: 8. 608; 53-61: 3. 221; Canto 8: Argument: 1. 213; 5: 1. 195; 21: 4. 215; 42: 4. 239; Canto 9: moral allegory: 3. 272-3; 5: 2. 227; 5. 202; 20: 4. 242; 8. 472; 27: 2. 227, 383; 8. 432; 33: 8. 509; 37: 2. 217; 41: 2. 199; 45: 8. 507; 46-9: 2. 397; 48: 2. 309; 49: 2. 243, 306; 50: 2. 308; Canto 10: 3: 2. 206; 7: 4. 234; 6. 222; 8: 2. 231; 22: 2. 442; 29: 6. 309; 31: 6. 192; 40: 8. 342; 44-5: 1. 240, 59: 8. 487; 60: 8. 482; Canto 11: 4. 241; 8. 513; 1: 3. 272-3; 5. 207-8; 22, 25: 7. 519; 28-46: 3. 394, 397-9; 28-41: 3. 393; 30: 8. 401-2; 32: 8. 498; 35: 8. 548; 36, 44: 2. 247; 41: 8. 396; 42: 4. 214; 43: 8. 484; 45: 8. 488; 46: 5. 341; 47: 4. 229; 6. 186; 8. 396; 51: 4. 229; 53: 1. 260; 4. 208; 54: 6. 276; Canto 12: 1. 339; 7. 509; 8. 446, 513, 647; allegory: 3. 300-1, 357-8; analyzed: 3. 359; date: 3. 300; 1-5: 3. 356-7; 3: 8. 437; 6: 8. 657; 7: 2. 373; 9-18: 1. 365; 10, 12: 4. 225; 12: 1. 199, 277; 2. 258; 13: 1. 286; 23: 1. 374; 39: 6. 192; 24: 4. 181; 45: 2. 231

Book 4: allegory: 4. 205-7, 290, 294-6, 305; analyzed: 4. 294-6, 298-301; bibliography: 4. 357; climax: 4. 306; other Books of F. Q. compared and related: 4. 281-2, 286-91, 301, 307, 309-11, 314, 334; complicated: 4. 281; composition: 4. 298, 314-6; compounds in: 8. 676; conclusion of cantos: 6. 198; contrast in: 4. 299-300, 302, 309-12; date: 4. 315-7; formless: 1. 344; 4. 282; friendship, its opposites: 1. 347; 4. 294-6, 300, 302; friendship, little to do with: 4. 290; plan: 4. 281-313, 333; praised: 4. 276, 299-302; least satisfactory and comprehensible of F. Q.: 4. 289; a sequel: 4. 301; sources and analogues, index of: 4. 335-9; symmetrical: 4. 299-301, 305, 309-10; text, critical notes on: 4. 350-5; unity: 4. 299-392, 309-10, 333; unity lacking in Books 4-6: 3. 312; unity lacking in Book 4: 4. 282-5; variant readings: 4. 340-49; variation on themes: 4. 294-6; weakest, most inconsequent: 5. 283; Proem: 5. 309; 1: 3. 303-4; 7. 660; 8.

303, 544, 559; 2-3: 4. 305; 4: 8. 459; Canto 1: 3. 355-6; 13: 3. 278; 4. 242, 285; 14: 8. 414; 17-54: 5. 323; 18: 6. 326; 19-26: 2. 233, 266; 4. 297; 23: 2. 373; 25: 8. 434; 28: 1. 364; 46: 3. 207; Canto 2: 1: 2. 237; 4. 169; 8. 434; 5: 8. 422; 13: 4. 332; 16: 2. 199; 8. 308, 396; 18: 4. 332; 28: 4. 330; 29: 4. 305, 327; 32: 3. 249; 41: 6. 186; 43: 4. 330; Canto 3: 2: 6. 192, 341; 3: 8. 352; 9: 5. 176; 17: 8. 473; 19, 20: 6. 218; 37: 8. 437; 38-51: 4. 283; 39: 8. 472; 42: 4. 330; 8. 305; 49: 5. 201; 8. 471; Canto 4: 1: 4. 295, 332; 24: 2. 235; 29: 1. 247-8; Canto 5: 1, 26: 4. 216; 5: 8. 483; 13: 8. 472; 14: 8. 500; 32-46: 1. 367; 38: 1. 365; 44: 8. 387-8; Canto 6: cardinal canto: 4. 285, 299-301, 306; masterpiece of allegorical narrative: 4. 301; 13: 1. 200-1; 14: 1. 257; 19-44: 4. 285; 20: 8. 413; 24. 6. 295; 28: 4. 174; 31: 4. 327; 46: 4. 327; Canto 7: 36: 3. 377-8; 40: 6. 309; Canto 8: 20: 1. 268; 26: 3. 276; 30-4: 4. 311, 334; 5. 155; 33: 6. 185; 48: 4. 202; Canto 9: 1: 5. 176; 8: 4. 208; 14: 8. 371; 16: 6. 295; 22: 2. 248; 27: 4. 332; 39: 3. 304; 45: 4. 201; Cantos 10-12: 4. 306; 6. 630; Canto 10: 3. 254; 7. 521; some of Spenser's finest poetry: 4. 308; 1-2: 7. 510; 3-10: 8. 444; 5-25: 4. 228; 12: 8. 422; 16-20: 1. 366; 16: 3. 302; 21: 6. 295; 23: 8. 449; 26 ff.: 4. 216; 28: 2. 461; 29, 44: 4. 216; 37: 8. 464; 38: 2. 231; 39 ff.: 6. 411; 40: 4. 331; 42-3: 5. 254; 42: 4. 203; 44-7: 2. 245; 4. 308-9, 333-4; 6. 413; 8. 421; 45: 8. 466; 47, 56: 4. 165, 201; 6. 412; 51: 6. 192, 341; 52: 3. 379; 6. 246; 58: 8. 344; Canto 11: 1. 371; 2. 301, 303, 399; 8. 515, 670-3; 10: 1. 514; 8. 328; 11: 8. 472; 13-5: 1. 363; 8. 548; 16: 2. 308; 20: 8. 406; 22: 5. 304; 26: 8. 502; 28: 6. 191; 8. 382; 29: 5. 173; 37-8: 2. 309; 40-4: 6. 424; 8. 463, 510; 41: 8. 308, 459; 45-6: 8. 472; 44: 4. 330; 5. 173; 46: 4. 242; 8. 299, 472; 47: 7. 330; 48-51: 8. 463; 52: 6. 302; Canto 12: 9: 6. 231; 11: 8. 498; 27: 2. 307; 33: 8. 474

Book 5: allegory: 5. 273, 282, 284; 7. 254; and Amoretti: 8. 422; and Aristotle: 5. 281-2; bibliography: 5. 153, 375; biographical background: 5. 282-4; 6. 385; other Books of the F. Q. compared and related: 5. 269-74, 276, 282-4, 292, 303, 306, 315-6, 322-4; 6. 346, 440; 8. 459; charming romance: 5. 306; close: 6. 345; date: 5. 207, 234, 248, 282; Elizabethan

spirit in action: 5. 312; episodic: 5. 287, 292-3; historical: 5. 273, 280, 285-6, 299-335; isolated: 1. 344; patchwork: 5. 293; plan and conduct: 5. 269-98, 303; a political pamphlet: 5. 343-4; sources and analogues: 5. 350-5; text, critical notes: 5. 366-73; text, variants: 5. 356-65; theme: 5. 303-10; verse: 5. 271; and *View of Ireland*: 5. 326; 6. 363-4; shows waning power: 5. 298; Proem: 2. 461; 3. 342; 4. 311; 5. 178; 6. 275, 311-2, 404, 406; 4-8: 6. 424; 5: 3. 293; 8. 401; 6: 6. 305; 10: 8. 376; Cantos 1-3 schematized: 5. 193; Canto 1: 2: 6. 305; 7, 11: 5. 176; 11: 8. 505; 12: 1. 365; 13-30: 5. 303-4; 23: 6. 191; 25-8: 5. 304; 6. 200; Canto 2: 4. 332; 5. 294; 8. 353; and *Mother Hubberds Tale*: 5. 342; 8. 352; political allegory: 5. 335-47; Argument: 5. 314; 1-28: 5. 303-4; 10: 1. 365; 19: 8. 308, 500, 669; 20: 5. 298; 33, 53: 5. 261; 36: 5. 156; 40: 8. 450; 41: 8. 376; 47: 5. 296; 49: 5. 295; Canto 3: 1. 307; 8: 6. 193; 17: 6. 185; 18: 6. 199; 22-4, 35: 5. 304; 23: 2. 296; 8. 474; 32-40: 2. 211; 37: 2. 210; 40: 8. 462; Canto 4: 5. 295; 2: 8. 314; 4-20: 5. 304; 28: 6. 240; 42: 8. 397; 43: 6. 191; 49: 5. 314; Canto 5: 5. 295, 302; 1: 7. 491; 2: 3. 278; 3: 2. 205; 12, 23-5: 5. 304; 24: 8. 305; 25: 5. 297; 34: 6. 191; 42: 8. 435; Canto 6: 5. 314; 1: 5. 304; 7: 5. 301; 28: 2. 205; 42: 8. 447; Canto 7: 5. 295, 305-6; 1: 5. 156, 293; 12: 4. 231; 23: 3. 369; 31-6: 5. 316; 37-41: 5. 304; 41: 6. 207; 45: 5. 298; Canto 8: 5. 305; 1: 2. 384; 5. 304; 28-44: 8. 540; 45: 5. 303; 47: 2. 373; cantos 9-12, lowest point in poem: 5. 232; Canto 9: 5. 302-3, 316-7; 8. 579; 1: 5. 280; 6. 194; 6, 19: 5. 303; 8-19: 5. 305; 25-50: 5. 321; 28: 6. 246; 30: 5. 296; 38, 41: 5. 322; 45: 3. 302; 46: 5. 293; 47: 2. 266; Canto 10: 5. 317-8; 8: 1. 453-4; 16: 1. 363; 2. 205; 23: 8. 487, 507; Canto 11: 5. 318; 20: 1. 254; 22: 4. 220; 25: 8. 305, 333; 31: 1. 364; 34: 5. 201; 8. 471; 35: 8. 397; 41: 5. 298; 43-65: 5. 329; 53: 3. 237; 56: 5. 309; 6. 199; Canto 12: 5. 297, 318-9; Argument: 5. 331; 1: 2. 370; 3: 5. 302; 13: 4. 278; 14: 5. 312; 24-7: 5. 313; 26: 5. 302; 28-42: 2. 461; 29, 39: 1. 221; 4. 231; 30: 2. 227; 36: 5. 202; 37: 6. 188, 385; 40: 5. 301; 41: 6. 385; 43: 6. 194, 205; 8. 513

Book 6: allegory: 6. 318, 334-5, 345-8, 349-64, 365; and *Amoretti*: 8. 441; auto-biographical: 6. 318-21, 349; bibliography: 6. 505-6; and Book 5 of *F. Q.*: 6. 345-6, 349, 360, 363; 8. 459; and other Books of *F. Q.*: 6. 214, 317, 320, 322, 325, 328, 333, 346, 348, 365, 376; date: 6. 364; disjointed: 1. 344; 6. 322; distinctive: 6. 328; like Sidney's *Arcadia*: 1. 345-6; like *As You Like It, Cymbeline, Winter's Tale*: 1. 348; lowly life: 1. 348; plan and conduct: 6. 317-48; simplicity: 6. 317-8; sources and analogues, index of: 6. 452-7; structure: 6. 333-4; text: 6. 201, 458-79; text, critical notes: 6. 470-9; text, variants: 6. 458-67; uneven in quality: 6. 324; Proem: 1-2: 8. 451; 1: 5. 193; 3, 7: 6. 191; 4: 6. 337, 340; 8. 504; 5: 6. 324; 8. 313, 475; 6: 6. 342; 8. 434; Canto 1: 1: 6. 191, 329; 2: 6. 330-1, 352, 361; 3: 6. 322, 352; 4: 6. 331; 7: 6. 333; 9: 6. 342; 11-47: 6. 365-7; 22-3: 6. 354; 41-2: 6. 335; 8. 330, 439; Canto 2: 1-39: 6. 367-71; 1: 6. 191, 327, 341, 345; 2: 6. 331, 347; 3: 3. 188; 6. 331; 4: 8. 473; 12: 7. 505; 24: 6. 329; 32: 8. 397; 40: 6. 191; 44: 8. 626; Canto 3: 6. 198; 1: 6. 327, 330; 7. 320; 5: 2. 460; 15: 6. 324; 16: 6. 342; 21: 6. 186; 25: 6. 354; 40: 6. 322, 326; 47: 6. 191; 51: 2. 247; Canto 4: 1: 5. 181; Canto 5: 6. 198; 1-2: 6. 334; 4-6: 6. 191; 13: 6. 345; 19: 4. 202; 31: 1. 221; 33: 6. 201; 36: 6. 330; 37: 6. 211; 38: 8. 657; Cantos 6-8, 11, 12: 6. 214; Canto 6: 4: 4. 277; 9: 2. 252; 6. 188; 10-11: 4. 205; 15: 6. 342; Canto 7: 6. 198; Argument: 6. 214; 1: 6. 198, 322; 18: 6. 345; 27: 6. 214; 29: 8. 422; 32-7: 8. 513; 33: 8. 396; 42: 8. 364; 44: 2. 261; 47: 2. 276; 4. 202; Canto 8: 6. 198; 1: 4. 203; 2, 20-1: 4. 234; 8. 474; 6: 6. 327; 7: 8. 461; 19-24: 1. 366; 8. 513; 42: 8. 519; 43: 2. 290; 46: 8. 426, 460; 49: 8. 336; Cantos 9-10: 7. 581-2; Canto 9: 6. 198; 4, 43-4: 6. 354; 7-9: 7. 281; 8. 473, 500; 18-9: 5. 156-7; 6. 362; 23: 7. 304; 29: 5. 196; 31: 6. 333; 35: 6. 351, 355; 39, 42: 6. 340; 45, 46: 6. 344; 45: 6. 339; Canto 10: 6. 198; 7. 588; 8. 654; 3: 6. 343; 5: 6. 295; 6-12: 8. 311-2; 7: 8. 463; 10-7: 6. 339; 8. 460; 12-28: 7. 536; 12-6: 2. 384; 13: 4. 168; 8. 474; 14: 3. 209; 8. 479; 15: 8. 648; 16: 6. 285; 7. 247; 17: 4. 216; 18: 6. 349; 20: 6. 347; 21: 8. 467; 22-4: 2. 273; 7. 284; 23: 6. 192, 339, 341; 25-7: 6. 349; 26: 8. 500, 679; 29: 6. 356; 30: 8. 470; 37: 6. 344; 44: 8. 450; Canto 11: 25-32: 6. 191; 44: 1. 210;

46: 3. 282; Canto 12: 1: 1. 338; 5. 181,
309; 8. 315; 4: 6. 349; 8. 579; 12-4: 6.
363; 19-22: 6. 381; 25: 6. 384; 26-8: 1.
364; 2. 370; 6. 324, 382-3; 31: 6. 188; 35:
2. 237; 8. 484, 487; 38-41: 6. 357; 39:
6. 188; 41: 5. 300; 7. 522; 8. 370, 544,
559, 569, 575, 583
  Book 7: 1. 232, 273; 3. 340, 342, 352;
4. 307, 310-2; 5. 284; 6. 346, 389-451;
8. 306, 662; allegory best of *F. Q.*: 6. 273,
313-4, 348; Arguments: 6. 435-7; bibliography: 6. 505-6; and other Books of the
F. Q.: 6. 348, 404, 416-9, 433-51, 445;
and Book 4: 4. 310-1, 334; 6. 407, 433,
449; Book 12, intended for the end of:
6. 419; date: 6. 312, 389, 433-51; and
Epithalamion: 8. 471, 650; *F. Q.*, a part
of: 6. 273, 404, 433-51; flexible movement:
6. 445-6; almost Homeric: 6. 273, 313;
an independent poem: 6. 433-6; Ireland its
theme: 6. 439; Ireland, written in: 6. 436,
441, 444, 448; mature: 6. 448-9; its moral:
6. 416; most sublime part of *F. Q.*: 6. 449;
music, composed like: 6. 423; sources and
philosophical significance: 6. 389-432; in
Spenser's best style: 6. 273, 313; peculiar
style: 6. 438, 445-7; text: 6. 297; text,
critical notes on: 6. 470-9; text, variants:
6. 458-69; and *View of the State of Ireland*: 6. 435-6; Canto 6: 1: 6. 400, 437;
2: 6. 439; 3: 3. 279; 5: 4. 310; 6. 406,
412, 427; 6: 6. 427; 14-36: 4. 310; 6. 404;
8. 376; 18: 6. 185; 22, 30: 8. 376; 32: 8.
414; 35: 6. 400, 412, 428; 36-55: 4. 173;
6. 424, 441-2; 8. 510; 37: 1. 507, 512-4;
2. 304; 6. 433, 436-7; 8. 451; 39: 8. 465;
40-55: 8. 396, 463; 41: 4. 183; 8. 408,
471; 52: 5. 201; 8. 471; 55: 6. 315; Canto
7: 8. 626; 1: 1. 507; 8. 328; 5: 2. 375; 6.
404; 6: 6. 412; 7-31: 6. 409; 7: 6. 412;
8-10: 6. 396-7; 13: 6. 397, 404, 413, 428;
14 ff.; 4. 277, 310; 15-6: 1. 233; 6. 411,
428; 18: 6. 402, 405; 19: 6. 394, 405,
439; 20: 6. 439; 24, 25: 6. 402; 25, 55:
6. 401; 31, 40: 1. 221; 32: 3. 293; 33:
2. 231; 34-43: 1. 365; 35: 6. 387; 7. 607;
8. 478; 36: 8. 345, 395; 39: 2. 204; 44:
1. 231; 8. 484; 46: 2. 304; 6. 313, 421;
47, 49: 6. 394-5, 405, 414-5; 52: 3. 297;
5. 159-60; 54: 6. 424; 58: 6. 397, 400,
402-3, 405-6, 416-8, 420, 434; 59: 6. 401;
Canto 8: 6. 403, 407, 415-6, 420, 429; 7.
568, 680; 8. 410; Spenser's intention: 6.
407-8; Spenser's last lines: 6. 314-5; text:
6. 315
  Book 12: 2. 411; 6. 378, 419. *See also*
Allegory; Spenser, Edmund

Faery, 3. 388
Faery Land, 1. 265, 305, 322
Fairchild, Hoxie N., 6. 202
Fairclough, H. R., 8. 336
Fairfax, Edward, 1. 225, 228; 2. 240, 278,
  384, 389; 4. 247; 7. 594; 8. 594; *Godfrey
  of Bulloigne*: 1. 174; *Jerusalem Delivered*:
  1. 182, 192, 300; 3. 240-1, 303; 4. 199;
  6. 309; 7. 271
Fairies, 1. 294; 3. 246, 278, 311; nymphs,
  same as: 2. 336; 8. 311-2, 338, 463
Fair Unknown. See Libeaus Desconus
Fairyland, 1. 290, 291, 292, 311-2, 316-7,
  352, 373, 482, 485; 2. 183, 371; is Eng-
  land: 1. 344; 2. 202; 3. 215; is Wales:
  2. 454-5
Fairy-mortal, 1. 245, 267
Fairy Mythology, 2. 334-6
Fairy Queen, 1. 251, 254, 265, 266, 296,
  309, 317, 334, 343, 352-3, 392, 480, 482,
  493; 2. 371; 3. 237, 363; 4. 212; 5. 269
Faith, 1. 254, 284, 287, 407, 424-31, 504
Falconry, 1. 231, 298; 3. 285-6; 5. 202; 6.
  195-6, 203, 218, 236, 239, 245; 7. 539,
  556; 8. 327, 397, 447
Falkiner, C. L., 3. 239, 247; 4. 265; 5. 265;
  6. 435-6
False Florimell. See Florimell
Falsehood, 1. 230-1
Falstaff, John, 2. 210
Fame, 1. 213, 415, 417-8, 514; 2. 220-1,
  253, 257, 461; 3. 223; 7. 319, 369; 8. 286,
  298-301, 313
Fanchin, 6. 286-90, 424-6, 441; 7. 454
Fancy, 2. 286; 3. 301, 358
Fanshawe, Richard, 2. 357
Fantasy, 2. 463
Faral, Edmond, 8. 459
Farleigh Wallop, 7. 475
Farmer, 1. 294, 424, 442; 8. 355, 357
Farmer, Richard, 5. 225
Farquhar, George, 7. 426
Fashion, 1. 215-6
"Fatal sisters," 7. 412
Fate, 1. 266; 2. 276; 3. 340; 6. 417-8; 8.
  597, 609
Fates, 4. 181-2, 259; 6. 281; 7. 416, 512;
  8. 493. *See also* House of Fates
Father Hubberds Tale. See Middleton
Fathers, Church: 2. 459; 6. 422
Faunus, 1. 242; 6. 285, 290-1, 428-32; 7.
  330
Faustulus, 7. 351, 354
Faustus Andrelinus, 7. 299, 356, 590
Fay, 1. 292, 352-3; 2. 334; 3. 240
Fear, 1. 339; 2. 257, 461; 3. 301-2; 4. 165,
  225; of self: 1. 199

Feast. *See* Annual Feast
"fee," 7. 301-2
"feed the eyes," 3. 279; 7. 536; 8. 432-3
Female, 2. 475, 482; 5. 215, 266
Feminine endings, 6. 436, 438, 445-7, 449, 450-1; 7. 267
Feminism, 5. 197-8, 223
Fenelon, François, 2. 394
Fenton, Elijah, 8. 396-7, 439
Ferdoman, 7. 456
"ferme," 3. 245
Fermor, Arabella, 8. 666
Fermoy, 6. 286, 425
Fermoy, Lord. *See* Roche
Ferne, John, 3. 339
Feronia, 4. 181
Ferrau, 1. 419; 2. 210; 3. 328, 374, 380; 4. 174-5; 6. 202
Ferrers, Edward, 3. 307; 7. 285
Ferrex, 2. 319-20
Ferrex and Porrex. See Gorboduc
Fescennine, 8. 470-1
Festus, 1. 259, 272
Feuillerat, Albert, 8. 317-8, 369
Fiachna, 1. 293
Fianna, 3. 278
Fiant, 8. 372-3
Ficino, Marsilio, 3. 318, 345, 350; 6. 390, 412; 7. 371, 492, 525, 528, 552-4, 560-1, 567, 662, 664, 670-1, 673-4, 676, 679; *Commentary on the Phaedrus*: 7. 552; *Commentary on Plato's Symposium*: 7. 665; 1. 1: 7. 510-1; 1. 3: 7. 512-3; 2. 2: 7. 525, 557-8; 2. 4: 7. 554; 2. 5: 7. 523, 525; 2. 7: 4. 317-8; 2. 8: 4. 330; 7. 532-3; 3. 1-2: 7. 517; 3. 2: 7. 511, 513-4; 3. 3: 4. 313; 7. 513; 4. 4: 7. 570; 5. 3: 7. 526-7, 530; 5. 4: 7. 523, 554; 5. 5: 7. 526-7; 5. 6: 7. 523, 529; 5. 10: 7. 511, 538; 6. 6: 7. 530, 532-5; 6. 7: 8. 468; 6. 11: 7. 514; 6. 13: 4. 320; 7. 557; 6. 17: 2. 377; 7. 558; 6. 18: 7. 570; *De Christiana Religione*: 7. 540, 552; *Theologia Platonica*: 7. 532-3, 552
Fidelia, 1. 284-5, 406, 430, 432, 501-2; 3. 399; most powerful person in *F.Q.* 1: 1. 430
Fidelity, 1. 285
Fidessa, 1. 427; 2. 229; her letter is last attempt of Papacy to regain England: 1. 457; is Mary Stuart's claim to the throne: 1. 465. *See also* Duessa
Fido da Toffia, Pietro, 2. 377
Field, John (astronomer), 5. 177-8
Field, John (divine), 6. 387; 7. 295, 325, 602; 8. 357-61, 591

Field, Richard, 1. 521-2, 525; 6. 480; 7. 706; 8. 507, 722, 736
Fielding, Henry, 5. 305
Fiery Dragon, Knight of the, 1. 400
Fights, 5. 172-3
"filed tongue," 7. 479
Finney, C. L., 7. 519, 657
Finn mac Cumaill, 1. 244; 6. 425-6
Fiordelisa, 1. 182; 6. 261-2
Fiordispina, 3. 371-3, 386
Fire, 2. 231-2, 346, 510; 3. 289-91, 300, 373; 6. 300-1; of love: 4. 228; 8. 429-30, 638; is Spanish artillery?: 3. 378
Firmicus Maternus, 3. 248-9
Firm Island, 3. 362, 365
First fruits, 8. 562
Fish, 4. 255, 257, 260, 264, 266; 6. 300; 7. 613; 8. 464
Fisherman, 3. 269-70, 313, 319, 327, 333, 374, 379
"fit," 7. 453
FitzGerald, Gerald, Earl of Desmond, 5. 163, 173-4, 233, 265, 312-4; 6. 426; 7. 454
FitzGerald, Henry, Earl of Kildare, 7. 475
FitzGeralds, 5. 265. *See also* Desmond
Fitzmaurice, James, 5. 314
Five Senses, 2. 338-41, 348, 351, 365-6, 412, 456-9, 468, 471
Flail, 5. 165, 167
Flaminius, 8. 347
Flanders, 3. 392-3
Flasket, John, 8. 507, 736
Flavia, 7. 477
Fleay, F. G., 7. 295-6, 375, 463, 465-6, 468-9, 472-3, 484, 499; 8. 364, 378
Fleming, C. S., 1. 201
Flesh, 1. 416
Fletcher, Giles, Jr., 1. 272; 2. 387; 7. 283
Fletcher, Giles, Sr., 2. 345; 5. 189; 7. 468
Fletcher, John, 1. 190; 4. 199; 6. 203; 7. 281, 286, 393, 594; 8. 485
Fletcher, Phineas, *Brittains Ida*: 2. 245; *Piscatory Eclogues*: 2. 357; 4. 199; 7. 248, 384, 468, 578, 594; *The Locusts*: 1. 283; *The Purple Island*: 2. 198, 352, 456, 458, 463, 470; 1. 23: 4. 186; 1. 44: 2. 289; 2. 30: 2. 291; 2. 33: 2. 293; 2. 36: 2. 292; 2. 39-62: 2. 371; 3. 4: 6. 478; 4. 7: 4. 186; 6. 15: 3. 277; 6. 51: 2. 298; 7-12: 2. 470; 7. 49-50: 3. 302; 7. 63: 4. 170; 7. 66: 5. 266; Canto 8 and Aristotle: 2. 470; 8. 12: 3. 302; 8. 27-30: 2. 255; 8. 30-1: 2. 262; 8. 45: 3. 212; 10. 29: 3. 215; 10. 31, 36: 2. 215; 10. 35: 2. 214; 10. 37: 2. 217; 10. 39: 2. 216; 11. 38: 5. 264; 11. 47-8: 2. 345; 12. 25: 3. 239;

12. 32 ff.: 1. 272; 12. 59: 1. 297, 305;
5. 199; 12. 64. 1. 211; 12. 85: 3. 278
The Fletchers, 7. 585
Flibbertigibbet, 8. 486
Flies. See Fly
Flight, 1. 254
Floating Island, 2. 243-4, 356
Flood, W. H. Gratton, 8. 649
Flora, 7. 273, 289-90; 8. 495
Florence, 1. 493; 3. 363; 7. 662-76
Flores Historiarum, 2. 331; 3. 230
Florimell, 1. 195, 248, 378, 480; 2. 436;
3. 202, 243, 262-4, 269-73, 311, 313-6,
324-5, 333, 373-5; 4. 239, 281-3, 296,
334; 5. 182-3, 187-90, 224, 273, 285,
304; 6. 205, 244, 257; 7. 665; 8. 364;
and Angelica: 3. 201-2, 205, 314-5, 375;
and Arthur: 3. 237; character: 3. 381-7,
389-90; 4. 288; False Florimell: 2. 211;
3. 268, 273, 329, 373-4, 378, 380, 385,
390; 4. 295, 300, 306; 5. 182, 187-90,
273, 278, 304; 6. 185; 7. 665; 8. 364;
and Florence: 3. 363; girdle: 3. 267, 327,
374, 390; 4. 175-6, 192-3, 195, 276, 286,
298, 300; 5. 169, 182, 190; is Ireland:
3. 380; is Mary Stuart?: 3. 263-4, 271;
5. 187; is true beauty: 4. 306; and Una:
4. 288; wedding: 5. 182-93, 302
Florindo, 3. 289; 6. 261
Florio, John, 6. 220; 7. 321, 419, 642, 652;
8. 292, 607
Floris, Frans, 8. 626
Floris and Blauncheflur, 1. 301
Flourdelis, 5. 260, 299, 326, 329
Flower, Desmond, 8. 420
Flower, W., 8. 500, 667-71
Flower and Leaf. See Chaucer (pseudo)
Flowers, 3. 259; 6. 200, 297, 398; 7. 282,
285-7; 8. 337, 347-9, 398, 404, 424, 441,
495, 497, 596-7; metamorphosis to: 3. 260;
7. 498-9
Flux, 6. 394, 404, 409
Fly, 8. 395, 397, 456-8; flies: 1. 192; 5. 261
Folger Shakespeare Library, 1. 517-9; 6. 458,
472; 7. 709; 8. 680-1, 697-8
Folio editions of Spenser's Works, 3. 403;
4. 340; 5. 356; 7. 692; 8. 687, 699; 1609:
1. 516, 525, 527, 546; 2. 486, 513; 4. 350;
8. 685; 1611: 1. 516, 525, 527, 546; 2. 486,
513; 4. 350; 7. 723; 8. 685-7; Drayton's
copy (?): see Drayton; 1617: 1. 516; 8.
686-7, 712; Milton's copy: see Milton;
1679: Dryden's copy: see Dryden
Folklore, 1. 203; 2. 436; 3. 221-2, 298; 5.
236; 8. 470, 480, 652; as source of F. Q.
1: 1. 389-90
Fontainbleau, 3. 394

Foot on neck of foe, 2. 236; 6. 219
Forbearance, 1. 289
Ford, Emanuel, 6. 203
Ford, John, 2. 460; 7. 499
Forde, Thomas, 6. 424
Forest, 2. 211; 3. 262; 6. 287-9, 299; 7. 505;
8. 344, 459-60, 496; symbol of worldli-
ness: 1. 434
Forester, 3. 379
Foresti, Jacobus Philippus, 2. 452
Form, 2. 479; 3. 260-1, 340-52; 7. 513, 525,
529-31, 566
Forman, H. B., 3. 248
Formula, 2. 211; 5. 206; 7. 248; 8. 306
Fornari, Simone, 1. 513; 2. 439-41; 3. 372-6;
5. 221, 349; 7. 552
Fort del Ore, 5. 314, 318-9
Fortitude, 1. 329, 446
Fortuna, 6. 400, 410
Fortune, 1. 417; 2. 262; 3. 269; 5. 252; 6.
240, 293, 400, 416; 7. 256; 8. 346, 459,
597; " Fortune, my foe ": 2. 281. See also
Castle of Fortune
Foster, John, 8. 374
Fountain, 1. 437; 2. 371, 381-3
Four Masters, 4. 268
" Four visions out of the Revelation of S.
John." See [Visions from Revelation]
Fowler, informer, 8. 606
Fowre Hymnes, 2. 397, 429; 3. 342; 6. 399,
402, 406; 7. 372, 614, 663-81; 8. 508-9,
603, 662, 674, 676; and Amoretti: 7. 656-
8. 660, 665; 8. 674; and Colin Clouts:
7. 449, 656, 660-1, 665; composition: 7.
657-62, 681; 8. 529-30; criticism: 7.
656-7, 659, 679, 681-2; date: 7. 657-62;
editions: 7. 712-3; and Epithalamion: 8:
674; experience, based on: 7. 656-60, 665;
and F. Q.: 7. 656-60, 665; First Pair: 1.
361; 3. 318; 7. 320, 375, 656-7, 662-77,
679; 8. 459, 518; form: 7. 676-81; 8. 542;
humor in: 8. 518; intention: 7. 679; inter-
relation: 7. 657-62, 667-81; metre: 7. 660,
662; and Paradise Lost: 7. 537, 656-7,
669; place in Spenser's work: 7. 664-5;
and Prothalamion: 8. 674; Second Pair:
7. 656-76; and Shepheardes Calender: 7.
656-8, 660; and S. C. October: 7. 665;
sources: 7. 662-70; style: 7. 656-7, 662,
681-2; 8. 676-7; symmetry: 7. 521-2, 549,
560-1, 564, 678; and Teares of the Muses:
7. 660-1, 665; 8. 539, 541-2; text: 7. 712-
4, 723; variants: 7. 713-4; Dedication:
3. 366; 7. 454, 474, 657-62, 680; 8. 431,
567, 663-4, 666
    Hymn of Love, 4. 163, 220, 306; 7. 387,
611, 664-5; 8. 325-6; 2: 8. 433; 25-6: 8.

299; 29: 8. 459; 34: 8. 478; 43-119: 7.
480; 43-9: 4. 203; 50-140: 7. 481; 57-60:
3. 348; 60: 4. 182; 65: 8. 423; 74 ff.: 1.
232; 4. 227, 308; 103-16: 7. 678; 107-
19: 6. 291; 115-6: 8. 498; 120-33, 190-
6: 6. 221; 120-6: 3. 280; 6. 255; 7. 680;
153-4: 6. 222; 162-72: 8. 422; 175: 4.
318; 176-96: 7. 675, 680; 176-82, 190-3:
3. 244; 183-4: 6. 217; 184-217: 7. 677-8;
185-6: 4. 319; 190-6: 4. 223; 7. 678, 680;
8. 422, 424, 476, 498; 197-217: 8. 427,
432; 226-9: 4. 318; 231-7: 4. 223; 259-
61: 4. 320; 5. 207; 263, 265, 278: 8. 519;
266-72: 5. 208; 280-300: 4. 175; 8. 442,
446, 449-50; 280-2: 8. 433, 488; 283: 8.
492; 287-93: 3. 261; 5. 216; 8. 396. *See
also above* First Pair

Hymn of Beauty, 4. 306; 7. 611; 8. 325-
6; 1-7: 6. 291; 7. 664-5; 11-4: 7. 680;
29-137: 7. 663; 29-54: 4. 211; 8. 472,
475; 38: 3. 345; 46: 8. 331; 48-60: 6.
221; 62-3: 6. 255; 64-70: 7. 682; 70-1:
3. 280; 108 ff.: 8. 420; 121: 8. 498; 132-
3: 8. 331; 141-7: 3. 348; 148-61: 4. 211;
5. 244; 163 ff.: 7. 680; 8. 498; 169-97: 7.
481; 176-189: 6. 221; 194-8: 4. 308; 197-
203: 7. 682; 211-31: 7. 677-9; 8. 427; 211-
24, 239-45: 6. 221; 7. 678, 680-1; 231-45:
8. 422, 439; 249: 8. 299; 254: 2. 216;
262: 8. 474; 267 ff.: 8. 493. *See also
above* First Pair

Hymn of Heavenly Love, 3. 223; 5. 284;
6. 399, 407; 7. 672-4, 676; 8. 493; criticism: 7. 537; and Milton: 7. 537, 656-7,
669; style and rhetoric: 8. 676; worst line:
7. 544; 1-21: 8. 416; 1-4: 4. 223; 7. 521,
680; 8-11: 4. 163; 13: 8. 459; 24: 8.
480; 28-9: 7. 676; 30-5: 8. 326; 64-70:
1. 310; 7. 623; 8. 493; 134: 8. 296, 325;
160 ff.: 7. 680; 8. 676; 166: 8. 461; 178-
85: 8. 676; 198-204: 5. 342; 267-86: 7.
680; 281-7: 7. 679. *See also above* Second
Pair

Hymn of Heavenly Beauty, 1. 433-4; 5.
284; 6. 266, 399, 407; 7. 672-4, 676; 8.
493, 675-6; style and rhetoric: 8. 676-7;
13: 8. 450; 15-21: 7. 680; 22-119: 8. 330-
1; 43-105; 8. 676-7; 82-4: 3. 345; 85-98:
1. 310; 8. 493; 109-11: 7. 676; 181: 6.
278; 183-301: 7. 680; 8. 313, 325; 197-
203: 6. 411: 204: 8. 472; 211-4: 8. 425;
231: 4. 195: 232-3: 8. 478; 244-52: 6.
241; 264-6: 8. 315; 274-6: 8. 423. *See
also above* Second Pair

Fox, 1. 263; 2. 341; 7. 266, 293-4, 304-5,
361, 603; 8. 352-3, 363, 373, 377, 561,
564, 570, 574, 576, 578-9, 586-92, 604,
606-7, 609

Fox, Richard, 1. 486

Foxe, John, 1. 287, 468-70; 2. 242; 7. 326;
8. 479

Foyle, 4. 267

Fra Angelico, 7. 267

Fradubio, 1. 205, 427, 431, 435; is Thomas
Cranmer: 1. 461, 465; represents insuf-
ficiency of faith: 1. 435; is Lord Guilford
Dudley: 1. 458

Fraelissa, 1. 205, 427; is Mrs. Cranmer: 1.
461; is Lady Jane Grey: 1. 458

Fragments, 8. 509-10, 709-10, 723; bibliography: 8. 736-45

France, 2. 250; 5. 246; 7. 586; 8. 364; is
Flourdelis: 5. 260, 299; is Sansfoy: 1.
449, 458. *See also* French

Francis, Duke of Guise, 1. 449, 459-60

Francis, St., 6. 321; 7. 672

Franklin, 1. 283-4

Fraud, 1. 205, 231

Fraunce, Abraham, 4. 314; 7. 465-6, 469,
474; 8. 284, 536; *Arcadian Rhetorike*: 1.
252; 2. 230, 399; 8. 709-10; *Countess of
Pembrokes Emanuel*: 8. 296; *Countess of
Pembrokes Ivychurch*: 7. 466; 8. 497;
Lamentation of Amintas: 7. 466; *Lawiers
Logike*: 7. 280, 287, 466, 643

Frazer, Sir James G., 5. 166, 217

" free," 6. 220

Freeman, Edward Augustus, 6. 196

Free will, 1. 266; 8. 609

Freinsheim, Johann, 8. 302

French, arms: 5. 241; fashions: 8. 364;
gaiety: 5. 192; kings: 8. 372; language:
8. 365; names: 7. 252; poetry: 8. 391;
Spenser, influence on: 4. 179-80; 7. 615-
7, 621, 625-7. *See also* France

French Revolution, 5. 175, 275, 289

Frere, Walter H., 7. 360

Friedrich, W. G., 7. 494

Friendliness, 1. 328-9, 342; 6. 325-7, 335,
345

Friendship, 1. 328-9, 337, 341-2, 347, 432;
2. 229; 3. 317-20; 4. 176, 223-6, 234,
281-313; 6. 326-7; 7. 665; according to
Aristotle: 4. 282-3, 288-9, 291, 296-7,
303-5, 307, 312, 328; 6. 379; according
to Bacon: 4. 291, 304; and Beauty: 4.
306-7; calumny, secure against: 4. 304;
and Chastity: 3. 318, 320; 4. 301, 305;
and Chivalry: 4. 293-4; according to
Cicero: 4. 291, 303-4, 312, 328; communion of souls: 4. 294-6, 330; Concord
in the State: 4. 297; cosmic force: 4. 307-
12, 327; and Courtesy: 3. 319; according

to Elyot, Edwards, Lyly, Greene: 4. 312; its enemies: 4. 295-6, 297, 299, 304-5; episodes, illustrated by: 4. 295; between equals: 4. 297, 304, 327-9, 333; false friendship: 4. 281, 284, 295-6, 299-300, 303, 307, 331-2; and Justice: 4. 291, 294, 301; kinds: 4. 282, 288-91, 296-99, 303; and Love: 3. 317, 319; 4. 181, 281-4, 293, 296, 306; according to Lucretius: 4. 312-3; according to Montaigne: 4. 291, 303-4, 328; mystical approach to God: 4. 290; according to Plato: 4. 291, 293, 303, 305, 307, 312, 328-9; according to Plutarch: 4. 291, 303, 312; a Renaissance virtue: 1. 345; 4. 289-96, 312, 328, 333; according to Shakespeare: 4. 290, 293; according to Sidney: 4. 293; one soul: 4. 181, 330-1; according to Spenser: 4. 327, 332-3; title: 4. 282; varieties: 4. 282, 288-91, 296-7, 303; and Vice: 4. 306-7; and Virtue: 4. 176, 284, 290, 293-4, 296-9, 303-4, 306-7, 327-8, 333; what it is not: 1. 347; 4. 294-7

Fright, 1. 268, 272

Frith, 4. 273

Frobisher, Sir Martin, 8. 540

Froissart, Jean, 2. 371; 3. 394; 4. 223, 294; 5. 192, 207; 6. 222; 8. 352

Frontino, 2. 342; 5. 191

Froude, James Anthony, 5. 201, 225, 233, 251, 264; 7. 403

Fuimus Troes, 7. 364

Fulgent, 2. 329-30

Fulgentius, 1. 512-4; 2. 347, 366; 4. 319; 7. 274, 333; 8. 301, 309, 324, 329, 470

Fulke, William, 6. 210; 7. 326

Fuller, Thomas, 2. 199; 6. 266, 268, 358, 387; 7. 331, 473, 573, 615, 652; 8. 359

Fulton, Edward, 7. 488

Fulwel, Ulpian, 4. 164; 5. 239, 321; 8. 591

Funsheon. *See* Fanchin

Furies, 8. 315, 332, 343, 388

Furnivall, F. J., 6. 315; 8. 318

Furor, 2. 184, 225, 227-9, 350, 401-2, 427; 3. 354

Fusberta, 5. 191

Fynmore, R. J., 7. 328

Gabbett, S., 8. 317-8

Gabrina, 4. 173, 205

Gain, 2. 414, 425-6, 471. *See also* Riches

Gairdner, James, 1. 389

Gaius, 5. 194

Galafron, 3. 204

Galahad, 1. 177, 347, 351, 399; 3. 204; 4. 223; 5. 309

Galantine, 5. 192

Galatea, 4. 269

Galathea, 7. 464, 475

Galen, 2. 292;

Galigari, G., 8. 465

Galileo, 5. 200; 6. 423

Galingale, 8. 399

Galland, René, 8. 612

Galle, Theodore, 2. 226-7

Galli, 5. 214-6; 6. 399

Galloglasses, 5. 233

Gallus, 7. 246, 597; 8. 297

Galtees, 1. 244; 6. 282-9, 425-6, 436; 7. 453-4, 495

Galtymore, 5. 255; 6. 247, 252, 282-9, 426; 7. 453

Games, pastimes, and sports, 3. 288; 5. 324; 7. 379; 8. 350-1, 357, 366

Gammer Gurtons Needle, 7. 305; 8. 321

Gandelin, 3. 360-1

Ganymede, 3. 397; 6. 308

Garden, Gardens, 2. 238, 262, 264, 371, 379, 381; 3. 258-9, 303; 8. 397, 441-2

Garden of Adonis, 1. 205; 2. 334, 374; 3. 248, 253-61, 326, 340-52, 366, 377; 4. 216; 5. 162, 215; 7. 448, 480, 521, 562; analyzed: 3. 352; and Mutability cantos: 6. 281, 389, 394, 400-4, 409, 413, 416-7, 419, 421, 433-4, 440-1

Garden of Alcinous, 2. 381; 3. 258

Garden of Armida, 2. 381, 398, 447

Garden of the Hesperides, 2. 264; 3. 258

Garden of Jove, 3. 261; 7. 480

Garden of Mirth, 1. 406; 4. 226

Garden of Pleasure, 3. 357

Garden of Sensual Delight, 2. 371

Garden of Venus, 2. 381; 3. 255

Gardiner, Stephen, 1. 458, 461, 463-5; 8. 592

Gareth, 1. |351, 379, 391-5; 6. 325

Garland, 6. 237

Garnier, Robert, 7. 504; 8. 284, 296, 528, 539

Garrod, H. W., 8. 649

Garter, Order of, 1. 256, 293, 491; 2. 202-3, 280; 4. 199-200; 5. 197, 203

Gascoigne, George, 2. 220; 3. 307; 4. 165; 7. 303, 469, 589, 624, 639; 8. 530, 600, 618; is Willy: 8. 319; *Certain Notes*: 7. 260, 405, 635-7; *Complaint of Phylomene*: 4. 350; 7. 405, 415-6, 446; 8. 343; *Defence of Rhyme*: 3. 284; *Hearbes*: 8. 600, 610; *Hundreth Sundrie Posies*: 7. 625; *Instructions concerning the Making of Verse*: 7. 405; *Jocasta*: 4. 324, 326-7; *Patience Perforce*: 2. 206; *Princely Pleasure*: 6. 304; 7. 285, 289; *Steele Glas*: 8. 591, 595; *Weeds*: 4. 164

Gate, 2. 373; 3. 345

Gate of Good Desert, 4. 276
Gates of Dreams, 1. 193-5
Gathelus, 1. 482
"Gather ye rosebuds," 2. 388-91; 8. 445
Gaultier, Thomas, 8. 586
Gawain, 1. 346-7, 401, 488-9; 2. 427; 3. 361-
    2; 5. 168, 192; 6. 187, 260
Gawain and the Green Knight, 7. 629
Gay, John, 7. 574, 576; 8. 578
Gayton, Edmund, 6. 309
Gefferon, Sir, 1. 391
Gelli, Giovanni B., 2. 394
Gemini, 8. 505
Gems, 3. 303
Genesis and Exodus (M. E.), 7. 639
Genii, 3. 250
Genius, 2. 351, 374-6, 433, 477; 3. 256, 340,
    345, 347, 350-2; 6. 398; 8. 285, 294, 389,
    468, 488, 491-2
Genre, 6. 290; 8. 602
Gentilis, Robert, 7. 468-9
Gentillet, Innocent, 5. 309; 8. 364, 368-9,
    375, 524, 589
"gentle spirit," 8. 317-20
Gentleman, 1. 336, 338; 2. 209, 223-4, 260,
    284, 403; 3. 337; 5. 175; 6. 191-2, 320-
    48; 8. 365-8; Christian: 1. 432-7; learned:
    1. 340. See also Breeding
Gentleman's Magazine, 8. 319-20
Geoffrey of Monmouth, 1. 486, 490, 493;
    2. 302, 304-34, 397; 5. 242; Historia
    Regum Britanniae: 1. 482-3; 2. 301, 449-
    52; 3. 286; 1. 3: 3. 281-2; 1. 11: 3. 283;
    5. 220; 1. 16: 2. 304-5, 307-8; 1. 17: 3.
    283; 2. 1-17: 2. 309-20; 2. 9: 3. 234;
    3. 1-20: 2. 321-4; 3. 17: 5. 161; 3. 18:
    3. 269; 4. 1-20: 2. 324-5; 5. 1-2: 2. 325-
    8, 332; 5. 2-16: 2. 329-32; 6. 10-7: 3.
    333; 6. 17: 3. 225; 6. 18: 3. 226; 7. 3:
    3. 235; 8. 1-14: 2. 333, 334, 512; 8. 16,
    18, 23: 3. 236; 8. 19: 1. 265; 3. 227;
    9. 1-5: 3. 228; 9. 4: 1. 251-2; 2. 275;
    9. 12: 3. 228; 5. 161; 10. 3: 6. 366; 10.
    13: 6. 190; 11. 4-5: 3. 229; 11. 7: 3.
    230; 11. 8, 10: 3. 231; 11. 12-13: 3. 232;
    12. 1-13: 3. 233; 12. 17, 18: 3. 234; 14.
    18: 3. 234
George III, 8. 508
George, St., 1. 177, 201, 207, 254, 256, 290-
    4, 301, 308-11, 366, 377, 379-90, 393, 400,
    498-500; 3. 237, 268; ballad of: 1. 390;
    and dragon compared with Christian and
    Apollyon: 1. 377; is Elizabeth: 1. 478;
    is England: 1. 430; etymology: 1. 389,
    424; legend: 1. 418; Protestantism, emblem
    of: 1. 478; religion, emblem of: 1. 477.
    See also Red Cross Knight

Georgione, 3. 395
Geraldine, 3. 216-7
Geraldus Odo, 1. 355
Gerard, John, 1. 205; 2. 263; 7. 498; 8.
    398-9
Gerard Mercator, 2. 252
Germanic, 3. 330-2
Germanicus, 8. 333
Gerson, John, 7. 672
Geryon, 5. 162, 249-51, 257
Geryoneo, 5. 291-2, 301-2, 312; 6. 213; is
    Charles V: 5. 317-8; is Philip II: 5. 249,
    301-2, 317-8; is Spain, Germany, America:
    1. 453-4; 5. 249-51
Gesner, Conrad, 1. 402; 2. 236, 359-63, 435;
    3. 263
Gesta Romanorum, 2. 260
Gesualdo, Giovanni Andrea, 7. 650
Geta, 2. 330
Gheeraerts, Marcus, Sr., 8. 626
Ghibellines, 2. 335
Ghosts, 2. 346; 4. 184; 7. 443
Giant with the scales, 4. 332; 5. 175-81, 275,
    277-8, 280, 282, 284-5, 289-95, 304, 336-
    45; 8. 353
Giants, 1. 248-9, 418; 2. 304-6, 308; 4. 197,
    281; 5. 169-70, 176, 219; 6. 225, 394,
    415; 8. 384
Gibbon, Edward, 8. 380
Gibraltar, 8. 504
Gideon, 8. 390
Gifford, Katherine, 7. 475
Gigli, Antonio and Silvestro, 1. 484
Gilbert, Humphrey, 2. 358; 5. 308
Gildas, 1. 483, 486-7; 2. 450-1; 8. 290-1
Gildersleeve, Basil, 2. 223
Gildon, Charles, 7. 575
Gilfillan, George, 1. 181
Ginevra, 2. 228, 441
Giotto, 1. 271; 2. 414, 416; 7. 238, 267
Giraldi Cinthio, Giovanni Battista, 1. 329,
    342-3, 348-9, 354, 356, 359-60; 2. 397,
    459; 3. 321; 8. 529; Tre Dialoghi della
    Vita Civile: 1. 356; 3. 227; 4. 291-6
Giraldus Cambrensis, 2. 323, 452; 3. 224-5,
    229; 4. 269
Girardin, St. Marc, 8. 610
Girdle. See Florimell
Giulio Romano, 2. 228; 3. 395
Giuntoni, J. D., 1. 187
Glamorgan, 2. 318
Glanworth, 6. 286
Glasenapp, G., 2. 279
Glass, 3. 216-7
Glastonbury, 1. 487; 2. 446-7
Glatissant Beast, 6. 236, 268-9, 271, 382,
    384

Glauce, 3. 217, 219-22, 236, 325, 330, 334-6, 370, 388, 390; 4. 173-4, 283, 285; is Faith: 4. 320; is Reason or Prudence: 3. 321
Glaucon, 5. 292
Glaucus, 4. 243
" gleam," 8. 411
" glen," 7. 278, 312
Glendalough, 5. 303
Glenmalure, 4. 271-2; 5. 174; 7. 462
Gloriana, 1. 266, 291, 305, 317, 323, 334, 337, 343, 345, 359, 391, 497, 500; 2. 236, 334-5; 5. 258; 6. 330; is Elizabeth: 1. 449, 450, 485; 2. 409; 4. 319; 5. 197, 310; 6. 186; 8. 503; fairy: 1. 353; heroine of F. Q.: 3. 369; 6. 427; is Platonic Truth: 4. 319-20
Gloucestershire, 7. 312
Glover, T. R., 8. 517
Gluttony, 1. 410-3; 2. 414, 422; 5. 266; 6. 304, 307-8
Glyn Cothi, Lewis, 1. 484; 3. 235
Gnats, 2. 282; 8. 396
Gnome, 1. 189, 202; 8. 372. See also Proverb
Gnostics, 7. 558-9, 561, 563, 567
Goat, 1. 411, 413, 416, 418; 3. 286-7; 5. 232; 7. 242, 293
Göbel, Heinrich, 8. 402
Gobbelines, 2. 334-5
Goblin, 7. 322; 8. 486
God, 6. 392; 7. 333, 551, 557, 667-9; Beauty absolute: 7. 539, 552; Beauty, source of: 7. 523-4, 554, 663-4, 667; Father and Son: 7. 539, 547; and Nature: 6. 296, 412, 418, 422, 428; 7. 669-70
" God of my life," 1. 207
" godded," 7. 481
Godfrey, 1. 293, 345; 2. 428
Gods, 3. 311; 6. 281, 283, 310, 392, 394, 405, 414-5, 420, 427, 429; 7. 551; 8. 493; genealogy: 1. 230-1
Goemot, Goemagot, Gogmagog, 2. 307-8
Goethe, Johann Wolfgang von, 8. 586
Gog and Magog, 2. 187, 307-8
Gold, 1. 287; 6. 239; 8. 411, 425
Golde, 7. 469
Golden Age, 2. 255; 3. 258; 4. 311; 5. 154-7, 160, 342; 6. 401, 419, 423, 444, 449
Golden Apples, 2. 252
Golden Bough, 1. 357-8
Golden Fleece, 4. 169; 8. 339
Golden Legend. See Voragine
Golder, H., 1. 275-7, 282, 290-1
Golding, Arthur, 2. 295; 3. 340, 346-9; Ovid's Metamorphoses: 3. 345, 347-9; 6. 421; 7. 461, 469; 8. 312, 343; Prefatory Epistle: 3. 347, 349, 352
Goldsmith, Oliver, 5. 305; 6. 290

Goliath, 8. 306
Gollancz, Sir Israel, 3. 428; 7. 361; 8. 419, 582
Goneril, 2. 315-7
Good and Evil. See Psychomachia
Good Operation, 1. 285
Goodman, Christopher, 1. 470
Googe, Barnabe, 4. 228; 7. 264, 465-6, 514, 552, 582, 586; 8. 546, 618; Cupido Conquered: 3. 354; Eglogs, Epitaphs, and Sonnets: 7. 464, 589, 592-5; 8. 459
Gorboduc, 2. 320; 7. 465, 480, 578; 8. 528, 621
Gorbogud, 2. 319
Gorboman, 2. 323
Gordon, Alexander, 2. 450; 4. 261
Gorgeous Gallery of Gallant Inventions, 7. 239; 8. 332, 538
Gorges, Ambrosia, 7. 403, 433-7, 442
Gorges, Arthur, 7. 430, 432-5, 437-8, 466-7, 486, 501
Gorges Family, 7. 433-5, 439
Gorges, Thomas, 7. 433-5, 437
Gorges, William, 7. 433-4
Gorgias Leontinus, 2. 274
Gorgon, 1. 251, 254
Gorlois, 2. 453; 3. 227-8
Gormund, 3. 231-2
Gorphorost, 6. 380
Gortnatubrid, 4. 271
Gospel, 1. 295, 301, 444; 7. 537
Gosse, Edmund, 7. 589
Gosson, Stephen, 6. 304; 7. 608; 8. 321, 591
Got Amur, 2. 355-6
Gothic, 2. 421-2; architecture: 1. 315, 324, 331; 4. 281; classic, contrasted with: 1. 324-7, 337
Gotland, 3. 231
Gottfried, R. B., 6. 429-32; 8. 418
Gouge, William, 1. 276
Gough, A. B., 5. 155-268, 282-5, 311
Goulart, Simon, 1. 276
Governar, 3. 362-3
Gower, John, 1. 189; 2. 365; 7. 237, 258, 337, 615-7, 620, 626; 8. 370; Ballad to King Henry: 7. 321; Confessio Amantis: 3. 353; 6. 410; Prologue: 8. 595; 1: 1. 237; 1. 5: 1. 238; 1. 1777-80: 1. 218; 1. 1883-6: 1. 406; 1. 2315: 8. 312; 2. 479-81: 7. 264; 3. 1701-5: 7. 481; 3. 2217-8: 4. 278; 4. 979-1034: 5. 230; 5. 515-6: 7. 357-8; 6. 470-5: 6. 195; 7: 2. 279; 8. 442; 7. 477: 2. 292; 8: 3. 211; Mirror de L'Omme: 1. 405, 407-13; 5. 172; 8. 595; possible source of F. Q.: 1. 407-13; 2. 286; Vox Clamantis: 8. 595
Grace, 1. 301; 3. 379; 7. 506, 525-7; 8. 344,

635; of bearing: 6. 330; saving: 7. 568. *See also* Castle of Grace

Graces, 1. 363, 371; 2. 215-6, 273; 6. 245, 247, 249-54, 309, 318, 323, 328; 7. 276, 280, 284, 289, 309, 316, 322; 8. 327, 332, 467-8, 479, 482, 495; Christian: 1. 347, 504; are inspiration: 6. 347

Gradasso, 2. 276

Gradatio, 6. 189

Grafton, Richard, 2. 302, 305, 314-5, 322, 324; *Abridgement*: 2. 315, 324, 452; 3. 232; *Chronicle at Large*: 2. 305, 314, 322, 453; 3. 237; *Manuell of the Chronicles of England*: 2. 452

Graius, 4. 316

Grammar, 6. 188, 207; 7. 269, 271, 305, 316-8, 329, 349, 453, 463; 8. 293, 351, 395. *See also* Dative Case; Omission of expletive; Participle; Relative omitted; Sentence order; Syntax; Tenses; "thou" and "you"; Vocative; "you, ye"

Grandeur, 1. 250, 295

Grand opera, 8. 340

Grange, John, 8. 600

Granger, James, 8. 361

Granta, 4. 258

Grantorto, 5. 163, 267, 282, 290-2, 303, 312; is the Desmond rebellion: 5. 312-3; is the Pope: 5. 318

Grapes, 2. 381

Grasshopper, 7. 379-80

Gratian, 2. 331-2

Graund Amour, 1. 176, 407, 415, 417; 5. 213. *See also* Hawes, Stephen

Gray, 7. 346

Gray, Arthur, 7. 473-4

Gray, M. M., 1. 261-2, 274; 2. 281-2, 339; 5. 172-3; 6. 233, 256

Gray, Thomas, 1. 216; 7. 264, 344, 412, 627, 635; 8. 461, 661, 674

Gray's Inn, 4. 316

Great Mother, 2. 375; 6. 398-9

Great Records of Munster, 8. 633

"gree," 1. 228

Greek, conception of Truth: 1. 433; ethics: 2. 420; idea of Friendship: 4. 333; and "Gothic": 5. 169; idiom: 1. 233; 2. 364; quality: 7. 499; Spenser's knowledge of: 1. 356; 2. 264; 6. 402; 7. 408, 589, 595-6, 670; 8. 376

Greek Anthology: 7. 266; (following reff. to ed. Paton in *Loeb Library*) 5. 74: 2. 391; 5. 123: 8. 489; 5. 256: 6. 201; 6. 222; 7. 294: 5. 195; 6. 336: 7. 337; 9. 39: 3. 253; 9. 66, 506, 571: 6. 252

Green, 7. 297, 346

Green, Henry, 7. 392; 8. 375

Green leaves, 6. 304

Greene, H. E., 2. 412

Greene, Maurice, 8. 643

Greene, Robert, 6. 242, 376, 379; 7. 464; 8. 534, 536, 540; *Carde of Fancie*: 6. 214; *Ciceronis Amor*: 4. 328; *Greene's Arcadia*: 1. 225; *Looking Glasses for London*: 1. 276; 7. 468; *Menaphon*: 8. 318; *Morando*: 4. 328; *Mourning Garment*: 7. 594; *Mucedorus*: 7. 464; *Pandosto*: 6. 203-4, 237, 262, 371, 374-7; *Perimedes the Blacksmith*, Pref.: 1. 252; *Quip for an Upstart*: 6. 186; *Scottish History of James IV*: 8. 369

Greenfield, B. W., 7. 403

Greenham, Richard, 7. 352-3

Green Knight, 1. 394

Greenwich, 8. 498, 663-4, 666, 671; Palace: 1. 291; 8. 495, 567

Greg, W. W., 1. 522; 7. 321, 390, 398, 410, 449, 593, 632; 8. 420

Gregory Nazianzen, 2. 187

Gregory the Great, 1. 310; 7. 674

Gregory Thaumaturgus, 7. 559-60

Gregory XIII, 5. 167; 7. 243

Grendel, 1. 292

Greville, Fulke, 1. 341; 3. 307, 355; 5. 302; 7. 375, 466; 8. 281; *Caelica*: 8. 463; *Life of Sir Philip Sidney*: 1. 475; 5. 306, 308; *Sonnets*: 2. 385

Grey, Arthur, Baron de Wilton, 1. 459; 2. 186, 349-50, 398, 404; 3. 217-8; 4. 196, 271, 316; 5. 165, 167, 172-4, 201, 233, 258-9, 285, 335; 6. 321, 360-1, 384, 386; 7. 474; 8. 281, 531-2, 540, 648; is Artegall: 3. 217-8, 369; 5. 161, 163, 172-3, 244, 264, 271, 298, 300, 303, 310; 6. 318, 437; death: 5. 284, 313; defended by Spenser: 5. 265-8, 271-2, 276, 283, 307, 318-9, 325, 333; 6. 189, 191, 345, 356; policy: 5. 194, 244, 265, 280, 303-4, 311-3, 318-9, 332; is the "Salvage Knight": 5. 312

Grey, Edward, Viscount, 8. 467

"gride," 7. 265

Grief, 1. 365; 2. 460

Grierson, Sir H. J. C., 1. 378; 2. 198, 256, 350-1; 4. 163; 5. 156-7; 7. 370; 8. 599, 602

Griffin, 2. 346

Grille, 2. 377, 394-5, 422, 435

Grimald, Nicholas, 4. 223-4; 7. 242

Grinbert, 8. 588

Grindal, Edmund, 6. 210, 266, 272, 386; 7. 243, 261, 278, 290-3, 296, 300, 323-5, 335, 352, 354, 361, 404, 582, 602, 605-8, 612; 8. 357, 370, 373, 543; *Remains*: 7. 336. *See also* Algrind

Griselda, 1. 305, 496
Grosart, A. B., 6. 434; 7. 314, 353, 377, 393, 429, 485, 492, 511, 579, 590, 630; 8. 431, 434, 437, 520, 527, 531, 560, 567, 585, 633, 648, 689, 717
Grosseteste, Robert, 1. 310; 2. 286
Grotesque, 1. 184, 212, 217, 263; 2. 366, 395; 5. 275; 8. 346, 475
Grotius, Hugo, 6. 282, 400; 7. 657
Grove, Matthew, 5. 183
Grubb, Marion, 5. 234
Gualsever, 4. 261
Gualter d'Avignon, 3. 286
Guarini, Gianbattista, 2. 390; 4. 234; 6. 378; 7. 590
Guazzo, Stefano, 6. 187, 192, 204, 212, 214, 241, 244, 329, 341-2
Gudrun, 2. 355
Guelfs, 2. 335
Guendolene, 2. 310-1; 3. 236
Guerilla warfare, 5. 236
Guest, Edwin, 7. 635
Guide, 1. 406
Guiderius, 2. 324-5
Guido Reni, 2. 211
Guid' Ubaldo di Montelfetro, 6. 329
Guildford, Henry, 8. 662-4
Guile. *See* Malengin
Guillaume de Lorris, 2. 382
Guillaume de Machaut, 1. 407; 2. 352, 371; 3. 211; 4. 222, 278; 6. 222
Guillaume de Normandie, 1. 228
Guillim, John, 7. 423
Guilpin, Edward, 7. 236
Guinevere, 1. 488
Guinglain, Sir, 1. 391
Guinicelli, Guido, 7. 666
Guise, Dukes of, 1. 459; 5. 211-2, 302, 316
Guistard and Sismond, 7. 409
Guitheline, 2. 321
Guizor, 5. 171, 211, 213, 302, 329; is Duke of Guise: 5. 211-2, 302; is James Fitzmaurice: 5. 314
Gulf of Greediness, 2. 349, 353-4, 421-2, 429
Gulick, 2. 280
Gummere, Francis, 7. 275, 291, 338, 351, 362, 410, 636
Guns, 2. 341
Gunton, Simon, 6. 268
Gurgunt, 1. 482; 2. 321, 397
Gurgustus, 2. 319
Guy of Warwick, 1. 396-7
Guyon, 1. 346, 358, 366, 389, 396; 2. 183-5, 187-90, 192, 194, 199, 207, 213, 225, 231, 241, 243, 252, 268-9, 271-2, 274, 281, 295, 338, 350, 365-7, 371, 382, 394-5, 402, 404-5, 410-2, 421, 423, 425; 3. 314,
318, 363, 374; 4. 298; 5. 191-2, 208, 215, 289, 297, 341; 6. 310; 8. 363; and Aeneas: 2. 202; and anger: 2. 416; and appetite: 2. 417; and Arthur in Book 2: 2. 471; and Britomart: 3. 324, 368-9, 390; and Calidore: 6. 191, 319-20; Celtic elements in his story: 2. 445-7; character: 2. 411; is Coligny: 2. 403-4; and Collen: 2. 446; colorless: 2. 416; and Cúchulainn: 2. 445-6; elfin, Celtic: 1. 351-2; 2. 335, 445-7; is Essex: 1. 491-2; 2. 190, 278, 297, 400-1; 3. 203; and Ferrau: 3. 205; and his horse: 5. 191, 273, 285, 296, 304; imperfect: 2. 427; legend of: 2. 420-2, 427-31; 8. 513; and Medina: 3. 315; his name, meaning of: 2. 187; Red Cross Knight, surpasses: 2. 352; and Ruggiero: 2. 439-42; is Sussex: 3. 379; voyage: 8. 315
G. W. I., 8. 417-8
G. W. Senior, 8. 417-8, 632
Gynecia, 3. 246
Gyron le Courtoys. See Alamanni
Gysippus, 4. 223-4

Haarlem, 5. 319
Haclito, 8. 486
Hades, 2. 251-2, 254; 8. 377
Hadrian (Emperor), 8. 333
Hadrian Junius, 1. 483; 8. 626
Haemony, 2. 377
Haemus, 2. 378-9; 6. 299
Hagthorpe, John, 6. 424
Hair, 2. 217, 285, 384; 4. 275; 5. 171; 8. 425, 472, 497, 633, 639
Hakewill, George, 6. 423-4
Hakluyt, Richard, 1. 483; 2. 358
Hale, John, 5. 320
Hales, J. W., 314-5, 420, 617, 653; 8. 289-90, 308-10, 351, 484, 495-500, 502-4, 514, 527, 534, 670
Halifax, 7. 250
Hall, A., 8. 318
Hall, Arthur, 8. 614
Hall, Edgar A., 6. 365-71
Hall, Edward, 1. 488; 4. 165-6; 5. 193; 8. 351, 672
Hall, John, 6. 224
Hall, Joseph, 1. 484; 2. 394; 3. 216; 4. 219; 6. 227-8, 285; 7. 238, 340, 357, 545, 572, 594, 623
Hallam, Arthur, 8. 308
Hallam, Henry, 1. 178, 180; 8. 645
Halliwell-Phillips, J. O., 8. 318
Halpin, C. G. and N. J., 6. 220; 7. 652; 8. 441, 633
Hamer, D., 7. 312, 650; 8. 311, 649-51
Hamlet, 4. 290

Hammers, 4. 197-8
Hammond, E. P., 1. 386
Hammond, W. A., 2. 468
Hampton Court, 4. 222; 5. 237-8
Hancock, Thomas, 7. 260
Handful of Pleasant Delights, 8. 370
Hands, 1. 208
Hanford, J. H., 7. 286, 298, 483
Hanging, 5. 196
Hankins, J. E., 7. 465
Hannah, John, 3. 305
Hannibal, 1. 444; 2. 274; 8. 386
Hapax, 7. 495, 516
Harbledown, 7. 343-4
Harclay, Andrew, Earl of Carlisle, 5. 196
Hard, Frederick, 1. 284; 3. 208, 394-9; 4.
    219; 5. 217-8, 237; 6. 263-4; 7. 238; 8.
    288, 373-5, 401, 498
Harding, John, *Chronicle* (ed. 1812, cited by
    chapters): 1. 176; 2. 302, 450-2; 5: 2.
    356; 6: 2. 305; 11: 2. 307; 15: 2. 309;
    20: 2. 311, 314; 25: 2. 318; 26: 2. 314-7;
    29: 2. 315-8; 30: 2. 319; 31: 2. 320;
    35: 2. 321; 37-9: 2. 322; 5. 161; 42-4:
    2. 324; 45-6: 2. 325; 63: 2. 331; 70:
    2. 333; 78: 3. 228; 86: 3. 230; 90: 3.
    232-3
Harington, Sir John, 1. 418-20, 492, 522;
    2. 215, 290, 341; 3. 367, 372, 374, 376-
    7; 4. 166; 5. 235, 241; 7. 326, 464, 477;
    8. 362, 508; *Briefe View of . . . the Church
    of England*: 8. 543; Preface to translation
    of *Orlando Furioso*: 1. 312; 2. 441-2;
    translation of *Orlando Furioso*: 2. 290-1;
    3. 367, 372, 376; 6. 501
Harleian MS 6947, 3. 358
Harman, E. G., 5. 245; 7. 501; 8. 294, 500,
    533, 601
Harman, Thomas, 8. 354-5, 591
Harmony, 2. 477; 4. 294; 5. 287, 291; of
    arrangement: 2. 379-80; of style: 1. 260
Harold-Barry, Peter, 6. 210; 8. 464
Harp, 7. 384; 8. 307-8
Harpalus, 7. 464-5
Harper, C. A., 2. 303-34, 396-9, 449-53;
    3. 228-36, 281, 283
Harpies, 2. 258
Harrington, James, 3. 217
Harris, R. B., 8. 393, 578-80, 606
Harrison, G. B., 3. 306; 6. 206-7; 8. 708
Harrison, J. S., 1. 501-5; 2. 416-7; 7. 511,
    513, 523, 526, 528, 532, 534, 539, 546,
    663-4; 8. 422, 434, 473
Harrison, Robert, 7. 307
Harrison, T. P., 6. 242, 379-81, 408; 7. 268,
    271-2, 349, 407, 411, 441-3, 487-8, 490-1,
    495, 497, 499, 507, 672; 8. 295-7, 307

Harrison, William, *Description of Britain*.
    See Holinshed, Raphael
Harrison, William, Vicar of Radminster, 7.
    353-4
Harrowing of Hell, 1. 234, 288
Harsnet, Samuel, 8. 486
Hart, E. C., 2. 189, 195, 273, 340; 8. 660
Hart, John S., 8. 660
Harvard University Library, 1. 517, 519; 7.
    706, 708-9; 8. 681, 706
Harvey, Gabriel, 1. 329-30, 332, 351, 509;
    2. 230, 303; 4. 314; 5. 155, 271; 7. 252,
    376, 466, 468, 488-9, 586, 589, 650, 654-
    5; 8. 316, 576; and Book 7 of the *F. Q.*:
    6. 439-44; and Du Bartas: 8. 391; and the
    Earl of Oxford: 8. 313; is E. K. in part:
    7. 650; and Essex: 5. 329; is Hobbinol:
    1. 509, 511; 3. 305; 7. 245, 310-1, 321,
    325, 352-3, 362, 375, 447, 452; literary
    and critical faculty: 8. 506; and Spenser:
    5. 328-9; 6. 433-4, 439-44, 447-8; 7. 235,
    241, 309-10, 361-2, 375, 420-2, 608-9,
    643-4; 8. 506; Spenser's sonnet to: 7. 311,
    325, 462, 478, 588; 8. 506; *Advertise-
    ment*: 7. 608; *Anticosmopolita*: 7. 366;
    Four Letters: 2. 281; 4. 171; 5. 328-9;
    7. 295; 8. 707-8, 736; *Gratulationes*: 8.
    516, 528-9; Latin works: 8. 622; *Letter
    Book*: 5. 155; 6. 439-44, 447-9; 7. 235,
    241, 310, 314, 353, 366, 415, 608, 610,
    612; 8. 311, 328-31, 364, 437; Letter to
    Christopher Bird: 8. 375, 560, 570, 575,
    580; Letters to Spenser (references are to
    pages of vol. 9, *The Prose Works*, of the
    Variorum): 8. 622; 442: 7. 487; 8. 509,
    723; 444: 8. 603, 650; 447-8: 7. 650;
    449-50: 8. 650; 459: 8. 270, 283, 517-8;
    460: 7. 479, 670; 462: 7. 295; 463-76:
    7. 615; 463: 7. 487; 466: 7. 647, 651;
    467: 7. 366, 487; 8. 350, 364, 577; 469:
    7. 612; 470: 8. 270, 515; 471: 1. 330,
    348; 7. 374-5, 643; 8. 270, 273, 280, 319,
    414, 511, 516-8, 613; 476: 7. 651, 655;
    8. 436, 650; *Marginalia* (references are to
    pages in Moore-Smith's edition): 6. 439-
    40, 444; 16, 174: 7. 314; 114: 7. 353;
    151: 8. 537; 159-64: 7. 634; 162: 7. 415;
    8. 350; 178: 7. 615; 192: 7. 350; 197-8:
    6. 440; 199: 7. 310; 232: 7. 472; *Pierces
    Supererogation*: 2. 209, 510; 5. 296, 328;
    7. 295, 325; 8. 316, 506; *Rameidos*: 7.
    366; *Smithus vel Musarum Lachrymae*: 7.
    366; 8. 312, 324, 536-7, 540. *See also*
    Letters to Harvey from Spenser
Harvey, Richard, 1. 196, 483
Haslewood, Joseph, 8. 709-10, 737

Hastings, Henry, Earl of Huntingdon, 5. 320; 6. 353
Hate, 4. 217, 222, 226
Hatfield MSS, 5. 322; 7. 360
Hatton, Christopher, 8. 374, 571
" have at will," 4. 173
Havré, Marquess of, 5. 249, 299, 301, 317
Hawes, Stephen, 3. 394; *Exemple of Vertue*: 1. 176, 216, 283, 405, 407, 414-8; 6. 293; 7. 564; *Passetyme of Pleasure*: 1. 176, 283, 346, 405, 407, 414-8; 2. 243, 279, 294; 4. 226; 5. 174, 257; 7. 564; 275-80, 4929: 6. 255; 400 ff., 3230 ff., 3754 ff.: 4. 229; 477, 483: 5. 239; 1778-80: 7. 316; 2167: 5. 206; 2780-2864: 2. 286-7; 3487 ff.: 4. 211; 3750: 6. 223; 4755-9: 4. 221; 4963: 5. 213; 5479-80: 8. 479
Hawking. *See* Falconry
Hawkins, John, 5. 334; 8. 540
Hawthorne, Nathaniel, 1. 204; 3. 287-8; 5. 176
Hay any Worke for Cooper, 7. 299
Hayes, Edward, 2. 358
Hayward, J., 6. 267
Hayward, Sir John, 1. 474
Hazlitt, William, 1. 241-2, 244, 373-4, 442; 2. 211, 299, 371, 388-9; 3. 302-3
Hazlitt, W. Carew, 8. 312, 361, 370, 463
Healing Liquor, 1. 268
Hearne, Thomas, 6. 298; 8. 667, 671
Heart, burning: 1. 411-2; devour: 4. 200; 6. 244; gentle: 6. 198, 219, 229; ruby: 4. 300, 325; torn: 6. 258
Heavenly Beauty. *See* Beauty
Heavenly birth, 7. 281
Heavenly Grace, 1. 251, 414, 424; 3. 323, 371
Heavenly Love. *See* Love
Heavenly Wisdom. *See* Wisdom
Hebe, 8. 299, 488, 492, 512
Heber (son of Milesius), 5. 194
Heber, Richard, 8. 613
Hebrew Literature, 7. 560-68
Hebrus, 1. 302
Hecate, 1. 195, 205, 230, 233, 234; 3. 221; 4. 196; 6. 274-5, 277
Hector, 5. 222, 269; 8. 345, 384, 494
Hector Boece, 7. 336
Hecuba, 5. 232
Hedge-hog, 2. 341
Hedington, 8. 375
Heffner, Ray, 1. 473-82; 2. 337; 4. 248-9; 5. 324-35; 6. 357-64; 8. 502, 651
Heinsius, Daniel, 8. 489
Heinsius, Nicholas, 7. 242
Helen, 3. 270, 285; 4. 223; 8. 472, 667
Helen of Corinth, 3. 377

Helena, 1. 240; 2. 331
Heliades, 8. 311, 339-40
Helice, 8. 420, 431-2
Helicon, 7. 281; 8. 301, 324, 420, 541
Heliodorus, 3. 205; 5. 225; 6. 233-4, 257, 371-2, 379; 7. 466; *Ethiopics*: 1. 184-5, 214, 246; 2. 187, 193-4, 392; 6. 264, 376-7
Hell, 1. 312; 2. 237, 251; 5. 234; descent to: 1. 233, 235, 402-3; gate: 2. 258; Harrowing of: 1. 234, 288; mouth: 1. 297; 5. 234; rivers: 1. 234; 2. 267; tortures: 1. 235
Hell of Lovers; his Purgatory, 7. 520; 8. 270, 283, 519
Helle, 3. 292-3
Hellenistic, 7. 266
Hellenore, 1. 378; 3. 272-5, 280, 285, 313, 314, 320, 328; is Anne Cecil: 3. 380; is Mary Queen of Scots: 3. 378
Hellespont, 7. 519
Hely, 2. 323-4
Hemistichs, 2. 217
Henderson, William, 8. 469
Hengist, 2. 333-4; 3. 236
Henley, Pauline, 2. 349; 3. 246, 278, 301, 334, 380; 4. 175, 191, 196, 265; 5. 160, 163-5, 265, 312-5; 6. 187, 195, 239; 7. 454, 475; 8. 648
Henry II, of England, 2. 293-4
Henry II, of France, 1. 458, 460, 464; 2. 404
Henry III, 2. 307
Henry III, of France, 5. 246
Henry IV, of France, 5. 248, 259-61, 263, 280, 285, 299, 326, 329-30, 333; 6. 384
Henry V, 8. 365
Henry VI, 7. 652
Henry VII, 1. 390, 414, 417, 480, 483-4, 486, 488-90; 2. 323, 454; 3. 234-5; 6. 299, 310; 8. 672; is Elficleos: 2. 335
Henry VIII, 1. 207, 208, 211, 244, 340, 417, 441, 454-7, 462, 480, 484, 487-90, 492-4; 3. 357, 397; 5. 238; 6. 265, 386; 8. 497, 671; entertainments: 3. 357, 359; " greate shephearde": 7. 404; king of Faery Land: 2. 188; is the lion: 1. 461, 464, 467; and monopolies: 5. 170; is Oberon: 1. 480; 2. 334-6, 453; is Pan: 2. 384; 7. 274, 281-2; is Red Cross Knight: 1. 492; his will: 2. 338; *Assertio . . . adversus Martinum Lutherum*: 1. 466; *Certaine Statutes*: 1. 177; *State Papers*: 8. 453
Henry, Duke of Guise, 5. 171, 211-2
Henry, Matthew, 7. 331
Henry, Prince of Wales, 7. 490
Henryson, Robert, 2. 273; 3. 276; 6. 337; 7. 339; 8. 375

Hentzner, Pauli, 2. 382; 5. 238; 6. 298
Hephaestus, 2. 392-3; 6. 301. See Vulcan
Heraldry, 3. 203, 379; 5. 187, 240-1
Herbert, George, 7. 311
Herbert, Henry, Earl of Pembroke, 7. 354, 466; 8. 295
Herbert, Thomas, 6. 226
Herbs, 1. 205; 3. 321; 8. 398-9
Hercaean, 8. 347
Hercules, 1. 236, 299, 303, 306, 385-6; 2. 239, 308, 347, 359; 3. 301-2, 397; 4. 169, 223, 246; 5. 162, 168-9, 198, 200, 203, 224, 228; 6. 270; 8. 299, 328, 345, 395, 449, 484, 492, 548, 672; Pillars of: 8. 504
Herder, Johann Gottfried von, 8. 586
Herlle, informer, 8. 378-9
Hermes Trismegistus, 7. 562
Hermit, 1. 188; 6. 210, 212, 328, 342, 344, 346, 348; King: 1. 400
Hermitage, 1. 189
Hero and Leander, 6. 293
Herodotus, 1. 214; 3. 332; History: 1. 26-33: 1. 238; 1. 32: 3. 290; 1. 91: 4. 182; 1. 98: 2. 298; 1. 105: 4. 236; 1. 107: 3. 227; 1. 195: 1. 200; 2: 2. 299; 2. 37: 5. 217; 2. 123: 3. 257; 2. 141: 5. 221; 2. 142: 5. 159; 3: 1. 214; 3. 31: 1. 214; 3. 52: 7. 307; 3. 116: 1. 227; 4. 12: 1. 258; 4. 85: 2. 356; 7: 1. 214; 7. 22-5, 35: 8. 335; 8. 53: 8. 335
Heroic poetry, 2. 370
Heroicall Adventures of the Knight of the Sea, 4. 277
Heron, 6. 218
Herrera, Tordesillas Antonio de, 4. 248
Herrick, Robert, 2. 390; 7. 294, 491
Herzeléide, 6. 369-70
Hesiod, 1. 296, 514; 6. 413; 7. 380, 481, 510-1, 599; 8. 332, 449; Shield of Heracles: 8. 377, 652; Theogony: 1-84: 8. 229; 53 ff.: 7. 319; 61-3: 6. 245, 247; 77-9: 1. 510; 8. 312; 77: 1. 173-4; 8. 470; 116: 6. 279; 7. 481; 123: 1. 230, 232; 2. 232-3; 140: 4. 244; 149: 1. 249; 194: 6. 296-7, 413; 207, 411-52, 616 ff.: 6. 274-5; 211 ff.: 3. 244; 223: 8. 394; 224: 1. 231, 233; 230: 2. 266; 4. 169; 233-6: 4. 246-7; 243 ff.: 4. 273-5; 257: 3. 242; 265: 5. 190; 270-336: 4. 243; 281-4: 4. 245; 5. 165; 8. 309; 287-309: 1. 182; 5. 249-50; 6. 212-3, 295-305, 388; 332 ff.: 4. 247; 369: 4. 246; 453 ff.: 4. 253; 478 ff.: 6. 312; 507 ff.: 7. 508; 517-20: 7. 303; 571 ff.: 8. 428; 601: 1. 222; 768: 6. 293; 770: 1. 234; 811-2: 8. 461; 821 ff.: 6. 277; 900: 6. 308; 901-2: 5. 241-2; 6. 420;

907-11: 2. 273; 6. 251, 253; 918: 6. 194; 930: 4. 242; 950-5; 8. 299; 984: 1. 304; 1001-2: 3. 297; 6. 307; Works and Days: 60 ff.: 8. 428; 61: 2. 289; 73: 6. 253; 8. 468; 109-20: 5. 160; 121: 2. 271; 203 ff.: 2. 277; 250: 3. 271; 256: 5. 216; 287-91: 2. 222-3; 654: 2. 265
Hesione, 8. 344-5
Hesperides, 2. 264; 3. 258; 8. 448
Hesperus, 6. 255; 8. 481, 483
Hesychius, 2. 226
Heuresis, 2. 299
Hevenfield, 3. 233
Heyne, Christian Gottlob, 8. 348
Heywood, John, 8. 343-4, 353, 479, 605, 610
Heywood, Thomas, 1. 189; 3. 339; 7. 366; 8. 461
Hickey, Emily, 1. 308; 6. 209
" hidder and shidder," 7. 363-4
Higden, Ralph, 2. 302, 452
Higford, William, 2. 223
Higgins, John, 1. 269-70, 272; 2. 215
" high disdain," 1. 211
Highmindedness, 1. 341-2, 432; 445-6; 2. 418-9. See also Magnanimity, Magnificence
Hildebertus, 2. 425; 8. 380
Hileo, Hillo, Hilo, 8. 486
Hill of Hope, 1. 289
Hill, W. H., 1. 301
Hillard, G. S., 4. 206, 231, 241; 5. 158, 174, 226; 8. 406
Hills, 3. 278; 6. 398
Hills, Henry, 7. 707; 8. 737
Himera, 7. 288
Himerius, 8. 463
Hinckley, H. B., 2. 344
Hippocrene, 7. 281; 8. 301, 324
Hippodamia, 6. 251
Hippogriff, 2. 439-40; 3. 372
Hippolito, Cardinal, 3. 310; 6. 330
Hippolyta, 5. 200; 8. 299
Hippolytus, 1. 236; 3. 354
Hippomanes, 2. 264-5
Hirmus, 8. 372
Historia de Carlo Magno, 5. 164
Historical Manuscripts Commission, 7. 362
History, 8. 328; historical basis of the epic: 1. 349; and poetry: 1. 312-3, 325, 360, 480; 8. 314, 327
History of Barlaam and Josophat: 2. 448
History of Beryn. See Chaucer (pseudo)
History of King Leir, 2. 192
History of Palmendos, 2. 239; 4. 208
History of Prince Arthur, 1. 216; 2. 275, 301, 327; 3. 203, 237, 276
History of the Four Sons of Aymon, 3. 213
History of the Tryall of Chevalry, 6. 228

Hitchcock, Robert, 8. 354

Hobbes, Thomas, 6. 257, 281

Hobbin, 7. 468

Hobbinol, 7. 250, 275-7, 280, 309, 350, 448, 468, 482, 594, 631, 641, 643; 8. 319, 328, 569; is Harvey: 1. 509, 511; 3. 305; 7. 245, 310-1, 321, 325, 352-3, 362, 375, 447, 452

Hodnell, 7. 312

Hoffmann, Max, 2. 278, 338

Hoffmann, Oscar, 8. 643

Hogan, Frank J., 8. 420, 681, 706

Hogarth, William, 2. 259; 3. 328

Hogg, James, 7. 576

Holiness, 1. 329, 342, 431-2; 2. 420-1; 3. 323, 371, 390; medieval: 1. 345; recognized by Plato, not Aristotle: 1. 433. *See also* House of Holiness

Holinshed, Raphael, 1. 349; 2. 304-23, 325-33, 450-1; 4. 241, 250-1; 5. 309, 342; 8. 287-8, 672; *Chronicles*, including William Harrison's *Description of Britain*: Ed. of 1577: 2. 301-2, 322-3, 331-2, 397, 453; 4. 241-2, 250; 5. 309; Ed. of 1587: 2. 301, 305, 391, 453; 4. 241-2, 250; Ed. of 1807-8 (Harrison's *Description* 1. 1-421): Vol. 1: 6, 432: 2. 205; 4. 246; 9: 3. 237; 78-81: 4. 251; 80, 85-9: 4. 254-5; 90: 4. 272; 92, 173, 177: 4. 257; 98, 103-4, 115: 4. 255-6; 117: 2. 310; 129: 3. 224-5; 145: 4. 263; 156-7, 160: 4. 261-2; 162, 172: 4. 260; 169, 320, 328: 4. 264; 173-5: 4. 258; 196: 2. 309; 197: 2. 311; 214: 4. 261; 231, 234: 8. 361; 249-50: 4. 253; 272: 4. 199-200; 315: 1. 214; 317: 6. 298; 321-3: 8. 280, 284, 286-90; 330-1: 5. 240; 427: 2. 304; 432, 434: 2. 305-6; 443-4: 2. 307-9; 3. 283; 445-51: 2. 312-20; 456-9: 2. 321-2; 479-80, 484, 503: 2. 325; 488, 495-501: 2. 327-9; 8. 289; 504, 511: 2. 326; 521: 2. 330-1; 541-2, 552-5, 560-1: 2. 332-3; 582: 3. 229; 588: 3. 231; 695: 7. 365; 709: 7. 336; Vol. 2: 749: 8. 352-3; Vol. 3: 381: 7. 308; 974: 5. 344; Vol. 4: 10-2: 8. 289; 475-83: 4. 325-6; 640-51: 5. 319; 871: 6. 385; Vol. 5: 256: 7. 336; 344: 8. 465; Vol. 6: 20: 8. 465; 67: 1. 209; 90: 3. 231-2; 93-4: 2. 321; 304: 4. 171; 325: 6. 385; 412, 433, 446, 454: 5. 173

Holland, 4. 259; 5. 249; 8. 307

Holland, H. H., 8. 321

Holland, Philemon, 4. 251; 8. 436-7

Holles, Lord Denzil, 7. 403

Holme, J. W., 7. 666

Holme, Randle, 1. 247

Holy Ghost, 1. 271; 7. 539-40, 558-62, 668, 673; 8. 330, 450

Holy Grail, 1. 201, 351, 399-401, 488; 2. 326-7, 329; 3. 361-5; Castle of: 1. 400; 3. 361-2; *Conte du Graal*: 6. 367-71

Holy Water, 1. 303, 309, 365

Holy Wells, 1. 189; 301-2

Homer, 1. 250, 254, 296, 304, 314-6, 323-4, 327, 335, 360, 489, 510, 513; 2. 304, 435-6; 5. 311; 6. 211; 7. 393, 642; 8. 328, 332; additions to: 3. 238; allegory in: 1. 335, 340-1, 345, 511, 513; 2. 183; allegory explained: 1. 312; and Ariosto: 1. 333; *F. Q.*, compared with: 1. 316, 321-2, 337; 2. 301, 366-7, 436; 3. 310; 5. 269; 6. 273; favorite with Spenser: 2. 342; historical: 1. 359

Iliad: 1. 303, 321, 350; 2. 273; 5. 262; 7. 393; 8. 301; Renaissance interpretation: 1. 341, 345, 511, 513; Book 1: 1: 8. 394; 3: 4. 169; 6. 236; 4: 1. 232; 2. 274; 18: 1. 250; 63: 5. 221; 80: 4. 210; 85: 4. 173; 201: 5. 180; 243: 6. 258; 249: 1. 278; 8. 322; 250 ff.: 2. 299; 469: 2. 202; 5. 184; 474: 4. 214; 528-30: 3. 253; 6. 280; 8. 376; 593: 4. 193; 605: 8. 460; Book 2: 20: 1. 196; 89: 5. 199; 196-7: 7. 288; 8. 376; 217: 2. 226-7, 343; 235: 2. 240; 371-2: 1. 341; 394-5: 1. 299; 418: 3. 245; 469: 1. 188; 2. 285; 469-71: 5. 261; 6. 259; 488: 4. 246; 484-93: 4. 241; 6. 292; 490: 4. 200; 732: 6. 211; 851: 6. 211; Book 3: 220: 2. 372; 270, 295: 1. 225; 369: 2. 277; 380: 1. 228; 424: 4. 165; 8. 482; Book 4: 75: 6. 217; 139-40: 3. 213; 141: 2. 296; 440: 4. 165; 452: 2. 341; 539: 4. 191; Book 5: 1-6: 8. 505; 56-8: 5. 254; 60: 3. 201; 87: 2. 342; 265: 2. 342; 297: 1. 183; 300: 3. 291; 338: 3. 209; 6. 253; 345: 1. 228; 385: 2. 228, 388: 2. 230; 401, 900: 3. 242; 449-54: 1. 195, 196; 3. 268; 504: 4. 212; 509: 5. 163; 585: 5. 230; 618: 2. 236; 640-1: 2. 342; 646: 4. 183; 746: 3. 204; 749: 2. 259; 6. 308; 845: 8. 377; Book 6: 65: 2. 236; 202: 6. 244; 506: 2. 255; 8. 451; Book 7: 32: 2. 235; 89-91: 8. 494; 99: 2. 289; 210: 8. 371; 220: 2. 205; Book 8: 13: 2. 237; 18-27: 4. 170; 7. 513; 19: 1. 233; 2. 261; 69-72: 5. 176; 368: 6. 270; 539: 3. 301; Book 9: 14: 5. 167; 158: 2. 370; 257: 2. 187; 312: 4. 183; 498: 5. 241-2; 571: 2. 200; 646: 4. 200; Book 10: 91: 2. 192; 314: 5. 212; 8. 345; 360: 5. 228; 374: 1. 277; 457: 4. 212; 458: 5. 231; 485: 1. 183; 6. 259; Book 11: 1: 8. 466; 15-46: 8. 395; 37: 4. 165; 172: 6. 216; 241: 6.

239; 474-82: 1. 240-1; 492: 2. 342; 547-
53: 5. 228: 740: 3. 246; 832: 6. 211; Book
12: 156, 278: 2. 341; 293: 6. 259; Book
13: 1: 4. 182; 17-31: 3. 296; 137-42: 1.
305; 248: 6. 211; 294: 3. 291; 389: 1. 259;
471-80: 1. 248; 474: 1. 298; 570: 6. 230;
754: 1. 289; Book 14: 83: 2. 291; 201:
4. 247; 214-21: 4. 193; 5. 190; 231: 2.
259; 259: 1. 230, 232; 264-7: 1. 193;
276: 7. 289; 347: 6. 296-7; 394-9: 1. 299;
414-7: 1. 259; 418: 6. 211; 516-9: 5. 254;
Book 15: 69: 5. 181; 101-2: 5. 235; 119:
4. 165; 187 ff.: 1. 237; 189-92: 6. 253;
190: 2. 357; 192: 6. 308; 237: 6. 232;
323: 6. 216; 348: 2. 196; 579: 5. 228;
630: 6. 259; Book 16: 3: 5. 167; 233-5:
5. 219; 352: 4. 191; 384-92: 1. 258; 482-
4: 1. 259; 582: 5. 181; 641: 1. 188; 5.
261; 6. 259; 752-3: 6. 259; 763 ff., 4.
215; 775: 1. 297; 856: 4. 184; Book 17:
46: 5. 181; 51: 1. 252; 53-8: 1. 259;
263-6: 1. 299; 425: 4. 212; 520: 3. 239;
570: 1. 188; 5. 261; 6. 259; 593 ff.: 1.
253; 654: 8. 496; 657-64: 5. 228; 674:
6. 232; 755: 5. 181; Book 18: 35 ff.: 3.
239, 243, 271; 4. 274-5; 40: 4. 273; 50-2:
3. 241; 207-13: 1. 298; 318-22: 6. 259;
369 ff.: 6. 301; 370: 2. 242; 372: 2. 261;
383: 2. 273; 468 ff.: 2. 260; 410: 4. 197;
490-6: 8. 652; 493: 8. 495; Book 19:
12-8: 6. 197; 20 ff.: 7. 519; 38-9: 3. 242;
91: 2. 233; 4. 169; 373-4: 5. 200; Book
20: 164: 4. 191; 321: 1. 228; 325: 2. 210;
Book 21: 404: 2. 346; 407: 1. 297; 492:
3. 243; 6. 236; Book 22: 25 ff.: 1. 209;
3. 206; 139: 3. 243; 6. 236; 209-12: 5.
176; 261: 5. 222; 294: 3. 239; 308: 6.
232; 317-8: 1. 251; 8. 467; 320: 1. 200;
345: 2. 209; 359: 8. 345; 369-75: 1. 306;
8. 384; 386: 1. 232; Book 23: 20-4, 181-
3: 1. 211; 340: 3. 265; Book 24: 5, 10:
4. 197; 41-3: 6. 259; 129: 4. 200; 6. 244;
8. 371; 205: 4. 200; 359: 1. 204

Odyssey: 1. 325; 2. 353, 435-6; Book 1:
32-5: 6. 240; 48-62: 2. 380; 122: 5. 180;
Book 2: 92-105: 8. 428; 388: 1. 304; Book
4: 122: 8. 472; 221: 4. 186; 232: 3. 242;
274 ff.: 3. 285; 384 ff.: 1. 199; 3. 241; 399:
5. 236; 791: 4. 191; Book 5: 1-2: 1. 304;
47: 1. 223; 121: 2. 204; 136: 3. 301;
Book 6: 42: 2. 377; 102-9: 8. 472; 149 ff.:
2. 220; 3. 247; 232-4: 6. 251; Book 7:
1. 307; 20: 1. 207; 112: 2. 381; 117:
3. 258; 302-7: 1. 308; 6. 199; Book 8:
266 ff.: 2. 247, 273, 393; 4. 193; 8. 404;
283: 4. 193; 362-4: 4. 228; 6. 253; 8.
468, 482; 555 ff.: 2. 242; Book 9: 38 ff.:

8. 346; 94: 8. 338; 412: 4. 244; 415-20:
4. 205; Book 10: 2: 2. 357; 4: 4. 261;
81-96: 2. 370; 8. 346; 105: 1. 207; 136 ff.:
7. 426; 234-6: 2. 192; 469: 6. 308; Book
11: 13-8: 1. 193; 8. 323; 53: 1. 232;
242: 3. 243; 305 ff.: 8. 342; 324: 6. 251;
544: 6. 208; 576: 1. 297; 578: 8. 342;
582 ff.: 1. 235; 2. 266, 267; 601-4: 8. 299;
Book 12: 1. 341; 2. 348; 37 ff.: 8. 346;
39: 2. 365; 45: 2. 259, 366; 59-78: 2.
354; 165-200: 2. 365-7; 235-43: 2. 353;
Book 13: 1-2: 2. 204; 86: 6. 232;
Book 14: 156: 4. 183; Book 16: 176: 1.
233; Book 17: 266-8: 5. 170; 330: 1. 254;
Book 18: 1: 8. 328; Book 19: 296: 2.
239; 8. 411; 562-7: 1. 193, 194; Book
20: 302: 5. 235; Book 21: 22-30: 5. 198;
Book 23: 85-110: 5. 223; 96-100: 5. 222-
3; 159-61: 6. 251; 195: 7. 264; 233-8:
1. 209; 6. 259; Book 24: 1 ff.: 2. 370
Homer (pseudo) *Batrachomyomachia*: 8. 605
Homeric Hymns, *To Aphrodite*: 1. 304; 4.
277; 6. 253; 8. 468; *To Delian Apollo*:
2. 357; 6. 194; *To Demeter*: 7. 446; *To
Hermes*: 8. 483; *To Pythian Apollo*: 245:
1. 302
Homilies, 1. 380, 418
Honesty, 6. 335-6
Honey, 8. 322; honey and gall: 4. 216-7;
7. 272-3. 491, 507
Honor, 2. 220-1; Sir Honor: 1. 407
" hook or crook," 5. 174-5
Hooker, Richard, 1. 466; 4. 324; 5. 296;
6. 282, 400, 422; 7. 608
Hoole, John, 1. 277
Hooper, John, 5. 337
Hope, 1. 284-7, 365, 407, 424, 504; 3. 301,
302; 4. 237; 5. 243; Sir Hope: 1. 407
Horace, 1. 348, 357, 360; 7. 266, 372, 615;
8. 324; influenced Spenser's purpose: 1.
340
    Ars Poetica: 4: 1. 371; 2. 365; 146-
152: 1. 313; 210: 2. 376; 280: 7. 390;
361: 3. 392; 7. 256; 436: 8. 388
    Epistles: 1. 1. 4-5: 6. 210; 1. 1. 12: 8.
388; 1. 1. 76: 7. 359; 1. 1. 87: 8. 492;
1. 2. 39: 8. 371; 1. 2. 60: 2. 227-8; 1. 2.
63: 2. 228; 1. 2. 143: 2. 376; 1. 3. 24:
8. 388; 1. 5. 19: 7. 394; 1. 11. 2: 1. 238;
1. 16. 13: 1. 302; 1. 17. 30: 7. 251; 1. 17.
35: 6. 272; 1. 18. 9: 2. 194; 1. 18. 71:
5. 180; 2. 1. 5-8: 5. 162; 8. 328; 2. 1.
50: 4. 180; 2. 1. 55: 4. 214; 2. 1. 72:
6. 211
    Epodes: 5. 45: 3. 225; 5. 61-6: 2. 373;
5. 65: 2. 372; 5. 99-100: 2. 293; 7. 11-
20: 8. 387-8; 11. 6: 8. 397; 15. 2: 4. 195;

16. 2: 8. 382, 386; 17. 7: 3. 222; 17. 58: 2. 293

Odes: Book 1: 1. 5: 3. 239, 265; 1. 13, 26: 1. 258; 1. 26: 6. 253; 1. 29-36: 7. 390; 8. 312; 1. 36: 1. 249; 2. 34-5: 4. 232; 8. 402; 4: 6. 253; 8. 468; 4. 5-7: 7. 316; 7. 1-14: 8. 380; 7. 23: 2. 294; 8. 8: 5. 172; 8. 9: 1. 199; 7. 251; 10. 18: 2. 370; 12. 6: 8. 498; 12. 15-6: 8. 377, 669; 12. 21: 8. 328; 12. 46: 8. 500; 12. 57-8: 6. 255; 14. 15: 7. 356; 15: 3. 209-10; 4. 246-7; 17: 6. 239; 18: 8. 375; 19. 1: 4. 232; 23: 3. 262; 8. 450; 26. 2: 1. 258; 8. 314; 28. 8: 1. 304; 30: 6. 253; 8. 468; 33: 3. 275; 34: 2. 355; 35. 21: 1. 285; Book 2: 2. 1: 1. 182; 2. 13: 1. 220; 3: 2. 270; 4. 245-6; 3. 3: 2. 241; 3. 21-3: 8. 327; 4. 245-6; 10. 10: 7. 336-7; 16. 15: 3. 287; 17. 22-3: 2. 300; 3. 297; 19. 29-33: 1. 235; Book 3: 1. 5-8: 6. 280; 8. 376; 1. 37: 3. 287; 2. 31-2: 5. 255; 3. 5: 2. 254; 3. 9-13: 5. 162; 3. 53-6: 8. 388; 4. 1: 1. 512; 4. 9: 4. 211; 4. 73-6: 5. 219-20; 5. 13: 6. 211; 6. 46-8: 5. 156-7; 7. 27-8: 5. 172; 10. 18: 1. 258; 11. 15-20: 1. 234-5; 11. 17: 1. 234; 11. 35-6: 6. 199; 16. 1-3: 3. 275; 16. 7-8: 3. 293; 16. 15: 6. 239; 18. 1: 6. 290; 21. 11-2: 6. 211, 253; 8. 468; 26. 3-4: 6. 210; 28. 10: 4. 275; 29. 22: 1. 242; 30: 7. 426; 8. 297; Book 4: 1. 10: 2. 205; 5. 241; 8. 498; 2: 1. 212; 4: 2. 347; 4. 1: 8. 385; 4. 29-32: 6. 198; 4. 61-4: 8. 385; 5. 22: 1. 183; 6. 9-10: 1. 256, 259, 275; 8-9: 8. 297, 299; 8. 9: 7. 393; 8. 28-32: 8. 298-9; 10: 8. 428; 13. 4: 3. 275; 4. 173

Satires: Book 1: 1. 7: 3. 239; 1. 106: 2. 194; 3. 78, 118: 2. 194; 8. 10: 2. 293; 10. 20-1: 4. 180; Book 2: 3. 154: 2. 269; 3. 267: 2. 200; 7. 250, 272; 3. 314: 1. 222; 5: 8. 369; 6. 66-7: 6. 233

Horatio, 4. 290

Horden, Elisa, 7. 652

Horden, Thomas, 7. 652

Horn, 1. 320; 2. 283-4, 363; is the Bible: 1. 471; of cuckoldry: 3. 286-7; of justice: 1. 257; of salvation: 1. 257, 268

Horomazes, 3. 244

Horror, 1. 254

Horsa, 2. 333

Horse, 1. 412; 2. 207, 274, 342, 414, 440; 4. 177; 5. 191; 6. 330; 8. 279, 367

" horsefoot," 8. 324

Horsemanship, 1. 176; 2. 209, 223-4; 8. 366-7

Horses, 1. 229-31, 236; 3. 203; of Night: *see* Night

Hoskins, John, 5. 236

Hotspur, 2. 230; 4. 171; 5. 301

Houghton, Arthur A., 7. 696, 708, 719; 8. 680-1, 687, 697-8, 706

Hour, 3. 239

Hours, 5. 241-2; 6. 293, 302, 308-9, 391, 404, 420; 8. 467-8, 484, 495

Hours of the Lord, 8. 270, 283

House, 2. 300, 469

House of Alma, 2. 184, 197, 278-9, 285-301, 338-40, 436-8, 442-3, 456-7, 466, 469; 3. 365; 6. 396, 398; 7. 241; 8. 475, 513

House of Ate, 4. 281; 8. 513

House of the Blessed, 1. 287

House of Busirane, 3. 287-90, 292, 300-3, 353-66, 393-4, 397-9; 5. 237

House of Care, 1. 367; 2. 287; 4. 196-8, 281, 287; 8. 388

House of Commons, 5. 322-3

House of Correction, 2. 294

House of Dis, 2. 257-8

House of Fates, 4. 281

House of Holiness, 1. 238, 281-3, 404-7, 417, 424, 430, 457, 499, 504; 2. 184, 195, 287, 410; 6. 208; 7. 241, 674; 8. 513; represents accession of Elizabeth: 1. 457; represents growth of English Church: 1. 472; resembles medieval monastery: 1. 441, 472; is restoration of Protestantism: 1. 465

House of Love, 1. 406

House of Mars, 1. 213

House of Medina, 2. 184, 198, 350, 440-1

House of Pride, 1. 238, 404-7, 410, 423, 427-8; 2. 287; 3. 365; 5. 237, 270; 8. 305, 513, 622, 625; is Renaissance Court, high society: 1. 443; is Roman Catholic Church: 1. 459; is Roman Empire: 1. 455

House of Repentance, 1. 283

House of Salvation, 1. 283

House of Sleep, 1. 189-90, 192-3, 195, 312, 421

House of Temperance: 2. 278-9, 285-301, 459, 466; 5. 237

House of Venus, 7. 506

Houses, 1. 213-4, 238, 282-3; of gods: 1. 250

Howard, Charles of Effingham, Earl of Nottingham, 1. 449; 3. 240; 4. 277; 5. 227; 7. 461, 475; 8. 532

Howard, Douglas, 7. 402-3, 430, 433-7, 441, 465, 506

Howard family, 7. 433-5

Howard, Frances, Countess of Kildare, 7. 475

Howard, Frank, 1. 452-4; 2. 401

Howard, Henry, Earl of Northampton, 6. 350; 8. 302

Howard, Henry, Earl of Surrey, 3. 216-7; 6. 234; 7. 464, 576, 578, 583, 626, 637, 640; 8. 324, 618-9; *Aeneid*: 8. 371; *Songs and Sonnets*: 2. 297; 4. 224; 7. 409

Howard, Henry, Viscount Byndon, 7. 433-5

Howard, Philip, Earl of Arundel, 5. 245, 302; 7. 675

Howard, Thomas, Duke of Norfolk, 2. 403, 408; 5. 201, 324; is Malengin: 5. 279; is the Oak: 7. 254

Howe, George, 8. 463

Howell, James, 2. 206; 4. 209

Howell, Thomas, 8. 284, 353-4

Howleglas, 7. 362, 612

Hrotswitha, 7. 564

Huarte, John, 2. 463-5

Hub, 8. 486

Hubbard, W., 7. 291, 316, 580

Hudibras, 2. 198, 202, 313, 417, 421, 426, 461; represents Puritans: 2. 198; is θυμός: 2. 198

Hudson, Henry, 2. 363

Hudson, Hoyt H., 7. 493

Huetiana, 6. 306

Hugh de Paganis, 2. 187-8

Hugh of St. Victor, 7. 674

Hughes, J., 1. 217, 228; 2. 211, 248, 256, 301, 381, 385; 6. 254, 273; 7. 241, 290, 366, 425, 453, 458, 474, 574, 600, 611, 616; 8. 303, 414, 515, 559, 569, 628, 666, 688, 721

Hugo, Victor, 8. 535

Huguenots, 1. 455; 8. 391

Hulbert, Viola, 1. 353-7; 2. 424-6; 7. 354; 8. 603

Hulme, Frederick E., 2. 362-3

Humanism, 7. 371, 376, 384, 587

Human Nature, 1. 245

Humber (chieftain), 2. 309-10, 332

Humber (river), 4. 261

Hume, David, 5. 346

Hume, Joseph, 1. 372

Humility, 1. 405, 417-8, 424; 4. 237; 6. 256, 348

Humors, 2. 475-6, 483; 7. 527; 8. 387

Humours and Conversations of the Town, 7. 478-9

Humphrey, Lawrence, 6. 337

Hunnis, William, 8. 319, 520

Huns, 2. 331-2

Hunsdon, Lord. *See* Carey, George, Henry

Hunt, 4. 202; 5. 232; 6. 425-7; 8. 326-7, 412, 443

Hunt, Leigh, 1. 189-90, 192, 194, 206-7, 288; 2. 228, 262, 265, 271, 382

Hunter, Joseph, 2. 329; 7. 439-40, 442, 468, 472, 475, 646; 8. 613

Hunterian Museum, 7. 708; 8. 680, 682

Hunting of the Fox and the Wolf, Hunting of the Romish Foxe. *See* Turner, William

Huntingdon, Earl of. *See* Hastings, Henry

Huntington Library, 1. 516-9; 5. 369; 6.458, 472; 7. 696, 708, 719, 769; 8. 681-2, 697-8, 706-7

Huon, 2. 187-8

Huon de Meery, 4. 223

Huon of Bordeaux, 1. 254, 283, 296, 298, 301, 488; 2. 188, 352-3, 355; 3. 215, 228; 4. 213; 5. 298; possible source of *F. Q.*: 1. 393, 396, 404

Hurault, Jaques, 2. 295

Hurd, Richard, 1. 324-7, 331; 4. 192; 5. 169; 6. 187

Hurstwood, 7. 250, 306, 311, 313-4, 382, 616, 631

"hurtle," 1. 216

Hussites, 5. 167

Hutton, James, 8. 456-8, 489

Hycke-Scorner, 1. 289

Hyde, Arthur, 7. 454

Hydra, 2. 359; 8. 383

Hyena, 3. 263

Hyginus, 1. 230, 236, 238, 249; 4. 244, 274; 5. 158; *Fables*: 1. 191; Preface: 2. 232-3, 365; 4. 239; 6. 213, 252; 14: 4. 245; 8. 339; 25: 2. 372; 30: 6. 270; 32: 5. 198; 38: 6. 279; 47: 1. 236; 59: 8. 339; 82-3: 2. 268; 92: 2. 266; 107: 7. 274; 109: 2. 298; 118: 3. 241; 130, 138: 3. 296; 140: 2. 357; 6. 312; 141: 2. 365; 151: 5. 250; 6. 213; 152: 6. 213; 157, 186: 4. 214; 168: 1. 235; 188: 3. 293, 296; 195: 2. 204; 202: 1. 237; 3. 295; 252: 6. 204; *Poeticon Astronomicon*: 1. 209; 2. 204; 3. 293; 4. 186; 5. 158, 164; 6. 251, 305; 8. 309, 339, 505

Hylas, 3. 301-2

"Hymen, Hymenaeus," 1. 196; 8. 461, 471, 488, 492, 652

"hymn," 7. 454, 666-7

Hymn of Love, etc. *See* Fowre Hymnes

Hyperbaton, 7. 308

Hyperbole, 6. 191; 7. 246

Hyperion, 8. 395

Hypnerotomachia, 6. 361

Hypocrisy, 1. 406

Hyssop, 8. 399

Hysteron-proteron, 8. 469, 530

Iago, 2. 319

Iambicum Trimetrum, 8. 508-10, 709-10, 723

Iamblichus, 4. 224; 5. 163

Iambulus, 2. 448

Ice, 8. 429-30, 638

Iceland, 3. 231

Iceni, 8. 288-9

Icon, 7. 246; 8. 425, 474

Iconography, 7. 564

Ida, Mount, 2. 273; 7. 336-7

Ide, 3. 215

Idea, 7. 546-7, 553-4, 654-5, 657; 8. 434-5, 453-4, 637

Identical lines or phrases, 5. 256; 7. 296, 460; 8. 321, 326, 397, 404, 433

Idleness, 1. 406, 410-3; 2. 433; 3. 355

Idolatry, 1. 240

Idyll, 6. 250, 290; 7. 267, 271-2, 280, 583-4; 8. 335, 655

Ignaro, 1. 260, 366, 460

Ignorance, 1. 260, 366; 8. 319, 322-4, 532, 535, 538, 540

Igrayne, 1. 265; 3. 227

Ile d'Or, 1. 393

Il Juditio di Paridi, 3. 285

Illuminations, 1. 413; 7. 270, 273

Il Schifanoya, 5. 238

Imagery, 1. 239, 284; 3. 238-9; 4. 172, 242; 6. 188, 204, 234-5; 7. 259, 386, 481, 537; 8. 380, 387, 396, 424-5, 428, 431, 483; auditory and visual: 3. 247; favorite: *see* Spenser, Edmund, s. v; Hebraic: 7. 477; inappropriate: 5. 209; occidental and oriental: 8. 448-9; odious: 5. 258; Platonic: 6. 258; 7. 477, 538; religious: 8. 427, 440; Scriptural: 5. 178; 6. 257-9, 314-57, 477, 538; Spenser's: 1. 175, 178, 187-8, 209, 221; 2. 244, 259; 4. 172, 242; 5. 202, 206, 209, 244, 252; 6. 188, 204, 234-5, 237, 242, 296; 7. 539; 8. 300-1, 305, 315, 499, 618. *See also,* Metaphor, Simile

Imagination, 1. 181, 190, 197, 209, 277-8; 2. 352, 463-5, 468, 481; 4. 212; 8. 404

Imago. *See* Icon.

Imitation, 7. 371, 429-33. *See also* Spenser, s. v.

Immerito, 6. 448; 7. 645, 648, 651

Immortality, 1. 208, 273, 301; 3. 259; 7. 370-1, 391, 514; 8. 294, 297-302; poetic: 8. 297-302, 307, 328, 332, 423, 429, 442, 494, 522, 524-6, 535, 537-8, 639, 661

Imogen, 1. 305, 496

Impatience, 2. 343

Imperialism, 5. 303-10, 333-5; 7. 448

Impotence, 2. 227, 343

Imrama, 2. 447-8

Imram Curaig Maelduin, 2. 373-4, 381, 383

Inachus, 4. 245

Inconsistency, 1. 297, 303; 2. 511

Incontinence, 1. 337; 2. 418, 426; 3. 319, 322-3, 325, 328-9; 5. 291

Incubatio, 5. 218

Indelicacy, 1. 221

Indians, 2. 343; 6. 202

" in evil hour," 6. 218

Infamy, 6. 222

" Infant," 2. 278; 6. 196, 232

Infernal Spirits, 1. 204-5

Influence. *See* Spenser, Edmund, Imitators

Ingleby, C. M., 8. 318

Injunctions of 1539, 1. 468

Injustice, 5. 214, 225-6, 259, 297

In medias res, 1. 334, 337, 350-1, 360; 2. 202

" inn," 6. 200

Ino, 5. 231

Inobedience, 1. 406

Inogene, 2. 308-9

Inquisition, 5. 253-4, 257

Inscriptions, 2. 376

Insects, 8. 598

" insolence," 7. 478

Inspiration, 1. 181; 7. 366-7, 369-70, 376, 389, 391, 490, 523, 588

Institucion of a Gentleman, 6. 337-8, 341

Instructions for Parish Priests, 1. 222

Intelligences, 2. 477; 7. 553-4; 8. 329, 493

Interpositio, 6. 285

Interrogatio, 6. 285; 7. 444, 504; 8. 285, 372, 644, 677

Invention, 1. 221, 248; 7. 241

Inventory, 6. 235; 7. 477; 8. 424, 474

" Io Hymen." *See* Hymen, Hymenaeus

Iole, 5. 203-4

Ireland, 1. 188, 196, 209, 244, 275, 335, 347; 2. 281-2, 284, 339, 399; 3. 278; 4. 185; 5. 209, 244, 280; 6. 189, 205, 385; 7. 360, 475; 8. 354, 543-4; in Book 5 of *F. Q.*: 5. 312-5, 331-3; 6. 363, 384, 435; in Book 7 of *F. Q.*: 6. 435, 440; cliffs: 3. 287; desolation: 1. 261-2; 5. 233; 8. 543; dogs in: 5. 232; Elizabethan view of: 5. 265, 303-5; 6. 435, 444; another epic, subject of?: 6. 205; in *Epithalamion*: 8. 648-52; in *F. Q.*: 3. 380; 4. 172, 174-5; 5. 161-2, 173, 306, 312-5, 331-3; 6. 252, 257, 282-9, 317, 363, 384, 435, 440; Harvey in?: 7. 452; " the salvage Iland ": 5. 259; in *Shepheardes Calender*: 7. 355; one of the " six islands ": 3. 231; Spenser, influence upon: 2. 349-50; 3. 262, 301; 4. 185-6, 241; 5. 255; 6. 202, 231, 233, 282-9, 424-7, 441, 444; 8. 397, 408, 463, 487; Spenser's view of: 5. 305, 315; 6. 289-91; 8. 543; wolves in: 7. 278, 462. *See also* Irish; Spenser, Edmund

Irena, 5. 161-2, 267, 269, 298, 300-2, 312, 329; 6. 189, 361
Irenaeus, 7. 559
Irenius, 5. 162
Iris, 5. 190
Irish, 2. 281-2, 284; 5. 235; administration: 8. 373; bogs: 8. 487; devotion to holiness and learning: 6. 285; family: 5. 294; foot-soldier: 5. 264; legend: 1. 293; 2. 350; 4. 268-70; 6. 424-7; 7. 455-6; outlaws: 6. 257; 7. 462, 495; poetry: 2. 367, 373-4, 381, 383; 3. 301; 6. 218; 7. 454-6; rebels: 3. 379; 5. 303, 305; Records: 8. 311; rivers: 4. 250, 264-72; 6. 424-7, 429-32. See also Ireland
Irish Ecclesiastical Record, 1. 244
"iron," 1. 262; 4. 200; 5. 165, 167, 177, 253; 6. 239, 304; 8. 314, 356, 395
Irony, 5. 196, 233; 6. 235; 8. 357, 595
Irus, 8. 327-8
Isabel, Countess Roos, 6. 263
Isabella, 1. 239; 3. 272; 4. 205; 6. 257, 371, 374
Isidore of Seville, 2. 424-5; 7. 285; 8. 421
Isis, 4. 229-31, 319; 5. 213-20, 295; 6. 294, 399; 8. 513
Isis (river), 4. 252; 7. 287; 8. 671-2
Isis Church, 3. 364; 5. 217-8, 244, 270
Islands of the Blest, 6. 202
Ismeno, 3. 226, 291
Isocrates, 8. 548
Israel, 3. 224
Isumbras, 1. 346
Italian, allegory: 1. 333, 335-7, 345, 366; critics: 1. 348-51; 7. 626; influence on Spenser: 7. 615-7, 621; 8. 402; language: 8. 365; luxury: 2. 381; manners: 3. 212; painting: 3. 392-4; poetry: 1. 209, 316, 325, 331; 2. 215, 384; 3. 239, 393; 4. 202; 6. 234; 8. 391; romances: 1. 509-10; 3. 272, 291, 332, 367-76; 5. 258; 348-9; romantic epic: 1. 330-1; Spenser's knowledge of: 8. 274-7, 614, 622
Italy, 1. 359; 6. 314; 7. 615
Itys, 8. 343
Ivory, 6. 233; 8. 449
Ivory gate, 2. 371-3
Ivy, 1. 242, 363; 2. 193-4, 382-3; 6. 304; 7. 271, 273, 344, 390; 8. 339-40, 348
Ixeutas, 7. 267, 272
Ixion, 6. 280

Jackson, William A., 8. 626-7, 735
Jacob, 1. 291; 7. 332; staff: 7. 438
Jacobs, Joseph, 8. 610
Jael, 3. 238
James I of England, 1. 263, 492; 2. 402; 3. 259; 5. 244, 246, 321; 7. 636; 8. 502, 618; is Alcon: 7. 469; is the Ape: 8. 578-9; is the kid: 7. 304; is Ruddymane: 2. 402; is the spider: 8. 605; Essayes of a Prentise: 8. 643
James I of Scotland, The Kingis Quair: 2, 262, 392; 4. 229; 7. 427; 8. 466
James IV of Scotland, 1. 486; 2. 338; 4. 164
James V of Scotland, 2. 338; 3. 397
James, St., 1. 247
Jamyn, Amadis, 8. 486
"jane," 3. 267
Jansenism, 1. 448
January, 7. 242-4
Janus Vitalis, 8. 381
Jaques, 2. 202; 7. 488
Jar, 1. 230; 2. 231-2
Jason, 2. 346, 351, 371-4; 4. 223; 8. 383, 472
Javellus, Chrysostomus, 1. 355
Jealousy, 1. 220, 239; 2. 257; 3. 272-3, 286-8, 301, 314, 372; 4. 196, 201, 234, 295, 305; 5. 207, 349; 6. 269, 333; 7. 519-20; a theme of F. Q.: 5. 208
Jean de Meun, 6. 428; 8. 492
Jeanroy, Alfred, 8. 466
Jehan Le Bel, 1. 354
Jenynges, Edward, 4. 224
Jerome, St., 1. 256; 8. 469
Jerram, C. S., 7. 242
Jerusalem. See New Jerusalem
Jesuits, 1. 448; 7. 353, 360
Jesus Christ, 1. 293, 295, 301, 303, 308-10, 347, 351, 363, 400-1, 477; 2. 325-7, 339, 348, 429-30, 435; 7. 332, 357, 537, 539-40, 546-7, 558-64, 666-7, 672-3; 8. 279, 357-8, 444; the Logos: 7. 558, 668; is Pan: 7. 281, 299; Passion: 7. 544; Temptation: 2. 271, 429; Transfiguration: 6. 412, 428; Victory: 1. 390; is Wisdom: 7. 561-4, 566, 668
Jeu de Saint Nicolas, 6. 227
The Jew and Ptolome, 8. 440
Jewel, John, 1. 470; 6. 210
Jewels, 8. 424
Joannes Cesarius Juliacensis, 1. 355
Jocante, 3. 211
Jocularity, 1. 328-9, 342
Jodelle, Etienne, 8. 624
Johannes Secundus, 2. 261
John the Baptist, St., 1. 401
John of Damascus, 1. 240
John the Evangelist, St., 1. 291, 370; 7. 672; 8. 279-80
John, L. C., 7. 494; 8. 423, 456
John Rylands Library, 7. 708; 8. 682, 697-8
John of Salisbury, 1. 513

John of Whethamstede, 1. 483
Johnson, F. R., 8. 679-80, 685-6, 706, 707
Johnson, Samuel, 2. 203, 511; 4. 353; 6. 213-4; 7. 242, 470, 488, 490, 575, 615, 617, 627, 693; 8. 369, 478, 508, 655
Johnson, William, 8. 319-20
Joinville, Jean de, 4. 294
Jones, Inigo, 2. 256
Jones, Sir William, 7. 576; 8. 507
Jones, William (translator), 8. 507, 708, 736
Jonson, Benjamin, 2. 264; 3. 355; 6. 277; 7. 320, 324, 371, 406, 615-7, 619-20, 682; 8. 525, 658-9, 669; *Conversations with Drummond*: 1. 481-2, 492; 5. 325; 6. 359, 364, 382, 386; *Elegy on the Lady Anne Pawlet*: 7. 540; *Epithalamion*: 8. 464, 472-3, 658-9; *Epode*: 6. 277; *Horace, Odes*: 7. 479; *Hue and Cry after Cupid*: 3. 252; 8. 488; *Hymenaei*: 8. 482; *Hymn to Diana*: 1. 174; *Masque of Hymen*: 6. 277; 8. 462-3, 467, 484-5, 487-8, 490-2; *Masque of Queens*: 3. 222; *Prince Henries Barriers*: 7. 285; *Sad Shepherd*: 7. 318; 8. 426, 505, 508, 709, 736; *Silent Woman*: 1. 198; *Tale of a Tub*: 5. 241; *Timber*: 6. 359; 7. 572-3, 575-6, 615-6, 619-20; *To the Memory of Shakespeare*: 7. 473; 8. 320; *Volpone*: 5. 193
Jordan, 1. 302
Jordanes, 5. 225
Joseph of Arimathea, 1. 176, 399; 2. 326
Joseph of Exeter, 2. 218
Josephus, Flavius, 1. 214; 2. 248
Joseus, 1. 401
Josian, 1. 207, 398
Jove, 1. 242, 265, 296, 304, 363; 2. 266; 3. 292-4; 6. 253, 278-82, 293, 303, 308, 311-2, 391-2, 411, 415; 7. 319; 8. 323, 376, 400, 407, 411, 468, 569; is Day: 8. 484; fame and immortality, giver of: 8. 298; Jupiter Stygius: 2. 254; loves: 3. 393-4, 397; 8. 400, 597. *See* Garden of Jove; Zeus
Joy, 4. 232; 8. 600
" joyance," 8. 478
Joyce, P. W., 4. 264-71; 6. 282-4, 286-9, 424
Judson, A. C., 6. 284, 289, 340-5; 7. 362, 404; 8. 419
Julian, Emperor, 2. 365
Juliet, 3. 219
Julius Caesar, 1. 292-3, 444; 2. 324; 5. 191, 263; 6. 293; 8. 328, 372, 386-7, 391
July, 6. 409; 8. 350
June, 8. 479
Junius, Francis, 6. 265; 7. 238

Juno, 2. 193, 266; 3. 282, 397; 6. 301; 8. 488, 490
Jupiter. *See* Jove
Jusserand, J. J., 1. 327-9; 7. 248, 293, 581, 650; 8. 275-6
Justice, 1. 257, 285, 328-9, 339, 342, 416; 2. 195; 3. 370; 5. 214, 227; 6. 379, 442; 7. 553; 8. 350; in Aristotle: 5. 272, 281-2, 287-90; not Aristotelian: 5. 285; is Astraea: 5. 163-4; classical: 1. 345; 5. 216-7; corrective: 5. 285, 288, 294-5, 345-6; Court of: 5. 243; Dame Justice: 6. 293; decay: 5. 155; defined: 5. 214; distributive: 5. 175-81, 285, 288, 294-5, 345-6; In *F. Q.* 5: 5. 269-98, 348-9; is Lord Grey: 5. 303; and mercy: 5. 247-8, 295-6; 6. 192, 345; is Nature: 6. 413; phases: 5. 282; and pity: 5. 247, 293; 6. 345; in Plato: 5. 287-8, 290-2; political: 5. 271-2, 285, 331, 336-47; Spenser's analyzed: 5. 284-5; and the stars: 5. 178, not universal: 5. 272, 284
Justin, Marcus Junianus, 2. 248; 6. 204
Justinian, 8. 352
Juvenal, 1. 357; 7. 373, 390; 8. 564; 1. 74: 7. 381; 3. 280: 4. 197; 6. 19: 5. 164; 6. 533: 5. 217; 7. 30-2: 7. 382; 7. 59-61: 7. 389; 7. 94: 7. 385; 8: 8. 313; 8. 88: 2. 228; 10. 2-5, 346-353: 6. 240; 12. 27: 3. 239
Juventus, 8. 492
Jynx, 2. 295-6

Kahun, H. A., 8. 492
Kalander, 3. 393
Kalendar of Shepherds, 1. 415; 7. 240-1, 581
Kalendrier des Bergiers, 7. 581-2, 594, 633-4
Kastner, L. E., 8. 436, 450, 640
Kearney, C. F., 8. 462
Keats, John, 2. 372; 6. 290, 314, 429; 8. 396, 445, 623, 645, 659, 674; Spenser's influence on: 2. 352, 360; 3. 248; 7. 657; 8. 293, 297, 400, 473, 475; " Bards of Passion ": 8. 297; *Endymion*: 3. 248; 7. 519, 657; 8. 460, 466-7; *Epistle to C. C. Clarke*: 8. 475; *Isabella*: 3. 219; *Ode to a Grecian Urn*: 7. 343, 368; *Ode to a Nightingale*: 8. 323
Keble, John, 2. 270
Keightley, Thomas, 7. 361, 436, 456, 482, 611, 654; 8. 373, 414, 569, 633
Keimaneigh, 6. 190
Kelton, Arthur, 1. 483-4; 2. 452
Kendall, Timothy, 8. 456
Kenilworth, 5. 199; 7. 284-5, 289; 8. 304
Kenmare, 4. 270
Kennet, 4. 254

Kent. 7. 312-3, 315, 322, 328, 336, 396, 402-3, 620, 651-2
Kent, William, 1. 212
Kenton, Edward, 8. 627
Kepler, Johann, 5. 159
Ker, W. P., 1. 391
Keraber, 6. 282
Kerke. *See* Kirke
Kerlin, R. T., 7. 499
Kerns, 1. 275; 5. 233
Kett, Robert, 5. 175-6, 342, 344
Kew, 8. 671
Keymis, Lawrence, 4. 249
Kid, 7. 293-4
Kilbeg, 4. 270
Kilbeheny, 6. 287
Kilcolman, 2. 282, 290, 399; 3. 239; 4. 174; 6. 210, 252, 257, 284-5, 299, 315, 425, 429, 441-2; 7. 451, 453-4, 458-9, 475, 495; 8. 440, 464-5, 487, 633, 636, 646-7, 650, 663
Kilcoran. 8. 648-50
Kilcredan, 8. 651
Kilhwch and Olwen, 4. 204
Killing of defeated adversary, 1. 211; 5. 201; 6. 218
Kilnemulla, 4. 271; 7. 451, 456
Kimarus, 2. 321
Kimbeline, 2. 324-5
Kinahan, G. H., 8. 480
King Arthur, poem projected by Spenser, 1. 323
King, Edward, 7. 646
Kingdom of Heaven, 1. 289
King Edward IV, Part 1, 2. 285
The Kingis Quair. See James I, of Scotland
Kings, English: 1. 211; Gothic: 1. 199; Saxon: 1. 442, 453
" kings and kesars," 5. 241
Kirbye, George, 7. 406
Kirke, Edward, 7. 236, 374-5, 415-6, 645-50
Kirke, Mistress, 7. 645, 649
Kirkrapine, 1. 414, 458, 461, 465, 467; 6. 265-6
Kirtle, 1. 411
Kirtling, 7. 312, 653
Kiffen, Maurice, 8. 508
Kisses, 8. 441
Kite, 1. 412-3
Kitson, Katherine, 8. 417
Kitson, Thomas, 7. 650
Kittredge, G. L., 8. 486
Kluge, F., 7. 326, 329-33, 337, 379, 385, 387, 393, 589
Knack to Know an Honest Man, 4. 211; 7. 481
Knife, 3. 241

Knight, Charles, 8. 316-7, 498
Knight Errantry, 2. 335
Knights, 2. 335; Chaucer's: 2. 274; of the Garter; *see* Garter; of Maidenhead: 2. 280; 3. 380, 390; 4. 189-90, 199-200; 5. 197; 6. 385; of the Round Table: *see* Round Table; Spenser's: 3. 383; of St. John: 8. 502; Templar: 8. 502; violation of code: 6. 217
Knockainey, 6. 426
Knocknadarriff, 6. 287-8
Knollys, Francis, 5. 182
Knollys, Letitia, 2. 403; 7. 402-3; 8. 394, 567-8, 606-7
Knowlton, E. C., 2. 375; 6. 422
Knox, John, 1. 470; 2. 402, 408; 3. 337; 5. 198, 278, 297; 7. 261, 326
Koellin, Conrad, 1. 355
Koller, Kathrine, 4. 206-7, 249; 7. 449, 451, 458, 474
Konrad von Wuerzberg, 2. 355
Koran, 3. 250
Kuersteiner, A. D., 7. 647
Kyd, Thomas, 8. 539
Kyffin, Maurice, 1. 266, 484; 5. 245

La Belle Dame sans Merci. See Chaucer (pseudo)
La Bel Pucell, 1. 415-6
La Beste Glatissant. *See* Glatissant Beast
Labor, 8. 565, 579
Labyrinth, 4. 222-3
" lace," 7. 285
Lacey, T. A., 8. 510
Lachesis, 7. 416, 512
Lactantius, Caelius Firmianus, 7. 514; 8. 329; *De Falsa Religione*: 7. 290; scholia on the *Thebaid of Statius*: 1. 191; 3. 294; 8. 396-7, 484; *De Phoenice*: 2. 257; *Divine Institutes*: 2. 375; 5. 164; 7. 273
La Dame du Lac, 2. 445
Ladder. *See* Platonic Ascent
" Ladies of the Lake," 7. 276, 280, 284-5
Lady Carey. *See* Spencer, Elizabeth
Lady Loyalté, 5. 240
Lady Meed, 5. 172-3, 294
Laelius, 4. 223, 316
Laestrigones, 5. 169
Laiazzo, 5. 349
La Mausolee, ou Les Tombeaux des Chevaliers . . . de la Toison d'Or, 1. 294
Lamb, 1. 389-90, 496-8; 7. 304, 343-4, 350, 362, 557; 8. 280; symbol of purity and innocence: 1. 433
Lamb, Charles, 2. 249, 389; 8. 502
Lambard, William, 1. 483; 7. 322, 328, 336
Lambers, Sir, 1. 391

Lambert, John, 1. 469
Lamentation of Marie Magdaleine. See Chaucer (pseudo).
Lamentation of Troy for the Death of Hector, 3. 271
Lamorack, 6. 271
Lamps, 6. 237
Lancashire, 7. 312-5, 387, 422, 616, 620, 653; 8. 501
Lancaster, James, 5. 248
Lancaster and York, 7. 282-3
Lancelot, 1. 347, 391, 488-9; 2. 445; 4. 223; 5. 168, 169, 203, 205, 211; 6. 365-6
Lancelot (Vulgate), 3. 361-2, 365
Land of Cockayne, 21448
Landi, Giulio, 1. 187, 355
Landini, Cristoforo, 1. 357-8, 493, 513; 2. 218; 3. 245
Landscape, 1. 194; 2. 366, 379, 382; 3. 259; 7. 630-1; 8. 596-7
Lane, John, 4. 177-8; 5. 325
Laneham, Robert, 2. 188; 7. 289
Langdon, I., 7. 369, 377, 380-2, 387-9, 455; 8. 425
Langham, William, 1. 205
Langland, William, 7. 620; 8. 486, 564-5; *Piers Plowman:* 1. 407, 415; 5. 345; 7. 237, 293, 295, 321, 427-8, 577, 615, 681; 8. 562, 567, 591, 595; A text, Passus 10. 1 ff.: 2. 286, 456; B text, Passus 2-4: 5. 172, 294; Passus 5: 1. 410; 5. 78-80: 1. 222; 5. 188-91: 1. 220-1; 5. 134: 1. 223; 6. 124-6: 8. 356; 12. 22: 7. 321; 20. 271-6: 8. 352; C text, Passus 8. 161-9: 1. 189; 11. 127-41: 2. 286, 456; 18. 126-7: 8. 463; 20. 291: 1. 272; 23. 100-1: 5. 241
Language. See Coined Words; Compound Words; Diction; *Faerie Queene,* language; Spenser, language, style.
Languet, Hubert, 6. 354, 356
La Nocle, Veauvoir, 5. 326
Lanquet, Thomas, 2. 324
Lansack, 5. 186
Laomedon, 2. 342
Lapithae, 4. 168-9; 6. 251
La Primaudaye, Pierre de, 2. 426, 463; 3. 249
"lapt in lead," 7. 385
Lapwing, 8. 343
Larivey, 1. 354
Larrabee, S. A., 7. 379
Latham, George, 8. 686
Latham, M. W., 8. 312
Latimer, Hugh, 1. 486; 5. 345; 7. 306; 8. 591
Latin Anthology, 4. 182; 7. 288, 440; 8. 312
Latin element, 1. 198-9, 232, 233, 421; 3.

209, 266; 4. 214; 6. 280; 7. 264, 469, 617, 626; 8. 293, 377, 386, 397, 487. *See also* Spenser, Edmund, style
Latmos, 8. 490
Latona, 3. 253
Lattice, 3. 302
Lauchert, Friedrich, 1. 208
Laughter, 1. 245; 3. 267; 4. 195, 207; 5. 235; 6. 290; 8. 317
Laura, 7. 393, 654; 8. 274, 392, 415
Laurel, 7. 393, 419
Lavardin, Jaques de, 8. 507, 708, 736
Lavater, Ludwig, 7. 307
Law, 1. 218; English: 5. 195; 6. 224; and equity: 5. 195, 295; of Love: 6. 292-3; Roman: 5. 194-5; Scottish: 5. 195
Law of Arms, 1. 225; 5. 203
Laws of King Alfred, 1. 240
Layamon, 1. 352; 2. 302, 318; 3. 233; 6. 366
Lay of Aristotle, 4. 277
Lea, 4. 264; 5. 173; 8. 308, 498, 500, 670
Leader, J. D., 5. 320
Leander, 4. 237; 7. 519
Lear, King, 1. 496; 2. 315-8, 396; 3. 238
Learned tradition, 7. 346
Learning, 8. 313, 535; and poetry: 8. 313, 332, 535; Renaissance: 1. 362
Le Bel Inconnu, 1. 394
Lechery, 1. 406, 410-3, 416, 418; 6. 307
Le Chevalier aux Armes Dorée, 6. 188, 236, 269, 382
Leda, 3. 397-8; 6. 303-4; 8. 498, 667
"ledden," 7. 479
Le Duchet (Le Duchat, Jacob?), 5. 234
"Lee," 4. 264; 5. 173; 8. 308, 498, 500, 669-70
Lee (rivers), 4. 254, 270-2; 5. 173; 8. 664, 667-70
Lee, R. W., 7. 509, 512, 515-6, 525-6, 529, 531, 535, 670, 678
Lee, Sir Sidney, 5. 346-7; 7. 483, 647; 8. 299, 318, 424-5, 432, 436, 438, 441, 443, 451, 456, 495, 637-9, 643
Lefevre, 1. 355
Le Franc, A., 7. 472-3; 8. 319
Legendes, 2. 303, 397, 399; 3. 299-300; 7. 241; 8. 513
Legh, Gerard, 5. 203
Leible, A. B., 8. 590-2
Leibnitz, Gottfried Wilhelm, 6. 390
Leicester, Earl of. See Dudley, Robert; *also* Leycester
Leicester House. See Essex House.
Leighton, Sir William, 8. 520
Leill, 2. 313
Leland, John, 1. 483-4, 486, 488; 3. 236;

7. 468; 8. 670-3; *Assertio*: 3. 235; *Collectanea*: 1. 390; 5. 182; 7. 604; *Cygnea Cantio*: 8. 290, 499-500, 502, 667, 671; *Itinerary*: 4. 256; 8. 515, 667
Lemaire, Jean de Belges, 6. 274
Lent, 8. 427
Leo (sign of Zodiac), 6. 305; 8. 350
Leo X, 6. 269, 384
Leone Hebreo, 7. 662, 670
Leopard, 2. 341; 8. 287
Lepanto of James the Sixth, 1. 231-2
Le Parlement d'Amour, 5. 243
Le Roy, Louis, 8. 529
Leslie, George, 6. 364
Leslie, John, Bishop of Ross, 5. 320, 322
Lessabeus, Jacob, 2. 312
Le Temple de Cupido, 3. 211
Lethe, 7. 269; 8. 301
Letter of the Authors, 1. 251, 264-5, 294-6, 312-3, 320-1, 324-5, 327, 329-30, 334, 337-8, 340, 342-5, 349, 351, 353-4, 360, 388-9, 392, 418, 433, 449-50, 466, 492, 510; 2. 197, 409-10; 3. 201, 227, 246, 321, 367; 5. 197, 243, 283, 287, 310-1; 6. 434; 7. 380, 458; 8. 364, 503, 526, 598; abandoned in *F. Q.* 4: 4. 289; second letter to Raleigh: 1. 481
Letters to Harvey from Spenser (references are to pages of vol. 9, *The Prose Works*, of the *Variorum*): 8. 622; 5: 7. 605, 613; 8. 544, 572-3, 575; 6-7: 7. 487, 612, 645; 6: 7. 648; 8. 270, 283, 514; 7-8: 8. 509; 7: 7. 296; 8-12: 7. 362, 648; 9: 8. 537, 650; 12: 4. 289; 7. 487, 610, 645; 8. 502, 571; 16: 4. 351; 7. 487, 647; 8. 509; 17: 1. 329, 332; 2. 398; 4. 242; 6. 439; 7. 651, 655; 8. 270, 292, 436, 511, 515, 670; 18: 7. 384, 416, 646, 648; 8. 270, 414, 516, 522, 527. *See also Two Other . . . Letters*
Lettice, 7. 269
Lettuce, 8. 399
Leucippe, 6. 233-4
Lever, Thomas, 8. 591
Leveson, Dora (Dorothy). 6. 221; 7. 654
Leviathan, 8. 407
" levin," 7. 346
Levinson, Ronald, 3. 343; 6. 400
Lewicke, Edward, 4. 224-5
Lewis, C. S., 2. 282-3, 346; 6. 208-9, 233, 250, 274, 281, 346-8, 427
Lewkenor, Lewis, 8. 505, 507-8, 709, 736
Leycester Correspondence, 5. 251
Leycester's Commonwealth, 5. 320; 6. 383, 7. 402
Leycester's Ghost, 8. 294
L'Homme Juste et L'Homme Mondain, 2. 433

L'homme sensuel moyen, 1. 245
L'Hospital d'Amours, 1. 405-7; 3. 211; 4. 221, 229-30, 237; 6. 221-2
Lhuyd, 1. 482-3
Liagore, 3. 242
Libation, 1. 209
Libeaus Desconus, 1. 201, 290, 293, 391-5
Libel, 6. 383-6
Liber Festivalis, 3. 250
Liberality, 1. 328-9, 341
Libraries, 6. 267-8
Library of Congress, 6. 458; 7. 708
Licentiousness, 3. 319-20
Lidia, 6. 221, 224
Liesse, 4. 237
Life, 3. 254-61; 6. 302, 420; 8. 315. *See also* Tree of Life
Life after death. *See* Immortality
Life and Death, 1. 407
Life and Death of Thomas Lord Cromwell, 1. 468
Liffar, 4. 267
Liffey, 4. 264-5, 267
Light, 2. 234; 6. 450-1; 7. 263; divine: 7. 557-8
" lightfoot," 8. 312
Lightning, 4. 184, 200; 6. 217
Ligridonia, 1. 248
" like," 7. 360
Lilius Giraldus, 8. 324, 329-30
Liljegren, S. B., 6. 400
Lilly, Josiah K., 8. 706
Lily, 5. 189; 7. 506
" lily-handed," 3. 242; 6. 305
Limbs, 6. 290
Limerick, 4. 186, 268; 6. 286-7
Linacre, Thomas, 1. 486
Lincoln, 4. 263-4; 6. 193
Lincoln green, 6. 193
Lindsay, Sir David, 1. 310; 2. 206, 273; 3. 204, 207, 262, 276; 7. 236; 8. 591, 594
Lindus, 4. 263-4
Linen, 4. 229-30
Lingua, 2. 248, 290-1, 299, 300, 339-40, 387
Linley, Paul, 8. 507, 736
Linocier, Geoffrey, 1. 514-5; 7. 415; 8. 313, 326, 329
Linus, 7. 429; 8. 297
Lion, 1. 206-8, 303, 396-8, 400, 412, 497, 499, 501; 2. 235-6, 341; 3. 358; 5. 228, 242, 299; 6. 214, 305, 381, 398; 8. 363, 371, 377, 408, 562, 567, 573, 586, 589-92; is Assyria: 8. 287; is common people: 1. 458; is Counts of Toulouse: 1. 449, 455; is Elizabeth: 8. 363, 573; is England: 8. 579; English: 1. 483; 5. 242; is Henry VIII: 1. 461, 465, 467; 6. 265-6; is in-

adequate holiness: 1. 431; is Law of
Nature: 1. 436; is Leicester: 5. 242; 8.
567, 571; is Netherlands: 1. 453; is simple
children of the Faith: 1. 436; is Thomas
Cromwell: 1. 467; is Violence: 1. 422
Liones, Dame, 1. 392
Lippo Lippi, 1. 305-6; 7. 267
Lipsius, Justus, 2. 341; 6. 401, 423
Liptote, 7. 444
Lisle, William, 3. 305; 8. 545. *See also*
W. L.
Lismore Papers, 8. 450
Litae, 5. 241-2
Literary conditions, 8. 531-41
Litigium, 2. 232; 4. 169
Littledale, H., 6. 352; 8. 512
Liturgies of King Edward VI, 5. 341
" live . . . die." *See* " dead . . . living."
Living water, 1. 205
Livre d'Arthur, 6. 366
Livy, 7. 426; 8. 409
Llewelyn ap Gryffydh, 3. 236
Lloyd, David, 5. 246, 301-2
Lloyd, Hugh, 7. 362-3, 612
Llwyd, Humphrey, 1. 266; 2. 323, 453; 3.
226, 232-3, 235. *See also* Price, Sir John;
Wynne, W.
Lobbin, 7. 395-6, 402-3, 479; 8. 318, 320
Loch Bel Draccon, 6. 426
Loch Gile, 7. 456
Loch Léin, 2. 350; 6. 425
Loch Meilge, 6. 426-7
Locrine, 2. 317, 396
Locrine, 2. 308; 8. 287, 315, 384, 406
Lodge, Thomas, 6. 376; 7. 468-9, 675; 8.
540; *A Fig for Momus:* 7. 468, 473;
Phillis: 5. 189; 7. 468; 8. 464; *Proso-
popeia:* 7. 675; *Rosalynde:* 7. 253, 594;
8. 318, 474; *Scilla's Metamorphosis:* 8.
495; *Wits Miserie:* 8. 320
Loegria, 2. 309
Logistilla, 1. 257, 268, 282; 2. 439-42
Logos, 7. 559, 563, 566
Logris, 2. 309; 4. 261
Lois of Savoy, 7. 398, 400-1, 410
Lok, Henry, 3. 306-9; 8. 519
London, 1. 256, 291; 2. 323, 335; 4. 253; 7.
451; 8. 288, 495, 500-2, 662-9, 673
Lone (river), 4. 263
Long, John, 4. 292-3
Long, P. W., 3. 309, 378-9; 7. 261, 263,
278, 296, 315, 336, 436, 451, 501, 522,
608, 620, 653, 655, 659; 8. 357, 443, 535,
576, 600, 634, 715
Longinus, 1. 184, 257; *On the Sublime:*
1. 229, 288; 2. 195-6, 274, 290; 4. 176

Longus, 6. 242, 262, 264, 371-2, 374, 376-9,
381; 7. 590
Longworth, Clara, Comtesse de Chambrun,
7. 652
Looney, J. T., 8. 319
Lord of the Isles, 6. 353
Lord President of the Council, 1. 214
" Lordings," 3. 274-5
Lord's Supper. *See* Communion
" lorel," 7. 330
Lorenzo the Magnificent, 6. 430-1; 7. 454
Lorraine, Cardinal of, 5. 211
Lostwithiel, 7. 451, 458
Lost Works by Spenser, 2. 397; 7. 241, 520,
538, 613; 8. 270, 283, 510-20, 527; dates:
8. 511
Lounsbury, T. R., 4. 178; 8. 593
louver, 6. 257
Love, 1. 407; 2. 213-4; 3. 238, 288, 311,
342, 385; and absence: 8. 453-4; an
affinity: 7. 512-3, 532-3, 542-3; allegory
of: 1. 405-6; 3. 261, 371-6, 391; 7. 368;
and Beauty: 4. 306-7; 7. 514-5, 539, 549-
50, 662-76; 8. 422; birth of: 7. 511-2;
bowers: 7. 510; chain of: 7. 537; code:
6. 231-2; complaint: 7. 424, 593-4; and
concord: 7. 512-3; contraries, described by:
4. 217; 6. 333; cosmic: 4. 226, 234, 324;
Courtly: 1. 378; 4. 163, 201-2, 214, 220-
3, 225, 228-33; 5. 206-7, 210, 213-4; 6.
221-4, 231-2, 255-6, 378; 7. 319-20, 480,
493, 652, 654-5; 8. 367, 393; the Creator:
7. 481, 517; and Cupid: 7. 509; dying
of: 1. 267; earthly: 2. 429, 431; 3. 223,
371; 4. 235; 7. 661-76; and friendship:
3. 317-8; 4. 163, 181; god of: 1. 407;
4. 203; heavenly: 2. 429, 431; 3. 223,
371; 7. 388, 547, 661-76; idealizes: 7.
518, 533-4; joys: 7. 521-2; king of: 1.
416; Lord and preserver: 7. 515; a madness: 7. 510, 523; melancholy: 5. 224;
pains and sufferings: 7. 516, 519-20, 522;
Paradise of: 2. 381; 4. 222; 7. 521-2; 8.
450; Platonic: 7. 368, 371-2, 493, 654-5;
8. 422; power of: 4. 223; prison: 8. 451;
and religion: 4. 427; religion of: 1. 378;
romantic: 7. 659; siege: 8. 424; Sir Love:
1. 407; slavery: 8. 442; Spenser's theory
of: 2. 294-5; 4. 306-7; 6. 332-3; 7. 662-
76; spiritualized: 8. 442; triumph of: 3.
301, 354, 359, 398; 7. 510; two kinds:
7. 517, 531-2; a warfare: 8. 423, 438.
See also Castle, House of Love
Low Countries. *See* Netherlands
Lowder, 7. 361-3, 612
Lowell, James Russell, 1. 197, 224, 263; 2.
203, 220, 286, 367; 4. 163; 5. 176; 6.

250; 7. 376, 381, 383, 385, 479, 578-9, 601, 615, 682; 8. 369, 439, 596, 645

Lowery, M. R., 8. 335, 443, 459, 469, 471, 481, 659

Lowes, J. L., 1. 407-13; 2. 286

Lownes, Humphrey, 8. 686

Lownes, Matthew, 7. 707; 8. 663; 685-6

Loyalty, 4. 237

Loys le Roy, 7. 523, 662, 670

Lucan, Marcus Annaeus, 3. 294; 8. 484; *Pharsalia*: 7. 434-5; Book 1: 1-3: 8. 388, 391; 28-32: 8. 390; 72-80: 8. 387; 92-3: 8. 372; 136-43: 8. 389; 185-92: 8. 529; 528: 3. 205; 651: 2. 300; Book 3: 175: 1. 302; 440-3: 1. 179; Book 4: 237-42: 4. 215; 377: 2. 255; 519: 7. 413; 593 ff.: 2. 347; 615 ff.: 2. 347; Book 6: 286-7: 5. 264; 499-504: 3. 226; 674: 8. 408; 744-9: 1. 191; Book 7: 125-7: 5. 264; Book 9: 303: 2. 198; 365-7: 8. 449; 836: 2. 204

Luce, Alice, 8. 283-4

Lucian, 1. 236; 6. 282; 7. 252, 514; *The Cock*: 4. 196; *The Dead Come to Life*: 5. 166; *Dialogue of the Sea Gods*: 3. 271; *Dialogues of the Dead*: 2. 370; *Dialogues of the Gods*: 3. 293; 7. 394; *The Fly*: 8. 397; *Philopseudes*: 1. 208; *Timon*: 2. 253-4; *True History*: 2. 357, 381, 385, 392, 435, 447, 449

Lucifer, 1. 292; 2. 247; 3. 360; 8. 565

Lucifera, 1. 405, 427, 443; 2. 371; 4. 167; is Mary Tudor: 1. 460-1; is material pride: 1. 432, 436; is the Scarlet Woman: 1. 459. *See also* Pride

Lucina, 2. 193; 8. 488, 490

Lucius, 2. 326, 330-1

Lucretius, 1. 186, 361; 3. 256, 340, 342-3, 347, 385; 6. 282, 311, 389, 393-6, 398, 401-4, 406-10, 413-5, 423, 449; 7. 240, 573, 669-70; 8. 387, 449; *De Rerum Natura*: Book 1: 1 ff.: 4. 233-6, 307-9, 312-3; 6. 413; 7. 523, 549; 8. 421; 7: 3. 201; 8: 6. 296; 35: 2. 383; 36: 3. 279; 73: 3. 255; 101: 6. 235; 117-8: 4. 180; 169-71, 205-7: 3. 254, 342; 188-91: 3. 340-1; 227-8: 3. 342; 251: 1. 178; 313: 8. 426; 403: 2. 186; 767-8: 3. 341; 792-3: 3. 342; 925-6: 6. 185; 958-1037: 3. 341-2; 1020 ff.: 6. 402; Book 2: 355-60: 4. 277-8; 419: 3. 279; 600-60: 4. 254; 609: 4. 253; 618-9: 1. 242; 1002-3, 1077-92: 3. 341; 1132: 3. 342; 1173-4: 8. 387; Book 3: 3-4: 4. 180; 7. 240; 18: 2. 377; 455-6: 4. 184; 946: 1. 280; Book 4: 181-2: 8. 486; 1055-6: 2. 243; 1059: 3. 218; Book 5: 2: 8. 388; 28: 5. 249; 119: 3.

255; 179-94, 418 ff.: 6. 402; 222-7: 8. 315; 234-5: 2. 245; 6. 394; 260: 8. 285; 509 ff.: 6. 394, 414; 655: 1. 304; 662: 3. 283; 737-47: 6. 302, 394; 783 ff.: 3. 341; 828-35: 4. 311; 6. 395, 414; 925-1104: 8. 352; 1019-26: 4. 312; 1183 ff.: 6. 395; Book 6: 94: 1. 512; 909: 2. 354

Lud, 2. 314, 323, 335

Ludlow Castle, 8. 310

Luis de Granada, 7. 675

Luna, 6. 275, 277

Lundy, 7. 462

"lurden," 7. 336

Lusignan, Count of, 1. 205

Lust, 2. 421; 3. 244-5, 266, 311, 319, 325-6, 373, 390; 4. 203-4, 206-8, 281, 295

Lustie huffe-cap, 8. 486

Luther, Martin, 1. 448, 456; 5. 343; 6. 269, 423

Lydgate, John, 1. 417; 2. 433; 3. 394; 7. 237, 281, 681; Spenser's knowledge of: 1. 388-9; 7. 615-6, 620, 626; *Ballad of Our Lady*: 6. 265; *The Churle and the Byrde*: 2. 240; *Court of Sapience*: 1. 415; *Defence of Peace*: 7. 235; *Devotions of the Foules*: 8. 466; *Falls of Princes*: 1. 237, 352; 3. 207; 7. 236, 427; *Life and Death of Hector*: 7. 264; *Life of Our Lady*: 7. 235; *Life of St. George*: 1. 386-9; *Proverbes*: 7. 235; *Reson and Sensuallyte*: 1. 417; 4. 220, 232; 6. 222, 410; 8. 492; *Serpent of Division*: 8. 528; *Story of Thebes*: 3. 276; *Temple of Glas*: 1. 415; 3. 208, 216, 292; 4. 177, 238; 7. 427; *Troybook*: 1. 175; 2. 219; 7. 235, 266, 281-2, 341, 427

Lyly, John, 1. 228; 8. 316-8, 405, 437, 517, 535-6; *Endymion*: 4. 328; *Euphues*: 1. 340; 2. 409; 4. 223, 291; 6. 292; 7. 467, 645; 8. 318, 320, 437, 477, 518, 534; *Galathea*: 3. 355; *Midas*: 1. 215; 8. 607; *Sappho and Phaon*: 8. 320; *Woman in the Moone*: 4. 324

Lyly, N. W., 7. 708

Lynde, John, 7. 652

Lynde, Rosa, 7. 652

Lyon, William, 8. 648-50

Lyonesse, 6. 194-5

Lyons, J. M., 8. 599, 601

Lyra, 8. 308-9

Lysippus, 8. 300, 390

Lyte, Henry, 3. 339; 7. 287; 8. 398

Lyte, Henry F., 6. 407

Maa, 7. 475

Mabbott, Thomas O., 8. 715

MacArthur, J. R., 1. 290, 396; 2. 352-3, 355-6
Macaulay, Thomas B., 8. 504
Maccabeus, Judas, 1. 292
MacCracken, Henry N., 1. 386
Macha, 3. 334
Machiavelli, Niccolo di Bernardo dei, 5. 306, 308-10; 8. 364, 368-9, 372, 516-8, 524, 589-90
Machyn, Henry, 5. 184
Macintire, E. J., 7. 372, 667; 8. 423, 433, 619
Mackail, J. W., 3. 221, 287; 5. 209, 223, 232, 284; 6. 194, 203, 255; 7. 584, 598; 8. 532, 655
Mackintosh, James, 5. 174
MacMahons of Ulster, 6. 204, 350
Macrobius, 2. 425; Saturnalia: 1. 7-8: 5. 160; 8. 354; 1. 10: 6. 301; 1. 12-3: 7. 243-4, 273; 1. 18: 8. 328; 1. 19: 2. 370; 8. 383; 1. 20: 1. 285; 1. 21: 3. 255; 8. 470; 3. 8: 4. 231; 5. 19: 8. 311; 6. 2: 1. 176; 7. 16: 1. 184; In Somnium Scipionis: 1. 2: 3. 345; 1. 6: 2. 284, 297, 480; 1. 8. 7: 1. 445; 1. 12: 2. 377; 1. 14: 6. 277; 8. 493; 1. 17. 2: 2. 479-80; 2. 3: 8. 329
Madan, 2. 310-1
Madden, Sir Frederic, 6. 187
Madness, 7. 510, 523
Madonna Coelia, 7. 252
Madrigal, 7. 276; 8. 326, 455
Maecenas, 7. 370; 8. 537
Maenads, 4. 205; 5. 231-2
Maev, 5. 314
Magic, 3. 221
Maglan, 2. 315
Magnanimity, 1. 323, 328-9, 334, 362, 445-8; 2. 253, 418, 438; 4. 307; most Greek of the virtues: 1. 445; equals will: 1. 446. See also Highmindedness; Magnificence
Magnet, 2. 354-5
Magnificence, 1. 250-1, 323, 328-9, 334, 337, 341-3, 362, 432, 466, 485, 495; 2. 418. See also Highmindedness; Magnanimity
Magoun, F. P., 4. 170
Maho, 8. 486
Mahomet, 3. 250; 6. 227
Mahoune, 2. 276; 6. 227-8
Maia, 8. 483
Maid Marian, 5. 223
Maidenhead. See Knights
Maire (river), 4. 270, 272
Majesty, 8. 484
Major, Georg, 7. 266, 272-3
"make," 7. 320-1, 347, 388-9, 459, 463
Malabar, 6. 226

Maladies, 1. 408-11; 2. 343
Malbecco, 1. 245, 378; 3. 272-5, 277, 286-7, 310, 313-4, 316, 319-20, 372; 5. 208, 275; is Earl of Shrewsbury: 3. 378
Malcontent, 2. 201-2
Maldon, 8. 288
Male, 2. 482; and female: 1. 222; 2. 475, 483; 4. 231-2; 5. 215, 266; 7. 562-3, 567
Malecasta, 2. 349; 3. 202, 208, 278, 313, 315-6, 320, 324, 329, 371-2, 386, 388, 390
Maleffort, 6. 326-8
Maleger, 2. 227, 338-41, 343-7, 403, 416, 427, 438, 442; 3. 314-5; 5. 232, 275
Malengin, 5. 233-4, 236, 273, 275, 279, 281, 348; 6. 346; is the wild Irish: 5. 302-3, 305, 316-7
Malfont, 5. 239
Malgo, 3. 230-1
Malice, 6. 207
Mallow, 4. 266-7; 7. 456
Malone, Edmond, 7. 402, 419, 434, 464-74, 479, 646, 652; 8. 317, 320, 505, 533, 709
Malory, Sir Thomas, Morte d'Arthur (reff. to book and chapter, in ed. Strachey): 1. 251, 349, 351, 488-90; 2. 199, 281-2, 336, 403, 415, 450; 3. 216; 4. 294; 5. 191, 225; 6. 188, 215, 271; 7. 616, 619; influence on Spenser strongest in F. Q. 6: 6. 348; possible source of F. Q. 1: 1. 391-5, 399; Caxton's Preface: 1. 347; 1. 1-2: 1. 265; 3. 236; 1. 9: 4. 213; 1. 15-6: 3. 237; 1. 17: 6. 268; 1. 18: 1. 264; 1. 19: 5. 194; 1. 21: 2. 246; 1. 22: 5. 186, 257; 1. 24: 6. 189-90, 366; 2. 17: 5. 187; 3. 4: 2. 243; 3. 8: 5. 168; 3. 14: 3. 225; 3. 15: 5. 194; 4. 1: 3. 225; 4. 13: 3. 226; 4. 20-1: 6. 271; 4. 26: 5. 167; 6. 3-4: 5. 205; 6. 10: 5. 169; 6. 11: 5. 187, 203; 6. 17: 5. 168; 7. 1-3, 5, 35: 1. 391; 7. 6-12: 1. 211, 261, 394-5; 7. 13: 186; 6. 271; 7. 15: 1. 278; 7. 19: 1. 307, 392; 7. 22: 3. 213; 7. 27: 4. 185; 7. 35: 5. 183; 8. 1-3: 6. 194-5, 368-71; 8. 3, 24-6: 6. 195; 8. 5: 4. 190; 8. 24: 3. 208; 9. 12: 6. 268, 271; 9. 20: 5. 167; 10. 5, 6: 6. 195; 10. 13: 6. 268; 10. 25: 5. 212; 10. 37: 6. 264; 10. 42: 2. 234; 10. 48: 2. 224; 10. 83: 4. 165; 11. 3: 3. 219; 11. 4: 1. 211; 12. 4: 5. 186; 12. 6: 4. 199; 13, 1: 1. 286; 13. 9: 1. 177, 399; 13. 12: 5. 194; 14. 6-8: 1. 397-8; 17. 12: 1. 261, 399; 18. 4: 5. 259; 18. 9: 5. 187; 18 .19: 3. 226; 19. 4: 5. 196; 19. 7-8: 5. 205, 211; 21. 5: 2. 273; 21. 12: 1. 293
Malvenu, 1. 495
Malvolio, 2. 421

Malynes, Gerard, 1. 478
Mammon, 1. 232; 2. 185, 248-60, 268, 272, 352, 412, 418, 428-9, 430, 471; 3. 365; 4. 287; 5. 275, 341; 6. 192; Cave of: 8. 622; Celtic origins: 2. 445; is Charles V: 2. 404
Manannan mac Ler, 1. 293
Man-Beast, 1. 244
Mandeville, John, *Travels*: 2. 435; 5. 197; 6. 213-4; Chapters 18, 30: 2. 354-5; 22: 4. 204; 26: 2. 344-5; 29: 1. 227; 33: 1. 255
Mandricardo, 2. 207-8, 210, 247, 276; 3. 218, 263, 268, 291; 6. 197
Mangys, 1. 391
Mania, 2. 414
Manilius, Marcus, 5. 158; 6. 185; *Astronomica*: 1. 126: 1. 250; 1. 211: 2. 479; 1. 317: 6. 251; 1. 485-6: 5. 178; 1. 677: 5. 165; 1. 726: 7. 551; 1. 727: 5. 229-30; 2. 442: 6. 305; 3. 334: 5. 165; 4. 14: 5. 178; 4. 259: 6. 308; 5. 726: 7. 551
Mankind, 1. 295
Manly, J. M., 8. 664
Manna, 9. 373
Manners, 1. 340
Manners, Edward, Earl of Rutland, 6. 353
Manning, Robert, of Brunne, 2. 302, 319; 3. 274-5, 286
Manningham's Diary, 8. 303
Manoa, 4. 248-9
Mansilia, 7. 448, 453, 474-5. *See also* Snachenbergh
Mansuetude, 1. 328-9, 342
Mant, Richard, 8. 477
Mantegna, Andrea, 1. 219
Mantles, 5. 235
Manto, 1. 204
Mantuanus, Baptista, 7. 368, 387, 393, 571, 573, 579, 582, 586-8, 589, 591-2, 595-6, 599, 610, 615; *Eclogues*: 7. 240, 266, 268, 601, 632, 650; 8. 281; 1: 7. 251; 1. 42-3: 8. 600; 1. 140: 7. 345; 1. 141: 7. 423; 3. 159: 7. 251; 3. 174: 7. 260, 385, 3. 180 ff.: 7. 249; 4: 7. 590; 4. 15: 7. 307; 4. 163: 7. 332; 5: 7. 373; 8. 313-4; 5. 1-52: 7. 378-9; 5. 18-9, 90-1: 7. 389; 5. 21-37: 7. 379; 5. 51-8: 7. 380; 5. 70: 7. 394; 5. 86-8, 89, 121, 157-9: 7. 385; 5. 126-8: 7. 383; 5. 146-69: 8. 313, 325; 5. 182-4: 7. 390-1; 6: 7. 255; 6. 8-9: 7. 357; 6. 19-25: 7. 257; 6. 38-40: 7. 260; 6. 106-11: 7. 265; 6. 178: 7. 332; 7. 10-22: 7. 331-2; 7. 14-31: 7. 332; 7. 27-31: 7. 333, 392; 7. 59: 7. 270; 7. 185: 7. 590; 7. 190: 7. 251; 8: 7.

323-6, 330, 337; 8. 1-14: 7. 327; 8. 42-3: 7. 330; 8. 45-57: 7. 328-9, 337; 9: 7. 350-3, 590; 9. 1-2: 7. 354; 9. 5-11: 7. 351, 355; 9. 11, 46-7, 54-8: 7. 356-7; 9. 13-7: 7. 365; 9. 32: 7. 365; 9. 38: 7. 364; 9. 42-3, 78-80, 192-7: 7. 357; 9. 143-52: 7. 363; 9. 179: 7. 365; 9. 199: 7. 365; 9. 201: 7. 310; 9. 220: 7. 260; 10. 8-9: 7. 318; *Life of St. George*: 1. 297, 304, 307, 380-6
Manuscripts, 7. 656; 8. 511
Marcellus, 8. 306
March, 6. 303; 7. 242-4
Marchese dal Caretto, 3. 358
Marchesi, C., 2. 423
Marchetus of Padua, 2. 201
Marco Polo, 2. 344-5; 4. 204
Marcus Aurelius, 2. 479; 3. 257
Marfisa, 2. 207; 3. 202, 332, 334, 371; 4. 166, 188-9; 5. 221, 349
Marganor, 6. 189
Margaret of Anjou, 3. 339
Margaret of Navarre, 7. 674
Margaret of Parma, 5. 198, 297
Marie de Champagne, 6. 292
Marie de France, 3. 394
Marin, 7. 459
Marinell, 3. 239-40, 267, 269, 318, 320, 325, 385, 388, 390; 4. 251-4, 296, 334; 5. 199; is Lord Howard: 3. 240, 379; 4. 277; is Raleigh: 3. 379; is sea power of Spain: 3. 380
Marino, Giovanni Battista, 1. 239; 2. 292; 8. 461
Marius, 2. 325-7
Mark, King, 2. 208; 6. 215
Marlowe, Christopher, 1. 346, 378; 2. 260, 287; 3. 240; 4. 314; 7. 390, 464, 473-4, 619; 8. 320, 396, 531, 534, 536, 539-40; *Doctor Faustus*: 1. 203, 276; 5. 158; 7. 439; *Edward II*: 2. 189; *Hero and Leander*: 7. 464, 474; *1 Tamburlaine*: 8. 321, 621; Prologue: 8. 533; 2. 1: 2. 247, 306; 2. 4: 2. 276; 3. 3: 8. 460; 5. 1: 1. 255; 2. 237; 5. 2: 1. 250; *2 Tamburlaine*: 8. 621; 2. 3: 2. 237; 2. 4: 2. 270; 3. 4: 2. 191; 4. 1: 2. 393; 4. 2: 1. 258; 4. 3, 4: 2. 399; 4. 4: 1. 252-3; 7. 474; 5. 2: 2. 254
Marot, Clement, 7. 240, 251-2, 268, 270, 314, 339, 361, 449, 578, 582, 584-6, 588-9, 592-3, 595-7, 601, 641, 647; 8. 380, 434, 511, 629, 643-4; *Chant rustique*: 7. 318; *Complaincte de Madame Loyse de Savoye*: 7. 247, 249, 251, 255, 270, 279, 281, 286, 310, 317-8, 366, 395-401, 403-14, 421-2, 442, 496, 590, 632; *Com-*

plaincte d'un Pastoureau Chrestien: 7. 251, 281, 298-9, 335, 419, 590, 598, 632; *De Cupido et de sa Dame*: 2. 273; 4. 221; 8. 456; *De Diane*: 2. 273; 8. 456; *Eclogue au Roy*: 7. 276, 281, 310, 417-25, 590, 614, 632; *Elegie*: 7. 341; *impresa*: 7. 416, 634; *Le Temple de Cupido*: 3. 256, 292, 303; 4. 229; 6. 222; 7. 481; translation of Virgil, *Ecl.* 1: 7. 315; *Visions de Pétrarque*: 8. 274-7, 415, 611-21, 623-4; sonnets: 8. 643-4

Marprelate controversy, 6. 266, 383, 386-8; 7. 261, 295, 299, 326, 582; 8. 316-7, 534

Marquand, Mrs. Allan, 7. 498

Marriage, 1. 309-10; 3. 310, 326-7, 356, 371-2, 384; 4. 238, 281; 7. 287; 8. 442, 461. See also Wedding

Marriage of Wit and Science, 1. 446-7

Marriage of Wit and Wisdom, 1. 446-7; 8. 591

Mars, 1. 213; 3. 297, 394, 397; 5. 159-60; 6. 389; 7. 383; 8. 383, 440; planet: 6. 310-12

Marsh, E., 8. 662, 722

Marshal, 5. 238-9

Marston, John, 3. 275, 284; 6. 270; 7. 238; 8. 462

Martano, 2. 207-8; 5. 192

Martial (Marcus Valerius Martialis), 3. 279; *Epigrams*: 3. 221; 4. 182; 7. 252, 394; 8. 299, 381; *On the Spectales*: 2. 378

Martianus Capella, 2. 375; 8. 424

Martinists. See Marprelate Controversy

Martinus Magister, 1. 355

Martyrs, 1. 472

Marullus, 8. 448

Marvell, Andrew, 2. 359

Mary Magdalene, 2. 434

Mary of Lorraine, 5. 198, 297

Mary Queen of Scots, 1. 263, 424, 452, 472, 481; 2. 338, 407; 4. 256, 316; 5. 198, 279, 297, 299, 303-7; 7. 586; 8. 391, 525; is Acrasia: 2. 402-3, 408; is Amavia: 2. 402; is Amoretta: 3. 249; character: 5. 323; claim to the throne: 6. 299; is Duessa: 1. 459-60, 465-6, 481, 492; 5. 244-7, 273, 286, 317; and Elizabeth: 5. 225, 243-7, 276, 303-7, 316, 325; is false Florimell: 3. 378; is Florimell: 3. 263-4, 271; is Hellenore: 3. 378; intended marriage to Leicester: 3. 263; 5. 320; is Munera: 5. 174; portrait: 3. 392; and Radigund: 5. 201, 221, 316; is Roman Church: 1. 452; is the spider: 8. 605; trial: 5. 243-7, 303-7, 319-24

Mary Tudor, 1. 457-66, 474, 483, 490; 2. 335; 3. 339; 5. 198; is Duessa: 1. 460,

470-2; 5. 286; *F. Q.* 1. 7. 1-16 represent her persecutions: 1. 450, 460; is Lucifera: 1. 461

Masaccio, 1. 305-6

Maspero, Gaston, 8. 485

Masque, 1. 450, 491, 493-4; 2. 256; 3. 287, 299-301, 353, 355-7; 4. 165-6, 324; 5. 184; 6. 202, 432; 8. 437, 461, 646-7

Masque "before the Queenes Majestie," 2. 404-5; 5. 324

Masque of Cupid, 3. 287, 299-303, 328-9, 353-66, 385, 389; 4. 234; 5. 207; 8. 437, 647; contrasted with other pageants: 1. 441

Massachusetts Historical Society, 1. 517-8; 7. 708; 8. 681

Massacre of St. Bartholomew, 2. 404; 7. 308; 8. 391

Massinger, Philip, 1. 190, 276; 3. 275; 5. 239; 7. 312

Master Steven, 3. 363-4

Mater Deum, 5. 215

Materialism, 3. 340-4, 349; 6. 389, 393-6, 401-3, 407, 421

Matilda, 3. 226, 339; 6. 204, 334

Matrona, 7. 561, 565, 568

Matter, 2. 479; 3. 260-1, 340-52; 6. 390; 7. 513, 525, 529-31

Mattes, Edmund, 8. 736

Matthew of Westminster, 2. 452

Matthew Paris, 5. 199

Matthieu de Conci, 1. 324

Mausoleum, 8. 305-6

Mausolus, 8. 300

Mavis, 8. 466

Mawde, Mother, 8. 351, 593

Maximilian, 1. 459

Maximinian, 2. 331-2, 397

Maximus Tyrius, 4. 217; 6. 199; 7. 252

Maxwell, W. C., 6. 438; 8. 675

May Day, 3. 357; 7. 294, 296-7; 8. 445

May Queen, 5. 223

Mayenne, Duke of, 5. 211-2, 316

Maynadier, Howard, 1. 251

Maynard, Theodore, 4. 180

Mayne, Cuthbert, 7. 360

Mazer, 7. 342-3

McElderry, B. R., 7. 620, 627-9

McKenzie, Kenneth, 7. 444

McKerrow, R. B., 1. 522; 8. 706

McLane, P. E., 7. 296, 354

McManaway, J. G., 2. 226

McMurphy, Susannah, 2. 438-43; 3. 371-6; 4. 317; 5. 221, 348

McNeill, E., 5. 312

McPeek, J. A. S., 8. 461-2, 464-5, 469-71,

473, 476, 478-9, 481, 483, 488-9, 492, 494, 653

Mean, 2. 409-26; 5. 296-7; 7. 324-5

Medaewart, 2. 275

Medea, 2. 346, 351, 366, 371-4; 3. 246; 4. 223

Medieval, 4. 228-9; 7. 281, 515, 662; symbolism: 8. 448; women, view of: 3. 317

Medina, 2. 183-5, 195, 198, 201, 350, 411, 416-7, 419, 421, 425-6, 427; 3. 315; 8. 518. See also Castle, House of Medina

Medoro, 3. 246, 374-5

Medusa, 1. 254; 8. 475

Medwall, Henry, 2. 432-4; 8. 591

Medway, 1. 363, 371; 2. 303; 4. 252, 272-3; 7. 329-30; marriage with Thames: see Thames

Meekness, 1. 407

Meetkercke, Adolf, 5. 249, 299, 301, 317

Megaera, 8. 315

Meiosis, 8. 293

Mela, Pomponius, 1. 184-5

Melampode, 7. 330

Melancholy, 1. 275-7; 2. 459; 4. 234; 6. 423-4; 8. 281

Melanchthon, 1. 466; 2. 423; 3. 321-3

Meleager (king of Calydon), 2. 343

Meleager (poet), 1. 230

Meliboe, 5. 284; 6. 238-9, 318-20, 327, 339, 342-3, 348, 375, 381; is Walsingham: 6. 349-52, 355, 359, 362-3; 7. 472

Meliboeus, 7. 309, 311, 315, 321, 472

Melicerta, 5. 231

Meliodas, 6. 368

Meliogras, 6. 194, 370

Melissa, 1. 205; 2. 394; 3. 231, 370; 6. 261-5, 381

Melizius, 1. 416

Melkinus Avalonius, 2. 326

Melmoth, William, 8. 306

Melody. See Cadence; Music; Sound

Melpomene, 7. 406-7, 415; 8. 312, 321, 394, 532

Melusine, 1. 182-3, 205

Melville, James, 2. 384

Melvin, Lough, 4. 268; 6. 282-3

Melyas, 5. 194

Memoirs of Ancient Chivalry. See Sainte-Palaye

" memories," 8. 359

Memory, 2. 278, 287, 300-1, 438, 463-6, 468, 481

Memprise, 2. 311

Menage, 2. 327; 3. 245

Menalcas, 7. 321, 338-9, 400, 412, 590, 651-3; 8. 453

Menander, 6. 378

Mendacio, 2. 340

Mendoza, Bernardino de, 5. 316, 324; 7. 360

Menelaus, 2. 277, 289; 3. 213, 270, 285

Menevia, 3. 236

Mercenaries, 8. 372

Merchant Taylors' Company, 7. 343

Merchant Taylors' School, 7. 315, 362, 404, 420, 599, 616; 8. 479, 623

Mercilla, 5. 236-7; 6. 246, 293; is Elizabeth: 1. 449; 5. 225-6, 244, 270, 273, 296, 305-6, 321-2; is Justice: 5. 272, 291; palace: 5. 237-9

Mercury, 2. 370, 393; 3. 354; 4. 186-7; 6. 277, 293, 389; 8. 309-10, 376-7, 483, 667

Mercury (planet), 6. 310-2

Mercutio, 4. 290

Mercy, 1. 406-7, 424; 5. 295; Dame Mercy: 1. 407; and Justice: 5. 247-8, 296; 6. 192; Seven Works of: 1. 424

Meres, Francis, 7. 377, 387-8, 468, 473, 572; 8. 317

Meriflure, 7. 434, 467

Merionethshire, 1. 265-6

Merismos. See Distributio

Merlin, 1. 264-7, 292, 399; 2. 275, 449, 453; 3. 224-7, 229-31, 234-5, 310-1, 369-70, 388; cave: 3. 364; and Master Steven: 3. 363; prophecy: 3. 370-1; 4. 259-60

Merlo, Filippo?, 8. 438, 475

Mermaid, 2. 351, 363-5, 421-2

Mermen, 2. 363

Mertia, 2. 321; 3. 236

Metamorphosis, 1. 205, 206, 248; 3. 260, 287, 291-7; 6. 414, 429-32; 7. 484, 498-9; 8. 339, 396, 400, 505, 610. See also Transformation

Metaphor, 7. 264, 298, 682; 8. 499; falconry: 3. 286; nautical: 1. 310-1; ships: 8. 387, 431; shower: 5. 199

" Metaphysical," 7. 470

Metempsychosis, 3. 340; 4. 184. See also Reincarnation

Meteor, 6. 217

Metonomy, 1. 301

Metre, 1. 210; 2. 199, 205, 217, 389; 3. 205, 247, 312; 4. 180, 225; 5. 177, 180, 182, 194, 199, 249, 256; 6. 445, 471; 8. 274-5, 547, 618-21; Anglo-Saxon: 7. 275, 292; heroic: 7. 292; 8. 618; hypermetric: 3. 239; 6. 215; 8. 715; polysyllabic: 8. 494; quantitative: 1. 357; 4. 240; 7. 367, 488-9; 8. 509-10, 515, 538, 709-10, 723; tumbling: 7. 292, 635-6- 639. See also Rhyme; rime couée; Run-over lines; Sestina; Spenserian Stanza; Stichomythia; Verse

Meyrick, Sir Samuel, 1. 452-3

Michael, Archangel, 1. 176, 309-10; 2. 235; 8. 565
Michelangelo, 2. 228; 7. 491
Micyllus, Jacobus, 8. 459
Midas, 7. 319
Middle Ages, 1. 275; 8. 532. *See also* Medieval
Middle English, 7. 618, 630
Middleton, Thomas, 7. 361; 8. 355, 375, 581-2, 584
Mid Lent, 1. 243
Midsummer Night, 7. 316
Milesians, 4. 269-70; 5. 194
Milesius, 2. 349; 5. 194
Milky Way, 5. 229; 8. 512
Mill, 5. 258
Millican, C. B., 1. 266, 482-5; 2. 312; 3. 235, 338-9; 7. 315
Milligan, Burton, 8. 355
Milton, John, 1. 315, 378, 418, 421; 2. 365, 382, 442; 3. 368; 4. 288; 5. 157, 179; 6. 280, 407, 428; 7. 371, 626-7; 8. 322, 331, 377, 661, 672-4, 720; Arthur, meditated story of: 1. 359; at Harefield: 8. 310; and Spenser: 2. 427-31; 3. 238; 4. 176-7, 255; 5. 218, 244, 250; 6. 202-4, 212, 214, 218, 275-6, 297, 302, 309, 428, 449; 7. 251, 280, 290, 301, 441, 537, 578; 8. 296, 388, 506, 543, 596, 630; his copy of *Spenser*: 7. 301
   Animadversions: 2. 256; 6. 253, 475; 7. 290, 301; *Apology for Smectymnuus*: 7. 518; *Arcades*: 1. 178-9; 2. 278, 480; 7. 280-1, 471; 8. 310; *Areopagitica*: 1. 341; 2. 256, 388; 7. 557; *At a Solemn Music*: 7. 520, 533, 543, 549, 554; 8. 332, 471, 658; *At a Vacation Exercise*: 4. 253, 260; 6. 275-6; 8. 331
   Comus: 2. 246, 349, 365, 377; 3. 287; 6. 428; 7. 471, 537, 664; 8. 310; Ms.: 2. 264; 50: 6. 285; 73-7: 2. 193, 395; 92: 2. 341; 101: 8. 472; 107: 8. 316; 143: 1. 240; 155: 7. 328; 157: 7. 394; 189: 2. 193; 212: 7. 547; 214: 7. 554; 265-70: 2. 220; 321-6: 6. 187, 297; 324: 1. 214; 331: 3. 211; 370-1: 1. 286; 373-5: 1. 182; 377: 1. 289; 398-9: 2. 252; 444: 2. 214; 457-8: 4. 319; 517: 5. 234; 541: 7. 409; 604: 1. 192; 621: 8. 399; 638: 2. 275; 651: 2. 381; 704-5: 2. 255; 710: 2. 245; 733: 3. 240; 743: 2. 391; 756-91: 2. 222, 254-5; 812: 1. 196; 847-8: 7. 384; 848-51: 3. 209; 872: 7. 558; 877: 4. 242; 880-3: 4. 181; 890: 8. 465; 934-5: 5. 237; 972: 2. 210; 992-1011: 7. 521; *Elegies*: 6. 298; *Epitaph on Shakespeare*: 8. 449; *History of Britain*: 2. 306, 312, 319, 450;
3. 238; *Il Penseroso*: 4: 4. 205; 32: 1. 286; 45: 1. 195; 52: 1. 289; 57-8: 3. 307; 79-80: 1. 183; 107: 4. 200; 5. 253; 109-12: 4. 176-7; 116-20: 1. 492; 146: 1. 190; 161: 8. 477; *In Quintum Novembris*: 1. 231; 2. 255-6; *L'Allegro*: 7. 255; 8. 645; 1-2: 2. 233; 6-7: 2. 369; 6. 235; 7. 316; 25-7: 1. 175; 119-24: 5. 183; 128: 5. 184; 135: 8. 371; 136: 7. 392
   Lycidas: 6. 448; 7. 282, 286, 288, 290, 324, 352, 397-8, 400, 580; 8. 675; and *Epithalamion*: 8. 654; and *Ruines of Time*: 8. 286, 291, 296-7, 300, 306, 530; 1: 8. 459; 6: 8. 461; 8-38: 8. 296; 9: 7. 491; 11: 8. 388; 15-6: 8. 311; 50-5: 7. 496, 558; 63: 1. 302; 64-84: 8. 286, 306; 70-84: 8. 300; 71: 5. 262; 75: 8. 388; 76-7: 7. 381; 86: 4. 255; 111: 3. 256; 113-31: 7. 298; 117: 7. 491; 125: 7. 298; 128 ff.: 7. 301, 306; 138-9: 7. 280; 139-51: 7. 286; 8. 398; 151-3: 8. 291; 161: 7. 328; 165-81: 7. 412, 414, 506; 8. 297; 183: 7. 601; close: 7. 483
   Nativity Hymn: 22-3, 53-4, 59-60, 155-6, 163-4: 5. 158; 6. 297; 29, 31: 8. 718; 31 ff.: 8. 470; 69-72: 1. 239; 6. 276; 77-84: 7. 283; 89: 7. 299; 123: 8. 383; 136-8: 1. 183; 205-10: 5. 256; *Of Reformation*: 1. 289; 6. 309; *On the Death of a Fair Infant*: 7. 441; *On Time*: 7. 547
   Paradise Lost: 1. 276; 2. 428-30; 3. 343; 7. 669; and *Hymn of Heavenly Love*: 7. 537, 656-7, 669; more heroic than *Iliad* or *Aeneid*: 1. 335; Book 1: 11: 1. 302; 16: 6. 185; 17-26: 7. 540; 22: 6. 478; 27: 6. 292; 45-9: 7. 514; 8. 412; 63: 2. 237; 98: 1. 211; 193: 1. 298; 195: 1. 297; 196: 1. 371; 225: 1. 298; 262: 5. 262; 287-91: 5. 200; 292: 3. 265; 354: 2. 310; 392-6: 5. 256; 423: 6. 281; 510-2: 6. 279; 527: 2. 280; 591: 2. 277; 683-5: 2. 255; 690-2: 2. 255; 702-4: 2. 260; 711: 3. 210; 5. 217-8; 714: 4. 219; 783: 2. 224; Book 2: 40-3: 6. 278; 90: 8. 314; 185: 2. 304; 245: 2. 214; 351-3: 6. 280; 396-7: 8. 461; 406: 6. 257; 574: 1. 234; 579: 2. 267; 580: 2. 232; 597: 1. 205; 637: 1. 194; 650-66: 1. 183; 656: 5. 244; 666-73: 6. 309; 686-7: 6. 270; 689-90: 6. 214; 691: 1. 229; 708: 3. 205; 714-6: 2. 254; 4. 173, 184; 746: 1. 283; 823: 1. 234; 242: 1. 303; 846: 5. 255; 878: 6. 304; 884: 2. 258; 891: 1. 232; 894: 1. 230; 898: 7. 481; 911: 3. 257; 8. 285; 927-30: 1. 298; 940: 1. 296; 959: 2. 233; 962: 1. 230; 964: 2. 370; 972: 1. 232; 1014-6: 6. 260; 1016:

4. 168; 1024-30: 2. 258; 1051: 1. 233; Book 3: 1-55: 2. 252-3; 6. 185; 7. 460, 540; 8. 402; 93: 3. 268; 231: 6. 309; 276-83: 2. 270; 320: 1. 310; 353-9: 3. 248, 259; 364: 3. 263; 377-94: 7. 558; 412: 3. 238; 489: 4. 191; 594: 6. 304; 736: 1. 188; 2. 278; 741: 1. 299; Book 4: 49: 1. 215; 121: 2. 187; 141-2: 3. 247; 147: 3. 258; 218-22: 1. 300-1; 248: 1. 182; 264 ff.: 2. 381; 266: 3. 258; 268-75: 8. 306; 288: 1. 288; 2. 288; 304: 4. 166; 332: 2. 380; 337: 3. 268; 568; 1. 299; 614: 1. 189; 649: 7. 540; 690-703; 6. 296; 700 ff.: 8. 464; 764: 7. 270; 797 ff., 977: 2. 270; 858: 4. 202; 7. 440; 965-7: 4. 208; 990-1015: 5. 176; Book 5: 7, 17-21: 8. 466; 41: 8. 467; 44: 3. 297; 193: 6. 296; 205-6: 6. 241; 254: 2. 259; 277-85: 2. 272; 300: 8. 470; 321: 1. 290; 344: 2. 381; 358-61: 2. 278; 451: 5. 184; 472: 3. 260; 569: 1. 232; 749: 1. 310; 896: 2. 304; 897: 6. 309; Book 6: 7. 541; 3: 6. 308; 15: 1. 225; 33: 4. 188; 100: 1. 225; 196-8: 3. 276; 305-7: 2. 198; 325: 2. 235; 329: 7. 256; 332: 1. 227; 337: 6. 198; 534: 1. 297; 545-6: 5. 199; 635: 6. 202; 749: 2. 242; Book 7: 7. 541; 1-39: 7. 428, 540, 564; 31: 7. 428; 358: 7. 551; 370: 8. 460; 526: 2. 395; 205: 2. 259; 390: 1. 298; 502-3: 1. 300; Book 8: 94 ff.: 8. 470; 162: 1. 207; 351: 3. 265; 471-4: 4. 195; 513: 6. 296; 519-20: 8. 481; 521-643: 2. 429; 588: 3. 223; 589: 3. 244; 7. 518; 618: 2. 296; 635-41: 2. 430; Book 9: 280, 1067: 6. 218; 452: 2. 246; 509: 5. 220; 513-6: 6. 260; 647: 2. 265; 719: 2. 245; 1009: 2. 220; Book 10: 53: 4. 183; 59: 5. 247; 257: 2. 198-9; 449-54: 6. 278; 460: 7. 541; 478: 1. 232; 540: 1. 304; 572-7: 1. 204; 581: 6. 253; 617-9: 6. 275; 687: 1. 239; 774-8, 855-8: 7. 445; 999: 1. 279; 1012 ff.: 1. 272; 1086: 6. 212; Book 11: 410-1: 5. 250; 432: 6. 235; 565: 6. 304; 625: 2. 220

Paradise Regained: 2. 429-30; Book 1: 1. 173; 7: 8. 342; Book 2: 109-11: 2. 253; 208: 2. 246; 258: 2. 253; 289-98: 2. 238; 361: 6. 271; 422-31: 2. 254; Book 3: 29: 7. 547; 322-5: 2. 344; 5. 199; 387: 3. 423; 429: 2. 304; 6. 309; Book 4: 51-4: 5. 237; 203: 2. 254; 409-38: 8. 433; 427: 1. 218; 497: 1. 188-9; 564: 2. 347; 629: 1. 192; *Psalms*: 80: 6. 194; 136: 1. 199: 4. 203

Samson Agonistes: 100-5: 2. 274; 235,

906: 5. 244; 620: 6. 212; 7. 272; 1053-60: 5. 223; 1134: 1. 223; 1323 ff.: 4. 209; 1422: 6. 309; 1529: 4. 191; Sonnets: 1. 296; 2. 357; 3. 305; 6. 302; 7. 444; 8. 426; Trinity College MS: 4. 255; 8. 389; *Upon the Circumcision*: 8. 658

Mind, 7. 562-3; is Form: 2. 479; and Matter: 3. 261

Mind, Will, and Understanding, 1. 446-7

Mine, 7. 525

Minerva, 1. 254, 407, 416-7; 2. 266; 3. 279, 397, 425; 7. 394; 8. 400-1, 475, 597, 603-4, 606-8

Minor Poems, 1. 249; bibliography: 7. 725-34; 8. 737-45; realism in: 1. 249; Sources and Analogues indexed: 7. 683-91; 8. 724-34

Minos, 5. 163, 298

Minsheu, John, 1. 219-20; 7. 322

Minstrels, 1. 225; 5. 201

Minto, William, 3. 203, 241, 243; 7. 473, 580; 8. 317-9, 321, 516, 629, 655

Minturno, Antonio, 1. 348-50, 359-60; 7. 368, 370; 8. 332

Minucius Felix, 7. 273

Mira, 3. 377

Mirabella, 3. 300, 319; 6. 191, 207, 223-4, 229, 231, 324, 326, 333-4; 8. 396; is the lady of *Amoretti*: 8. 633; is Rosalind: 6. 214, 219-21, 318

Miracle plays, 1. 297, 380; 2. 247; 7. 592

Mirk, John, 1. 380

Mirror, 2. 400; 3. 216-7, 370, 387, 391; 6. 186; 7. 388, 518, 532, 554-6; 8. 434-5, 638

Mirror for Magistrates (specific references are to Haslewood's edition, and in parenthesis to Campbell's): 1. 237, 269-70, 272, 277-9, 478; 2. 302, 309-11, 314, 317-8, 320-1, 324, 330, 333, 450-2; 3. 305; 7. 285, 409, 465, 645; *Induction*: 1. 277-9; 2. 257; 3. 308; 6. 303; 7. 248-9, 581; 8. 328; 1. 55 (2. 80): 2. 309; 1. 58 (2. 83): 2. 310; 1. 86 ff.: (2. 111 ff.): 2. 311; 1. 89 (2. 114): 6. 241-2; 1. 112 (2. 138): 2. 314; 1. 173 (2. 250): 2. 320; 1. 213-9 (2. 185-90): 2. 321; 1. 286-90 (2. 311-4): 2. 324; 1. 322-3 (2. 409): 2. 330; 1. 401 (2. 427): 2. 333; 2. 760 (*Edward II*, st. 132): 4. 199. *See also* Sackville, Thomas

Mirth, 2. 285; Dame Mirth: 1. 407; Sir Mirth: 6. 371

Misery, 2. 257

Mitchelstown, 6. 286

Mitre, 1. 200

Mnemon, 3. 283

Mnemosyne, 1. 296
Mock epic, 8. 394, 487, 518
"mocks and mows," 6. 228-9
Mode. *See* Mood
Moderation, 2. 184-5, 424-5; 7. 352-3
Moderns vs. Ancients: 5. 155
Modesty, 1. 342; 2. 294; 3. 355, 383; 4. 237; 6. 290
Moffet, Thomas, 8. 284
Mohl, Ruth, 8. 353, 594
Molanna, 1. 507, 515; 4. 271; 6. 246, 273, 286-90, 425-6, 429-32, 441; 7. 454
Mole (mountain), 6. 252, 283-9, 299, 424-6, 429-30, 441; 7. 453-5
Mole (rivers), 4. 256-7, 267, 271; 6. 413
Moloch, 5. 256-7
Moluccas, 5. 248
Moly, 2. 370; 8. 428
Mombritius, Boninus, 4. 274-5
Mommsen, Theodor, 7. 273
Momur, 1. 290, 291
Mona, 3. 235-6
Monarchy, 7. 462-3
Monasteries, 1. 441, 458, 465, 467; 6. 265-8, 298
Moneannymy, 8. 633
Monoceros, 2. 361
Monodante, 2. 241
Monopolies, 5. 170-1, 345-7
Monox, Will, 8. 319
Monsters, 2. 359-64; 3. 263-5
Monstrelet, Enguerrand de, 1. 324
Montaigne, Michel eyquem de, 4. 291; 5. 191; 8. 380
Montemayor, George de, 6. 372, 379-81; 7. 407, 595; 8. 485, 492, 494, 652
Montgomerie, Alexander, 8. 643
Months, 1. 365; 6. 293, 302-8, 391, 420-1, 429, 436; 7. 630-4
Mood (musical), 2. 201; 7. 392
Moon, 5. 200, 217; 6. 310, 409, 439, 447; 7. 553; 8. 472, 489-90; "horned": 4. 203; moon-rainbow: 7. 463
Moore-Smith, G. C., 7. 293, 415, 720; 8. 506
Moorman, F. W., 7. 459, 583; 8. 398
Moors, 6. 226; 8. 571
Mopsus, 7. 412
Moralities, 1. 339, 347, 415, 418, 431, 446-7; 2. 224; and Spenser: 2. 432-4; 6. 209; 8. 591
Morals, intrusive at times: 4. 287; Renaissance interest in: 1. 340-1
Mordant, 2. 184, 194, 410, 415-6, 418-9, 421, 440, 443; 5. 191
Morddure, 1. 251; 2. 207, 275-6; 5. 192
Mordred, 4. 223

More, Henry, 1. 225, 272, 278; 7. 265, 268-9, 271, 359, 594
More, P. E., 8. 448
More, Sir Thomas, 1. 461-2, 467, 486; 2. 216; 5. 198, 294, 297, 306, 336; 6. 321; 7. 293; 8. 564; *Dialogue of Comfort*: 8. 351, 593
Morel, Leon, 2. 383
Morgan, 2. 318
Morgan le Fay, 1. 204, 292-3, 352, 399; 2. 229, 446
Morgan Library, 1. 519; 7. 708; 8. 680-1
Morgan, Thomas, 5. 320
Morglay, 5. 192
Morindus, 2. 321-2
Morison, Fynes, 6. 196, 239; 8. 465
Morley, Henry, 2. 481-2; 7. 361, 395, 414, 417-24
Morning, 3. 250; 4. 199
Morpheus. *See* Sleep
Morrell, 7. 296, 323-5, 329, 354, 601-3. *See also* Aylmer
Morris, William, 7. 629; 8. 396-7
Mors, 2. 361-2
Mortal-fairy, 1. 245, 267; 8. 397
Mortdant, 2. 402
Moschus, *Idylls*: 1: 2. 273; 3. 251-2; 7. 267, 271; 8. 497, 513; 2. 3. 240; 7. 350; 8. 401-2, 497; 3: 7. 249, 397, 400, 407-8, 412-3, 486, 590, 596; 8. 307; 5: 2. 391
Moses, 1. 291; 2. 186, 364; 7. 332-3, 8. 358
"most and least," 6. 213
"mote," 7. 359
Mother Hubbard, 8. 351
Mother Hubberds Tale, 1. 336; 2. 186, 208; 5. 156, 342; 6. 386; 7. 324, 432, 583, 594-5, 602, 605, 611, 614; 8. 283, 349-77, 459, 511, 518; allegory in: 8. 560, 562, 564, 568-80; Augustan passages: 8. 594; "calling in": 5. 309; 8. 560, 573, 580-5, 686; and *Colin Clouts*: 7. 447-8; 8. 364, 560, 575, 585, 593-4; composition: 8. 349, 363, 369, 373, 377, 564, 566-8, 571-4; contemporary allusion: 8. 568-71, 578; criticism: 8. 559-66, 573, 715-6; date: 7. 295; 8. 349, 364, 373, 559, 563, 566-8, 578, 590; diction: 8. 562-4, 595; and *Epithalamion*: 8. 593; and *F. Q.*: 8. 562, 580-1; and Emblems: 8. 626; form: 8. 564, 593-4; humor: 8. 518; in MS: 8. 560, 579, 582-4, 687-8; medieval: 8. 562, 564, 566, 571, 594-5; metre: 7. 635, 639; 8. 562-4, 570, 593-4; and *Muiopotmos*: 8. 564, 597-9, 601, 605; parts: 8. 565-6, 579, 590-1; proverbs in: 8. 351; publication: 8. 282, 561, 576, 580, 583, 585, 685-7, 737; purpose: 8. 573-4; re-

vised: 8. 559, 563-4, 567, 572-4, 579;
rhetoric in: 8. 595; and *Ruines of Time*:
8. 564, 570, 581, 583, 595; as satire: 8.
560-6, 568-71, 578-9, 594; and *Shepheardes
Calender*: 7. 605, 611; 8. 563, 566, 577,
590, 594; sources: 8. 562, 564, 572, 585-
93; style: 8. 559-60, 564, 593-4; and
Teares of the Muses: 8. 534, 536, 539;
text: 8. 363, 683, 685-8; title: 8. 349;
variant readings: 8. 693-5; and *Virgils
Gnat*: 8. 543-4, 547; and *Vision* poems:
8. 562; *Dedication*: 8. 282, 349-50, 393,
539, 561, 567, 635; 1-3: 8. 331; 5: 1. 209;
45-574: 8. 586-7; 109: 4. 183; 8. 472;
129-49: 5. 338-9; 160: 8. 283; 235-45:
7. 304; 341 ff.: 7. 292, 607; 8. 587; 386-
91: 8. 563; 460-74: 7. 334; 475-9: 7. 359;
513-20: 7. 298; 521-34: 7. 607; 575-942:
7. 478; 8. 587-8; 619-30: 8. 567-8, 576;
624-6: 5. 242; 628-1224: 8. 572; 628:
6. 353; 8. 567-8; 637-49: 6. 332; 662-
793: 6. 329; 700-1: 5. 236; 717-52: 5.
172; 717-93: 6. 187, 337, 349, 354; 7.
487, 608; 8. 563, 595; 733: 6. 188; 739:
5. 191; 7. 495; 760-7: 8. 313, 595; 809-
38: 8. 325; 877 ff.: 2. 262; 891-914: 6.
305; 8. 303, 496, 559, 568-9; 895: 5.
283; 901: 6. 271-2; 915-7: 8. 588; 942-
1388: 8. 578-9, 585; 1111-93: 8. 570;
1137-1388: 6. 272; 8. 578, 580; 1258:
6. 277; 1378-80: 5. 193
Motion, 2. 458; 6. 390, 420
Motley, John L., 5. 253
Motteux, Peter Anthony, 2. 206
Motubizanto, 8. 486
Mount of Olives, 1. 281, 368, 370
Mountain, 1. 290, 291; 7. 328
Mountjoy, Charles, Lord, 1. 390, 477-8; 4.
206
Mountjoy, William, Lord, 4. 206
Mount's Bay, 7. 451, 458
Mourning Muse of Thestylis. See Bryskett,
Lodowick
Mucedorus, 6. 203
Muiopotmos, 6. 438; 7. 505; 8. 281, 392-
404, 518, 636, 675-6; allegory: 8. 393-4,
597, 599-609; and *Amoretti*: 8. 600; and
Astrophel: 8. 604; and *Colin Clouts*: 8.
598, 601; composition: 8. 597, 601, 607;
criticism: 8. 398, 596-8; date: 8. 281, 393,
599-600, 601, 602, 604, 679; diction: 8.
610; and *F. Q.*: 8. 596-9, 602; humor in:
8. 518; incomplete: 8. 605; medieval
tragedy: 8. 608; metre: 8. 596; mock-
heroic: 8. 597, 599, 602-3, 605, 609; and
Mother Hubberds Tale: 8. 564, 597-9, 601,
605; most original poem, Spenser's: 8.

603; not picturesque: 8. 596; publication:
8. 281, 598, 679, 688; Renaissance Italian:
8. 597; rhetoric in: 8. 595; and *Ruines of
Time*: 8. 598, 610; and *Shepheardes Calender*: 8. 601; sources: 8. 602, 608-10;
style: 8. 597, 604, 610; and *Teares of the
Muses*: 8. 598, 602; text: 8. 395, 696,
717; and *Virgils Gnat*: 8. 599, 601;
Vision poems: 8. 392-3; *Dedication*:
8. 311, 392-4, 403, 599, 600, 605, 634;
1-147: 8. 608; 1-16: 8. 346, 600-1, 604-5,
608; 14-5: 8. 346; 22-139: 8. 606; 28:
8. 407; 57-144: 8. 517; 92-6, 101: 3. 298;
105-440: 8. 605; 161-216: 8. 603; 177-9:
6. 420; 185-434: 8. 609; 187-200: 8. 348,
497; 243-56: 8. 600; 246-434: 8. 606;
261 ff.: 2. 259; 277-96: 3. 293; 293:
8. 461; 370: 4. 193; 8. 283; 401: 7. 304;
8. 607
Mulcaster, Richard, 7. 378, 421, 586; 8. 619,
623
Mulciber, 3. 291
Mule, 5. 242; 8. 362-4, 564, 585
Mulla, 4. 268-72; 6. 288-9, 424-7, 429-32,
441; 7. 448, 453-6; 8. 633, 647
"mum," 4. 208-9
Munby, A. N. L., 8. 420
Munera, 1. 365; 5. 171-4, 277-8, 294, 345-
7; 6. 192; is Mary Stuart: 5. 174; is
wealth of Spain and garrison at Smerwick:
5. 314
Munster, 1. 261; 2. 339; 5. 233; 6. 291,
431, 436; 8. 463, 633
Murals, 3. 208, 292
Murder, 4. 222
Muret, Antoine, 7. 650
Murmelius, 7. 374
Murray, Sir James, 2. 510
Murray, M. A., 8. 486
Murrough, 2. 445
Musaeus, 4. 217, 229, 237; 7. 322, 464, 519;
8. 297, 424
Muscaroll, 8. 395, 597, 600, 605-6
Muse, Christian: 8. 330; Spenser's: 1. 173-4,
296, 506-15; 6. 292; 7. 372, 390, 424-5,
654; 8. 327-8, 602
Muses, 2. 365-6; 3. 253; 7. 276, 284, 309,
319; 8. 301, 311-34, 367, 459, 462, 470,
517, 533, 535, 538, 540-1
Muses Gardin for Delights, 1. 181
Music, 1. 206-7, 241-2, 273, 305, 378; 2.
201, 366, 386; 6. 184, 249; 7. 276, 370,
381, 392, 429-30, 483, 541, 576, 578, 585,
594, 619, 638, 682; 8. 496-7, 500, 531,
661; Elizabethan: 8. 367; and *F. Q.* 7:
6. 423; identity with thought: 8. 295;
and running water: 4. 242; 8. 311; Spen-

ser's verse set to: 7. 406; 8. 643; of the
Spheres: 7. 533. *See also* Cadence; Metre;
Sound; Spenser, Edmund, his own myth-
ographer; Verse

Musidorus, 2. 401-2; 6. 242-3

Mutability, 1. 187, 417-8, 507, 512, 515;
2. 211; 5. 155-6; 6. 273-6, 278-9, 310-3,
390-1, 408; 8. 609; and Ate: 4. 310;
6. 278, 449; is corruption, sin: 6. 427;
and Fortune: 6. 293, 418, 437; 8. 346;
materialistic: 6. 393-4; and Nature: 2.
211; 3. 254; 5. 155; 6. 278, 292-6, 418;
place in Book 7 of *F. Q.*: 6. 427; Spenser's
conception: 6. 389-429, 444; 7. 438, 445-
6; 8. 400. *See also* Change; Vicissitude

Mutability Cantos. *See Faerie Queene*, Book
7

Muzio, Giralomo, 6. 329

Myles, 5. 194

Myrrh, 1. 181

Myrrha, 3. 220; 4. 205; 8. 340

Myrsine, 8. 340

Myrtle, 8. 340

My Slomber, 8. 270, 283, 512, 514-5

Mystery, 5. 254

Mystery plays. *See* Miracle plays

Mysticism, 7. 537, 539, 657, 666-9, 673-6,
679-82

Myth, 7. 682; of locality: 6. 429-32. *See also*
Ovidian myth

Mythology, 1. 230-1, 240, 249, 369-71; 2.
250, 265, 270, 273, 346, 373; 3. 260;
4. 223; 6. 414; 7. 268; 8. 329; allegory in:
5. 234; classical: 1. 331, 421, 484, 507;
2. 336; 3. 242, 357; 6. 247, 425; 7. 445-
6, 580; Elizabethan treatment of: 7. 599;
in Renaissance art: 3. 392-99; in similes:
6. 243; Spenser follows religiously: 3. 254;
6. 247. *See also* Spenser, Edmund, his own
mythographer

Nabal, 3. 275

Nadal, T. W., 7. 430-1, 438-41, 445-6; 8.
599, 608-10

Nadder, 4. 256

Nagle, Elizabeth, 8. 633

Naiads, 8. 334, 338

Nais, 6. 307

Names, 5. 199; 7. 267, 574, 578; 8. 333,
347; coinage of: 1. 202; 2. 209; 5. 186;
7. 454-5; feigned: 1. 264; 7. 463-77; more
for sound than meaning: 7. 491; 8. 311;
varied from original sources: 1. 264-5; 5.
186

Nangle. *See* Nagle

Napoleon, 2. 327

Narcissus, 3. 220; 6. 246; 8. 432, 548

Narwhal, 2. 359, 361

Nash, Thomas, 1. 492; 7. 650; 8. 299, 316,
393, 506, 582; Spenser, praise of: 3. 306;
7. 644; *Apology*: 8. 320; *Christs Teares
over Jerusalem*: 7. 379, 477; 8. 392, 634-
5; Greene's *Arcadia*, Preface: 7. 472;
Greene's Menaphon, Introduction: 1. 312;
7. 304; *Pierce Pennilesse*: 1. 255; 2. 353-
4; 3. 306, 428; 7. 419; *Strange News*:
8. 319, 375, 479, 575, 580-1, 584; *Summer's Last Will*: 8. 480; *Terrors of the
Night*: 8. 393; *To the Gentlemen Students
of Both Universities*: 7. 394; *Unfortunate
Traveller*: 2. 209

Natalis Comes, *Mythologia*: 1. 512, 514-5;
2. 251-2, 351; 4. 243, 274; Book 1: 1: 8.
376; 9: 2. 239; Book 2: 1: 3. 292-3;
5. 242; 6. 279, 312; 2: 3. 297; 5. 164,
167; 8. 350; 4: 2. 261; 6. 301; 5: 8. 492;
6: 2. 393; 4. 196-7; 8: 1. 236; 4. 242-5,
276; 6. 305; 9, 10: 5. 172, 212; Book 3:
Preface: 2. 251, 267; 1: 1. 234; 2: 5.
258; 3, 4, 10: 2. 357; 5: 2. 253; 6: 4.
182; 12: 1. 231; 2. 233, 257; 3. 244;
8. 323; 15: 1. 195; 4. 197; 6. 275; 17:
6. 276-7; 19: 3. 345; Book 4: 3: 2. 374-
6; 8. 491; 6: 8. 428; 7: 3. 213; 8: 7.
329; 9: 5. 252; 6. 410; 10: 3. 295; 7.
288; 8. 470; 11: 6. 211; 13: 2. 369; 4.
235-7; 7. 525, 567; 8. 327; 14: 7. 511;
15: 6. 252; 7. 289; 16: 5. 242; 8. 467-8;
Book 5: 1: 3. 266; 5: 2. 267, 370; 8. 483;
10: 1. 243; 12: 4. 276; 13: 3. 293; 5.
162, 215-7; 8. 328; 14: 8. 339; 16: 3. 208,
254; 7. 440; Book 6: 1: 3. 294; 5. 229;
8. 484; 6: 2. 359, 375-6, 394; 7: 2. 373;
9: 3. 293; 10: 5. 229; 16: 6. 280; 20-1:
1. 249; 5. 171, 219; 6. 279, 410; 8. 384;
22: 3. 266, 279: 6. 213, 277; 23: 3. 280;
7. 333; 24: 6. 285, 289-90; Book 7: 1:
4. 319; 5. 172, 203, 250, 255, 257; 2: 6.
307; 4: 4. 169; 6. 251; 7: 2. 264; 8.
449; 11: 8. 309, 377, 475; 13: 2. 364-6;
14: 4. 169; 8. 308; 15: 1. 514; 7. 288;
8. 312, 329; 18: 3. 293; Book 8: 1:
2. 384; 4. 276; 2: 4. 247; 8. 386; 3:
4. 242; 4: 4. 244; 5. 231; 6: 1. 208; 4.
247, 275; 8: 1. 199; 12: 2. 355; 8. 346;
13: 6. 306-7; 17: 5. 157; 19: 6. 301; 22:
2. 205; 4. 245; Book 9: 4: 8. 309; 5:
1. 242; 6: 2. 357; 12: 3. 240; 13: 3. 294;
6. 308; 18: 5. 257; Book 10; De Flumini-
bus Inferorum: 4. 196; De Faunis: 1. 240;
De Nymphis, De Baccho: 2. 193, 382-3;
3. 251

National Library of Scotland, 8. 682

Natura, 2. 374-5; 6. 397-8, 403

Nature, 1. 213, 507, 512, 515; 2. 244-5, 366, 390; 3. 259, 343, 345; 4. 310; 5. 155, 215; 6. 281-2, 284, 447; 7. 268, 550, 562, 566, 630-1; is *anima mundi*: 6. 412-3; and Art: 8. 397; beauty: 6. 397, 412; and Concord: 4. 334; cult: 6. 398; decay of: 8. 380; fecundity: 2. 211; and God: 6. 296, 412, 418, 422; 7. 669, 672; great grandmother: 6. 299, 398, 404, 428; island of: 3. 254; and Justice: 6. 440; Law of: 2. 251; 8. 353; and Mutability: 2. 211; 3. 254; 5. 155; 6. 278, 311, 410; mythologized: 7. 268; Neo-platonic conception of: 6. 411-3, 415-21; pageant of: 6. 302-10, 409, 420, 436, 447; poetry of: 4. 239; 7. 282; in *Shepheardes Calender*: 7. 630; Spenser's conception of: 6. 281-2, 422-3, 427-8; stepdame: 7. 443; sympathy with man: 1. 239; 7. 245, 249, 269, 425, 452, 505; truth to: 1. 180-1, 443; 7. 275, 282; 8. 398; veiled: 6. 294-6, 397-8, 403, 412, 415, 449; and Venus: 4. 310, 321, 333; 6. 411-2, 449; womb and grave: 3. 257; 8. 285. *See also* Court of Nature
Nauclerus, Johannes, 2. 330, 452
Naunton, Robert, 2. 281; 4. 206; 6. 358; 8. 292-3, 304
Nausa, 3. 281
Nausicaa, 1. 305, 496; 8. 472
Navigation, 2. 252, 358
Naylor, E. W., 2. 201, 485
" ne," 7. 357
Neaera, 7. 464
Nebuchadnezzar, 1. 238; 4. 167; 8. 305
Neckam, Alexander, 4. 259-60, 264; 8. 288
Nectar, 7. 416; 8. 433, 512
Needham, Lady. *See* Aston, Frances
Needham, Sir Robert, 4. 314-5; 8. 417-8, 455
Neff, M. L., 5. 170, 345-7
Neill, J. K., 2. 294-5; 5. 319-24
Neilson, William A., 3. 353; 6. 224; 8. 466, 541
Nembroth. *See* Nimrod
Nemesian, 1. 311; 7. 385, 423
Nemesis, 3. 269; 5. 243; 8. 394
Nene, 4. 260
Nenna, Giovanni Battista, 6. 344; 8. 506-7, 708, 736
Nennius (historian), 1. 176
Nennius (son of Hely), 2. 323-4, 332
Neo-Latin, 8. 566
Neologisms: 8. 676
Neo-platonism, 1. 357-9; 2. 382; 3. 245, 326; 4. 307; 6. 389-90, 400, 404, 410-21; 7. 524, 529, 540, 547, 563, 566, 659-61, 662-81; 8. 442, 450, 453-4, 493, 631, 639-43, 653; Academy: 7. 559; and courtly

love: 4. 223; key to allegory of *F. Q.*: 1. 358; mystics: 7. 557, 666-9, 673-6; Renaissance: 7. 524, 662-76
Nepenthe, 1. 331; 3. 246; 4. 186-7
Nepotes, 1. 232
Neptune, 1. 236; 3. 296, 393-4, 398; 4. 243, 246, 276, 316; 8. 400-1, 413, 597, 607
Nereids, 4. 242, 273-6
Nereus, 4. 246-7; 8. 413
Nero, 7. 463; 8. 289
Nessus, 1. 299
Nestor, 2. 299
Net, 2. 392-3; 3. 302; 5. 235-6; 8. 639
Netherlands, 1. 459; 5. 226-7, 244, 247-55, 279-80, 300-1, 303, 305, 317; 6. 384; 8. 304, 354; represented by Lion: 1. 453
Neve, Philip, 8. 708-9, 736-7
Neville, Alexander, 7. 463
Neville, Charles, Earl of Westmoreland, 2. 402; 3. 276, 279; 8. 374; is Paridell: 3. 378; 4. 171; 5. 245, 299, 301
New Abbey, 2. 399
New Custom, 8. 591
New Jerusalem, 1. 282, 290-2, 368, 370, 424, 503; 7. 561
New Law, 1. 399-401
New Poetry, 7. 371, 374, 390; 8. 333, 391, 532, 549
New Ross, 4. 269
New Testament, 1. 268, 285, 295, 407, 457, 466, 475; 8. 357-8
New Year, 2. 203; 5. 165; 6. 303; 7. 242-4, 435-8; 8. 421-2, 598, 633-4
New York Public Library, 1. 519; 8. 680-1, 706, 717
Newberry Library, 1. 519; 7. 709; 8. 681, 716
Newbolt, H., 7. 384
" newell," 7. 306
Newfangle, 1. 215-6; 8. 364, 577
Newre, 6. 424
Newton, A. Edward, 7. 708
Newton, Thomas (poet), 7. 468
Newton, Thomas (editor), 7. 544
Nibelungen Lied, 3. 332
Nicander, 1. 402; 2. 361
Niccols, Richard, 1. 478-9; 3. 275; 5. 329; 8. 580
Nichols, John, *Progresses of Queen Elizabeth*: 1. 473-5; 2. 407-8; 4. 324; 5. 184-5, 203; 6. 304, 309; 7. 475-6; 8. 403
Nichols, Josias, 6. 387
Nicholson, Brinsley, 7. 465; 8. 274-9, 411, 415, 616
Nicodemus, Gospel of: 1. 288
Nicolas, N. H., 7. 403
Nicole de Margival, 3. 353

Nicolo degli Agnostini, 2. 238, 390-1
Nicolson, M. E., 1. 249
Nicomachides, 5. 189
Nidd, 4. 262
Night, 1. 229-32, 250, 459; 2. 232-3, 257, 259; 3. 244; 6. 302, 308, 420; 8. 323-4, 468; is Countess of Salisbury: 1. 462-3, 468-9; Night's counsel: 1. 189; horses of: 1. 229, 366; 3. 302
Nightingale, 7. 405, 411; 8. 426, 434
Night-raven, 2. 369; 7. 316; 8. 487
Nile, 1. 184-7; 3. 251; 8. 406
Nimrod, 1. 444; 4. 167; 8. 305
Nine, 2. 480, 484-5
" Nine Comoedies," 2. 432; 6. 378; 8. 316, 437, 516-8; and Teares of the Muses: 8. 516, 534
Ninus, 2. 289; 8. 305
Niobe, 4. 207-8
Nisus, 3. 272
Nitze, W. A., 6. 366
Nobility, 6. 338. See Ancestry; Breeding
Noble, J. A., 8. 443
Noie, 7. 444
Nonnus, 1. 184; 4. 244
Noradin, 3. 286-7
Norden, John, 4. 257, 270
Nore, 4. 269
Norfolk, 7. 312
Norfolk, Duke of. See Howard, Thomas
Norfolk pamphlet, 5. 320
Norlin, George, 7. 408, 496
Norris, Sir John, 1. 449; 3. 308; 5. 248
North, Christian, 8. 665
North, Christopher. See Wilson, John
North, Eliza, 7. 312, 482, 653-4; 8. 665
North, Roger, 7. 653-4; 8. 665
North country, 7. 250, 253, 309-15, 331, 375, 386-7, 581, 651, 653-4
North, Thomas, 7. 653-4; 8. 300, 328, 353, 389, 585, 665; Diall of Princes: 5. 342-3, 345; Plutarch's Lives: 1. 489. See also Plutarch
Northampton, Earl of. See Howard, Henry
Northampton, Marquess of. See Snachenbergh
Northamptonshire, 7. 312, 315
Northbrooke, John, 7. 608
Northern dialect. See Dialect
Northumberland, Earl of. See Perey, Henry
Norton, Dan, 8. 503, 664-6, 722
Norton, Thomas, 7. 465
Norway, 3. 231
Norwegians, 2. 332
Norwich, 8. 362
Notcutt, H. C., 298-301; 5. 285-7
Notre Dame, 1. 294

Noun becomes a verb, 6. 258
Novels, 1. 340; 7. 260
Novius, 5. 213
Nowell, Alexander, 8. 418
Nowell, Robert, 7. 314; 8. 418
Noyes, Alfred, 8. 602
Nugent, Nicholas, 5. 319
Numa, 2. 320-1; 5. 163
Nun of Kent, 1. 461, 465, 467
Nyctelius, 8. 338
Nymphs, 2. 193-4, 3. 241-2, 251-2, 301-2; 4. 276; 6. 302, 413; 7. 276, 280, 309, 316; 8. 402, 464-5, 482; fairies, same as: 2. 336; 7. 297; 8. 311-2, 338, 463

Oak, 6. 209, 287-9, 299, 304, 398; 7. 369; 8. 304, 360, 389, 411; and briar: 7. 253-5, 260-6, 603; 8. 577; is Grindal: 7. 261; is Norfolk: 7. 254; is Romanism: 7. 603; is Watson: 7. 363
Oat, 7. 380
Oath, 1. 225-6; 5. 168, 225; 6. 227
Obedience, 1. 406, 424; 3. 385; 4. 237
Oberon, 1. 254, 290, 291-3, 480; 2. 187-8, 334-7; is Henry VIII: 1. 480; 2. 334-6, 453
Oblivion, 8. 301
O'Brien, Murrogh, 2. 398
Obscure origin, 1. 294; 6. 204. See also Breeding
Occasion, 1. 366; 2. 225-7, 350; 3. 392
Occleve, Thomas, 7. 616
Occupatio, 8. 265, 288
Oceanus, 4. 276; 8. 483
Ockland, Christopher, 7. 285
O'Connor, Matthew, 1. 379-89
Octa, 1. 321; 2. 319; 3. 236
Octavius, King of Britain, 2. 331
October, 6. 420
Odorico, 1. 239
Odysseus. See Ulysses
Oedipus, 5. 257-8
Oenone, 3. 281; 8. 285
Offensiveness, 1. 221
Ogier the Dane, 2. 355, 445
Ogyges, 4. 245
Olaus Magnus, 2. 364
Olcon, 7. 469
Old Age, 4. 182-3
Old English alliterative verse, 7. 634, 636-7, 639
Old men, 3. 273
Old stories, 6. 237
Old Testament, 1. 295, 457, 466, 475
Oldys, William, 6. 349; 7. 464; 8. 292, 294-5, 302, 317, 319-20, 501
Olimpia, 5. 247; 6. 234

Olive, 7. 285
Olivier de la Marche, 1. 324
Ollyphant, 2. 372; 3. 266, 313, 320, 327, 372, 390; 6. 437
Olympia, 3. 265-6; 8. 381
Olympias, 1. 238
Olympic Games, 3. 265-6
Olympus, 3. 265-6; 8. 381
Omission of expletive or pronoun, 1. 303; 7. 248, 270; 8. 314
Omphale, 5. 203-4
" One day . . . ," 8. 423
O'Neill, Hugh, Earl of Tyrone, 5. 263
O'Neill, Shane, 2. 400, 402; 5. 162, 167; 6. 233
O'Neills, 2. 191, 400-1
Onomacritus, 6. 274
Onomatopoeia, 1. 195, 227; 2. 368; 3. 268; 4. 221; 6. 208; 8. 415
Ooraxes, 4. 248
Opera Aliquot, 5. 219
Operinus, 7. 596
Oppian, 2. 360-1, 364; 8. 408
Ops, 6. 279, 301
Orc, 1. 295, 374-6; 3. 263, 270; 4. 203, 205
Orcus, 2. 254, 370; 8. 377
Ordeal, 5. 168
Order, 1. 225, 270; 4. 310; 5. 239, 243-4; 6. 293-5, 427, 429, 440, 449; 7. 254
Orestes, 4. 223-4, 303, 316
Organs, 8. 477
Orgoglio, 1. 199, 366, 368-9, 399, 414, 417, 437-8, 471; 2. 471; 6. 191, 225, 229; is Carnal Pride: 1. 423-4, 428; is Charlemagne: 1. 449, 485; his dungeon the Inquisition: 1. 441; is reign of Mary Tudor: 1. 470; fight with is a trial of faith: 1. 428-9; is persecution under Mary: 1. 453; is Francis, Duke of Guise: 1. 449, 460; Henry VIII, one trait of: 1. 456, 458; is Philip II: 1. 441, 458, 460, 465, 470; is Romanism: 1. 470; is Spanish marriage: 1. 460; is spiritual pride: 1. 432: victory over Red Cross Knight is triumph of Papacy: 1. 450, 455-6; is capture of Calais: 1. 459
Orguil, 1. 405
Orguilleus, 1. 254
Orichalcum, 8. 395
Origen, 7. 558
Orillo, 2. 346
Orimont, 3. 380; 5. 186
Orion, 1. 363; 2. 204-5; 6. 306
Orkneys, 3. 231
Orlando, 1. 295, 360, 374-6, 418-9; 2. 207, 229, 275-6, 279; 3. 264, 367, 369, 375; 5. 247; 6. 202

Ormonde, Earl of. *See* Butler, Thomas
Ormonde, Countess of. *See* Sheffield, Elizabeth
Orontea, 5. 197
Orpheus, 1. 239, 302; 4. 174; 7. 381, 446, 510-1, 518-9; 8. 297, 307-8, 311, 332, 344, 434, 459-60; *Argonautica*: 2. 373; 3. 293; 5. 166; 6. 274; *Hymns*: 1. 231; 7. 666; *To Adonis*: 3. 255; *To Aphrodite*: 7. 481; *To Natura*: 6. 295, 299, 412-3; *To Nereus*: 4. 247; *To Zeus*: 6. 281
Orpine, 8. 399
Orsilochus, 3. 238
Orson, 1. 293; 6. 201
Orthrus, 6. 213
Orwen, W. R., 8. 528, 607
Orwin, Thomas, 8. 584, 679, 735
Osiris, 4. 319; 5. 214-7, 295
Ossian, 6. 425-6
Oswald, 3. 233
Otes de Lisle, Sir, 1. 391
Othello, 5. 176
" other," 2. 226, 343; 5. 202
Otherworld, 2. 444-9; 6. 184
Oure (river), 4. 271
Our Lady's Bower, 7. 328
Outlaws. *See* Thieves
Ouze (rivers), 4. 252, 257-8, 260, 262
Ouzel (bird), 8. 467
Ouzel (river), 4. 257
Ovid, 1. 205, 404, 406, 421, 514; 3. 301, 345-9, 352, 393-6; 4. 180-1; 6. 398, 407, 414, 449; 7. 266, 394, 426, 448, 654; 8. 449, 564; Spenser, compared with: 3. 287; 5. 262; 6. 285; 8. 401-3
    Amores: Book 1: 1: 4. 203; 5. 206; 8. 297;2: 3. 299, 354; 5. 210; 7: 2. 205; 9: 8. 423; 13: 3. 293; 14: 7. 567; 15: 8. 532; Book 2: 4: 1. 304; 5: 2. 214, 296; 3. 279-80; 5. 189; 6: 8. 460; 9: 4. 202; 12, 13, 17: 7. 252; 12: 4. 190; 16: 8. 467; Book 3: 4: 3. 275; 7: 7. 394
    Art of Love: Book 1: 77: 4. 229; 95-6: 5. 199; 117: 3. 243; 6. 236; 118: 6. 216; 473-6: 8. 426; 772: 1. 311; Book 2: 439: 3. 212; 445: 5. 207; 598: 1. 310; 735: 6. 211; Book 3: 37: 8. 339; 69-70: 1. 198; 77: 7. 407; 83: 8. 490; 224: 2. 384; 7. 567; 396: 3. 265; 401-2: 4. 194; 549-50: 7. 389; 564: 5. 263; 653: 5. 206; *Ex Ponto*: 2. 314; 3. 262, 292; 4. 185; 6. 244; 7. 285; 8. 426, 505
    Fasti: Book 1: 65, 125: 4. 221; 89-112: 8. 352; 125: 6. 308; 233: 5. 160; 375: 4. 252; 425-32: 3. 213; 461: 1. 304; 555-6: 5. 234; 637-50: 4. 226; 645-6: 5. 171; Book 2: 83-105: 4. 249-50; 119:

2. 303; 175, 447: 3. 226; 207-10: 6. 259; 219: 2. 342; 305: 5. 198; 6. 270; 449 ff.: 2. 193; 457: 6. 308; 683-4: 8. 388; 806: 6. 258; Book 3: 1-13: 1. 174; 6. 303; 107-8: 8. 432; 255: 2. 193; 263, 275: 2. 321; 451-8: 8. 309; 507-16: 6. 251; 555: 5. 199; 720: 5. 162; 851-76: 3. 293; 6. 303; 891-2: 4. 226; Book 4: 23-30: 6. 303; 91: 7. 481; 201 ff.: 1. 242; 249: 4. 253; 429-42: 8. 496-7; 459: 4. 278; 5. 231-2; 715: 3. 293; Book 5: 19-25: 5. 241; 23: 8. 484; 111-28, 693-720: 6. 303, 307; 164: 3. 213; 195 ff.: 7. 289; 201 ff.: 2. 238; 8. 495; 419-20: 1. 198; 537: 2. 204; 541: 4. 244; 607-14: 3. 293; 617: 5. 158; 693-720: 8. 505; Book 6: 5: 7. 387, 391; 13-4: 7. 318; 292-306: 6. 301; 489, 497: 4. 244; 629: 1. 237; 637-48: 4. 226; 741: 1. 236; 745: 1. 237; 811: 8. 459

Heroides: 1: 1. 198; 3. 283; 5. 212; 2: 8. 339; 4: 1. 240; 3. 262, 298; 4. 277; 7. 366; 5: 6. 243; 8. 504; 9: 2. 294; 5. 198, 203; 12: 8. 471; 15: 3. 306; 7. 394; 17: 3. 280; 18, 19: 7. 519; 20, 21: 2. 265-6; 8. 474

Metamorphoses: and Book 7 of *F.Q.*: 6. 273; and Renaissance painting: 3. 395-6; Book 1: 5 ff.: 3. 257; 7. 512; 8. 330-1; 10: 7. 461; 17-20: 7. 481; 18-25: 7. 511-2; 21 ff.: 6. 295; 7. 550; 25 ff.: 4. 226; 85: 2. 288; 89-113: 5. 160, 166; 8. 354; 107: 3. 258; 138-40: 2. 255; 149- 50: 6. 305; 8. 350; 156-62: 6. 278; 168-252: 6. 276, 408; 175-6: 6. 277; 179-80: 6. 278, 280; 187: 8. 413; 190-1: 5. 247; 241: 2. 200; 253 ff.: 6. 280; 272-3: 2. 342; 3. 264; 336: 7. 461; 399: 5. 157; 416-37: 1. 186; 419: 3. 340; 422-33: 1. 184; 3. 251; 8. 470; 452 ff.: 2. 379; 468-73: 3. 294; 7. 480; 492: 3. 211; 498: 8. 467; 505: 6. 216; 506: 3. 243; 6. 236; 521-4: 4. 199; 7. 424; 533: 5. 228; 543-7: 8. 429; 548: 2. 196; 570: 8. 498; 601 ff.: 7. 382; 623-722: 7. 392; 625-7: 7. 333; 649: 7. 337; 662: 3. 242; 668-77: 8. 376; 689-712: 7. 248, 281; 748: 5. 229; 750-2, 329: 8. 311; Book 2: 1-300: 6. 276; 1-3: 3. 208; 4. 229; 5-18: 2. 373; 3. 292; 4. 189; 23-4: 5. 240; 25-30: 6. 293, 302-3, 305-6; 31-380: 6. 408; 69: 2. 364; 112-5: 8. 466; 119: 5. 229; 153-5: 2. 342; 5. 229; 195-200: 5. 229; 225: 8. 498; 296-7: 7. 303; 340-66: 8. 339; 342: 6. 217; 344: 3. 226; 362: 1. 202; 392: 1. 305; 397: 6. 258; 457 ff.: 6. 283, 409; 542 ff.: 3. 295; 592: 1. 194; 623: 5. 231; 640: 6. 185; 760-832: 5. 266-7; 768-96: 1. 221-

2; 833: 3. 293; 846-75: 8. 401; 867-8: 6. 303; Book 3: 31-45: 1. 296; 69-73: 1. 299; 131 ff.: 6. 285; 138-252: 3. 253; 157-62: 2. 238; 4. 222; 6. 290, 295; 173, 180: 6. 283, 409; 184: 1. 216; 5. 241; 253 ff.: 3. 293; 303-6: 6. 277; 339-510: 1. 221; 3. 22, 247, 259; 6. 246; 7. 365; 8. 349, 432; 568-71: 3. 264; 701: 5. 231-2; Book 4: 1-166: 3. 268; 11: 3. 212; 20: 5. 162; 26-7: 1. 218; 46: 1. 235; 122: 6. 201; 176-89: 1. 175; 2. 393; 185: 4. 193; 190: 3. 295; 192: 3. 295; 8. 395; 228: 1. 207; 241: 8. 395; 285 ff.: 1. 248; 330-2: 2. 296; 8. 474; 416 ff., 512, 519-21: 4. 244; 432-3: 2. 256; 449: 1. 234; 458 ff.: 1. 235; 461: 6. 280; 480: 5. 190; 495 ff.: 3. 288; 528: 5. 231; 756: 6. 277; 8. 310; 782: 1. 254; 785-6: 8. 309; 797: 3. 296; Book 5: 5-7: 1. 299; 104: 4. 212; 158: 4. 185; 177-80: 1. 253; 254-63: 8. 301, 324, 459; 339-84: 1. 511-2, 514; 7. 497; 388--91: 6. 245-6; 533: 2. 268; 538-52: 4. 196; 570: 3. 278; 572 ff.: 6. 283, 290, 409, 430; 604 ff.: 3. 243; 6. 236; 618-21: 2. 196; 642 ff.: 8. 339; Book 6: 1-145: 3. 396-7; 8. 400-3, 607, 610; 37-8: 2. 210; 70-7: 8. 403; 87: 2. 378-9; 97: 8. 486; 101: 8. 403; 103-28: 3. 291-6, 394; 4. 214; 6. 303, 307; 8. 397, 498; 127-30: 8. 402; 143-5: 8. 403; 146 ff.: 4. 208; 7. 284; 152-5: 5. 249; 173: 2. 268; 174-5: 7. 303; 176 ff.: 2. 298; 186: 2. 357; 412 ff.: 8. 343; 424-674: 7. 349: 429: 8. 468; 455: 3. 211; 516-8: 2. 277; 527: 1. 241; 6. 216; 529: 3. 243; 6. 236; 558: 4. 212; 674: 8. 343; 685-6: 5. 262; 695: 6. 217; Book 7: 2. 374; 1 ff.: 2. 373; 225: 8. 498; 408-15: 6. 270; 530: 3. 226; Book 8: 176-82: 6. 251; 303, 405-6: 4. 224; 339: 6. 217; 373: 8. 505; 422-4: 1. 306; 452-4: 4. 182; 561: 3. 242; 695: 1. 299; 761: 1. 202; Book 9: 46-9: 4. 189; 71: 6. 270; 140: 5. 203; 153: 1. 300; 191: 4. 169; 194-6: 5. 228; 229-72: 8. 299; 429: 4. 182; 453: 3. 220; 722: 8. 461; 735-44: 3. 220; 782: 4. 238; Book 10: 8. 344; 1: 1. 287; 8. 460; 11-77: 1. 234; 76: 2. 232; 86 ff.: 2. 378; 6. 245; 90-104: 1. 179, 181; 3. 258; 91, 263: 8. 339; 120 ff.: 1. 243; 130: 1. 242; 155: 3. 294; 162-219: 3. 259, 295; 197-200: 8. 339; 298 ff.: 3. 220; 312 ff.: 4. 205; 372-3: 1. 259; 452: 2. 369; 500: 1. 182; 519-739: 7. 486-7, 497-8; 519: 3. 208; 535-45: 3. 208-9; 560-605: 2. 265; 634: 1. 307; 705: 3. 209; 717-8: 8. 498; 728 ff.: 3. 208; 734-

9: 7. 498; Book 11: 50: 1. 302; 51-3: 8. 307; 73: 3. 212; 142-5: 4. 201; 146 ff.: 7. 319; 194-220: 8. 345; 200: 2. 342; 217 ff.: 3. 240; 6. 254; 229: 6. 299; 237, 249-56: 3. 241; 312: 6. 277; 8. 310; 384-478: 7. 432, 434, 439; 435: 6. 217; 554: 8. 498; 592 ff.: 1. 192-3, 195; 617-21: 1. 195; 647: 5. 190; 771: 3. 262; 5. 181; Book 12: 44-6: 3. 256; 50-2: 1. 299; 102 ff.: 6. 207; 210 ff.: 4. 169, 224; 6. 251; 536-41: 4. 169: Book 13: 25: 8. 344; 162 ff.: 3. 240; 241-6: 5. 212; 8. 345; 262-5: 5. 189; 394-8: 3. 295; 404-7, 565-71: 5. 232; 415: 2. 298; 547: 6. 259; 806: 3. 262; 870: 5. 231; 904 ff.: 4. 243; Book 14: 116-7: 2. 370; 122: 2. 256; 255: 2. 370; 291-2: 8. 428; 403-5: 1. 231; 639: 1. 242; 694: 8. 394; 767-9: 3. 278; 7. 497; Book 15: 6. 409; 54: 4. 259; 103-42: 6. 300; 132: 3. 239; 165-478: 6. 300; 165-7, 249: 3. 257; 196: 6. 312; 197-213: 6. 302-3, 409; 212: 7. 256; 234-7: 6. 300, 310; 241-51: 6. 423; 249-58: 6. 313; 252-60: 3. 340, 347; 298: 3. 277; 317: 1. 248; 362-4: 1. 186-7; 375-8: 1. 186; 497: 1. 237; 5. 231; 504, 524-9: 5. 230-1; 517: 1. 236; 553: 1. 294; 603-5: 1. 299; 781: 4. 182; 808: 4. 182; 845-6: 4. 184; 871-2: 7. 427; 8. 297; *Remedia Amoris*: 2. 433; 3. 212; 6. 260; 7. 270, 272; 8. 339

Tristia: 1. 1: 7. 394; 1. 2: 7. 460; 1. 4: 8. 314; 2. 13: 8. 459; 2. 299: 8. 490; 2. 568: 1. 512; 3. 5: 8. 426; 3. 7: 1. 238; 3. 9: 2. 373; 3. 11: 6. 216; 4. 3: 7. 355; 4. 6: 8. 425; 4. 10: 7. 252; 5. 1: 7. 355; 5. 8: 3. 269; 8. 9: 8. 394. *See also* Golding

Ovidian myth, 6. 252; 7. 454; 8. 401-2
Owl, 1. 412; 2. 296, 369; 4. 196; 8. 486
Owst, C. R., 5. 172
Ox, 3. 239
Oxford, 4. 252-3, 259-60; 6. 298-9; Reformers: 7. 674
Oxford Book of Proverbs, 8. 351-3, 356, 479
Oxford, Earl of. *See* De Vere, Edward
Oxymoron, 1. 243; 8. 285, 296, 407, 482, 500
Oza, 2. 319; 3. 236

Pacuvius, 2. 392; 6. 256
Paeon, 3. 242
Pagan and Paganism, 1. 200, 244; 5. 157; 7. 562, 591, 601-2; blended with Christian: 1. 273, 363; 7. 601, 667; 8. 493; kings: 1. 296. *See also* Classical
Page, 6. 196

Page, William, 7. 609
Pageantry, 1. 212, 410, 413; 2. 190; 3. 287; 4. 167, 239-40; 5. 184-5; 6. 184, 302-10, 409, 420, 433, 438; 8. 304, 437, 646-7, 672; lacking in *F.Q.* 6: 6. 317-8
Pageants, 1. 390, 415, 441, 450, 473-82, 493-4; 2. 190-1, 224; 3. 355-9; 4. 203-4; 5. 319; 6. 202, 302, 432; 7. 390, 608; 8. 304, 307, 461
Pageaunts, 2. 399; 3. 299-300, 393; 4. 324; 6. 436; 7. 322; 8. 304, 405, 512, 514, 526-8
Painless birth, 3. 253
Painter, William, 1. 488
Painting, 1. 207, 219, 225, 241, 277, 286, 288, 294-5, 305, 367-9, 413, 418; 2. 211, 213, 216, 217, 228, 259, 270-1, 277, 293, 373, 379; 3. 237, 309, 392-4, 399; 8. 402, 602; Flemish: 2. 366; Italian: 2. 366, 379; 6. 254; 7. 238, 267, 282: of St. George (possible source of *F.Q.* 1): 1. 390; miniature: 8. 397; mural: 3. 208; 4. 168, 209; 6. 298; Roman: 1. 512
Palaces, 5. 237-9; 8. 374
Palamon and Arcite, 4. 303; 5. 214; 6. 203
Palemon, 4. 243; 7. 345, 464, 469, 517
Palici, 8. 311
Palin, 7. 464, 467-8
Palingenius, 3. 340, 345; 4. 228; 7. 513-4, 552; 8. 281, 391
Palinode, 6. 359; 7. 290-6, 300, 306-7, 323, 334, 468, 584, 643; 8. 357; is Youth: 7. 603
Palladine, 3. 266, 328
Pallans, 5. 171
Pallas. *See* Minerva
Palmer, 1. 189; 2. 197, 230, 350, 352, 365, 370, 377, 393-5, 410, 427, 431, 471; abstract quality of temperance: 2. 429; type of Christ: 2. 429; is Conscience, God's Word, Sobriety: 2. 192; is John Knox: 2. 402; is prudence: 2. 188; Paphael, corresponds to: 2. 429; is reason: 2. 188, 192, 442-3; 3. 323; is Sir Henry Palmer: 2. 404; is Whitgift: 1. 492; 2. 188, 278, 401
Palmerin D'Oliva, 2. 394
Palmerin of England, 2. 230, 237, 348; 6. 201; 8. 342
Palm Sunday, 1. 243
Palomides, 6. 271
Pamela, 2. 402
Pan, 1. 243; 2. 295-6; 6. 281, 291; 7. 248, 319, 419, 598, 647; 8. 490; is Christ: 7. 288, 299, 601; is Francis I: 7. 418, 422; is God: 7. 333; is Henry VIII: 2.

384; 7. 274, 281-2, 288; is the Pope: 7. 288, 334

Pandemonium, 5. 217-8

Pandora, 8. 333

Pandora (Drayton's), 8. 451

Pandosto. See Greene, Robert

Panope, 3. 271

Panthea, 1. 291, 514; 2. 334-5

Panther, 8. 437

Pantomime, 2. 224-5; 3. 299-301, 356

Panwelt, 2. 332

Papacy, 1. 178, 423-4; 5. 314; 7. 586, 609; 8. 412. See Popery

Paradise, 3. 258; 7. 322, 397. *See also* Earthly Paradise; Love, Paradise of

Paradise of Daintie Devices, 7. 318; 8. 286; 332, 370

Paradox, 1. 177; 6. 240; 8. 294, 676

Paranomasia, 7. 247, 251

Parcae. *See* Fates

Parenthesis, 6. 485; 7. 246-7

Parhelion, 5. 188-9

Paridell, 1. 480-1; 2. 372; 3. 273, 276, 279-85, 313, 319-20, 328; 4. 188, 284, 299, 330; 5. 322, 324; is Earl of Arundel: 5. 245; is Earl of Oxford: 3. 380; is Westmoreland: 3. 378; 4. 171; 5. 245, 299, 301

Paris, of Troy, 2. 273, 277; 3. 240, 280-1, 320; 4. 223; 6. 293; 7. 333, 347, 392

Paris and Vienna, 4. 221

Parisiles, 6. 381

Parison, 7. 246, 444; 8. 484, 595

Parius, 3. 281

Park of Pride, 1. 416

Parker, Matthew, 1. 484; 7. 298, 300, 302, 359; 8. 361-2

Parker, R. E., 7. 625

Parkinson, John, 2. 263; 7. 498

Parlante, 3. 211

Parma, Prince of, 5. 226-7, 252

Parmenides, 7. 481

Parmenter, M., 7. 243, 248, 256, 304, 316, 346, 355, 404, 634

Parnassus, 1. 368, 370; 7. 319; 8. 313, 541

Paros, 3. 281

Parr, William, 7. 433, 435

Parry, William, 5. 320, 324

Parsons, Robert, 7. 360, 402

Part, W. M., 7. 616

Partheneia Sacra, 2. 368; 3. 284; 6. 200

Parthenius, 6. 380

Parthians, 2. 344

Participle, 7. 337

Pasiphae, 2. 366

Pasithea, 7. 289

"Pasquill," 1. 173; 3. 307

Passerat, Jean, 8. 434

Passions, 2. 458-62; 5. 287

Pastimes. *See* Games.

Pastoral, 1. 242; 3. 252; 5. 156-7; 6. 242-3, 255, 258; 7. 237, 240, 251, 390, 422, 447; 8. 594; Alexandrian: 7. 484; allegory: 7. 580, 582, 597; and chivalry: 7. 495; close of pastoral poem: 7. 251, 287, 482; convention: 6. 238, 362; 7. 248, 338, 397-401, 407-8, 417, 429, 442-3, 448, 478, 483, 485, 496, 591-2; 8. 296-7, 307, 381, 459; disguise: 7. 399, 483-5, 571, 576, 580-1, 585, 590, 593, 597, 604, 8. 629; elegy: 7. 395-401, 407-8, 432, 442, 483-6, 590; expressions: 6. 239; in *F. Q.* 6: 6. 317, 319-20, 347-8, 355, 360; French: 3. 253; 7. 277, 595-7; grief: 7. 278; Italian: 7. 595-7; language: 7. 614-30; native English: 7. 268, 277, 592-5; panegyric: 7. 275-7, 590; poets: 7. 240; Portuguese: 7. 590; romantic: 7. 644; satire: 7. 292, 590-1, 600, 604, 607; Spanish: 7. 590; tradition: 7. 571-6, 579, 581-2, 584, 587-99, 615, 618, 622, 625, 637, 644, 654

Pastorella, 3. 263; 5. 284; 6. 255-7, 260-1, 318-20, 325-6, 334, 340, 344, 349, 360, 371-81; is Elizabeth Boyle: 6. 318; is Frances Walsingham: 6. 350-3, 355, 363

Pastourelle, 7. 590

Patch, H. R., 4. 240; 5. 252

"pate," 7. 311-2

Patent Rolls, 5. 346

Pater, Walter, 7. 382; 8. 397

Pathetic Fallacy, 1. 239; 7. 245, 249, 321, 400, 443, 592, 597

Pathos, 1. 256; 2. 229

Patience, 1. 405-7, 424; 2. 206; 4. 237

Patmore, Coventry, 8. 659

Patmos, 2. 373

Paton, L. A., 1. 267

Patrick, Simon, 8. 589

The Patriot, 5. 177

Patriotism, 1. 266

Patroclus, 4. 316

Patronage, 8. 533-4, 537, 567, 584

Patrons, 7. 501

Pattison, Bruce, 7. 346

Paul of Perugia, 8. 387

Paul, St., 1. 308, 414, 416, 418, 422, 425, 435; 3. 324; 5. 338-9; 7. 672

Paulinus, 2. 327

Paulus Jovius, 8. 498

Pausanius, 2. 375; 3. 333; 4. 237, 246-7; 5. 166; 6. 398

Peace, 5. 244; 8. 649; Dame Peace: 1. 407

Peace, Tristram, 8. 649-51

Peacham, Henry, 5. 325, 367; 6. 337, 359; 8. 464, 508-9

Peacock, 1. 416; 8. 396

" peal," 5. 244

Pearl, 4. 226

Pearl, 7. 444; 8. 462, 469, 472

Pearson, A. S. F., 7. 325

" peasant," 6. 200, 255-6

Peasants' War, 5. 175, 342

" Peece," 3. 284

Peele, George, 4. 314; 6. 360; 8. 536, 540, 621; *Anglorum Feriae*: 1. 476; 6. 359; *Arraignment of Paris*: 3. 285; 7. 468, 594, 643; *David and Bethsabe*: 1. 224; 2. 399; *Eclogue Gratulatorie*: 6. 359-61; 7. 468, 594, 643; *Farewell to Drake and Norris*: 1. 476-7; *Old Wives Tale*: 2. 205; *Poly-hymnia*: 2. 203; 6. 361

Pelasgus, 4. 246

Pelerinage de Vie Humaine, 1. 277; 2. 253

Peleus, 2. 266; 3. 240; 6. 253-4, 299; 8. 345, 401, 652

Pelham, William, 5. 174

Pelion, 6. 299

Pelleas, 6. 271

Pelles, King, 1. 400

Pellite, 2. 318

Pelops, 2. 267

Pembroke College, Cambridge, 4. 259; 7. 361, 362, 404, 571, 610, 646, 650; 8. 317

Pembroke, Earl of. *See* Herbert, Henry

Penance, 1. 406-7; 6. 208, 210

Penda, 3. 233

Pendle, 7. 313, 362, 386, 616, 631, 653

Pendragon. *See* Arthur, Uther

Penelope, 1. 208; 5. 222; 8. 428

Peneus, 2. 378; 8. 499

Penia, 8. 468. *See also* Penury

Penitence, 2. 229

Penn, William, 2. 206

Penshurst, 4. 273; 7. 329-30, 371, 378, 395-6, 402, 489, 611

Pensioners, 1. 305

Pentecost, 1. 313

Penthesilea, 2. 218-9; 3. 238, 332, 336-7; 5. 200

Pentheus, 5. 231

Penthia, 7. 498-9

Penury, 3. 261; 7. 511. *See also* Penia

Penzance, 7. 462

Pepys, Samuel, 8. 666

Perceforest, 2. 451; 6. 382

Percival, 1. 293, 397-8, 399-401; 6. 367-71

Percy, Henry, Earl of Northumberland: 2. 402-3; 3. 307; 5. 304; 8. 374; is Blanda-mour: 3. 378; 4. 171; 5. 245, 299, 301

Percy, Thomas, *Folio Manuscripts*: 1. 259,

272, 391; *Reliques of Ancient Poetry*: 4. 213; 1. 4: 1. 188, 199; 1. 6: 6. 227-8; 2. 8: 1. 181; 5. 4: 7. 459; 5. 11: 2. 246; 5. 13: 2. 240; 5. 22: 8. 504; 6. 4: 7. 636; 8. 9: 1. 181; 9. 1: 1. 177

Percy, William, 7. 296

Peredur, 6. 369

Pérez, Alonzo, 6. 379-81

Pérez de Moya, Juan, 2. 375

Peridure, 2. 323; 3. 269

Perigot, 7. 338-40, 342, 344-6; 8. 319

Periphrasis, 8. 549, 677

Perissa, 2. 197, 201-2, 411, 417, 421, 425-6

Peristera, 8. 396-7

Perkinson, R. H., 8. 508

Perlesvaus, 1. 399-401; 6. 365-71

Perne, Andrew, 7. 293, 295, 606

Perodia, 6. 260-1

Perotto, Niccolò, 7. 289

Perrett, Wilfrid, 2. 314-6

Perrot, John, 1. 244, 464-5, 469; 5. 236; 6. 384-5; 7. 475

Persant of Inde, Sir, 1. 395

Persephone, 7. 416, 446; 8. 315-6, 343. *See also* Proserpina

Perseus, 1. 253, 293, 379; 4. 243; 8. 309, 377

Persia, 1. 214, 217, 293, 344

Persius Flaccus, 1. 357; 2. 223, 376; 4. 241; 6. 211; 7. 318-9, 390

Personification, 1. 339-40; 2. 230, 256-8, 412-3; 3. 287, 292, 299-303, 354-5; 4. 203, 237; 8. 294, 389. *See also* Prosopo-poeia

Perturbations, 1. 357-8; 2. 233-4, 284, 458-62; 6. 212

Pervigilium Veneris, 1. 178; 7. 440

Pessimism, 8. 293. *See also* Disillusion; Spen-ser, Edmund

Peter Cantor, 2. 425-6

Peter Lombard, 1. 310

Peter, St., 1. 423, 428; 3. 256

Petitus, 5. 198, 200

Petowe, Henry, 7. 473-4

Petrarch, 1. 418, 513; 3. 325; 4. 163; 7. 242, 246, 268, 320, 347, 373, 442, 492, 587, 589, 592, 596, 621, 650, 661, 675-6, 679; 8. 380, 393, 404, 413-6, 628-32, 634, 637-40; " the English Petrarch": 7. 468; and Spenser: 8. 530, 628-30, 638; *Africa*: 7. 240, 289; *Eclogues*: 1, 2, 11: 7. 249; 1: 7. 590; 3: 7. 317; 6, 7: 7. 359; 11: 7. 355; *Sestine*: 7. 347-9; *Son-nets*: 8. 455, 628, 631, 634, 637; *Sonnets and Canzoni*, ed. Carducci: 2, 3: 8. 423, 425; 4: 7. 279; 14: 8. 432; 17: 8. 438; 20: 8. 421; 21, 86: 7. 481; 8. 423, 432,

438-9; 23, 28, 37: 8. 656; 38: 7. 393;
42: 2. 246; 45: 8. 434; 49: 8. 421; 55:
5. 206; 76: 8. 433; 77: 8. 425; 79, 212,
214: 8. 440; 86: 8. 439; 90: 8. 474; 115:
7. 283; 121: 8. 423; 125: 8. 421; 126-7:
8. 450; 128: 2. 310; 130: 8. 454; 133:
8. 432, 451; 134: 8. 428; 150: 8. 432;
151, 154: 8. 422, 427; 159: 8. 474; 171:
3. 211; 173: 8. 428; 187: 7. 393; 8. 302;
189: 8. 431; 190: 8. 443; 192: 7. 331;
8. 433; 193: 8. 432; 203: 8. 426; 206:
8. 453; 215: 8. 423, 434; 237: 7. 348-9;
242: 8. 436; 248: 8. 382; 263: 7. 289;
264: 8. 654-6; 265: 8. 425, 430; 268:
7. 432, 445; 278: 7. 441; 292: 8. 474;
323: 8. 273-7, 413, 415-6, 438, 611-9,
622-5, 627; 343: 7. 721; 348: 8. 474;
353: 8. 454; 362: 7. 557; *Triumph of
Chastity*: 3. 354; *Triumph of Love*: 3.
298-9, 301, 354; 4. 217; *"Visions"*: 8.
414, 511-2
Petrarchans, 7. 370
Petrarchism, 3. 325; 7. 515, 535, 583, 618,
654, 661, 663-4, 669, 675; 8. 422, 429,
431, 435, 441, 448, 630-4, 637-40
Petre, Anne, 8. 666
Petre, Robert, Lord, 8. 666
Petre, William, 8. 662-3, 665-6
Petronius Arbiter, 2. 228; 3. 222; 7. 360
Pforzheimer, Carl H., 7. 696, 708; 8. 681,
697-8, 706
Phaedra, 1. 236-7; 2. 366
Phaedria, 1. 347; 2. 183, 199, 234, 241-5,
349, 352, 415, 425, 430, 435; 6. 216;
and Armida: 2. 445; and Dame du Lac:
2. 445
Phaedrus (fabulist), 1. 243; 2. 225; 7. 304
Phaedrus (Plato's), 4. 164
Phaer, Thomas, 8. 312
Phaethon, 5. 229; 8. 311, 339
Phantastes, 2. 297, 299, 438, 458
Phao, 4. 273-6
Phaon. *See* Phedon
Pharos of Alexander, 8. 305
Phasis, 4. 248
Phedon, 2. 229, 402, 411, 441, 471; 5. 169
Philautas, 4. 223
Philemon, 2. 229
Philip, Alexander, 7. 243
Philip II, 1. 454, 459-60, 471-2; 5. 225, 246,
260, 280, 285, 329; 8. 607; is Arachne:
8. 607; is Dolon: 5. 211-2, 316; is Gran-
torto: 5. 163, 261, 302, 312; is Geryoneo:
5. 249, 301-2; is Jove: 8. 607; is Neptune:
8. 607; portrait: 3. 392; is Proteus: 3.
379-80; is Sansjoy: 1. 449, 459-60; is the

Soldan: 5. 225-7, 302; is the spider: 8.
605, 607
Philips, Ambrose, 8. 460
Philisides, 6. 351, 373; 7. 491, 585; 8. 307.
See Sidney, Philip
Phillips, Edward, 2. 398; 4. 177-8; 7. 466,
468, 477, 488
Phillips, Gerald, 8. 605
Phillira, 3. 296
Phillis. *See* Phyllis
Philo Judaeus, 6. 423; 7. 514
Philobone, 1. 406
Philoclea, 3. 393
Philodemus, 8. 489
Philomela, 7. 349, 415-6; 8. 343
Φιλοφίλιππος, 7. 494
Philosophy, 1. 289; 4. 235; 7. 662; 8. 329
Philotime, 1. 356; 2. 252, 260, 262, 415,
418, 427-8, 434, 436; 6. 191
Philotimus, 2. 262
Philpot, 8. 486
Philpot, W. B., 7. 425; 8. 397, 593, 654
Philtra, 5. 195
Philyra, 6. 307
Phlegethon, 1. 230; 2. 231, 237, 248
Phlegeton, 2. 404
Phlegra, 2. 304
Phoeax, 4. 246
Phoebe, 6. 437
Phoenix, 1. 196; 2. 196; 4. 246
Phoenix, 2. 448; 8. 460
Phoenix Nest, 7. 485
Phorcus, 4. 243
Phornutus, 1. 514; 8. 541
Phyllis, 7. 266, 472, 476-7; 8. 338-9, 392,
497, 635. *See also* Spencer, Elizabeth
Physician's Prologue. See Chaucer (pseudo)
Physiologus, 1. 303
Physiology, 2. 468-70, 482
Pibrac, Guy du Faur, 8. 281
Piccolomini, Aeneaus Silvius, 8. 321
Piccolomini, Alessandro, 1. 329-30, 343, 354,
356; 2. 459; 3. 321; 4. 292-3
Piccolomini, Francesco, 3. 321
Pico della Mirandola, 6. 390; 7. 492, 528,
540, 551, 553, 559, 673-4; 8. 641; Com-
mentary on Benivieni: 3. 346; 7. 650, 661,
662, 671, 676-80; 1. 4: 7. 562-3; 2. 4:
7. 542; 2. 10: 7. 566; 2. 11: 7. 553, 566;
2. 13: 7. 553; 3. 2: 7. 568; 3. 8: 7. 569-
70; 3. 10: 7. 526-7, 531, 533; 6. 8: 7.
533; *Heptaplus*: 7. 552
Picts, 2. 331-3
Picturesque. *See* Spenser, Edmund
Pienaar, W. J. B., 1. 254, 8. 274-7, 280,
413-4, 621-2
Pierce, William, 7. 261

Piers, 6. 359; 7. 243, 290-6, 300-1, 334, 352, 358, 368, 370, 373-6, 382, 384-6, 388-9, 391, 468, 501, 584, 602-3, 643; 8. 319
Piers, John, 7. 296
Piers Plowman, 7. 293
Piers Plowman. See Langland, William
Piers Plowman's Creed, 6. 298; 7. 271; 8. 356
Pigna, Giovanni Battista, 1. 349, 359-60
Pilgrim, 1. 189
" Pilgrimage of life," 7. 674
Pilgrimage of the Life of Man, 2. 434
Pilgrimage to Parnassus, 8. 464
Pilkington, James, 1. 472
" pill and poll," 5. 171-2, 346; 8. 375
Pillars, 2. 269
Pinabello, 1. 259; 3. 288-9, 373; 6. 200, 216-7
Pinçon, Yanez, 2. 185
Pindar, 7. 393; 8. 299, 324; frag. 233 (257): 7. 307; *Isthmian*: 2. 366; *Nemean*: 8. 504; *Olympian*: 2. 252, 267; 5. 242; 8. 479, 504; *Pythian*: 1. 237; 2. 226, 356, 373; 4. 245; 7. 307
Pindarics, 8. 658, 675
Pindus, 8. 498
Pippin, 8. 486
Pirates. *See* Thieves
Pirithous, 4. 223-4, 316; 6. 251
Pisces, 7. 405, 414-5
Pisgah, 1. 291
Pity, 1. 405; 5. 247, 295-6; 6. 219, 345; 7. 517
Placidas, 4. 213, 284, 323; 6. 379
Plagiarism, 1. 252-3, 298
Planché, James R., 1. 247
Planetary year, 8. 440
Planets, 2. 480, 483; 6. 310-2; 7. 528, 539, 551, 553; 8. 440
Plantin edition of Virgil, 8. 342, 347
Plato, 1. 178, 329, 435, 446; 2. 264, 279, 459; 3. 343; 4. 235; 5. 297; 6. 345-6, 422; 7. 369, 381, 560, 599, 646-7, 662-74, 678, 680; doctor of Protestants: 6. 209; ethics: 1. 342; 2. 197, 365; idea of life as moral warfare: 1. 433; influence on Renaissance allegory: 1. 341, 346; soul, division of: 2. 416; Spenser's debt to: 1. 361; 2. 264, 416-7; 6. 390; 7. 369, 371, 376, 381, 387-8; State, theory of: 8. 303; *Alcibiades*: 5. 206; 6. 240; 7. 252; *Apology*: 2. 298; 8. 297; *Charmides*: 1. 194; 2. 189; *Ion*: 1. 173; 6. 277; 7. 371, 376; *Laws*: 7. 371, 391-2; *Lysis*: 4. 291, 295, 329, 332; *Minos*: 5. 165, 167; *Parmenides*: 2. 186; *Phaedo*: 1. 205; 2. 263-4;

57A: 1. 303; 62: 1. 279-80; 7. 413; 70-2: 3. 256; 82, 83: 1. 503; 111-13: 1. 234; 2. 267-8; 114: 2. 248
Phaedrus: 1. 175, 503; 2. 414, 429; 4. 163-5, 291; 5. 287; 7. 372, 510, 516-7, 665, 674; 8. 301, 421; 230: 4. 164; 233: 7. 520; 240: 4. 329; 243: 7. 482; 245: 7. 523; 246-7: 7. 371; 247-9: 7. 529, 553; 249-50: 7. 548-9; 250: 1. 502; 7. 515, 524, 538, 555; 8. 285; 251: 1. 224, 505; 252: 7. 518; 255: 4. 331-2; 7. 532; 256: 4. 216; 7. 521; 259: 8. 326, 329; 276: 3. 253; *Philebus*: 4. 217; *Protagoras*: 1. 433; 2. 210, 417
Republic: 1. 313; 5. 198, 215-6, 287, 290, 294, 336; 6. 385; 7. 371, 533, 537; 1. 337: 5. 235; 1. 337 (schol.): 5. 166; 2: 5. 291-2; 2. 361: 7. 543-4; 2. 383: 6. 299; 3: 3. 338; 3. 390: 5. 206; 3. 398-9: 7. 392; 3. 415 ff.: 8. 352; 4. 439: 2. 198, 226; 4. 442: 2. 416; 8. 476; 4. 443: 5. 214; 6. 508: 7. 557; 8. 470; 7: 7. 525; 7. 509, 516-8: 7. 557; 7. 529: 7. 552; 7. 532: 1. 503; 7. 533: 7. 553; 8: 5. 290; 8. 560: 2. 284, 287, 297, 483-5; 8. 338; 8. 586: 5. 188; 9: 5. 292; 9. 571: 2. 252; 9. 580: 2. 198, 416; 9. 586: 5. 190; 10: 3. 257, 340, 345; 8. 329; 10. 617: 6. 240; *Sophist*: 2. 479
Symposium: 1. 444, 503; 4. 163-5; 7. 537, 659, 665, 668, 674; 178-80: 7. 518-9; 178, 195, 203: 7. 511; 178: 7. 481, 512; 179: 4. 223; 180-1: 4. 216; 188, 206-9: 7. 514-5; 197: 7. 510; 201: 7. 530; 202: 7. 480; 203: 3. 261; 7. 552; 8. 468; 204: 7. 567; 206: 1. 224; 209-10: 7. 524; 210-1: 7. 546-50, 568; 8. 473; 211-2: 7. 539; 211: 7. 518; 8. 331; *Theaetetus*: 1. 224; 2. 261
Timaeus: 2. 284; 3. 348; 6. 395, 423; 7. 511, 533; 28-9: 7. 523-4; 29: 7. 539, 543; 30: 7. 550; 32, 33: 2. 479; 37: 8. 476; 42: 6. 240; 44: 2. 482; 45: 2. 344; 49: 3. 258, 260; 50: 3. 351-2; 53-4: 2. 478, 482; 65 ff.: 2. 290; 69: 2. 483; 79: 3. 257; 91: 1. 224
Platonic Ascent, 1. 514; 2. 431; 3. 223; 7. 372, 518-9, 521, 534-5, 537, 546-7, 550, 552-3, 556, 564, 568, 661, 667-81; 8. 424, 427, 432, 434-5, 439, 441-2, 445-7, 449, 641-3
Platonic Commonwealth, 6. 385-6
Platonic ethics. *See* Plato
Platonic Great Year, 3. 345; 6. 397, 406; 8. 387
Platonic Ideas, 3. 345, 350; 6. 390, 411;

7. 524, 546-8, 551, 553, 557; 8. 434, 454, 493

Platonic imagery, 7. 538; 8. 491

Platonic Ladder. *See* Platonic Ascent

Platonic Millennium, 3. 345

Platonic myth, 5. 187-8

Platonism, 1. 246, 432, 484, 501-5; 2. 214, 224, 287, 339, 348, 403, 414, 416-7; 3. 217, 256, 260, 349; 4. 195, 211; 6. 237, 407, 422-3; 7. 281, 489, 493, 506, 537, 546-7, 658-9, 662-81; 8. 324, 373, 422, 424, 434, 440, 453-4, 491, 631; in *Amoretti*: 8. 630, 639-42; Aristotelianism, mingled with: 2. 427; 6. 403; Bible, mingled with: 7. 541-2; Christianity, mingled with: 2. 416; 6. 403, 423; 7. 537, 539, 559, 666, 670-6; 8. 493; French: 8. 639; Italian: 1. 432; 3. 317-8; 7. 368, 665, 670, 674; 8. 435, 639; Ovid, mingled with: 3. 349-352; Renaissance: 1. 501; 2. 429, 436; 7. 368, 371, 492, 511, 662-76; 8. 639-40; Spenser more Platonic than Aristotelian: 2. 417-8; Spenser's: 7. 509-70, 601, 662-76. *See also* Plato

Plautus, Titus Maccus, *Amphitruo*: 5. 256; *Casina*: 5. 167; *Cistellaria*: 4. 217; 7. 273; *Menaechmi*: 5. 232; *Pseudolus*: 4. 217; 6. 240-1; *Rudens*: 5. 252; *Trinummus*: 6. 241

" Play," 3. 275; 4. 173

Pleasant Historie of Palladine of England, 6. 203

Pleasure, 1. 365; 3. 256, 261; 7. 521; 8. 488; pleasure-pain: 4. 216-7; 7. 272-3, 491, 507

Plectrum, 2. 304

Pléiade, 1. 378, 493; 3. 239; 7. 320, 340, 342, 370, 378, 488, 596-7, 599, 621-5, 667; 8. 323, 332, 379, 391, 455, 534-5, 538, 620, 640-2, 653-4, 658

Plenty, 3. 261; 7. 511. *See also* Poros

Pleonasm, 4. 195; 8. 463

Plexippus, 6. 243

Plim, 4. 255

Pliny the Elder, *Natural History*: 3. 250; 8. 398; 2. 22: 2. 480; 2. 25: 3. 205; 2. 106: 1. 302; 3. 5: 8. 409; 5. 2: 8. 348; 3. 16: 2. 248; 6. 32: 1. 226; 7: 2. 199; 7. 1: 443; 7. 29, 108: 7. 393; 7. 49: 2. 297; 8. 5: 8. 348; 8. 10: 8. 408; 8. 23: 8. 437; 8. 25: 8. 406; 8. 80: 7. 301; 9. 6: 8. 406; 9. 8, 15: 2. 362; 10. 3: 7. 336; 10. 12: 8. 486; 10. 70: 1. 227; 16. 18: 8. 461; 16. 79: 8. 407-8; 19. 4: 3. 254; 20. 10: 8. 398; 25. 8: 8. 428; 25. 37: 8. 499; 25. 40: 7. 498; 32. 1: 8. 408; 33. 12: 8. 336; 34. 2: 8. 395; 34. 19:

1. 225; 35: 2. 228; 35. 10: 4. 194; 7. 567; 35. 26: 7. 567; 36. 5: 4. 231; 37. 2: 8. 407

Pliny the Younger, 2. 244; 8. 306

Ploce, 6. 231, 285; 7. 499, 505-6; 8. 285, 295, 381-2, 389, 469, 498, 530, 595, 658, 677

Plomer, H. R., 7. 507

Plotinus, 2. 377; 4. 318; 6. 411-2, 417, 419-21; 7. 552, 562, 664, 671-2

Plots, 1. 464-5; 5. 201, 211, 225, 244-5, 297, 302, 304, 316, 320, 324

Plowman's Tale. See Chaucer (pseudo)

Pluralism, 8. 362

Plutarch, 1. 489, 514; 2. 382, 435; 8. 389; *Alcibiades*: 3. 290; 4. 172; *Alexander*: 7. 393; 8. 300, 302; *Apophthegms*: 2. 259-60; *Brute Beasts Make Use of Reason*: 2. 394; *Brutus*: 8. 353; *Cato Major*: 8. 387; *Crassus*: 2. 198; *How the Young Man should Study Poetry*: 1. 236; 7. 256; *Isis and Osiris*: 5. 214-9; 6. 399; 2-6: 5. 216, 219; 2-8: 5. 218; 3: 5. 215; 8: 4. 231; 9: 4. 230-1; 6. 295; 13: 5. 214-5; 32: 1. 209; 41, 43: 3. 251; 46: 3. 244; 50, 52, 81: 5. 216-7; 56-7: 3. 261; *Lives*: 8. 314, 328; *Marcellus*: 8. 300; *Moralia*: 8. 436; *On Cessation of the Oracles*: 7. 307; *On Envy and Hatred*: 5. 267; *On the Fortune or Virtue of Alexander*: 7. 392; *On Large Acquaintance*: 4. 291, 329; *On Names of Rivers and Mountains*: 2. 378; *On Progress in Virtue*: 8. 476; *Parallels*: 1. 236; *Politics*: 5. 255; *Roman Questions*: 1. 309; *Symposiacs*: 1. 184, 511-2; 8. 329-30; *Theseus*: 5. 170; 7. 285

Pluto, 2. 252, 254; 5. 212-3; 8. 485

Plutus, 2. 254, 258; 5. 172, 212-3

Plymouth, 2. 307; 7. 462

Podalyrius, 6. 211

Poeana, 4. 214, 286, 323; 5. 208

Poet, 7. 320-1, 366-9, 373-6, 380-2, 387-9. *See also* " make "

Poetical Rhapsody. See Davison, Francis

Poetry, as art: 7. 370; 8. 332; contempt of: 7. 372, 374; courtly: 8. 367-8; and emblems: 8. 625; function: 8. 381; heroic: 2. 370; 6. 249; 7. 368-9, 390; 8. 327; and history: 1. 313, 325, 360, 480; 8. 314, 327; and inspiration: 7. 366-8, 376; and learning: 8. 313, 332, 535; and love: 7. 368, 387-9; lyric: 7. 583; and passion: 8. 326; and the poet: 8. 367-8; praise of: 7. 594; 8. 538; and praxis: 7. 538; and religion: 2. 270; 8. 332; and rhetoric: 8. 349; to teach and delight: 1. 311, 314, 348-9; 6. 249; and technical discipline:

8. 332; topographical: 6. 429-32. *See also* French; Italian; New Poetry; Pastoral
Poets, aged: 7. 418; Augustan: 8. 331; bad: 7. 238-9; 8. 325-7, 330, 332-3, 368; Court: 8. 333; humanists, more than: 8. 391; position and influence of: 7. 594; as teachers: 7. 588
Poet's poet, 1. 206; 7. 371
Poggio Bracciolini, 8. 380
Pole, Margaret, Countess of Salisbury, 1. 462-3, 468-9
Pole, Reginald, 1. 458-9, 462
Politian (Angelo Poliziano), 2. 273, 390; 3. 252; 7. 239, 250, 271-2, 281-2, 596; *La Giostra*: 1. 193; *De Violis*: 4. 194; *Stanze*: 8. 597
Political Economy: 5. 175
Pollard, Albert F., 5. 304
Pollente, 5. 170-4, 213, 275, 277, 280, 282, 288, 292, 294, 345-8; is Charles IX?: 5. 302; is Sir John of Desmond: 5. 313-4; is Spain: 5. 314
Pollio, 7. 597
" Polliticke vertues," projected poem on: 1. 296, 343, 345
Pollux, 7. 592. *See also* Castor
Polychronicon, 2. 320
Polydore Vergil, 1. 482-4, 486-9; 2. 315, 452
Polydorus, 1. 202-3, 206; 2. 370; 7. 415
Polyhymnia, 7. 370; 8. 312, 331-2, 531
Polynices, 3. 276
Polyphemus, 4. 205
Polyphony, 6. 423
Polyptoton, 1. 227; 5. 202, 236, 266; 6. 208, 259; 7. 247, 618; 8. 331, 372, 381-2, 404, 469, 530, 595, 658, 677
Polysyndeton, 7. 246; 8. 372, 658
Pomerius, 2. 424-5
Pompeius, Gnaeus, 6. 293; 8. 387, 389, 391
Pomponius Mela, 4. 246
Ponsonby, William, 4. 314-5; 7. 725-6; 8. 281-3, 393, 417-8, 507, 511, 514, 517, 528, 602, 608, 613, 615, 632, 663, 679, 687, 707, 709, 725-6
Pontanus Jovianus, 4. 194; 6. 431; 7. 423, 590, 596; 8. 309, 448, 487
Ponticus Virunnius, 2. 322, 331, 452
Pontius Pilate, 1. 363; 2. 268, 326
Pope, 1. 199, 471, 475; 5. 318; 7. 334; 8. 525
Pope, Alexander, 1. 489; 3. 268; 4. 193, 213; 5. 212; 7. 411, 421, 576, 615, 625, 627; 8. 281, 331, 560, 563, 659; *Discourse on Pastoral Poetry*: 7. 573; *Eloisa and Abelard*: 3. 207; *Epistle to Dr. Arbuthnot*: 8. 371; *Essay on Criticism*: 3. 292; *Essay on Man*: 5. 176; 6. 277, 300; *Pastorals*:

7. 412, 496; 8. 397, 460; *Rape of the Lock*: 5. 176, 224; 8. 395, 602; *Spring*: 8. 497
Pope, E. F., 7. 258, 626-7
Pope Jone, 2. 242
Popery, 8. 279. *See also* Papacy
Poplar, 2. 239, 294; 8. 339-40
Populace, 5. 175, 181. *See also* Rabble
Porch, 2. 350
Poris, 4. 273-5
Poros, 8. 468. *See also* Plenty
Porphyrion, 5. 219
Porphyry, 2. 377
Porrex, 2. 319-20
Porte Noire, 3. 363-4
Porter, 1. 214, 260, 283, 405-6, 417; 2. 291
Portrait, 8. 425, 435
Portugal, 5. 263; 8. 363
Poseidon. *See* Neptune
Poseidonos, 5. 312
Post of the World, 5. 321
Postern, 5. 255
Poteat, Hubert N., 8. 463
Potts, A. F., 8. 659, 677
Poupo, Pierre, 8. 473
Poverty, 3. 301
Powell, C. L., 2. 456-7
Powell, David, 1. 266, 483
Powers, 1. 310; 7. 553
Praeteritio, 8. 288
Prasutagus, 2. 325
Praxis, 7. 538
Praxiteles, 3. 201; 4. 231; 6. 379
Preaching, 8. 358-9
Predestination, 1. 266; 2. 275-6; 7. 609
Pre-Raphaelite, 1. 294; 2. 216
Presbyterianism, 1. 437; 2. 276
Pre-Socratics, 6. 422-3
Preston, Thomas, 7. 293, 296, 325
Presumption, 2. 371
Previté-Orton, C. W., 8. 594
Price, Fanny, 8. 510
Price, Sir John, 1. 483; 3. 232-3. *See also* Llwyd, Humphrey
Price, Richard, 1. 483
Price, W. H., 5. 347
" pricking," 1. 176
Pride, 1. 213-5, 237, 248, 260, 364, 371, 406, 408, 410, 412, 416; 4. 167; 5. 349; 6. 191, 229. *See also* House of Pride; Lucifera; Park of Pride
Pridwen, 2. 275; 5. 192
Priests of Isis, 5. 214-7, 219
" prime," 1. 205
" primrose," 7. 477
Primum Mobile, 7. 551, 553
Princedoms, 1. 310; 7. 553

Princeton University Library, 8. 548
Printing, 1. 517; 7. 693-6; 8. 680
Prior, Matthew, 2. 285; 8. 578
Priscilla, 6. 324, 327-8
Prisoners, 4. 214
Prisoner's base, 3. 288; 5. 224; 7. 379. *See also* "bidding base"
Privation, 3. 261
Privy Malice, 1. 416-7
Priwen, 1. 251
Processions, 5. 184
Proclus, 7. 514, 533
Procne, 8. 343
Procrustes, 6. 279-80
Progress, 6. 314
Prometheus, 2. 334, 336-7; 6. 280, 423
Promos and Cassandra. *See* Whetstone, George
Promptorium Parvulorum: 7. 297; 8. 359
Pronunciation, 2. 248, 262, 308, 313, 357; 4. 204, 214, 225, 247; 5. 194, 204, 213, 226; 6. 194, 211, 216, 234, 249, 258, 304, 475, 479; 7. 258, 264-5, 279, 321, 401, 422, 640; 8. 341, 345, 347, 352, 366, 371, 423-4, 428, 459. *See also* Disyllables, Trisyllables
Proper names, 1. 252; 4. 288; 6. 243, 253-4, 279, 289, 475
Propertius, 2. 273; 3. 252, 301; 1. 20: 3. 302; 2. 3: 8. 467; 2. 24. 4: 8. 475; 2. 34: 6. 230; 7. 452; 3: 8. 297; 3. 9: 8. 474; 3. 10: 5. 202; 3. 11: 8. 381; 3. 12: 7. 271; 3. 22: 8. 390; 4. 1-10: 8. 385; 4. 86: 2. 300
Proserpina, 1. 195; 2. 264, 445; 6. 293-4; 7. 445-6; 8. 339, 485, 497, 548. *See also* Persephone
Proserpyne, 3. 363-4
Prosody. *See* Metre
Prosonomasia, 8. 331, 409, 595, 677
Prosopopoeia, 2. 286; 3. 299; 7. 246, 504; 8. 349. *See also* Personification
Protestant, 1. 275, 305, 456, 459, 474, 480; 2. 280, 346, 403-4; 5. 157, 167, 225-6, 258-61, 302, 325, 330, 333-4, 343, 345; 6. 208-9, 249; 7. 290-5, 337, 427, 539, 592, 601-4; 8. 486, 566, 618, 620
Proteus, 3. 241, 269, 271, 313, 320, 327, 333, 374; 5. 190, 236; 7. 461; *Masque of*: 4. 315-6; 5. 236; is Philip II: 3. 379-80
Prothalamion, 5. 169, 284; 6. 392; 7. 246, 641, 654; 8. 495-505, 660-77; allegory: 8. 666-7, 676; and *Amoretti*: 8. 674; bibliography: 8. 735, 737-45; biographical significance: 8. 662-6; composition: 8. 495, 662-6; criticism: 8. 662-6; date: 8. 662-6, 672; decorative: 8. 499; epic type: 8. 673;

and *Epithalamion*: 8. 657-62, 670, 674-6; and *Hymnes*: 8. 674; influence: 8. 677; metre: 8. 661, 674-7; refrain: 8. 660-1, 664, 675; rhetoric: 8. 676; sources: 8. 667; Spenser's last poem: 8. 496, 661; structure: 8. 661, 674-5; style: 8. 499, 674-7; text criticism: 8. 687, 706-7, 721-2; title: 8. 495; worst poem: 8. 662; 1-18: 8. 668, 677; 5-11: 6. 240; 16-34: 8. 462; 18: 4. 189; 19-20: 8. 661; 21-3: 4. 275; 8. 472; 29-34: 8. 348; 38, 115: 5. 173; 40-6: 8. 667, 669; 62-5: 8. 667; 64-6: 8. 472; 68-9: 8. 668; 73-80: 2. 209; 8. 462, 483; 78-82: 8. 467; 87-109: 8. 464, 676; 105-6: 8. 658; 112-3: 8. 460; 114-28: 8. 668; 117-62: 8. 676; 121: 8. 671; 140: 8. 496; 146-60: 5. 334; 6. 354, 359; 150-4: 1. 259; 6. 352; 157-8, 177: 8. 669; 173, 176: 8. 667
Proto, 4. 273, 275
"protract," 8. 453
Proverb, 1. 202, 303; 2. 206, 242; 3. 219, 274; 4. 172, 181, 195, 327-33; 5. 174, 206, 256, 263; 7. 256, 258, 302, 307, 319, 356, 358, 360, 365, 382, 446; 8. 351-3, 355-6, 362, 370, 430, 432, 479, 594. *See also* Gnome
Prudence, 1. 329, 407; 2. 188, 405, 414; 3. 358
Prudentius, 1. 205, 225; 2. 287, 375, 464; 3. 221; 7. 285, 561
Prurience, 6. 234
Pryene, 2. 229
Psalms, Spenser's translation. *See Seven Psalms*
Pseudo-Dionysius, 1. 310; 2. 270; 4. 260; 7. 539-40, 551, 553, 672, 674-5
Psyche, 3. 256, 261; 7. 521; 8. 396, 488, 606-7
Psychology, 2. 458-71
Psychomachia, 1. 310; 2. 422, 463-4; 7. 674
Ptolemaic system, 6. 310-1, 401; 7. 528, 551; 8. 493
Ptolemy, Claudius, 2. 281, 300; 3. 344; 5. 157-8, 312; 6. 277, 311; 8. 309, 440
Publilius Syrus, 7. 258, 266, 272
Puck, 1. 292; 8. 486
Pulci, Luigi, *Driades*: 6. 430; *Morgante Maggiore*: 1. 513; 6: 4. 199; 11: 5. 228; 14: 1. 289; 17: 3. 211; 19: 1. 305; 21: 1. 241; 22: 6. 255; 23: 6. 232; 24: 5. 224; 25: 6. 217; 26: 1. 299; 27: 5. 262
Pullain, John, 8. 519
Pun, 2. 265, 508; 5. 239; 7. 256, 264; 8. 479, 499, 503-4, 594
Punctuation, 1. 177, 226, 237, 298, 525-7, 544-9; 2. 507, 509-11; 3. 240; 5. 229;

6. 445, 480-503; 7. 501-2; 8. 699, 707, 711-23
Punishment, 1. 287
Purcell, J. M., 6. 450; 7. 493
Purchas his Pilgrimes, 2. 448
Purgatory, 1. 205
Puritanism, 3. 386; 4. 234; 5. 157; 6. 214, 249; 7. 254, 307, 367, 488-9, 600-1, 604-9, 658, 661, 665, 669; 8. 279, 561, 573
Puritans, 1. 259, 275, 343, 481, 488, 490-1; 2. 195, 198, 201, 345, 349, 420, 443; 5. 173; 6. 304, 382, 386-8; 7. 290-6, 299-304, 325-6. 334-5, 353-4, 358, 360; 8. 357-8, 362, 571, 573-4, 607
Purity, 1. 263
" purple," 1. 216; 2. 205; 5. 24.
" Purposes," 3. 284
Purslane, 8. 399
Purves, D. L., 7. 281
Puttenham, George, 1. 513; 3. 212; 5. 184; 7. 236-7, 320-1, 367, 459, 465, 467, 608, 615, 623-4, 635; 8. 321, 327, 349, 618, 657
Pylades, 4. 223-4, 316
Pyramids, 8. 305-6
Pyramus, 4. 223
Pyrochles, 1. 230; 2. 208, 231-4, 276-7, 350, 401, 403, 411, 417, 427, 471; 5. 343; in the *Arcadia*: 2. 401; 6. 380; is Charles IX: 2. 404; is Philip Sidney: 2. 401-2
Pysma, 8. 285, 298
Pythagoras, 3. 257, 340; 6. 300, 409, 424
Pythagorean " Y," 2. 222-3
Pythagoreans, 1. 209; 2. 344, 478-9, 483; 5. 163
Pythias, 4. 223, 225

Quadrate, 2. 475, 481, 483
" Quae rara chara," 1. 202
Quaritch, Bernard, 7. 708
Quarles, Francis, 2. 357; 5. 165; 7. 594
Quarrel, 6. 216
Queen Hester, 2. 434
" queint," 7. 394
Quekett, A. E., 1. 291
Quest, 1. 351
Questing Beast, 6. 268-9, 271
Quiet, 1. 193-5
" quill," 7. 319
Quiller-Couch, Sir Arthur, 8. 484
Quin, Walter, 8. 580
Quintilian, 5. 262; 7. 239, 443, 615; 8. 383
Quintus Curtius, 2. 285; 4. 168, 186; 5. 226; 8. 372
Quintus Smyrnaeus, 3. 238; 4. 182; 5. 200

Rabanus Maurus, 2. 426; 4. 260

Rabble, 2. 282, 284-5, 339-40, 412; 5. 175, 181, 260, 262, 290, 294, 304, 342-3
Rabelais, François, 2. 361; 6. 358; 7. 299
Radcliffe, Thomas, Earl of Sussex, 2. 401-2; 3. 379; 8. 374, 568
Radcot Bridge, 8. 672
Radegund, St., 8. 361
Radigund, 1. 347; 3. 363, 371, 390; 5. 196-9, 201, 259, 273, 288, 297, 304; 6. 191, 229; and Arthegall: 5. 302, 349; and Britomart: 5. 214, 221-2; character: 5. 273; is Elizabeth?: 5. 202; is Ireland: 5. 314; is Mary Stuart: 5. 201, 221, 306
Rahilly, T. A., 4. 265
Rainbow, 8. 396
Rait, Robert, 5. 246
Raleigh, Sir Walter, 1. 264, 296, 327, 330, 481; 2. 185, 224, 343, 399; 4. 314; 5. 197; 6. 205, 325, 350, 382, 425; 7. 433-5, 437, 451, 461, 466-7, 471, 473, 478, 514, 645; 8. 362-3, 504, 531, 570; and Burleigh: 8. 574; character: 8. 601; is Clarion: 8. 601, 606; colonizer: 2. 358; 5. 248, 307-8; Commendatory Verses, author of?: 3. 305; and Elizabeth: 3. 326; 4. 205-8, 210-11, 249; 6. 207; 7. 451, 458-9; 8. 489, 574, 601; and Essex: 6. 205-6; 7. 457; 8. 393, 598-9, 601, 603; is Marinell: 3. 377, 379; Milton, imitated by: 3. 305; is Scudamour: 3. 378; " Shepherd of the Ocean ": 3. 377; 5. 308; 7. 447, 448, 453, 461, 467; and Spenser: 2. 186; 3. 240; 4. 205-7, 210, 249; 5. 248, 271, 304, 308, 325; 6. 255, 440; 7. 448-50, 461, 474, 485; 8. 321, 528, 574, 601, 631, 663; is not Tarquin: 6. 206; is Timias: 1. 340; 2. 345, 401; 3. 201, 246, 377-9; 4. 205-8, 211, 286; 6. 318, 350, 363; is " water ": 7. 453; *Cynthia*: 3. 305, 309, 377; 4. 207; 7. 446, 453, 458; *Discoverie of Guiana*: 4. 248-9; 5. 199; *History of the World*: 1. 236; 2. 185; 3. 265; 4. 232, 249; 6. 424; 7. 480; Spenser's letter to: *see Letter of the Authors*
Ralph Royster Doyster, 7. 271
Ram, 3. 292-3
Rambaldo, 1. 228
Ramsay, Allan, 7. 576
Ramus, Petrus, 7. 366
Ramusio, Gian Battista, 6. 226
Randolph, Thomas, 7. 594; 8. 474-5
" rankling," 6. 202
Raoul de Houdan, 1. 406
Raphael, Archangel, 2. 272, 429-30
Raphael Regius, 7. 337
Raphael, Sanzio, 1. 277, 288, 310, 366; 2. 271; 8. 532

Rare Triumphs of Love and Fortune, 6. 293, 392-3
" rascall," 5. 262
Rastell, John, 2. 452
Rathborne, I., 6. 274; 8. 397, 403, 605
Ratherius, Bishop of Verona, 2. 425
Ravenscroft, Thomas, 1. 240
Ray, John, 8. 370
Reading, 8. 671
Reason, 1. 417, 432; 2. 370, 416-7, 438, 462-3, 468, 481; 5. 215, 282, 287; 6. 199, 327, 447-8; 8. 352; Divine: 7. 563, 566; Red Cross Knight deficient in: 1. 432; is Glauce: 3. 321; is the Palmer: 2. 188, 192, 442-3; 3. 323, 366
Recorde, Robert, 5. 177
Red Cross, 1. 177, 399; 2. 187
Red Cross Knight, 1. 234, 250, 259, 268, 272-3, 311, 346, 358, 371, 388-93, 399, 401, 405-7, 414, 416-9, 422-6, 449-51, 501-5; 2. 207, 231, 274, 339, 352, 410, 420-1, 423, 427; 3. 262, 315, 387, 389; 5. 222, 258, 261, 292; 7. 363, 367, 471, 557, 661; British: 1. 353; and Britomart: 3. 324; and Calidore: 6. 320; character: 1. 299, 429, 435, 498; 5. 208, 222; is Christian people: 1. 455; complacency, surrenders to: 1. 438; conviction of sin: 1. 438; Defender of the Faith: 1. 425-6, 428-30, 455-7, 466; 6. 384; emotion, follows his: 1. 432, 442-4; experience, learns by: 1. 434, 504; 3. 383-4; is Henry VIII: 1. 466, 492; immature: 1. 498; is inadequate holiness: 1. 432; 2. 427; jealous: 5. 208; legend of: 8. 513; man of few words: 1. 429; a " morality hero": 1. 431; is Sir John Norris: 3. 379; origin: 1. 294; 3. 229; 6. 204; Pelagian heresy, inclined to: 1. 448; same as " Pietas " of St. Mark's and " Devotio " of Orcagna: 1. 422; is Pure Religion: 1. 478; reason, deficient in: 1. 432; royal blood with humble nurture, combines: 1. 442; Saxon-born: 1. 495; is Sir Philip Sidney: 1. 449, 451; is spirit of English People: 1. 458, 466; spiritual discernment, lacks: 1. 435; 3. 365; suicide, condemns: 1. 280; 6. 365; transformed by armor of Christ: 1. 433; separation from Una is return to Popery under Mary: 1. 441; union with Una symbol of Reformation: 1. 441, 457
Red Knight, 1. 395, 400
Redman, R., 6. 265
Reed, Edward B., 8. 661
Reformation, 1. 246, 378, 425, 440, 457-8; 5. 339; 6. 265, 383; 7. 666; 8. 532; shadowed forth in *F. Q.* 1: 1. 449

Refrain, 7. 395, 397-8, 430, 641; 8. 294, 460, 494-7
Regan, 2. 315-7
Regeneration, 1. 301
Regius, Raphael, 3. 296
Rehm, W., 8. 380
Reincarnation, 3. 340. *See also* Metempsychosis
Relative omitted, 6. 259
Religion, 1. 422, 475, 482; 7. 462, 480, 657; 8. 566; and love: 8. 427; of love: 1. 378; and poetry: 2. 270; Renaissance: 1. 362; 7. 506
Reliquiae Antiquae, 5. 172
Rembrandt, H. van Rijn, 1. 306; 3. 392
Remedy of Love. See Chaucer (pseudo)
Reminiscence, 7. 524
Remora, 8. 408, 625
Remorse, 1. 366, 406-7
Remus, 1. 293; 6. 204
Renaissance, 1. 224, 273, 306; 2. 423, 459; 3. 238; 5. 306; 6. 404, 441; 7. 347, 367-8, 388, 395, 605; 8. 363, 532; allegory: 1. 340-1; 7. 368; art: 1. 362; 3. 392-99; 7. 681; disapproved communism: 4. 332; comprehensive: 1. 362; 8. 297; convention: 7. 283, 494, 588; criticism: 1. 312-3; 6. 249; 7. 255-6, 376, 393, 664; 8. 313, 327, 332; dirge of: 8. 378; eclecticism: 8. 329; educational treatises: 1. 340-1; English: 2. 249; 3. 386; 8. 333; Epic: 1. 493, 513; 5. 306; ethics: 1. 312, 340-1; 3. 281; and Fortune: 6. 437; French: 7. 339-40, 342, 368, 391; ideals: 1. 418; ideas: 5. 342; 6. 404, 407; 7. 567; idyll: 7. 271-2; Italian: 7. 368, 391; literary art: 1. 378; 5. 306; love, theory of: 1. 347; 3. 366; 7. 663, 666; and melancholy: 6. 424; mysticism: 7. 673-6, 681; mythography: 6. 412; Neo-platonism: 7. 524, 662-76; pessimism: 8. 293; and poetic immortality: 8. 297-8, 328; poetry and painting, relation of: 8. 304; politics: 5. 306; religion of beauty: 7. 681; reverence for human body: 2. 279; scepticism: 3. 342; " sentences," love of: 8. 394; stoicism: 8. 314-5
Renard. *See* Reynard
Renaud de Beaujeu, 1. 391
" rencounter," 3. 204
René, King, 2. 352
Repentance, 1. 287, 303, 406-7; 3. 392; 4. 181. *See also* House of Repentance
Repetition, 4. 277; 5. 202; 6. 211, 240; 7. 483, 491, 506, 557
Reproach, 4. 181
Requiem, 2. 194
Retiarius, 5. 236

Retractation, 7. 537-8, 657-63, 668, 675, 678-80, 682; 8. 274, 416

Retrospective Review, 8. 628

Return from Parnassus, 1. 272; 8. 361, 536, 565

Reuchlin, Johann, 6. 316; 7. 559, 561

Reuter, W., 8. 321, 324, 327, 531

Revelation Sonnets. *See* [*Visions from Revelation*]

Revenge, 2. 257

Reverence, 1. 406-7, 424; 5. 241

Reyher, Paul, 3. 252; 4. 240; 5. 236, 324; 8. 461

Reynard the Fox, 2. 341; 8. 352, 375, 562, 564, 569, 572, 574, 585-90, 594

Reynolds, Henry, 6. 424

Reynolds, Sir Joshua, 2. 414

Rezia, 2. 188

Rhamnusia, 3. 269

Rhea, 1. 242; 6. 279, 301

Rhee, 4. 258

Rhesus, 8. 345

Rhetoric, 1. 295; 5. 223, 372; 6. 188-9, 231, 285, 445-6; 7. 239, 246-7, 251, 264, 277, 287, 394, 503-4, 552, 581, 618; 8. 331, 421, 465, 484, 530, 542, 595, 658, 676-7; and poetry: 8. 349

Rheusa, 4. 269

Rhine, 8. 390

Rhodope, 2. 378-9

Rhone, 4. 247

Rhyme, 2. 189, 191, 194, 227-8, 309, 385; 4. 196, 211; 6. 192; 7. 279, 321, 340, 360; 8. 274, 276-7, 424, 498, 538, 547, 657; careless: 1. 209; 5. 205; 6. 477; in *Epithalamion*: 8. 657; "eye": 2. 316-7; 4. 185; feminine: 7. 641; forced: 4. 272; 7. 250, 523; 8. 411, 423; identical: 1. 544; 2. 235; 4. 258; 6. 186, 191; 7. 279, 317; 8. 445, 462, 549; internal: 8. 372; late: 7. 657; linking: 5. 254; 6. 204; 8. 643-4; "riding": 7. 635-6; 8. 594; royal: 7. 430, 433, 487, 640, 660; more rumbling than rural: 7. 574; rhyme, Spenser's gift: 8. 409-10, 547. *See also* Metre; *rime couée*

Rhythm, 1. 242; 7. 258; 8. 410, 413, 457, 547

Rich, Barnaby, *Adventures of Simonides*: 2. 240, 297; 4. 190; 5. 174; *Faults and Nothing but Faults*: 1. 216; 2. 201-2, 210; 3. 212; 6. 228; 8. 365-6, 406; *Roome for a Gentleman*: 8. 355

Rich, Penelope. *See* Devereux, Penelope

Richard I, 5. 242

Richard of St. Victor, 7. 672, 674

Richard Rolle of Hampole, 7. 668, 672

Riches, 2. 251-5, 260, 433-4; 5. 340-1; 7. 506, 518, 567, 569. *See also* Gain

Richmond, 1. 291; 8. 671

Rich Strand, 3. 377, 380; 5. 225

Rickert, Edith, 8. 463

Riddles, 3. 284; 6. 377-8

"riding rhyme," 7. 635-6; 8. 594

Ridley, Nicholas, 1. 471

Ridolfi plot, 5. 201, 244, 324

Rigomer, 1. 347; 3. 365

rime couée, 7. 640

Rinaldo, 1. 246, 249, 277, 289, 345, 419; 2. 238, 428; 3. 289, 368-9, 374

Ring, 6. 186-7, 191

Ripa, 1. 365

Rising in the North, 5. 221, 241, 245, 304, 316, 320, 324

Ritho, 6. 190

Ritson, Joseph, 4. 213; 6. 193, 227-8; 8. 312

Rivallo, 2. 319

Rivers, 4. 311; 6. 186, 437; English: 4. 250-64, 272-3; 8. 667-72; Irish: 4. 250, 264-72; Spenser's love of: 4. 250-73, 311; 6. 437; 8. 291

Rix, H. D., 7. 246, 444, 503-5; 8. 286, 288, 292, 296, 298, 357, 395, 433, 474, 495, 595

Roan, 1. 251; 5. 192

Robert, A. C. M., 8. 406

Robert of Gloucester, 2. 307, 324; 3. 234, 286

Robert the Devyll, 1. 200, 292; 7. 409

Robin, 7. 418-9, 421, 479, 590; 8. 318, 320

Robin Hood, 6. 193

Robinson, Richard, 8. 591

Robinson, Thomas, 7. 287

Robinson, W. H., 7. 708

Robortelli, Francesco, 1. 348, 513

Robsart, Amy, 2. 403

Robson, Simon, 6. 341

Robin, P. A., 2. 292, 359-62, 364, 369, 482-5

Robin Good-Fellow, 8. 470, 485-6

Roche, Maurice, Lord Fermoy, 7. 454; 8. 453, 605

Rochester, 7. 330, 353; 8. 665

Rock of Reproach, 2. 349, 354, 422, 429

Rodomonte, 2. 207; 5. 172, 348

Roest, Theodore, 8. 273-80, 612-4, 621, 623-4

Roffet, Pierre, 7. 361

Roffy, 7. 296, 350, 352, 361, 366, 404, 601. *See also* Young, John

Rogers, Daniel, 1. 483

Rogers, Thomas, 5. 337, 340

Rogue literature, 8. 591

Roland, 1. 257; 5. 191

Rolland, John, 5. 243; 6. 293

Rolle. *See* Richard Rolle

Rollins, Hyder, 8. 318, 321, 370, 610, 709
Roman Catholic, 1. 365, 426; 2. 402-3; 5. 267, 319-20; 7. 243, 303-4; 8. 360; allegory: 6. 208-9; Church: 1. 201, 423, 426, 452, 470-2; 8. 279, 359, 592; clergy: 6. 267, 269; 7. 306, 350-3, 357-60; conspiracies: 5. 225-6, 316; doctrine in *F. Q.*, Book 1: 1. 439; 2. 270; League: 5. 248, 260, 326, 330; priesthood: 8. 279; reaction: 8. 532; Virgin Mary, conception of: 7. 568
Roman Catholicism, 1. 456, 490; 2. 346, 402; 3. 256; 5. 157, 163, 167, 249, 251, 253, 258-61, 312, 316, 318; 6. 265-6, 384; 7. 254, 261-2, 290-6, 323, 331, 334, 337, 360, 367, 427, 541, 559, 600-1, 603-6, 608, 667, 677; 8. 279, 360, 516-7, 525, 561, 566, 612
Romance, 2. 224, 244, 259, 335; 4. 221, 303; 5. 182; 7. 619; epic, distinguished from: 1. 359
Romances, 1. 178, 183, 196, 199, 207, 210, 211, 216, 225-6, 250-1, 254, 257, 260, 282, 320, 332, 334, 346, 359, 369, 418; 2. 183, 193, 281, 326; 3. 217, 241, 365; 5. 183, 187, 205, 263; 6. 204, 216; of Alexander: 5. 197; allegory mixed with: 1. 367; 2. 427-8; 3. 371-6; 6. 371-2; Arthurian: 1. 346-7, 349, 351, 488-9, 493, 509; 7. 289; in Book 6 of *F. Q.*: 6. 365; of Charlemagne: 1. 509; chivalric: 1. 415; 2. 428; 3. 310-1, 357; 4. 322; 5. 169-70, 225; English: 7. 616-7, 626; 8. 365; French: 3. 332; 6. 228, 365-71; 8. 363; of Galahad: 2. 287; Greek: 1. 488; 5. 225; 6. 374, 376-9; ground-work of *Orlando Furioso*: 1. 367; more important to *F. Q.* than Ariosto or Tasso: 1. 351; less important to Spenser than Italian romances: 2. 283; Irish: 6. 218; Italian: 1. 509-10; 3. 272, 291, 332, 367-76; 5. 258; '6. 372, 374; medieval and Renaissance: 1. 431; of Perceval: 2. 287; 6. 365-71; Renard: 8. 363, 375; Spanish: 6. 374; of Troy: 3. 332; 5. 196-7
Roman de la Rose, 1. 181, 208-9, 378; 2. 261, 371, 373-4, 382; 4. 221, 306; 6. 296, 336, 371
Roman de la Violette, 4. 210
Roman Empire, 8. 412
Romans, 2. 329-32; 8. 372, 409
Romans of Partenay, 1. 205
Romantic epic, 1. 330
Rome, 1. 490; 2. 324, 327; 3. 283; 8. 284, 365, 380-91, 522
Romei, Annibale, 7. 524-5, 666
Romeo, 4. 290; 5. 222; 7. 604, 655

Romulus, 1. 293; 6. 204
Rondelet, Guillaume, 2. 361
Ronsard, Pierre de, 1. 332, 359; 2. 390; 3. 253; 7. 276, 285, 340, 342, 372, 391, 410, 439, 488, 586, 588, 596-7, 622-6, 641, 650, 667; 8. 299, 391, 398, 448, 455, 481, 534-6, 631, 639, 642, 658; contrasts poet and historian: 1. 360; and Spenser, compared: 8. 631, 640; *Adonis*: 7. 268, 410, 487, 491, 495, 497, 499; *Amour Oyseau*: 7. 268, 271-2; *Amours*: 7. 650; 8. 425-6, 429, 431, 433, 441, 444-5; *Art poétique*: 7. 622-4; *Astrée*: 8. 429; *Au Seigneur de Carnavalet*: 8. 428; *Cassandre*: 8. 423, 428, 433; *Chanson*: 8. 423; *Continuation du Discours des Misères*: 8. 529; *Dialogue entre les Muses Deslogées et Ronsard*: 8. 325, 328, 332; *Eclogues*: 7. 345, 407; *Elegies*: 8. 428; *Epithalame de M. de Joyeuse*: 8. 445, 487; *Epithalame de Prince Anthoine*:' 8. 482; *Hélène*: 8. 423, 427, 429, 444-5, 453, 631; *La Franciade*: 1. 361; Preface to *La Franciade*: 1. 313; 7. 622, 625; *Marie*: 8. 423, 428; "Mignonne, allons voir": 7. 443; *Odes*: 7. 650; 8. 297-8, 322-3, 428, 441, 444-5, 455-8; *Stances*: 8. 428
Roos, Countess. *See* Isabel
Roosevelt, Theodore, 8. 467
Root, R. K., 5. 168
Ros, Richard, 6. 224
Rosalind (Shakespeare's), 3. 388; 4. 284
Rosalind (Spenser's), 3. 300; 6. 252, 254; 7. 245, 250, 277, 279, 308-9, 312-5, 321, 338, 400, 406, 417-8, 425, 451, 482, 488, 521, 574, 579, 613-4, 620, 632-3, 656-7, 660, 679; 8. 422, 436, 444, 453, 635; in *Amoretti*: 8. 637-8; is Elisa Horden: 7. 652; is Elisa Leveson: 7. 654; is Elisa North: 7. 653-4; 8. 665; and Elizabeth Boyle: 7. 654; is imaginary: 7. 652, 654; is Mirabella: 6. 214, 219-21, 318, 349; 7. 652; is a "moreland maiden": 7. 652; 8. 648; is Rose Daniel: 7. 652; is Rose Dinley: 7. 653
Rosalindula, 7. 651, 655; 8. 436
Roscher, W. H., 8. 470
Rose, 2. 285, 351, 383; 5. 264; 7. 263-4, 282-3; and lilies: 5. 189; 7. 506
Rosenbach, A. S. W., 7. 708, 723; 8. 420, 681, 688
Rosenthal, Bruno, 1. 213, 307; 4. 213, 217; 7. 251
Rosenzweig, Sidney, 7. 262
Roses, War of, 1. 488-90; 7. 282-3
Rosinante, 2. 342; 5. 191
Rosmarine, 2. 364

Ross, John, 2. 450
Rossetti, Dante Gabriel, 7. 444
Rota, Bernardino, 6. 431
rote, 4. 213-4
Rother, 4. 257
Rouen, 5. 263
Round Table, 1. 488-9; 2. 203; 3. 269; 6. 267-8, 271
Roundelay, 7. 340, 345-7
Rousseau, Jean Jacques, 6. 281
Rowe, F. E., 1. 295
Rowe, K. T., 6. 354-7
Rowe, Nicholas, 5. 264; 8. 317, 319-20
Rowena, 2. 333-4
Rowland, 7. 473
Rowlands, Samuel, 1. 298
Rowley, Ralph, 8. 317
Rowne, 4. 258
Roxburghe Ballads, 7. 409
Royal Scottish Museum, 1. 285
Roydon, Michael, 6. 206; 7. 464
Royster, J. F., 7. 237, 322
Rubel, V. L., 8. 331, 356, 372, 380, 382, 384, 389-90, 395, 400, 404, 409-10, 465, 469, 484, 530, 542, 549, 595, 610, 644, 658, 676-7, 712
Rubens, Peter Paul, 1. 219, 244, 306; 2. 250; 3. 392
Ruddock, 8. 467
Ruddymane, 2. 183, 195-6, 234, 350, 398, 400-1, 410-11; is James I: 2. 402
Rude Entendement, 1. 414
Rudel, Jaufre, 5. 206
Ruggiero, 1. 182, 202, 205, 254, 289, 336, 360; 2. 275; 3. 269, 369-71, 373; 8. 309; and Guyon: 2. 439-42; and Britomart: 3. 213, 315; 5. 348-9
Ruins, 5. 224; 6. 210; 8. 378, 380, 409, 523
Ruines of Rome, 8. 378-91, 617-20, 625; authorship: 8. 378-9, 618; composition: 8. 378-80; criticism: 8. 378-80; date: 8. 378-80; and *Faerie Queene*: 8. 379, 388; metre: 8. 379; and *Teares of the Muses*: 8. 380; text criticism: 8. 716; variant readings: 8. 695-6; and *Visions of Bellay, Petrarch, and the World's Vanity*: 8. 378-9, 404-5, 529, 626; 13-28: 8. 305; 24-42: 8. 285, 378; 48: 8. 283; 50: 8. 507; 71-84: 4. 253; 89-96: 8. 411, 507; 121-6: 6. 273, 404; 127-30: 2. 373; 135: 8. 498; 327-8: 4. 199; 345-78: 8. 285, 287, 378, 380; 405-6: 8. 494, 499; 421-34: 8. 529; 449-62: 8. 379; 459-60: 8. 329
Ruines of Time, 6. 439; 7. 503, 614; 8. 283-310, 393, 510, 645; and *Astrophel*: 7. 484, 486-8; 8. 295; "calling in": 8. 303; commentary: 8. 283-310; criticism: 7. 486;

8. 295, 521-6; and *Daphnaida*: 8. 295, 645; date and composition: 8. 526-30; and *Doleful Lay of Clorinda*: 7. 500-1, 503; 8. 296; and *Dreames*: 8. 512, 526-8; and *Epithalamion*: 8. 295; influence: 8. 530; and *Lycidas*: 8. 286, 291, 296-7, 300, 306; 8. 530; manuscript: 8. 687; and *Mother Hubberds Tale*: 8. 564, 570, 581, 583, 595; and *Muiopotmos*: 8. 598, 610; and *Pageaunts*: 8. 512, 526-8; publication: 8. 679; revision: 8. 686, 712; rhetoric: 8. 530, 595; source: 8. 522-3, 525, 529; and *Stemmata Dudleiana*: 2. 397; 7. 402; 8. 326, 516, 522, 526-8; structure: 8. 527, 529-30; style: 8. 530; and *Teares of the Muses*: 8. 326, 525, 528-30, 533, 535-6, 539; text, notes on: 8. 711-2; title: 8. 409; variant readings: 8. 689-90; and the *Vision* poems: 8. 405, 409, 512, 622, 626; *Dedication*: 7. 485, 487-8; 8. 282-4, 539; 9-10, 16, 19, 22-3, 26, 40: 8. 509; 17: 8. 311; 22-3, 41: 8. 285; 36-80: 8. 523; 43-56: 6. 439; 8. 394; 43-9: 1. 280; 2. 196; 8. 346; 50-6: 2. 194; 78-84: 8. 529; 85-6: 8. 285; 106-12: 2. 328; 127-8: 6. 245; 135, 603: 5. 173; 166-75: 4. 251; 169-75: 1. 483; 181: 4. 182; 186-7: 8. 285, 498; 188: 8. 325; 204-7: 8. 523, 216, 447-55: 6. 272; 8. 570; 239-80: 7. 508; 8. 525; 244-52: 7. 474; 8. 285; 274-343: 7. 487; 8. 459; 281: 8. 320; 316-9: 7. 500; 322: 8. 285; 325: 8. 311, 460; 331: 8. 320; 351-2: 8. 285; 368: 8. 470; 384-99: 8. 505, 512; 390-2: 8. 344; 400-7: 7. 370; 8. 498; 405: 3. 276; 411: 8. 512; 435-55: 8. 524; 436: 6. 350; 440: 5. 283; 8. 375; 441: 7. 608; 449-55: 8. 559, 574, 583-4; 473-7: 8. 473; 489-90: 3. 355; 8. 512; 507: 8. 507; 589-600: 8. 512; 589-600: 7. 393; 603-16, 673: 6. 351; 7. 487-8; 8. 500, 669; 631-5: 8. 482; 659-72: 8. 512; 675: 7. 506; 684: 8. 420
Rumor, 2. 253
Run-over lines, 6. 445-7; 8. 644
Ruskin, John, 1. 271, 286, 422-4, 428, 440, 456; 2. 258, 343, 414-5; 6. 305; 7. 400
Russell, Anne, Countess of Warwick, 3. 306-7; 7. 465, 474, 476, 490, 658-9, 661; 8. 294, 508, 736
Russell, Edward, 3d Earl of Bedford, 8. 295
Russell family, 8. 527
Russell, Francis, 2d Earl of Bedford, 8. 294-5
Russell, Francis Lord, 8. 295, 605
Russell, I. W., 8. 358-60
Russell, Margaret, Countess of Cumberland, 7. 508, 658, 661

Russell, Sir William, 8. 417
Russians, 2. 344
Rutland, Dukes of, 6. 262-3. *See also* Manners
Rutland, Earl of. *See* Edward, Lord Roos
Rutland MSS, 5. 184
Rutter, Joseph, 7. 410-1
Ryence, 3. 237; 5. 220; 6. 189-90, 366

Sabaoth, 6. 315-6, 392, 403, 410, 416-7, 421, 479; 7. 568
Sabbath, 6. 315-6, 479; 7. 570
Sabra, 1. 207
Sabrina, 2. 310
Sacchetti, Franco, 7. 590
Sackville, Robert, 7. 476-7; 8. 350
Sackville, Thomas, Lord Buckhurst, 3. 306-8; 4. 182-3; 5. 231; 7. 248-9, 398, 464-5, 472-3, 476-7, 577, 579, 581, 621-2, 627, 638, 640; 8. 388, 618-9. *See also Mirror for Magistrates*
Sacraments, 1. 301-2; 3. 280; 8. 358-61
" Sacred," 2. 370
Sacrifice, 6. 233-4
Sacrifice of a Sinner, 8. 270, 283
Sacripante, 1. 246, 248, 419; 3. 371
Sacro Bosco, Johannes de, 5. 178
Saffron Walden, 7. 343, 353, 366
Sages, Three, 2. 299-301
Sails, 1. 297; 5. 199
Saint Alban's, 8. 286-93
Saint Bridget's Bower, 7. 328
Saint Clement Danes, Church of, 8. 648
Saint John's Eve, 7. 316
Saint Margaret's Church, Westminster, 8. 651
Saint Michael's Mount, 7. 328, 462
Saint Paul's Cathedral, 8. 310
Sainte-Palaye, Jean Baptiste La Curne de, 1. 214; 5. 192
Saints, 7. 331; 8. 280, 427, 440
Saintsbury, George, 7. 267, 324, 398, 447, 639; 8. 479, 594, 618, 630, 674
Salamander, 9. 430
Salic Law, 5. 223
Salisbury Cathedral, 7. 475
Salisbury, Countess of. *See* Pole, Margaret
Salisbury MSS, 5. 185; 6. 364
Sallust, 2. 478-9; 3. 264; 6. 241; 8. 348
Salmasius, 8. 489
Salmon, William, 7. 238
Salvator Rosa, 2. 341; 7. 238
Samient, 5. 226, 298, 305-6, 316; 6. 205
Sammes, Aylet, 2. 311, 314, 323, 325
Sancho Panza, 2. 208
Sanctus, 1. 201
Sanders, Nicholas, 7. 360
Sanderson, William, 7. 238

Sandison, Helen, 3. 251, 300; 7. 434-5, 437, 466, 475; 8. 299, 511-7
Sandys, Edwin, 1. 471; 7. 326
Sandys, George, 1. 173, 302; 2. 248; 3. 255; 4. 194; 5. 256; 8. 459
Sanglier, 5. 277, 280, 282, 285, 292, 297; 6. 191, 200
Sannazaro, Jacopo, 3. 402; 6. 430-1; 7. 571, 578-9, 596, 615; 8. 454, 629; *Arcadia*: 6. 431; 7. 240, 249, 269, 279, 317, 342, 349, 385, 406-8, 423, 443, 590, 631-2; 8. 297, 460; *De Partu Virginis*: 3. 250; *Eclogae Piscatoriae*: 6. 431; *In Morum Candidam*: 6. 431; *Rime*: 8. 385; *Satires*: 6. 431
Sans = Saint, 1. 201-2
Sansfoy, 1. 230, 394-5, 422, 426-8, 432, 435; 6. 346; is France: 1. 449, 458, 460; oldest of three brothers: 1. 436; is paganism: 1. 455; is Sir Thomas More: 1. 461-2, 465, 468; is Thomas Wolsey: 1. 468; is the Turks: 1. 449
Sansjoy, 1. 230, 394-5, 405, 423, 427-8, 432, 443; 6. 346; is Philip II: 1. 449, 459-60; is Reginald Pole: 1. 462, 465; represents separation of Empire from Church: 1. 455; youngest of three brothers: 1. 436
Sansloy, 1. 230, 394-5, 419, 422-3, 432, 436, 499, 500; 2. 199, 202, 417, 421, 426, 461; 3. 383; 6. 346; is Duke of Alva: 1. 449, 458-60; is Edward Courtenay: 1. 463, 465; is Simon de Montfort the elder: 1. 455; is Stephen Gardiner: 1. 468. *See also* Saracen Brothers
Sapience, 1. 433-4; 7. 552-3, 558, 568-70, 673-6, 677, 679; 8. 330, 450; is Venus: 6. 411. *See also* Sapientia; Wisdom
Sapientia, 7. 668, 678. *See also* Sapience; Wisdom
Sappho, 4. 217; 6. 252, 310; 8. 299, 426, 483, 652, 657
Saracen Brothers, represent Earl of Oxford: 1. 449, 451; are Gog and Magog: 2. 187; represent Spain: 1. 453-4; 5. 305. *See also* Sansfoy; Sansjoy; Sansloy
Saracens, 2. 274, 276; 5. 169; 6. 227-8
Sasso, Panfilo, 8. 442
Satan, 1. 276, 304, 309, 364, 402, 414, 424, 471; 5. 200; 8. 486. *See also* Devil
Satire, 5. 212; 6. 304; 7. 290, 292-4, 334, 350-1, 358, 375, 447; 8. 560-6, 568-71, 578-9, 594
Saturn, 2. 300; 3. 296-7, 394, 397; 5. 159-60; 6. 279, 307; 7. 559; 8. 400; Age of: 5. 342; 8. 354; planet: 6. 310-2; 7. 528; his tears: 1. 209
Satyrane, 1. 245, 311-2, 419, 423, 437; 2.

210; 3. 264, 266-7, 276, 279, 313, 327; 4. 175-6, 189; 5. 182; is Cranmer: 1. 469-70; is Huguenots: 1. 455; is Sir John Perrot: 1. 454, 464, 469; is Prince of Orange: 1. 459; 3. 380

Satyrs, 1. 423, 431, 499-501, 503; 3. 355; 6. 381; 8. 413; are Beggars of the Sea: 1. 459; are the brutish multitude: 1. 454; are the humble children of the earth: 1. 437; are the Waldenses: 1. 455

Saul, 8. 357

Saurat, Denis, 2. 211, 244-5, 390; 3. 344; 6. 273, 404-6; 7. 538, 565-6, 568, 657

Savage Man, 4. 203-4, 281; 6. 201-2, 232, 304, 328, 334, 338, 340, 342, 345, 350; is Lord Savage: 6. 201, 350; the "Noble Savage": 6. 201-2, 348; is people of Ireland: 5. 315

Savage, Richard, 8. 666

Savages, 5. 169; 6. 201-2, 233-4, 326, 334

Savile, Henry, 1. 483

Sawles Warde, 2. 424-5, 456-7

Saxon Kings, 1. 442, 453, 454

Saxons, 1. 486; 2. 205, 332-4; 3. 228; 6. 285; 8. 289-90

Saxton, Christopher, 4. 252, 254, 257-8, 261, 273; 5. 237

"say," 7. 306-7

Sayce, A. H., 5. 159

Sayers, Dorothy, 8. 479

Scales, 5. 176-8, 180

Scaliger, Joseph Justus, 1. 200; 6. 310; 7. 288

Scaliger, Julius Caesar, 1. 187, 348-50, 358, 513; 2. 218; 4. 194, 212; Poetices: 3. 227; 7. 256; Virgil: 8. 545

Scamander, 3. 281

Scandal, 1. 364, 367; 6. 188, 203, 205-7, 350, 383-6; 7. 292

Scanderbeg, George Castriot, 8. 507, 708, 736

Scarabee, 8. 407, 625

Scarlet Letter, 5. 176

Scarlet Woman, 1. 199, 250, 259, 368; 8. 279-80, 392

Scatterlings, 2. 332

Scepticism, 3. 342; 6. 393-5, 399, 405, 407

Scève, Maurice, 7. 439; 8. 427, 430, 434, 610

Schekhina, 7. 558, 561-2, 565-6

Scheld, 2. 312

Schelling, Felix, 8. 498, 505

Schipper, J., 7. 636; 8. 656, 658, 674

Schoembs, Jakob, 2. 209

Schoeneich, Georg, 2. 189, 191, 237, 247, 254, 270, 276, 306

Schofield, W. H., 2. 208, 415

Scholasticism, 1. 310, 445; 2. 418; 6. 419; 7. 540-1

Schopper, Hartmann, 8. 590

Schramm, Richard, 3. 238, 258; 4. 215

Schröer, Arnold, 8. 412

Schrötter, Wilibald, 6. 221

Schulz, Herbert, C., 8. 420

Schulze, I. L., 1. 390; 5. 182-6, 197, 203, 319

Science, 2. 346, 478; 6. 391, 399, 405, 407; 7. 657

Scipio Africanus, 1. 406; 4. 223, 316; 5. 220; 7. 393; 8. 328, 387

Scipio Nasica, 8. 387

Scolopendra, 2. 359-61

Scorn, 6. 328, 350

Scory, Edmond, 8. 509

Scot, Thomas, 8. 582

Scotists, 1. 448

Scotland, 2. 309, 320; 5. 246; 7. 304

Scots, 6. 256

Scott, Janet, 8. 421, 423, 427-8, 430, 432, 434-8, 442-4, 446-8, 450-2, 454, 640, 644

Scott, John, 8. 489

Scott, Reginald, 1. 204

Scott, Sir Walter, 1. 450, 491; 3. 428; 6. 383; 7. 253; 8. 582

Scourge of Venus, 7. 283

Screech-owl, 2. 369

Screen, 5. 238-9, 254-5

Scudamore, Lord, 3. 290; 4. 172

Scudamour, 1. 367, 425; 2. 454; 3. 288-9, 303-4, 310-2, 318, 326, 329, 355-6, 361, 372-3, 381, 385, 388-90; 4. 173-4, 198, 201, 215-6, 218, 229, 233, 237, 276, 281, 283; 6. 319; 7. 510, 521; 8. 388, 444, 446; is Essex: 3. 380; jealous: 5. 208; the average lover: 4. 320; name: 4. 171-2, 216; is Raleigh: 3. 378; suspicious: 4. 305; a type: 4. 220

Scudéry, Mlle. de, 1. 263

Sculpture, 1. 219; 2. 212-3, 373, 379; 3. 392; 6. 305

Scylla, 2. 183, 348, 351, 354-5; 3. 334

Sea, 1. 194, 287; 2. 199, 211, 216, 234, 244, 252, 254, 356-68; 3. 238-9, 271; 6. 447; 8. 448, 646

Seal, 2. 359, 362-3

Seasons, 1. 365; 6. 293, 302-3, 391-4, 404, 409-10, 414, 420-1, 439, 447; 7. 592; 8. 437

Seckerstone, Richard, 8. 649

Seckerstone, Roger, 8. 648-51

Sedition, 1. 250

Seed, 6. 417

Segar, William, 5. 182; 6. 264, 337

Selden, John, Notes on Drayton's Polyolbion:

1. 265-6, 293, 477; 4. 239-40, 259-60; 5. 158; 6. 285; 8. 285, 288-90

" self," 7. 327

Self-control, 1. 328, 341; 2. 278, 404, 415

Selimus, 1. 250; 2. 191; 8. 287, 384

Selinis, 1. 252-3; 8. 408

Selloi, 5. 219

Semele, 3. 397

Semiramis, 2. 289; 8. 305

Seneca, Lucius Annaeus, 1. 279; 2. 425; 3. 257; 4. 235; 6. 365; 7. 336; 8. 536; *Agamemnon*: 3. 242; 8. 372; *Consolatio ad Marcam*: 1. 280; *Consolatio ad Polybium*: 8. 315; *De Beneficiis*: 6. 251, 254, 282; 7. 289; 8. 327; *De Clementia*: 5. 295-6; *De Ira*: 1. 222-3; *De Tranquillitate*: 8. 315; *De Vita Beata*: 5. 256; 8. 315; *Hercules Furens*: 2. 257, 281; 8. 299; *Hercules Oetaeus*: 3. 210; 5. 224; 8. 299, 310; *Hippolytus*: 1. 236; 2. 227; 8. 480, 504; *Medea*: 8. 463, 473, 480; *Moral Epistles*: 2, 4: 6. 238, 241; 8, 50, 68: 6. 212; 9, 25, 63: 6. 214; 50?: 6. 189; 81: 5. 256; 90: 8. 352; 98: 6. 241; 102: 8. 286; 114: 8. 476; *Naturales Quaestiones*: 4. 226; 7. 463; *Oedipus*: 1. 179; *Thyestes*: 7. 415, 446; 8. 372; *Troades*: 2. 187; 7. 439, 446; 8. 304

Senecan tragedy, 3. 301

A Senights Slumber. See My Slomber

Senses. *See* Five Senses

Sensuality, 1. 249; 2. 414

Sensuousness, 1. 238, 297; 8. 364

Sentence-order, 7. 628

Sententia, 8. 394

Sentimentality, 5. 201, 233

Serafino dell' Aquila, 8. 425, 434

Seraphim, 1. 310; 7. 553-4

Serena, 1. 378; 5. 315; 6. 205, 233-6, 317, 325, 327, 329-30, 334, 338, 371, 376, 384; is Elizabeth Throckmorton: 6. 384; is Elizabeth Vernon: 6. 363

Sergis, 5. 258-9, 302

Serpent, 1. 391, 398, 411

Serraglio, Christoforo, 8. 460

Servius, 1. 236; on the *Aeneid*: 3. 282; 1. 31: 2. 266; 1. 317: 2. 378; 1. 491: 2. 219; 1. 539: 2. 204; 1. 720: 4. 194; 6. 247, 254; 7. 289; 8. 327, 483; 1. 741: 7. 307-8; 2. 337: 2. 200; 2. 632: 1. 174; 4. 232, 236; 7. 480; 2. 770: 2. 187; 3. 23: 8. 340; 4. 122: 6. 301; 4. 167: 1. 310; 4. 242-4: 8. 377; 6. 57: 7. 274; 6. 121-2: 8. 299; 6. 603: 8. 492; 6. 743: 2. 375; 7. 662: 5. 250; 7. 761: 1. 236; 8. 276: 2. 294; 9. 585: 8. 311; 12. 87: 8. 395; 12. 119: 1. 310; on the *Eclogues*: 2. 31:

6. 281; 4. 63: 8. 490; 7. 61: 2. 239; on the *Georgics*: 1. 12: 7. 290; 1. 20: 1. 242; 1. 302: 2. 376; 3. 391: 7. 337; 8. 490; 4. 403: 4. 247

sestina, 7. 338, 347-9, 640-1

" set a price," 7. 306

Setual, 8. 399

Seven, 2. 480, 484-5

Seven Ages of the World, 2. 284

Seven Champions of Christendom, 1. 202, 205, 207, 294, 301, 320; 2. 259; 3. 268, 290, 301; 4. 181

Seven Deadly Sins, 1. 217, 237, 347, 351, 364, 371, 405-15, 418, 423, 427, 436; 2. 412; 7. 241; 8. 437; College of Cardinals (six): 1. 459; emblems: 1. 411-3; maladies: 1. 411; mount: 1. 411-3; order: 1. 410; pageant composed as separate *jeu d'esprit*: 1. 440-1; symbolized in rabble of *F. Q.* 2. 11. 5-25: 2. 339-40, 412

Seven Liberal Arts, 1. 417

Seven Psalms, translated by Spenser, 8. 270, 283, 520

Seven Wise Masters, 8. 586

Seven Wonders of the World, 8. 305-6, 380

Seven-headed beast, 8. 279, 412

Severn, 7. 439

Severus, 2. 329-30; 4. 261

Seymour, Lord Thomas, 1. 458; 3. 379

Seymour, St. J. D., 8. 486

Shafer, Robert, 7. 486, 495-9

Shakespeare, William, 1. 372, 488-90; 2. 287, 303; 7. 367, 428, 663; 8. 281, 284, 393, 398, 445, 531-2, 637, 659, 661, 720; is Aetion: 7. 472-3; Elizabeth, looking over her shoulder: 1. 491; epitaph: 2. 194; historical allegory in: 1. 490; the sea in: 1. 194; and Spenser: 1. 306, 316, 496; 3. 240, 384, 388; 4. 195, 290; 5. 274, 310, 344-5, 369; 6. 212, 346; 7. 385, 575, 620; 8. 321, 483-4, 504, 518, 565, 628-31, 637, 639, 717; vocabulary: 7. 619-20, 629; is Willy: 8. 317-21; *All's Well that Ends Well*: 8. 316, 437, 482; *Antony and Cleopatra*: 2. 253; 3. 212; 6. 241; 8. 389, 524; *As You Like It*: 1. 216; 2. 202, 284; 4. 209; 7. 253, 720; *Comedy of Errors*: 6. 246; 7. 263; 8. 316; *Coriolanus*: 5. 189, 344; 7. 359, 481; *Cymbeline*: 7. 379; 8. 467; *Hamlet*: 1. 273; 2. 346; 1. 1: 7. 443; 1. 2: 2. 460; 8. 337; 1. 3: 7. 720; 1. 5: 5. 157, 225; 6. 309; 2. 1: 4. 226; 2. 2: 2. 279; 7. 302; 3. 2: 2. 189, 276; 4. 5: 7. 305; 8. 353; 5. 1: 2. 194; 7. 302, 321; 8. 482-3; *1 Henry IV*: 1. 284; 2. 230; 6. 193, 239, 246; 8. 309; *2 Henry IV*: 7. 269; *Henry V*: 1. 255; 3. 213;

4. 213; 7. 341; 8. 309; *1 Henry VI*: 2. 189, 220; 4. 214; 5. 261; 6. 216; 8. 460, 486, 719; *2 Henry VI*: 2. 273, 340; 6. 246; 7. 392; 8. 719; *3 Henry VI*: 4. 212; 8. 492; *Henry VIII*: 1. 190; 2. 246; 7. 258, 341; *Julius Caesar*: 1. 216; 2. 235; 5. 194; 7. 349; 8. 372; *King John*: 6. 246; 8. 372; *King Lear*: 1. 1: 7. 297; 1. 4: 4. 181; 7. 331; 3. 4: 6. 196; 3. 6: 6. 265; 4. 6: 2. 196; 3. 287; 7. 269; 8. 315; 5. 3: 6. 212; *Love's Labors Lost*: 3. 284; 7. 297; 8. 316, 466; *Macbeth*: 1. 306; 2. 299; 1. 1: 4. 212; 1. 4: 1. 239; 2. 2: 1. 287; 8. 486; 2. 3: 2. 369; 3. 2: 7. 272; 4. 1: 3. 268, 370; 5. 1: 2. 196, 268; 5. 3: 6. 212; 8. 436; *Measure for Measure*: 1. 302; 5. 252; *Merchant of Venice*: 5. 195, 218, 247; 8. 355, 364, 436, 487; *Merry Wives of Windsor*: 2. 281; 3. 284; 4. 166, 209; 7. 265; *Midsummer Night's Dream*: 1. 316; 2. 190; 8. 321, 598; 1. 1: 6. 246; 2. 2: 7. 346; 3. 2: 1. 229; 8. 465, 475; 5. 1: 7. 473; 8. 327, 541; 5. 2: 8. 484; *Much Ado About Nothing*: 2. 228, 369; 3. 298; 7. 278, 316, 340-1; *Othello*: 1. 239, 496; 5. 176; 8. 474; *Passionate Pilgrim*: 4. 202; 7. 385; *Pericles*: 7. 251-2; *Rape of Lucrece*: 2. 228; 4. 212; 6. 187, 206-7, 244; 7. 577; *Richard II*: 1. 226; 5. 193, 201; 6. 246; 8. 719; *Richard III*: 1. 294; 3. 240; 6. 194, 239; 7. 383; 8. 372, 449, 486; *Romeo and Juliet*: 3. 219; 1. 1: 8. 472; 1. 2: 4. 166; 1. 4: 3. 359; 1. 5: 2. 206; 6. 251; 8. 477; 2. 2: 5. 209; 8. 447, 476; 2. 3: 6. 239; 8. 285; 2. 4: 8. 355; 2. 5: 8. 477; 2. 6: 8. 483; 3. 1: 5. 222; 3. 2: 7. 327; 8. 483; 3. 5: 5. 369; 8. 466; 4. 1: 1. 247; *Sonnets*: 8. 628-31, 637, 643; 18, 55, 63, 81: 8. 299; 18: 8. 433; 130: 8. 472; 146: 7. 479; 8. 429; *Taming of the Shrew*: 3. 395; 5. 167; 8. 316; *Tempest*: 1. 275; 2. 191; 6. 217, 228, 243; 7. 340; 8. 288, 491; *Timon of Athens*: 2. 235; 8. 483; *Titus Andronicus*: 6. 239; *Troilus and Cressida*: 4. 324; Prologue: 7. 305; 1. 3: 4. 227; 5. 157, 160, 177, 185; 1. 6: 7. 720; 2. 2: 8. 483; 3. 2: 8. 460; 3. 3: 4. 195; *Twelfth Night*: 1. 243; 5. 193; 7. 530; 8. 426, 436; *Two Gentlemen of Verona*: 7. 379, 386; 8. 316, 465; *Venus and Adonis*: 7. 379, 577; 8. 321; *Winter's Tale*: 4. 198; 6. 371, 378; 1. 2: 7. 272, 282; 3. 3: 6. 203, 264; 4. 3: 1. 215; 8. 460; 4. 4: 7. 285; 5. 2: 3. 395

Shakespeare's England, 8. 355

Shame, 1. 328, 342; 3. 319; 4. 181

Shamefastness, 2. 286-8, 294-5, 297, 418, 426, 434; 3. 355, 385; 4. 237

Shannon, 4. 185, 264-8

Sharp, Thomas, 1. 390

Sharpham, Edward, 8. 509

Sheep, 6. 216; 8. 375, 562, 571

Sheffield, Lady Douglas, 8. 606

Sheffield, Elizabeth, Countess of Ormonde, 7. 475-6

Sheffield, Robin, 7. 402-3

Sheldon, Edward W., 6. 458

Shelley, Percy Bysshe, 3. 325; 4. 239; 6. 277, 347, 420; 7. 397, 400, 408, 412, 481, 491, 493, 496, 525, 529-30, 560; 8. 599, 623; *Adonais*: 8. 295-6; *Homeric Hymn to Mercury*: 8. 545; *Revolt of Islam*: 8. 460; *Witch of Atlas*: 8. 372, 395, 603

Shene, 1. 291; 8. 672

Shepherd, 7. 463

Shepheardes Calender, 6. 317, 386, 399, 406, 440; 7. 466; 8. 418, 533-4, 566, 669; allegory in: 7. 600, 606; anonymity: 7. 235, 641-5; archaisms: 7. 614-30; circulation in MS: 7. 415; close or finale of eclogues: 7. 251, 482; and *Colin Clouts*: 7. 447-9, 451, 482; combines classic and romantic: 7. 644; composition: 7. 243, 250, 334, 418, 574, 591-9, 606-7, 610-4, 658; core and heart: 7. 427, 603; criticism: 7. 377, 571-88, 589, 592-3, 600-1; 8. 517; date: 3. 393; 7. 295, 362, 607, 610-4; decorum: 7. 631; dedication: 7. 581, 613; design: 7. 630-4; dialect: 7. 312-3, 315, 571-5, 578-81, 614-30; and *Doleful Lay of Clorinda*: 7. 501, 503; drama in: 8. 517; editions: 7. 641, 643-5, 692-6; "Emblems" in: 7. 633-4; 8. 626; more English than Renaissance: 7. 580; and *F. Q.*: 7. 574, 579, 581-2; fame: 7. 605, 641-5; form and content: 1. 350; 7. 574, 582-3, 630-4; grouping: 7. 607, 611, 616-8, 630-4; humor in: 8. 518; and the *Hymnes*: 7. 656-8, 660; inconsistencies: 7. 613-4; influence: 7. 427, 576, 593-4, 644-5; language: 7. 589, 595-6, 614-30; 8. 562, 676; licensed: 7. 612; metres: 7. 235, 244, 573-4, 580, 583-5, 595, 603, 607, 634-41; the "Moral Eclogues": 7. 235, 254-5, 291, 323-5, 351, 427, 454, 589, 592, 600-12, 614, 634-41; 8. 356; and *Mother Hubberds Tale*: 7. 605, 611; 8. 563, 566, 577, 590, 594; motives: 7. 594-5, 611, 613; and *Muiopotmos*: 8. 601; new style: 1. 330; 4. 178-9; 7. 580-1, 583-4, 586-8, 605; originality: 7. 594, panegyric: 7. 398, 591; pastoralism, summary

of: 7. 592; plan: 7. 251, 573-4, 589, 592-4, 610; poets, inspiration to: 7. 427; more polemical than pastoral: 7. 600; popularity: 7. 601, 605; publication: 7. 538, 576, 583-4, 605, 609, 644; Puritanism: 7. 669; purpose: 7. 427; realism: 7. 589, 592; "Recreative Eclogues": 7. 353; Renaissance studies, composed of: 7. 605; Rosalind its theme: 7. 602; satire: 7. 591, 600-9; 8. 590; Shepherd's or Shepherds'?: 7. 235; and *Sonets*: 8. 618; sources: 7. 589-99; style: 7. 575, 585, 614-30; success: 7. 452; symmetry: 7. 633; and *Teares of the Muses*: 8. 553, 539; text, critical notes on: 7. 715-20; text, variants: 7. 696-706; time sequence: 7. 277, 630-4; title: 7. 235, 581; unity: 7. 582-3, 632-3; and *Virgils Gnat*: 7. 605

"To his Booke," 7. 235, 487; 8. 459; *Dedicatory Epistle*: 2. 399; 3. 299-300; 4. 178-9; 6. 223; 7. 487, 611-3, 647-8; 8. 270; Spenser's hand in: 7. 238, 599, 647-8; §§ 12-15: 7. 599; 8. 325, 332; § 17: 8. 332, 538; § 21: 6. 431; 7. 587; § 22: 7. 655; § 24: 8. 270, 283, 512, 527; § 28: 7. 650; 8. 536; *General Argument*: 7. 391, 436-7; § 4: 7. 647; § 11: 4. 221

January: 7. 630-4, 653, 655; 8. 459, 537, 542; and *August*: 7. 246, 340, 641; characterized: 7. 244-7; and *December*: 7. 245-6, 418, 424, 585; metre: 7. 244, 246; rhetoric: 7. 246-7; Arg.: 7. 651; 1: 7. 613; 8. 404; 9: 8. 314; 49-54: 7. 654-5; 50, 60: 7. 651; 54: 6. 257; 7. 601; 65: 1. 199; 72: 8. 333; 73-8: 7. 591; 8. 480; 75: 7. 627; 80: 7. 245; E. K. *1*: 7. 647

February: 6. 209; 7. 243, 294, 583-4, 600-9, 613, 618, 630-2, 634; 8. 577; and *March*: 7. 267; metre: 7. 253, 255, 265, 275, 291, 398, 634-41; and *November*: 7. 405, 414-5; 1: 4. 239; 17: 7. 613; 32: 5. 181; 35-40: 6. 236; 59-60: 7. 255; 62: 7. 618; 80: 6. 239; 91-3: 7. 402, 604; 98-246: 7. 625; 102-14: 8. 389; 115: 8. 577; 169-71: 7. 578; 205-10: 8. 389; 215: 8. 411; 222, 237: 8. 577; 246: 7. 591; E. K. *102*: 8. 577; E. K. *119, 128*: 7. 647; gloss on Embleme: 7. 599

March: 7. 596, 613, 630-1; criticism: 7. 266-8, 272; and *February*: 7. 267; metre: 7. 266-8, 635, 638, 641; 5: 3. 276; 13: 8. 336; 22: 6. 304; 37-42: 7. 591; 73: 2. 191; 79-102: 6. 255; 79-89: 3. 298; 106-11: 5. 235; 115-7: 7. 591; 121-2: 4. 216; 6. 257; E. K. *16*: 2. 378; 7. 599; E. K. *25*: 7. 647; E. K. *79*: 2. 272; 3.

252, 298; 6. 310; 8. 270, 396; E. K. *97*: 3. 238; 7. 599; 8. 301; E. K. *116*: 8. 549

April: 2. 385; 4. 239; 7. 243, 572, 584-5, 590, 613, 630-6, 633; 8. 319, 459, 643, 673; composition: 7. 276-7; criticism: 7. 275-7; and *Epithalamion*: 7. 274, 280; 8. 657; gem of *S. C.*: 7. 641; metre: 7. 274-7, 310, 636, 638, 641; and *November*: 7. 395, 398, 401-2; 8. 643; structure: 7. 280; 14: 7. 591; 21-6: 6. 220; 7. 612-3, 651, 653, 655; 30-2: 7. 591; 37-45, 136-44: 7. 579; 42: 8. 324; 52-3: 8. 498; 55: 6. 237; 57: 8. 473; 61: 8. 469; 64-72: 8. 474; 68: 2. 384; 100-12: 8. 311, 327-8; 109-12: 6. 252; 8. 479; 125: 7. 627; 129-30: 8. 468; 131-4: 8. 465; 136-44: 8. 348, 398, 463, 497; 140: 8. 464; 160-1: 7. 591; E. K. *26, 50, 104*: 7. 647; E. K. *41*: 8. 470; E. K. *50*: 7. 281; 8. 376; E. K. *86-7, 110, 122*: 7. 273; E. K. *100*: 1. 509-15; 8. 312; E. K. *109*: 6. 253; 8. 327; E. K. *120*: 8. 312, 462

May: 7. 584, 600-10, 613, 618, 630-2, 635; composition: 7. 296; criticism: 7. 290-4; language: 7. 290, 304; metre: 7. 291-2, 627, 634-41; 1-2: 3. 355; 9 ff.: 7. 583; 17-8: 7. 296; 33: 8. 312, 463; 37-54: 7. 602; 54: 7. 281, 601; 73-131: 7. 602; 75-309: 7. 358; 103-29: 7. 602, 607; 119-25: 8. 358; 172-3: 7. 591; 187: 7. 627; 257, 266: 7. 601; 308-10: 8. 357; 315-7: 7. 591; 8. 480; E. K. *69, 257*: 7. 647; 8. 510; E. K. *142*: 7. 273

June: 7. 572, 574, 612-3, 631-2, 634, 655; 8. 319, 459; criticism: 7. 308-9; date: 7. 310; metre: 7. 309-10, 641; 8: 6. 247; 8. 470; 7-9: 8. 506; 18-22: 7. 612, 651; 23-4: 8. 487; 25-6: 2. 336; 8. 312, 327, 463; 41, 49 ff.: 7. 279, 591; 8. 500; 52: 8. 460; 57-61: 1. 509-11, 514; 8. 328; 65, 79: 7. 239; 70: 6. 185; 81-8: 7. 604; 82: 7. 592; 102-12: 7. 651; 118-20: 6. 237; 7. 591; 123: 7. 607; E. K. *25*: 2. 215-6, 399; 3. 299, 393; 6. 253; 8. 270, 510, 514; E. K. *59*: 7. 647

July: 5. 295; 7. 584, 600-9, 612-4, 631-2; 8. 370, 575; composition: 7. 327; criticism: 7. 323-4; metre: 7. 323-5, 638; 17-24: 1. 305; 6. 305; 8. 350; 47: 6. 185; 49: 7. 281, 601; 59: 7. 599; 83: 4. 242; 117: 7. 601; 145-51: 7. 347; 159: 8. 465; 165-96: 7. 602; 186: 7. 591; 197: 7. 607; 219-28: 8. 396, 409; 228: 7. 612; 230: 7. 614; E. K. *21*: 8. 350; E. K. *64*: 8. 490

August: 7. 309, 572, 574, 584, 596-7, 613-4, 631, 633; 8. 319, 459; composition: 7. 339; criticism: 7. 338-40, 345;

and *January*: 7. 246, 340, 641; metre: 7. 338, 340, 344-9, 636, 638; and *November*: 7. 395; sources: 7. 339-50; 25 ff.: 7. 591; 30: 7. 627; 49-53: 7. 591; 80: 8. 465; 138: 4. 216; 141-89: 7. 651, 655; 169-71: 6. 222; 198: 7. 591

September: 1. 381; 7. 295, 584-5, 607-9, 612-4, 631-2; criticism: 7. 350-2; metre: 7. 351, 627, 634-41; sources: 7. 350; 1-4: 7. 575; 36: 7. 607; 42-3: 7. 602; 56, 74: 7. 468; 57-60: 7. 614; 90-101: 7. 609; 106-61: 7. 603; 123: 8. 351; 124: 6. 272; 7. 602; 171-225: 7. 612; 238-9: 7. 369, 603

October: 1. 381; 7. 293, 574, 585, 594, 602-3, 612-3, 631-2, 658; 8. 313, 319, 528, 535, 540; and *Colin Clouts*: 7. 481, 665; criticism: 7. 366-71; and the *Hymnes*: 7. 665; metre: 7. 276, 366, 374, 430, 640-1; sources: 7. 371-4; text: 7. 392; Arg.: 7. 490; 8. 270, 332, 538; 25-30: 8. 326, 344; 37-48: 7. 296, 612; 46-7: 8. 576; 55-78: 7. 603; 8. 314, 321, 539, 602; 91-6: 7. 627; 8. 326; 114: 1. 296; 118: 5. 235; 119-20: 7. 287; E. K. *65*: 7. 648; 8. 302; E. K. *90*: 7. 640; 8. 270; E. K. *114*: 3. 279; E. K. *114*: 7. 647

November: 7. 243, 582, 613, 631-4; and *April*: 7. 395, 398, 401-2; 8. 643; and *Astrophel*: 7. 399; and *August*: 7. 395; composition: 7. 243, 395-6, 414-5; criticism: 7. 395-401; and *December*: 7. 425-6; and *Epithalamion*: 8. 657; and *February*: 7. 405, 414-5; metre: 7. 395, 397-8, 400-1, 406, 410, 412, 636, 638, 641; rhetoric: 7. 503, 506; source: 7. 395-7, 399-401; Arg.: 7. 252, 647; 9-22: 7. 613; 19-20: 3. 355; 21-41: 7. 591; 22: 3. 304; 38, 44, 63: 7. 651-2; 44: 7. 655; 53: 8. 394; 71: 7. 491; 8. 333; 75: 6. 237; 83-92: 7. 596; 93: 7. 506; 98: 7. 620; 105: 2. 277; 143-4: 8. 463; 148: 4. 182; 175: 7. 601; 206-10: 7. 252, 591, 633-4, 647; E. K. *13, 153, 170*: 7. 647; E. K. *38*: 7. 651; E. K. *53*: 8. 312; E. K. *179*: 4. 222; E. K. *148*: 4. 181-2; E. K. *164*: 8. 315-6; E. K. *195*: 8. 270, 283, 512

December: 7. 582, 631-4, 655; 8. 459, 537, 542; composition: 7. 417-8; criticism: 7. 417; and *January*: 7. 245-6, 418, 424, 585; and *November*: 7. 425-6; metre: 7. 418, 425, 636; source: 7. 417-25; 4: 7. 592; 7: 7. 601; 14: 7. 591; 57: 6. 305; 95-6: 6. 222; 104: 8. 492; 137: 7. 506; 155-6: 7. 651, 653; 157: 8. 300, 549

Envoy: 7. 584

Sherman, S. P., 7. 497, 499

Shield, 1. 177, 250, 425, 427; 2. 205, 230, 235, 237; 3. 290; 4. 171-2, 218, 220, 320; 5. 187, 192, 200, 228-9, 264; 6. 197-8; of Love: 3. 356; 4. 171, 216, 218, 220-1; 8. 444

Shipley, J. T., 7. 640

Shippe of Safegarde, 2. 352

Ships, 1. 310; 2. 199, 242; 5. 181, 258, 275; 6. 242; 7. 258; 8. 315, 387, 431, 441, 638

Shirley, James, 7. 262

Short, Peter, 7. 502; 8. 735-6

" shoulder," 8. 385

Showerman, Grant, 6. 398

Shrewsbury, Earl of. *See* Talbot, George

Shure, 6. 424

Shylock, 3. 314

" sib," 7. 305

Sibyl, 1. 233, 234, 359; 3. 227

Sibylline Oracles, 6. 315-6

Sidney, Ambrosia, 7. 402-4, 415

Sidney, Elizabeth, 7. 490

Sidney, Frances. *See* Walsingham, Frances

Sidney, Henry, 2. 295, 408; 5. 258-9; 6. 233, 356, 384-6, 442-3; 7. 355, 402-3, 648; 8. 284, 295; is Palmer: 2. 401

Sidney, Mary, Countess of Pembroke, 3. 309, 392; 4. 256; 6. 353-4; 7. 435, 453, 474, 487, 489-90, 499, 500-5, 594; 8. 283-4, 295-6, 307, 451, 526-7, 539; " Dialogue in Praise of Astrea": 7. 500, 502-4; Garnier's *Antonie*: 7. 504; 8. 284, 296, 528; Mornay's *Discourse of Life and Death*: 8. 284, 296; translation of the Psalms: 8. 284, 520; is Urania: 7. 474; 8. 284

Sidney, Sir Philip, 1. 173, 340, 351, 488, 513; 3. 307, 309, 343; 5. 185, 225, 302, 335, 343; 6. 242-3, 321, 393; 7. 367, 372, 375, 399, 408, 448, 453, 465-7, 469, 476, 504, 506, 581, 585, 590, 642; 8. 284, 295-6, 299, 363, 371, 398, 418, 503-4, 530, 539, 544, 637, 639, 665; is Amyntas: 3. 260; 7. 471; is Arthur: 5. 299-300; is Astrophel: 6. 351, 355; 7. 443, 453, 463, 474, 490, 492, 497, 499; 8. 307; is Calidore: 1. 340; 6. 187, 252, 267, 318, 349-51, 354-7; career: 8. 304, 604; is Clarion: 8. 604-6; on comedy: 8. 317; " courtier, the brave": 8. 349, 365, 570; death: 7. 489, 494; 8. 296-7, 307-10, 534, 540, 604; and the Earl of Oxford: 8. 313, 320, 569, 599, 603-4; elegies in *Colin Clouts* volume: 8. 527-8; and Elizabeth: 8. 573-5, 584; and *The English Poet*: 7. 370, 377-8; on epic and poetry: 8. 328; lamented: 3. 259; 7. 483-99, 501, 503; 8. 296-7, 307-10, 393, 522-30; " nectar-

tongued": 8. 321-2; and Penelope Devereux: *see* Devereux; Philisides: 6. 351, 373; 7. 491; 8. 307; political ideas: 5. 308; 7. 608; portrait: 3. 392; pride his besetting sin: 1. 451; is Red Cross Knight: 1. 449, 451-2; retractation: 7. 658; Spenser, compared with: 8. 629-31, 639, 644; Spenser, criticism of: 7. 620, 623, 643, 645; 8. 584; Spenser, influence upon: 3. 386, 393; 5. 320, 343; 6. 242-3, 252, 351, 371-6, 378-81; 7. 349, 585; 8. 652; Spenser, relations with: 1. 451; 2. 398; 3. 355; 4. 273; 5. 271, 307, 320, 325, 343; 6. 250, 255, 272, 357, 371-6, 380-1, 385, 440; 7. 291, 349, 396, 483-90, 538, 571, 579, 600, 604-5, 611, 613; 8. 297, 328, 349, 459, 514, 521, 523-4, 531-2, 536, 559; and Stella: 7. 350, 484, 489-95, 497, 499; vocabulary: 7. 619; is Willy: 8. 317, 320

Arcadia: 1. 279, 340-1, 345-6, 451-2; 2. 194, 224, 231, 401; 3. 318, 377-8, 392-3; 5. 308; 6. 187, 233, 242-3, 250, 255, 349, 356, 360; 371-6, 380, 408; 7. 340, 489-91, 581; 8. 296, 307; (numbers in parenthesis refer to volume and page of Feuillerat's edition): 1. 3. 1 (1. 17-8): 3. 393; 1. 3. 3 (1. 20): 3. 378; 1. 5. 1 (1. 30): 5. 342; 1. 8. 3 (1. 53-4): 8. 473; 1. 10. 1 (1. 60): 4. 211; 1. 12. 2 (1. 75): 2. 216; 1. 12. 5 (1. 78): 3. 223; 1. 13. 5 (1. 88-9): 2. 218, 253; 1. 13. 6 (1. 90): 2. 217; 5. 189; 1. 16. 1 (1. 105): 4. 218, 220; 1. 19. 3 (1. 121): 1. 398; 3. 246; 1. 19. 6 (1. 123): 2. 213; 1, *First Eclogues* (1. 126): 3. 284; 2. 2. 4 (1. 150): 2. 281; 2. 4. 1 (1. 167): 6. 218; 2. 7. 3 (1. 191): 3. 223; 2. 9. 3 (1. 203): 1. 222; 2. 11. 4-5 (1. 217-8): 3. 393; 2. 11. 6 (1. 218-22): 8. 474-5; 2. 14. 2 (1. 239): 7. 481; 2. 26. 3 (1. 315): 5. 343; 2. 29. 11 (1. 339-40): 2. 464; 2, *Second Eclogues* (1. 345): 7. 345; 3. 3. 1-2 (1. 367-8): 3. 393; 3. 11. 9 (1. 418): 2. 277; 3. 12. 11 (1. 426): 7. 409; 3. 12. 13 (1. 426): 6. 239; 3. 13. (1. 432): 1. 226; 3. 18. 6 (1. 458): 2. 234; 3. 25. 3 (1. 497): 2. 247; 3, *Third Eclogues* (2. 63-5): 8. 485, 652; 4, *Fourth Eclogues* (2. 141): 7. 283; 5 (2. 197): 3. 223; poems first printed in Folio of 1593 (2. 53): 2. 300; (2. 218): 2. 235; (2. 234): 1. 289

Astrophel and Stella: 4. 214; 7. 492-5, 499; 8. 296, 454, 535; 24, 35, 37: 7. 493-5; 49: 4. 277; 82: 8. 475; 100: 5.

189; 106: 5. 183; Defence of his father: 6. 442-3; Defence of Leicester: 6. 383

Defence of Poesie (references are by page to the text in G. Gregory Smith's *Elizabethan Critical Essays*, vol. 1, pp. 150-207): 1. 312; 7. 370, 377-8, 440; 8. 321, 536; p. 150: 2. 224; pp. 151 ff.: 8. 332; p. 154: 1. 225; p. 155: 7. 320, 459; p. 158: 7. 256; pp. 167, 185: 7. 599; pp. 177, 199: 7. 608; p. 179: 3. 265; p. 183: 2. 300; p. 192: 7. 368, 599; pp. 193-4: 8. 333; p. 195: 7. 490; p. 196: 7. 487-8, 571, 605; 8. 332, 538; pp. 199-200: 8. 317; p. 201: 7. 662; p. 204: 7. 623; pp. 205 ff.: 8. 332, 538; "Doubt you to whom": 8. 474; *Lady of May*: 8. 317; "Leave me, O Love": 8. 416; "*Madrigal*": *see Arcadia, 4th Ecl.*; masques: 8. 316; "*Nico and Dorus*": see *Arcadia, 2d Ecl.*; Psalms, translation of: 8. 296, 520; *Wooeing-stuff*: 7. 272

Sidney, Robert, Viscount Lisle, 8. 295
Sidney State Papers, 5. 184, 331; 7. 450
Sidonius, 1. 310; 2. 377; 4. 252
Sight, 1. 297; 2. 344
Signet Library, 7. 708; 8. 682
Silena, 1. 381-2
Silence, 1. 260, 262; 3. 385; 4. 237; 6. 207-8, 224, 232
Silexedra, 8. 318
Silius Italicus, *Punica*: 1. 429-31: 2. 274; 2. 68: 3. 215; 4. 85: 4. 174; 4. 522: 2. 342; 5. 141: 1. 252; 5. 398: 7. 266; 9. 383-4: 3. 245; 10. 354 6: 1. 223; 13. 663: 5. 256; 13. 845: 5. 250; 15. 284: 1. 229; 15. 800: 2. 277; 17. 122: 2. 342; 17. 417-8: 5. 226
Siloam, 1. 302
Silva Gadelica, 2. 373
Silvani, 7. 330
Silver, 4. 242; 6. 219, 239, 246, 278; 8. 411, 466
Silver bower, 6. 185
Silver sound, 7. 318; 8. 344
Silver stool, 2. 269
Simichidas, 7. 592
Simier, Jehan de, 1. 452; 2. 206, 219; 8. 568; is Ape: 8. 571, 574, 577-9; is Trompart: 2. 207, 219, 401-2; 5. 302
Simile, 1. 187-8, 199, 209-10, 226-7, 240-1, 252-3, 257, 258, 259, 295, 297, 303, 304, 307; 2. 199, 277, 282, 338, 341-2, 344; 3. 205, 207, 238, 243, 264-5, 271, 277, 278; 4. 172-3, 202, 207, 253, 277, 278, 285-6; 5. 181, 188, 190, 201, 202, 209, 258, 261, 264, 275; 6. 214, 216-9, 226-7, 230, 231, 243-4, 259, 290; 7. 236; 8. 377,

390; Aesopic: 8. 404; cattle: 6. 279; dream: 8. 377; epic: 8. 404; garden: 8. 442; horse: 7. 440; Milton's and Spenser's: 8. 306; peacock and rainbow: 8. 396; ships: 5. 275; 8. 387

Similitudo, 7. 246, 444

Simois, 3. 281

Simon de Montfort, the elder, 1. 455

Simonetta, 7. 281

Simonides, 8. 426

Simony, 7. 355; 8. 362

Simplesse, 4. 237

Simpson, Percy, 1. 522; 8. 711

Simpson, Richard, 8. 317

Sin, 1. 410; 2. 257

Sinadoun, 1. 391, 394

Sinai, Mount, 1. 281, 291; 7. 329

Sinann, 7. 456

Sincero, 7. 590

Singing-match, 7. 338-40, 344-6, 591, 597, 638

Singleton, Hugh, 7. 314, 609, 613

"singulf," 3. 426; 5. 369; 8. 712-3

Sion, 8. 285

"Sir," 2. 278

Sir Cauline, 1. 188, 199

Sir Cliges, 1. 346

Sir Gawayne, 7. 263

Sir John, 7. 306, 358

Sir Perceval of Galles, 6. 368

Sir Thomas More (tragedy), 5. 179

Sirens, 1. 363; 2. 183, 348, 351, 364-6

Sirius, 8. 350

Sisilius, 2. 321-2

"sit," 7. 300

Six Articles, 1. 468

Sixteenth Century, 5. 175, 341-2

Skeat, W. W., 3. 280; 5. 172; 7. 413, 415-6

Skell, 4. 262

Skelligs, 2. 349

Skelton, John, 1. 188, 228; 3. 286, 394; 7. 636, 681; 8. 321; *Boke of Philip Sparrow*: 7. 271; *Bowge of Court*: 3. 302; 6. 224; 8. 591; *Colin Cloute*: 1. 214; 5. 174; 7. 247, 299, 334, 479, 609, 614; 8. 591; *Elegy on the Earl of Northumberland*: 7. 383; *Garlande of Laurell*: 7. 235, 281, 305, 427; *Magnificence*: 1. 270, 276, 340, 346; *Tunning of Elinor Ruming*: 6. 193, 215; 7. 258, 305; *Ware the Hauke*: 5. 172; *Why come ye not to Court*: 6. 227; 7. 422; 8. 591

Skialetheia. See Guilpin, Edward

Skinner, Stephen, 4. 179-80; 7. 322

Slander, 1. 417; 2. 195; 3. 327; 4. 287, 295-6, 326; 5. 283, 292; 6. 323-4, 341-2; 363-4; 8. 453. *See also* Detraction

Slaney, 4. 264-5

Sleep, 2. 257, 259; 6. 233, 239; 8. 340. *See also* Law of Sleep; House of Sleep

Sléibe na Caillted, 7. 455

Slieve Bloom, 1. 244; 4. 269-70; 6. 425; 7. 455

Slieve Cullinn, 6. 426

Slieve Fuad, 6. 426

Slieve Lougher, 4. 266; 7. 455

Slievenaman, 6. 426

Slievenamuck, 6. 283

Slievesmole, 6. 425

Sloth, 2. 425

"smallage," 7. 443

Smell, 1. 297

Smerwick, 2. 349-50; 3. 380; 5. 181, 305, 314, 318-9, 332; 7. 458

Smith, Charles, *History of Cork*: 4. 268, 270; 6. 286; 7. 453, 457

Smith, Charles G., 4. 306-13, 324-34; 5. 188; 6. 275, 278, 449; 8. 450

Smith, J. C., 6. 436; 8. 598-9, 712-3, 718

Smith, Joseph, 1. 390

Smith, Nowell, 8. 489

Smith, Reed, 8. 395-6, 400, 404, 610

Smith, Richard, 3. 305

Smith, Sir Richard, 8. 463

Smith, Roland M., 6. 424-7; 7. 455-6

Smith, Thomas, 7. 252, 256, 366; 8. 528

Smith, William, 7. 339; 8. 460

Smithfield, 8. 501

Smól, 6. 426

Smolkin, 8. 486

Snachenbergh, Helena von, Marquesse of Northampton, 7. 433-5, 437, 474-5; 8. 622. *See also* Mansilia

Snake, 1. 199, 222, 285; 3. 288; 4. 186-7; 5. 267

Snám Dá Én, 7. 456

Snow, 1. 178

Social problem, 8. 565-6

Socialism, 5. 175-81

Socrates, 1. 279-80, 303; 2. 263-4, 298, 429; 4. 164; 6. 225; 7. 514

"soil," 8. 412

"Solamen miseris . . . ," 7. 439

Soldan, 1. 254; 5. 225-8, 292, 316; 6. 194, 227

Soldiers, 8. 302-3, 354-5

Solerti, Angelo, 7. 666

Solinus, 3. 330; 5. 312

Solomon, 5. 168, 193, 282, 304; 7. 563; 8. 303

Solon, 2. 273; 5. 216

Somerset, 7. 439

Somerset, Catherine, 7. 654; 8. 662-3, 665

Somerset, Edward, Earl of Worcester, 8. 663-5

Somerset, Elizabeth, 7. 654; 8. 662-3, 665

Somerset House, 8. 665

Somerville, John, 5. 320, 324

Sommer, H. O., 7. 242, 391

Sommers Collection, 5. 333

Somnolence, 1. 412

Sonets (in *Theatre for Worldlings*), 2. 359; 8. 277-80, 410-4, 512, 595, 611-27; authenticity: 8. 273-4, 611-24; and *Shepheardes Calender*: 8. 618; text, criticism: 8. 711; text, variants: 8. 678; 1-6: 8. 619, 621; 78: 8. 493; 128-41: 8. 322-3, 413

Songs . . . of Uncertain Authors, 7. 328

Sonnets and Sonneteering, 1. 247; 2. 379; 3. 305; 4. 216; 6. 229, 231; 7. 492-4, 664; 8. 274, 391, 405, 416, 535, 611-24, 628-31, 637, 639-43; English: 1. 247, 664; 8. 535, 628-31, 641; French: 7. 492; 8. 435, 441, 611-24, 628-31, 639-42; Italian: 8. 611-24, 628-31, 637, 639-42; portrait sonnet: 8. 425; "Shakespearian": 8. 422, 507, 620, 643; Spenserian: 7. 641; 8. 379, 391, 393, 404-5, 409, 415-6, 507, 539, 544, 615, 631, 643; Spenser's finest sonnet: 8. 506

Sophistry, 1. 273, 277, 279

Sophocles, 7. 338; 8. 333; *Ajax*: 2. 186; *Antigone*: 6. 309; 8. 460; *Electra*: 8. 394; fragments: 5. 166; *Oedipus Rex*: 7. 285; *Trachiniae*: 4. 252

Σωφροσύνη, 2. 414

Sophy, 2. 280

"sops in wine," 7. 287

Sorcery, 3. 221

Sorrow, 2. 257

"Sory Mayd," 1. 366

Soul, 4. 184; 7. 528, 673, 677; and body: 2. 468-71, 473-8, 482-7; 3. 256-7; without burial: 2. 346; a circle: 2. 473; heaven-descended: 7. 527-9; parts: 2. 198, 427, 437, 458, 462-3, 468, 480-1; 7. 665; revolutions: 1. 205; 3. 256-7, 340, 342, 344-5, 351-2; after temptation: 2. 347

Sound, 1. 241-2, 260, 297, 304; 2. 359, 366, 368, 386-7; 3. 205; 5. 186; 6. 290, 312; 7. 286, 383, 491, 682; 8. 497. *See also* Cadence; Music

Sources, 1. 193-5, 197, 202-4, 209-10, 213, 223-4, 228-9, 235-6, 239, 242, 249, 254, 264, 270, 272, 293-4, 349, 363, 395, 410-1, 471; 2. 202, 218, 232, 265, 301-38; 3. 223-37, 240, 242, 270, 333, 362, 396-7; 4. 172, 324; 6. 224; 7. 371-4; and Analogues indexed: 3. 400-2; 4. 335-9; 5. 350-5; 6. 452-7; 7. 683-9; 8. 724-34;

of Ariosto: 1. 419-21; 3. 367-76; of faery lore: 6. 274; French Romances: 6. 365-71; of history: 2. 302-34, 396-7, 406-7; 3. 227-37; manifold: 6. 249; of philosophy: 4. 234-5; Plutarch: 5. 214-5; of psychology: 2. 466; Spenser's treatment of: 6. 408-9, 413; 7. 304, 671; 8. 400-3, 446-7, 589; Tasso: 1. 420; Virgil: 3. 334-7

Southampton, Earl of. *See* Wriothesley, Henry

Southey, Robert, 2. 195, 205-6, 242; 8. 370, 478

Southwell, Robert, 3. 305; 7. 293, 675

Spagnuoli. *See* Mantuanus

Spain, 1. 459-60, 475; 2. 249, 252, 260, 301; 5. 163, 246, 248-55, 303, 305, 307, 312-4, 316-9, 330-5; 7. 586, 615; 8. 525; fashion: 8. 364; king of: 1. 296, 323; language: 8. 365; manners: 3. 212

Spanheim, Ezechiel, 2. 365; 6. 302, 312

Sparke, John, 2. 357

Sparrow, 1. 413

Spear, 1. 182, 250; 2. 276; 3. 204, 237, 286; 5. 192, 257, 348

Spectator, 2. 257

Speculum Morale, 1. 354-5

Speculum Regale, 2. 363

Speed, John, 3. 285; 5. 263; 8. 672

Speght, Thomas, 8. 595

Spelling, 5. 302, 366; 6. 475; 7. 618-20; 8. 342, 618, 715, 720

Spelman, Henry, 7. 575

Spence, Joseph, 1. 363-6

Spencer, Alice, Countess of Derby, 3. 260; 7. 451, 471-2, 476-7; 8. 310-1, 437, 501, 531, 535, 539, 635, 651

Spencer, Anne, Lady Compton and Mountegle, 3. 259-60; 7. 451, 476; 8. 349, 393, 501, 635, 651

Spencer, Elizabeth, Lady Carey, 3. 260, 309; 7. 435, 476-7, 660; 8. 311, 392-4, 403, 416, 420, 437, 445, 501, 598-9, 600, 603, 605, 634-7, 651, 717; is Amoretta: 3. 309, 378-9; 8. 635; is the Lady of the *Amoretti*: 3. 309, 378; 6. 353; 8. 393, 634-5

Spencer Family, 7. 312-5, 476; 8. 310-1, 392, 501-2, 651-2

Spencer, F. C., 7. 313-4; 8. 392

Spencer, Henry, 8. 310

Spencer, John, of Hodnell (ancestor of Elizabeth Boyle and the Spencers of Althorpe), 8. 651

Spencer, Sir John, 3. 259-60; 7. 312, 476, 650; 8. 310, 349, 392, 417, 501, 651-2

Spencer, Sir John (son of preceding), 8. 501

Spencer, Mary, 8. 417

Spens, Janet, 4. 235, 239; 6. 419-21, 449; 7. 681; 8. 446, 453, 647

Spenser, Catharine (Wiseman), 4. 270

Spenser, Edmund, absurdities: 6. 193; aesthetics, theory of: 7. 664; affects enthusiasm: 8. 593; allegorical method: 1. 490-5; 2. 436; 5. 217, 240; 6. 350, 383; 7. 254, 375, 483-4; 8. 371, 402; allegorist: 7. 579-81, 669; 8. 625-6; not a good allegorist: 1. 440; 8. 363; his allegory is medieval: 6. 371; allegory, superior in: 1. 270; allegory, tires of: 6. 346; ambition: 1. 335, 344; 5. 283-4; 7. 369, 382, 604; 8. 496; amorous: 8. 603; amuses himself: 2. 287; ancestry, believes in: 6. 255, 329-30, 334, 337-8, 345; "ancient" in description: 4. 228; 5. 189; ancient and modern, combines: 7. 587; ancients, compared with: 1. 363; ancients, free use of: 1. 370-1; 3. 271; anger: 8. 370; angler: 4. 255, 257, 273; 5. 202, 206; 6. 300; 7. 330; 8. 463; animal in man, conscious of: 3. 272-3; anonymity: 7. 235, 641-5; antiquarian: 1. 493; 2. 301-2, 315, 407; 4. 260; 5. 321; 6. 345; 7. 262; 8. 501-2, 672; Aphrodite, worships: 3. 254; Apocalypse, interest in: 1. 368-70; 6. 279-80; architecture, interest in: 2. 379; 4. 219; 5. 217-8, 224, 237-8; Ariosto, prefers to Tasso: 1. 316-7, 332-3, 337; compared with Ariosto: 1. 336-7, 366-7, 373-8; 2. 438-43; 3. 201, 213, 227, 273-4, 314-7, 367-76; 4. 189, 192, 328; 5. 221; 6. 313-4; hopes to "overgoe" Ariosto: 1. 332, 335, 361, 366; 2. 221; 3. 371; takes Ariosto seriously: 1. 366, 418-9; 3. 367-76; and the aristocracy: 8. 327; aristocratic: 1. 437; 4. 332; 5. 175, 262, 275, 290, 293, 341, 344; 8. 548; and Aristotle: see Aristotle; his art complex: 1. 495; Arthur, projected poem on: 1. 323; artificiality: 7. 571; artist, not philosopher: 1. 442; 3. 255-6, 345; artistic power: 1. 306; 2. 379-80, 386-7; 3. 252-3, 365; not ascetic: 3. 254; and astronomy: 6. 310-2; 7. 405, 415-6; and atheism: 6. 402, 406; his audience: 7. 428, 588; authority and independence, combines: 7. 593; autograph: 8. 419-20; awkward: 1. 284; bathos: 7. 259; Beauty, philosophy of: 4. 307; physical beauty, love of: 2. 296-7; 3. 254; 4. 195; 7. 294; beauty, prefers to truth: 1. 374; beauty rare: 2. 367; beauty, sense of: 2. 272, 296-7, 371; 3. 313; 4. 195; 7. 579; "better teacher than Aquinas": 2. 428, 431; 7. 371; biographical: 4. 287, 289; 5. 282-4; 7. 436, 439, 447-8; 8. 430-1, 435-6, 439-40, 443, 445-6, 449, 452-3, 561, 569, 601; birds, love of: 8. 466; birth: 8. 421, 439, 501; birthplace: 7. 419; bitterness: 8. 543; Boiardo, compared with: 2. 283; 3. 202; bold, could be: 7. 609; bored: 6. 346; borrowed from modesty, not need: 2. 371; botany: 7. 285-7; 8. 398; brief strokes, works in: 3. 243-4; and Bryskett: 7. 457; Bunyan, compared with: 1. 377; 2. 256, 339; and Burleigh: see Cecil, William; is Calidore: 6. 318; 7. 582; Calvinistic: 1. 437; 5. 175, 342-3; 6. 266; at Cambridge: 2. 424; 6. 386; 7. 254, 465, 586; 8. 518, 613, 620-1; Camden, regard for: 8. 291; caprice: 8. 311; careless: 2. 397; 3. 202, 208, 244, 264; 4. 189, 255, 258, 282; and Catholicism: 5. 343; 6. 266; changes his mind: 6. 266, 391-2; character: 1. 268-9; 7. 367; 8. 544; character, portrayal of: 1. 245; 2. 206; 5. 207, 274-5; charms the imagination but balks the intelligence: 1. 442; and Chaucer: see Chaucer; children: 4. 270; 8. 635, 648-51; children, love of: 3. 216; 6. 325; chivalry, passion for: 1. 336; 7. 254, 275; a Christian: 6. 428; chronology of his Works: 4. 312-6; as churchman: 1. 473; 5. 341; 6. 266; 7. 255, 564, 579, 608; Cicero, thought most formed by: 1. 361-2; classical: 5. 262; 7. 583; coarse sometimes: 1. 184, 221, 263, 364, 372; 3. 286; comedy, idea of: 8. 319; not commonplace: 4. 223; common sense: 5. 176; and communism: 4. 332; 5. 175-81, 336-47; 8. 352; composition, joy and exhaustion in: 8. 451; composition, manner of: 3. 314; 4. 323-4; 6. 427-9; 7. 438, 671; 8. 529-30; condescending: 7. 323, 340; conflict within: 7. 294, 367, 369; confused: 3. 340; 4. 289; 6. 280, 389, 404-6; 7. 302-3, 511, 551; 8. 364, 382; conscious art: 7. 421; conservative: 5. 155, 175, 343; 7. 254; consistent: 1. 264, 311; 5. 307; 6. 444; and contemporaries: 2. 186; 8. 288, 327, 333, 521, 531-40, 570; contemporary estimate: 5. 328; 7. 642; 8. 291-2, 302, 431; contentment: 6. 244; on the Continent: 7. 649; Cork, house in: 8. 649; courage: 8. 375; and the Court: 6. 238, 281, 319-20, 343; 7. 462, 478, 488, 629; 8. 303, 451, 495, 560-1, 566-7, 569, 603, 635, 662-3, 665; criticism, undeterred by: 7. 619, 624; critics, followed: 7. 626; dance, delights in: 7. 442; surpasses Dante: 2. 343; and Francis Davison: 5. 236; death: 8. 541; most delicate, yet vivid: 4. 287; 5. 222; and democracy: 5. 341-4; "de-

parture over sea ": 7. 611, 614, 649; 8. 281-2; depth and mellowness: 7. 316; *De Rebus Gestis Britanniae*, author of?: 1. 482; despondent: 5. 282-3, 292; 7. 309-10; 8. 293; despotism, warns against: 2. 250; dialect: 7. 331, 614-30; diction: *see* s. v.; diffuse: 5. 246; disappointed: 5. 308; 7. 478-9; 8. 593; disillusion: 1. 444; 3. 300, 327; 6. 319; 8. 281, 369; disproportion: 4. 172; distinguished most by his verse and painting: 6. 273-4; distrust of men: 6. 185; and divine right of kings: 8. 376; drama, interest in: 2. 432, 434; 3. 355-6; 6. 304; 7. 390; 8. 316-21, 426, 437, 516-8; dramatic power: 1. 271; 2. 224-5; 3. 220; 5. 274; 6. 205, 321; and dreams: 8. 377; dream with reality, combines: 2. 249; drops into poetry: 5. 209; Du Bellay, taste for: 8. 379-80; dull sometimes: 5. 273; Dutch, knowledge of: 8. 273-80, 621-2; early promise: 7. 605; 8. 388; early reading: 1. 417; 8. 278; echoes original, rarely: 7. 565-6; eclectic: 3. 343-4, 365; 4. 169; 6. 423-4; 7. 669; education: 6. 189; 7. 420; is E.K.: 7. 242, 278-9, 288, 307, 416, 599, 645-50; and Elizabeth: *see* Elizabeth; Elizabethan: 1. 305; 3. 349, 352, 354; emblem-writers, surpasses: 8. 309; emotional: 2. 324; enchanting: 2. 373; and English history: 5. 303-10; 6. 384; and English language: 8. 531; prefers English to alien setting: 7. 589-90, 592; envy, fear of: 7. 235, 450; 8. 403, 453; epigrammatic: 4. 202; escape: 1. 305, 335; 6. 275, 319; 8. 405; and Essex: *see* Devereux, Robert; ethics: 6. 391; evasive: 7. 531; expansive: 1. 224; 2. 203-4; 3. 203; experience, drew upon: 5. 273; 6. 238, 242; 7. 422, 517; experimenter: 7. 598, 636-7; extravagant: 1. 294-5, 297, 314-5; fabulist: 7. 599; fact, keen sense of: 6. 395; failure: 4. 176, 178; fair hair, liked: 8. 472-3; faith: 3. 383; 6. 311-4, 403, 407; falconry, love of: 1. 298; 3. 286; 5. 202; 6. 195-6, 218, 239, 245; 7. 539; 8. 327; and fame: 7. 367, 369, 641-5; family: 7. 312-4; 8. 310-11; farmer, respects: 8. 355; favorite ideas and images: 4. 202; 5. 186, 201, 206; 6. 192-4, 202, 205, 242, 258; 7. 344, 408, 539; 8. 337, 347, 364, 397, 400, 431, 439, 446, 452, 493, 498, 522, 614; favorite words and phrases: 6. 202, 214, 246, 291; 8. 335, 344, 381, 390, 403, 410, 432, 443, 463, 467, 478, 498, 500; feelings noble: 1. 320; fickle: 6. 404; a fighter: 6. 392; finest passages in: 2. 211,

270, 299; first of English heroic poets: 1. 314; flagging interest in *F. Q.*: 5. 205; forest, love of: 6. 235; 8. 296, 344, 459-60; freedom: 7. 624; 8. 620-1; French, knowledge of: 8. 273-80, 614, 617, 619, 623; *see also* Spenser, translator; and friendship: 4. 285; 5. 271, 276; 7. 291, 293, 465; 8. 503; "gentleman": 8. 311, 501-2; "gentle spirit"?: 8. 319; Golden Age, believed in: 5. 342; Greek, knowledge of: 1. 356; 2. 264; 6. 402; 7. 408, 589, 595-6, 670; 8. 376; Greek quality: 7. 499; hardships: 1. 268; harmony, great inventor of: 7. 638; and Harvey: *see* Harvey, Gabriel; hasty work: 8. 274, 277, 279; hates corruption: 8. 370; hates despite: 6. 207; hates disdain: 8. 364; hates flattery and servility: 6. 305; hates injustice, peculation: 5. 174, 283; 8. 370; hates slander: 6. 341-2; 8. 453; hates treachery: 5. 212; head and heart: 5. 311; health: 6. 275; heretical: 7. 538-9, 551; historical poet: 1. 485-6, 488; history, treatment of: 2. 302, 396-9, 406-7; 5. 312, 318; 6. 195, 383-5; 8. 327; hoarse: 7. 469; homeliness: 3. 220; 7. 349; Homer, compared with: 1. 337; 3. 301, 366-7, 435-6; 5. 269; 6. 273; humaneness: 2. 416; 5. 222; human interest, lacks: 1. 374, 378; humanist: 7. 292; human nature, could portray: 1. 496; 2. 410; 3. 313-4, 382-3, 386; 4. 285; 5. 207, 209; 6. 200, 205, 216; 8. 563; humor: 1. 306, 336, 378, 451; 2. 208, 299, 411; 3. 220-1, 267, 286; 5. 156, 235; 6. 204; 7. 255, 293; 8. 504, 516-8, 598, 601; hunting, fond of: 4. 202; 5. 202, 232; 6. 239, 300, 425-7; 8. 326-7, 443; hyperbole, delights in: 6. 191; idealism: 1. 336, 339, 362, 373; 3. 381-91; 5. 176, 233; 6. 346; 7. 291-2, 383; 8. 356, 370, 374, 646; idyllic power: 1. 271; 8. 629, 655; illness: 5. 284; illusion and disillusion, subject to: 1. 444; 6. 319; imagination: 1. 339, 373, 377; 2. 212, 238, 257, 260, 288, 334, 338, 352, 371, 416; 3. 215-6, 273, 313; 4. 196; 5. 271, 312; 6. 225, 313; 7. 284, 580; 8. 308, 404, 437; imagination, impresses reader's: 8. 309; imitates himself: 7. 503; imitates others: 7. 571, 592; imitators of: 1. 272-3, 278, 298; 2. 248, 261, 352, 360, 367, 371, 377, 383, 387, 399; 3. 301-3, 305; 4. 240; 5. 234; 7. 253, 255, 262, 268-9, 271, 276, 290, 324, 339, 352, 369, 399, 470, 593-4; and immortality: 6. 403, 405; imperialist: 5. 303-10; impiety: 1. 369-70; impropriety: 6. 281; inaccurate: 8.

378; incoherent: 6. 399; inconsistent: 2.
315, 511; 3. 344-5, 350-1; 6. 313, 406;
7. 334, 480, 545; indifference: 7. 561;
influence: 1. 477-82, 497; 2. 190, 211,
248, 285, 296, 299; 3. 211, 238, 288;
4. 315-6; 5. 224; 7. 238, 520, 585-6, 644;
8. 397, 405, 578; injustice: 5. 203; in-
scrutable: 7. 655; inspiration: 7. 621; intellectual and sensual, unites: 8. 674; intellectual aristocrat: 1. 437; intention: 2.
405; 4. 163; 5. 311; 6. 357, 442-3;
interest, power to sustain: 1. 377-8; in-
terests rich and varied: 1. 339; intimacy:
8. 530; invention: 1. 363-6; 2. 250, 266,
368, 381; 3. 271; 5. 267; 7. 582; in
Ireland: 4. 185-6, 241, 265-6; 5. 233,
255, 265, 280; 6. 231, 244, 282-9, 424-7,
441; 7. 459, 462, 485; 8. 281-2, 408, 463,
496, 531, 534-5, 544, 565-7, 632, 648-52;
see also Ireland; and Irish poetry: 2.
367, 373-4, 381, 383; 6. 218, 424-7;
irony: 1. 336; irrelevance: 2. 271; Italian,
knowledge of: 8. 274-7, 614, 622; Italian
poets, prefers as models: 1. 315-6; 2. 283;
Italian poets, vies with: 8. 518; Jonson,
compared with: 7. 617; joyous: 8. 645;
his knights: 3. 383; lame and impotent:
6. 201; language: 1. 206; 2. 364; 4. 178-
80; 6. 213, 302; 7. 238, 360, 571-3, 575-
6, 581, 586, 614-30; 8. 410-6, 531; see also
Vocabulary; last lines: 6. 315; learning: 5.
225; legal terms: 6. 223; and Leicester: see
Dudley, Robert; love, ideas of: 3. 366;
6. 399; 7. 662-76; love his prevailing
theme: 7. 669; in love: 5. 284; 7. 422,
482, 517, 579; low sometimes: 2. 278,
287; loyal: 8. 663; lyric power: 2. 270;
3. 345, 352; 7. 345; his magic: 4. 306;
manliness and sympathy: 5. 311; man of
action, would be: 5. 307; and Marlowe:
5. 344; and Marot: 8. 380; marriage: 7.
429, 439, 451, 487, 614, 655; 8. 463,
476, 479, 633, 636, 647-52; and Mary
Stuart: 4. 316; materialism: 6. 389, 393-5,
399; the mean, prefers: 5. 341; medieval:
2. 287; 7. 598-9; 8. 532; melancholy:
5. 154-6, 186, 283; 6. 275; 7. 245, 396,
417, 429, 560; 8. 523, 531-4, 621, 626;
mental health, yields: 6. 274; metres,
master of: 7. 398-9; his militant philosophy: 2. 195; and Milton: see Milton,
John; mingles acute observation with
strange lore: 2. 199; 4. 192; misrepre-
sents: 5. 260; mistakes: 3. 295-7; 4. 164-5,
184, 189, 196, 298; 5. 158, 203-4, 229,
262; 6. 251, 307-8; 7. 445; 8. 315-6, 348,
380-1, 385; modern, more than Shake-

speare: 7. 620; modern poetic diction,
creator of: 7. 627, 629; moral intention:
2. 371-2; 6. 249-50, 378-9; 8. 626; his
Muse: see Muse; the Muses' best pupil:
1. 266; mysticism: 6. 399; 7. 555, 560;
mystification: 8. 281; his own mythographer: 1. 203, 248, 340; 2. 365; 3.
249, 255, 271, 281, 295; 4. 169; 5. 166,
217; 6. 213, 247, 251, 283, 308, 394, 414,
429-32; 7. 284, 580; 8. 301, 396-7, 407,
484; narrative method: 1. 228-9; 3. 373;
6. 214; Nash, praised by: 3. 306; 7. 477;
naturalizes: 7. 328; Nature, blends mutability and fecundity of: 2. 211; Nature,
conception of: 2. 366; 4. 310; 6. 281-2,
390-406, 410-24; 7. 579-80, 597-8; Nature,
love of: 2. 244; 3. 254; Nature, not true
to: 5. 213; 7. 275; 8. 398; Nature, treatment of: 1. 373; 2. 366, 371, 580-3;
3. 238, 247, 259; 7. 257-8, 576-7, 597;
8. 390; the New Poet: 7. 371, 580-1,
583-4, 586-8; 8. 530, 532; noblest and
deepest on Britomart: 4. 285; in the north
country: 7. 250, 253, 309-15; obscurity:
1. 208, 248; 4. 228; 5. 169, 180, 221, 222,
231; 6. 201, 210; 7. 412, 547, 553-4,
561; 8. 347, 360, 405, 487, 667; observation: 4. 192, 198, 213, 265, 273; 5. 232-
3; 6. 200, 202, 218, 289, 299; 7. 245,
282, 583; 8. 335, 390, 404, 408; oligarchy,
approves: 5. 175; opposites, illustrates
virtues by: 2. 419; original: 7. 582-3, 593,
595; 8. 631; oversights: 1. 248, 303, 454;
2. 209-10, 263, 281, 309, 341; 3. 203,
208, 214, 218, 225, 230-1, 244, 264, 267,
283, 286, 294-5; 4. 175-6, 189, 197, 202,
208-9, 211, 213, 252, 298; 5. 181, 191,
213, 254, 264-5; 6. 208, 218, 235, 255;
8. 363, 493; and Ovid: 3. 287; 5. 262;
6. 285; 8. 401-3; and Earl of Oxford: 3.
307; 8. 319, 320; pagan: 7. 657; and
pantheism: 6. 404-5, 428; parable, emblem,
symbol, myth, hovered between: 8. 405;
paradox in him: 6. 240, 249-50; 7. 657;
pathos: 3. 220, 310-1; patriotism: 1. 493,
512-3; 2. 301; 5. 310; 7. 604; 8. 374;
patrons: 7. 501; not pedantic: 7. 284;
penetration: 4. 197; 6. 200; pension: 6.
271-2; perfunctory and hasty: 8. 380;
pessimism: 3. 342; 5. 154, 186; 8. 306,
346, 406; not a philosopher: 6. 273-4;
philosophy: 1. 362; 3. 310, 342-5; 6. 389-
432; 8. 329; philosophy and poetry, unites:
3. 345, 352; pictorial imagination and
quality: 1. 211, 274, 284, 289, 305-6,
408, 413; 2. 224-5, 250; 3. 215, 252, 255-
6, 273-4; 6. 302, 378-9, 420; 7. 270,

280, 420; 8. 597; picturesque: 1. 188-9, 194, 244, 289, 374; 2. 382; 3. 237, 393; 6. 225; 7. 345; pithiest and most masculine lines: 8. 369; pity and justice contend in: 5. 247; plain speech: 3. 273; and plastic arts: 1. 284; 3. 392-9; 4. 219; 5. 217-8, 237; 7. 238; 8. 401, 498; Plato, knowledge of: see Plato, Platonism; poet of first rank: 7. 572, 577; "Poet Laureate": 7. 419; 8. 429; poet, a reluctant: 7. 643; poet vs. politician: 5. 315; 8. 647; poetic manner: 7. 664; 8. 559-60; poetic method: 1. 189, 193-4, 197, 204, 473-7, 479-82; 3. 375; 4. 207; 5. 240, 267, 274, 286; 6. 190, 193, 224-5, 440; 7. 268, 368, 429, 431, 463; 8. 305, 560, 564, 578; on poetry: 7. 369-82, 387-8, 391, 424, 428, 454, 579; his the poetry of a passing age: 1. 378; 8. 532; poetry, would renounce: 7. 515; political theory: 5. 194, 303-12, 325, 343; 8. 303, 352-3; politics: 7. 235; 8. 372, 571-5; popular, not esoteric: 3. 340, 348; 7. 339; portraiture: 1. 228-9, 245; 3. 252-3, 383, 393-4; praised: 3. 306; 7. 468, 470, 477; 8. 291-2; praises himself: 7. 317, 501, 646-7; 8. 319; not precise: 7. 534-5; precocity: 8. 612, 614-5, 623; primitivism: 6 .185; Prince of Poets: 7. 448, 490; prolix: 8. 644; promises: 4. 242; 6. 205, 232; 8. 350, 393, 635; prose, lapses into: 2. 286; 6. 194, 274; proverbs, loves: 8. 351; and publication: 7. 583, 611; and Puritanism: 3. 386; 5. 157; 6. 214, 249, 266-7, 304-5, 386-8, 399; 7. 290-6, 391, 488-9, 580, 582, 600-9, 643, 665, 669; 8. 357-8, 511, 561, 564, 567, 597; purity: 8. 370; quibbles: 4. 284; and Raleigh: see Raleigh; rapidity: 2. 324; 3. 243; reading: 3. 217; 4. 291; 5. 309; 6. 202, 213, 442; 8. 440; realism: 1. 188, 194, 207, 245, 249, 275, 335, 339, 373, 377; 2. 286-7; 3. 214, 262, 264-5, 272-3, 342, 359, 391, 395; 4. 172, 192, 213, 285-6; 5. 181, 254; 6. 224, 432; 7. 245, 420, 580, 589-90, 592; 8. 431; not a realist: 7. 483; reformer: 5. 171, 347; religion: 3. 342; 6. 393, 399, 400, 402, 404-6, 418; 7. 291, 600-1, 603, 656-9, 665, 676; 8. 329, 618; religio-social thinking: 1. 437; Renaissance poet: 5. 264; 6. 406; 7. 598-9; retirement, longed for: 6. 419, 422; 8. 506; retractation: 7. 537-8, 657-63; and Revelation: see Apocalypse, above; revised his work: 2. 397; 6. 224-5; 7. 612-4, 661; 8. 282, 369, 392-3, 409-16, 419, 529, 534, 563-4, 567, 572-4, 579; rhyme, gift for: 8.

409-10, 547; ritual, love of: 7. 601; rivers, love of: 4. 250-73, 311; 6. 437; 8. 291; and Roman Catholicism: 7. 261-2; 8. 360, 516-7; romance, strongly tinctured with: 2. 335; room, requires: 1. 250; 7. 268, 272; 8. 455; ruins, an eye for: 5. 224; 7. 456; 8. 378; rural life, no interest in: 7. 598; Sackville, debt to: 3. 308; 7. 627; sane amid seeming aberration: 2. 249; satirist: 5. 212; 7. 292; 8. 356, 370, 559-66, 568-80, 594; and scandal: 1. 364; 6. 383-6; 7. 292; scepticism: 1. 482; 3. 340, 342; 6. 393-5, 399, 401, 406; and science: 2. 472; 6. 399, 401; script: 8. 407; and the sea: 2. 356; 7. 459-60; 8. 346 (but see Sea); not a Sectarian: 7. 290; self, portrays: 2. 380; 8. 661; self-esteem: 7. 441; sensitive to the beauty of light on water: 2. 234; sensitive and serious: 7. 678; sensuality: 2. 349, 351, 371-2; not sensuous: 6. 420; not sentimental: 5. 233; and Shakespeare: see Shakespeare; Sheriff of Cork: 5. 315; and ships: 8. 315, 408 (see also Ships); and Sidney: see Sidney, Sir Philip; simplicity: 5. 200; 6. 198; sin and sensuality, antidote to: 2. 348; sincerity: 2. 208; 6. 357; 7. 380, 429, 501, 538; 8. 356, 573, 575; skill, delights in: 8. 596; social ideas: 1. 437; 5. 175-7, 181, 262, 289-95, 304, 340-5; 6. 194; social rank: 8. 409; sophisticated and conventional: 4. 239; and the Spencers: 7. 477; 8. 310-1, 349; most Spenserian in Book 6 of F. Q.: 6. 325; splendor, love of: 3. 240; and the stage (see above Spenser, drama); standard idiom, brought out: 7. 629; stanza-form, preferred: 8. 547; stock phrase: 5. 188-9; Stoicism: see Stoicism; is Strephon: 2. 401; style: see Style; not too subtle: 3. 350; and Tasso: see Tasso; technique masterly: 1. 413; tenderness: 3. 220-1; 4. 278; and the theatre: see Spenser, drama, dramatic power; theology: 1. 439; 7. 291, 323, 539, 555; theory of government: 5. 303-10; thinking not deep or clear: 7. 672; toleration: 7. 601; tomb: 7. 314, 470-1; towers, eye for: 5. 224; translator: 8. 273-80, 333-49, 378-91, 409-16, 446, 451-2, 545-50, 612-24; trees, love of: 7. 262; 8. 407-8; true to life: 1. 245; 2. 210-1, 287-8; unity: 1. 412-3; 3. 312; 7. 582; vague: 7. 357; 8. 308-9; vanity of things, meditates: 8. 279, 400; variety: 1. 306; 3. 313; and Virgil: see Virgil; vituperation, unequalled in: 2. 208; vivid: 4. 281; vocabulary: see s. v.; voluptuous pathos and

languid brilliance of fancy: 2. 388; walks abroad: 7. 438; 8. 495; warmth and movement: 8. 295; water, love for: 2. 234; 3. 243; 4. 239, 242, 250-73, 276, 311; 6. 231, 437; 7. 456; 8. 291, 311, 463; weak lines: 8. 331; wealth of words and colors: 6. 302; wedding: 8. 439; Welsh, knowledge of: 2. 312, 512; 3. 233; women, interest in: 1. 499; 3. 216, 310-29, 381-91; 4. 195; 5. 223; 6. 305, 313

Spenser, Elizabeth (the poet's mother), 8. 447-8, 501

Spenser, Florence, 8. 648

Spenser, Lawrence, 8. 650

Spenser, Peregrine, 8. 649-51

Spenser, Sarah, 7. 313

Spenser, Sylvanus, 8. 635, 649-50

Spenserian Stanza, 1. 210, 314; 2. 203, 233, 507; 3. 249, 252; 5. 246; 6. 191-2, 434; 7. 340, 641; 8. 644, 654

Spensers (Spencers), 7. 312-5; spelling: 7. 314

Speranza, 1. 284-5, 406-7, 430, 432; 3. 399

Speroni, Sperone, 1. 358; 2. 218; 7. 520, 662

"sperre," 7. 305

Spheres, 2. 485; 5. 157, 178; 6. 411; 7. 551-2; 8. 329; Crystalline sphere: 7. 551, 553

Sphinx, 5. 257

Spicer, Rose, 6. 220; 7. 652

Spider, 8. 396, 400-1, 403, 407, 600-1

Spinoza, Benedict Baruch, 6. 390

Spiritual discipline, 1. 292

Spondanus (Jean de Spande), 2. 342; 8. 376

Spontaneous generation. See Abiogenesis

"sponte sua," 6. 296

Sport, 8. 402

Sports. See Games

Spring, 6. 303-4; 7. 256; perpetual: 3. 258

Spumador, 2. 342

Squire, 6. 196; Arthur's: 1. 471

Squire of Dames: 1. 331; 3. 221, 267, 276, 313, 319, 328

Squire of Low Degree, 4. 213, 284, 323

Squire of Low Degree, 1. 226, 346; 4. 205, 213

Staff, 2. 364, 370, 377

Stafford, Anthony, 1. 280

Stage. See Drama; Theatre

Stamford, 4. 259-60

Stanley, Ferdinando, Earl of Derby, 3. 260, 306; 7. 450-1, 468, 471-2, 477

Stanley, William, 7. 476; 8. 319

Stanyhurst, Richard, 1. 357; 3. 305; 8. 547

Stanza, 1. 210; 8. 547. See also Spenserian Stanza

Stark Collection, 1. 517, 519

Starnes, D. T., 7. 273; 8. 316, 323, 326, 328, 330, 332, 468, 540

Stars, 1. 178, 239, 307; 2. 476; 3. 206; 6. 219, 391; 8. 667, 669; fixed: 7. 540

State Papers, 6. 233, 256, 364; Domestic: 7. 261, 722; Foreign: 7. 403; Ireland: 5. 173, 331, 347; Scotland: 5. 244; Sidney: see s.v.; Venetian: 5. 182, 238

Stationers' Register, 7. 243, 409, 648; 8. 439, 451, 528, 533, 584, 598, 627, 632-4, 663, 666, 679

Statius, Publius Papinius, 1. 421; 8. 498

Achilleid: Book 1: 134, 269: 7. 274; 8. 301; 159: 1. 246; 304-8: 2. 296; Book 2: 77: 8. 339; 102-25: 1. 246; Silvae: Book 1: 1: 8. 300; 2: 3. 209; 4. 238; 7. 252; 8. 324, 462, 466, 471, 473, 476, 478, 480, 482, 487, 491, 499, 500, 652; Book 2: 3: 1. 243; 6: 1. 251; 4. 195; Book 3: 4: 1. 188; 3. 209; 8. 490; Book 4: 4: 1. 310; Book 5: 5: 8. 324

Thebaid: Book 1: 27: 1. 305; 34: 4. 246; 41: 1. 514; 92: 6. 217; 129-30: 8. 372; 292-311: 8. 376; 338: 6. 276; 406: 3. 276; 419: 4. 185; 476-7: 4. 223; 548-51: 3. 294; Book 2: 48: 2. 355; 59: 1. 229; 144: 1. 190; 193: 1. 209; 6. 259; 269: 4. 193; 530-5: 1. 248; Book 3: 317: 6. 217; 432 ff.: 4. 215; Book 4: 6: 4. 190; 64. 2. 284; 240: 4. 248; 314-6: 6. 259; 514-6: 1. 190; 520: 6. 293; 622-4: 8. 301; Book 5: 61: 4. 228; 62-3: 4. 193; 164: 3. 262; 199: 1. 190; 390 ff.: 4. 185; 556-8: 1. 295; Book 6: schol. 6. 27: 1. 190; 98-106: 1. 179; 107-8: 5. 262; 186: 4. 278; 5. 231; 336: 2. 304; 386: 6. 217; 422 ff.: 4. 185; 578-82: 1. 251; 598: 3. 262; 665-7: 1. 253; 864-6: 4. 190; 893: 2. 347; Book 7: 40 ff.: 4. 168; 45: 1. 213, 253; 47-53: 2. 257; 50: 2. 258; 4. 169; 223: 4. 279; 440-6: 2. 298; 582: 6. 217; 744-9: 1. 259, 305; Book 8: 125-6: 8. 426; 303: 6. 278-9; 374: 1. 514; 432: 2. 218; 675: 6. 232; Book 9: 218: 6. 217; 375: 3. 241; 413-5: 4. 252; 437: 1. 250; 526 ff.: 5. 185; 532-6, 554-6: 1. 259; 4. 183; Book 10: 84 ff.: 1. 192; 85: 1. 179, 193-4; 89: 1. 195; 111: 1. 190; 121-8: 1. 195; 384: 2. 281; 535: 4. 185; 628-31: 1. 510, 514; Book 11: 114 ff.: 4. 215; 180: 2. 298; 234: 1. 300; 483: 6. 217; 520 ff.: 4. 175; Book 12: 301: 8. 484; 561-2: 6. 281; 650 ff.: 4. 215; 809: 1. 310; 6. 260; 810-9: 7. 427

Statuary, 1. 390

Statutes of the Realm, 5. 346
Steevens, George, 8. 359, 497
Stein, Harold, 7. 361; 8. 274-5, 277, 280, 287, 303, 316, 409-16, 527, 539, 544, 578-9, 584, 599
Stela, 6. 380
Stella, 6. 355, 373; 7. 453, 476, 484, 489-99; 8. 308. *See also* Devereux, Penelope
Stella, Aruntius, 7. 252
Stemmata Dudleiana, 2. 397; 7. 384, 402; 8. 326, 516, 522, 526-8
Stephanus, Charles, 8. 326, 468, 541
Stephanus, Robert, 7. 273; 8. 323, 326, 332, 468, 541
Sternhold, Thomas and John Hopkins, 6. 231; 8. 477
Stesichorus, 7. 288, 482
Stevenson, Burton, 7. 331
Stevenson, George, 8. 643
Stewart, Bain, 7. 248
Stewart, J. A., 2. 377
Stewart, Randall, 3. 287-8
Sthenoboea, 1. 238; 2. 318
Stichomythia, 1. 247; 5. 180; 7. 338
Stillingfleet, Edward, 2. 326
Stirling, Brents, 3. 347-52; 6. 416-9, 421-3; 7. 261; 8. 324, 538-9
St. Leger, Warham (Anthony?), 6. 385
Stoicism, 1. 448; 2. 382, 459; 3. 250; 4. 165; 6. 214, 282, 365, 419, 422, 441; 8. 314-5, 327, 476
Stoll, E. E., 2. 346
Stonehenge, 2. 333
" stoop-gallant," 7. 259-60
Stopes, C. C., 7. 474
Stopes, Maria, 8. 319
Stork, 8. 486-7
" stound," 7. 308
" stour," 7, 250, 308
Stour (rivers), 4. 255-8, 271
Stourbridge Fair, 4. 258
Stourton, Edward, Baron, 4. 256
Stovall, F., 6. 438, 445, 450; 7. 641
Stow, John, 1. 483; 2. 302, 310-3, 315, 319, 320, 322, 324, 328, 330, 332, 333, 450-1, 453; 3. 232; 4. 179; 8. 504, 672; *Annals*: 2. 453; 3. 233; Ed. of 1631, cited by page: 9: 2. 310-3; 10: 2. 314, 319-20; 12: 2. 322; 13: 2. 323; 32-3: 2. 327-8; 42-3: 2. 330; 48: 2. 332; 56: 2. 333; 459: 6. 227; 805: 6. 359; *Historical Memorials*: 5. 185; *Summary*: 2. 315, 324, 452; *Survey of London*: 1. 309; 3. 267; 5. 238-9
Strabo, 1. 242; 5. 161, 312
Strange, Lord. *See* Stanley, Ferdinando
Strange, Robert, 2. 271
Strangeness, 1. 417

Strathmann, Ernest A., 2. 329, 467-71; 7. 477, 480; 8. 393, 403, 501, 599, 604-5
Strength, 2. 346
Strife, 2. 230; 3. 342; 4. 167
Strife of Love in a Dream, 4. 220, 230, 232; 5. 240. *See also* Hypnerotomachia
Strophe, 7. 638, 640-1
Strutt, Joseph, 5. 223; 7. 379
Strype, John, 8. 504; *Annals*: 2. 407-8; 5. 324; 8. 359, 504; *Ecclesiastical Memorials*: 1. 467-8, 470, 472; 5. 342; *Life of Aylmer*: 7. 261; *Life of Cranmer*: 1. 469; *Life of Grindal*: 5. 278, 340; 7. 261, 300; 8. 357, 543; *Life of Parker*: 7. 359; *Life of Whitgift*: 5. 337
Stuart, Esmé, 7. 304
Stubbs, John, 2. 208; 7. 609; 8. 571, 573
Stubbs, Philip, 7. 285, 295-8, 334; 8. 359-61, 371, 591
Stupeo, 7. 590
Stuteville, Thomas, 7. 321, 482, 653
Stuteville, Mrs. Thomas. *See* North, Eliza
Style, 1. 261, 374, 421; 2. 203, 286, 324, 438; 3. 273, 292; 4. 178-80, 240; 5. 246; 6. 280, 433, 438, 445-7, 450-1; 7. 236-9, 245, 449, 575-6, 586, 614-30; 8. 300, 408, 455, 531, 545, 559-60, 616, 622, 624, 663; diffuse: 1. 261; homely: 7. 304, 312, 342, 349-51, 373; later: 7. 323; 8. 507; Latin: *see* Latin Element; style of Pléiade, Ariosto, Tasso: 1. 378. *See also* Diction, etc.
Styx, 2. 237; 4. 239; 8. 301
Subjectio, 8. 395
Sublimity. *See* Faerie Queene
Substance, 3. 340-52
Succession. *See* Elizabeth
Suckling, John, 7. 248
Sugar, 2. 240
Suggestion, 1. 305
Suicide, 1. 271, 273-6, 279-80; 6. 365; 7. 439
Suidas, 5. 166 ;7. 392
Suir, 4. 269; 6. 284, 424; 7. 475
" Suite" Merlin, 6. 366
Sulla, 1. 444
Summer, 6. 305
Sun, 1. 239, 305; 2. 280-1; 3. 249-51, 255, 348, 352; 5. 159, 217; 6. 244, 308-10; 7. 553; 8. 469-70, 472, 479-80; divine: 7. 558; lamp: 8. 460
Superstition, 1. 260, 263, 422; 5. 257
Surprise, 1. 308-9
Surrey, 3. 262
Surrey, Earl of. *See* Howard, Henry
Susceptibility, 5. 209; 6. 280
Suso, 7. 564
Suspect, 1. 339; 3. 302

Suspense, 1. 272, 294, 295-6, 321, 322, 350, 430; 4. 165, 227; 6. 225

Suspicion, 3. 372

Sussex, Earl of. *See* Radcliffe

Swag, Captain, 2. 210

" swain," 7. 327

Swale (river), 4. 262

Swans, 8. 307, 498, 503, 515-6, 666-9, 672-3

Swan, John, 2. 362

Sweet, Henry, 7. 423

Swift, Jonathan, 3. 270; 7. 341; 8. 281, 568, 578

" swim," 2. 220, 231

Swimming, 5. 172

Swinburne, Algernon, 2. 260; 5. 201, 217; 6. 252; 8. 370, 674

Swine, 1. 412; 2. 341

" swink," 7. 298

" swink and sweat," 7. 284; 8. 354

Sword, 2. 207, 235, 274-7; 3. 241, 286; 4. 210; 5. 163-4, 191-2, 225, 257, 264; of the Spirit: 1. 176, 295

Swordfish, 2. 359, 363-4

Sylvanus, 1. 363, 371; 6. 291; 7. 368, 373-4, 378, 382

Sylvester, Joshua, 2. 361; 4. 203; 6. 423, 472; 7. 464, 551-2; *Bethulia's Rescue*: 2. 296-7; *Divine Weeks and Works*: 1. 1: 7. 551; 1. 2: 3. 207, 350; 7. 551; 8. 387; 1. 6: 2. 291, 293; 6. 472; 7. 551; 2. 1, Pt. 1 (*Eden*): 4. 222; 7. 551; 2. 1, Pt. 3 (*Furies*): 1. 270, 276; 7. 414; 2. 3, Pt. 1 (*Vocation*): 1. 215; *Works*, ed. 1621, p. 841: 4. 199

Sylvius, 7. 590

Symbolism, 1. 200, 219, 223, 260, 339-40; 2. 194, 197, 225, 256; 6. 234-5; 8. 666-7; animal: 1. 406-13; 2. 341; of maladies: 1. 408-11; in masques: 3. 357-8; symbolic use of romances: 1. 347, 351

Symmetry, 7. 441

Symonds, John A., 2. 390

Symonson, Philip, 4. 273

Synathroismus, 6. 188-9; 7. 247; 8. 288, 356, 384, 400, 595

Synchysis, 1. 233; 4. 207

Synecdoche, 6. 199; 8. 346

Synesius, 8. 547-8

Synoeciosis, 1. 247; 7. 444; 8. 676

Synonymia, 8. 400, 484

Syntax, 1. 265; 2. 247; 8. 293, 342, 452. *See also* Grammar, etc.

Syrinx, 7. 248, 281; is Anne Boleyn: 7. 274-5; is Elizabeth: 2. 384; 7. 282

Tacitus, Cornelius, 2. 248, 325, 327-8, 450; 3. 279, 332; 5. 254; 7. 273; 8. 289, 386

Taenarus, 2. 354-5

Tages, 1. 294

Taine, Hippolyte, 1. 197; 2. 250; 3. 255-6

" Talassio," 8. 461, 495

Talbot, George, Earl of Shrewsbury, 3. 378

Talbot, Robert, 4. 259

Talus, 3. 370-1; 4. 200; 5. 165-7, 196, 207, 268, 281, 344-5, 347; 6. 216; is the English army: 5. 260, 344-5; career reviewed: 5. 277-80, 298; is executioner: 5. 165; is force: 5. 264; is Justice: 2. 427; 5. 345; is the Law: 5. 170-1, 276-80, 340; personality: 5. 209, 269, 284; is power: 5. 269, 272

Tam Lin, 5. 236

Tamar, 4. 255

" tamburin," 7. 318, 322

Tame, 8. 672

Tanaquill, 1. 174; 2. 303, 334-5; 3. 337

Tancred, 5. 202

Tankerfield, George, 8. 479

Tanner, Thomas, 6. 268

Tantalus, 1. 363; 2. 252, 266, 268; 7. 415, 518; 8. 418, 591

Tapestry, 1. 214, 284-5, 390, 413, 418; 2. 293; 3. 208, 291-7, 392-9; 6. 297-9; 8. 401-2, 498, 597, 607

Tarlton, Richard, 8. 317-9, 321, 437, 539

Tarquin, 1. 444

Tartars, 2. 344

Tartarus, 1. 255; 2. 354; 8. 341, 346

Tasso, Torquato, 1. 314, 324, 327, 361, 366, 378; 2. 212, 218, 274, 349, 351, 370-1, 374-6, 390, 394; 3. 205, 250; 5. 157; 6. 227, 242, 428; 7. 539, 573, 583, 590; 8. 405, 532, 640-1; and allegory: 1. 333, 345, 493; less important to *F. Q.* than romances: 1. 351; a source of *F. Q.*: 2. 428, 444; and Spenser: 1. 316-7, 332-3, 337, 413, 420; 2. 245, 349, 375-6; *Aminta*: 2. 216-7; 3. 251-2; 7. 272, 472, 574-5, 615; *Corinna*: 7. 408; *Discorsi e Lettere*: 1. 358, 361

    Gerusalemme Liberata: 1. 209, 332; 2. 398; 3. 288; allegory explained: 1. 312; 2. 438-43; Spenser's conception of: 1. 420; Spenser's use of: 1. 337, 420; Canto 1: 3. 205; 2: 1. 510; 11: 1. 310; 13, 14: 2. 272; 55: 6. 204; 71: 4. 192; 75: 2. 342; 80: 2. 276; 83: 6. 199; Canto 2: 5. 200; 61: 1. 278; Canto 3: 4: 1. 209, 210; 6. 259; 19: 3. 222; 21 ff.: 4. 200; 5. 202; 30: 4. 201; 32: 3. 207; 6. 226; 40: 2. 192; 73: 1. 181; 76: 1. 182; Canto 4: 8. 1-4: 1. 295, 304; 11: 1. 255; 18: 3. 276-7; 28: 3. 206; 29: 3. 278; 7. 497; Canto 5: 28: 1. 299; Canto 6: 73: 5. 205;

Canto 7: 6. 375, 379; 1: 3. 262; 10, 11: 6. 238-9; 12-4: 6. 239-40; 16: 6. 242; 18: 6. 219; 43-4: 1. 228; 51: 6. 199; 52-3: 3. 205; 55: 6. 207; 71: 4. 185; 99-100: 1. 196; 107: 2. 345; Canto 8: 49: 1. 289; 57: 6. 235; Canto 9: 2, 22: 5. 226; 22: 3. 277; 4. 200; 25: 1. 252; 2. 398; 39-43: 1. 259; 46: 2. 342; 4. 186; 52: 4. 215; 75: 8. 451; 70: 4. 184; 80. 2. 236; 81: 2. 392; 84: 4. 201; 88: 4. 212; 92: 4. 241; Canto 10: 62: 2. 248; 76: 3. 203; Canto 11: 17: 5. 184; 84-5: 4. 191-2; Canto 12: 10: 1. 191; 22: 3. 297; 29: 3. 205; 53: 4. 190; 69: 2. 214; 77: 8. 377; 94: 3. 201; Canto 13: 2: 2. 259; 3. 205; 5: 3. 226; 34-5: 3. 290-1; 41-2: 1. 202; 74: 6. 280; Canto 14: 37: 2. 259; 3. 243; 62-4: 2. 244-5; 66: 2. 383; 71: 3. 261; 73: 2. 364, 370, 394; 74: 1. 248; Canto 15: 2. 352, 381; 3: 2. 242-3; 9: 2. 378; 14: 1. 289; 48: 1. 252; 49: 2. 364, 370; 51 f.: 2. 394; 53-4: 2. 378; 55-63: 1. 307-8; 2. 194, 368, 382-4; 8. 504; Canto 16: 1 ff.: 1. 331; 2. 447; 2-7: 2. 372; 3: 5. 204, 224; 9-10: 2. 238, 381-2; 12 ff.: 4. 222; 12 ff.: 2. 385-6; 14-5: 2. 388-9; 17: 2. 383; 18-9: 2. 239, 392; 24: 3. 298; 4. 193; 8. 396; 30: 2. 393; 32, 33: 2. 240; 71: 2. 248; Canto 17: 61-3: 2. 221; Canto 18: 16: 4. 185, 278; 5. 264; 18, 24: 2. 387; 82: 1. 305; 96: 1. 310; 7. 541; Canto 19: 6. 375, 379; 11: 1. 199; 17: 2. 277, 347; 22: 2. 277; 90: 3. 215; Canto 20: 20: 4. 167; 50: 3. 262; 4. 186; 129: 5. 264; 136: 3. 247; 142: 3. 285; 144: 1. 293; 6. 210

Il Mondo Creato: 7. 564; doubtful madrigal in *Opere*, 1754: 8. 430

Rime (reference numbers as found in vols. 2-4 of A. Solerti's edition): 8. 640-1; 1: 8. 442; 10: 8. 427; 14: 8. 427; 15: 8. 424; 17: 8. 451-2; 21: 8. 447; 35: 8. 421; 36: 8. 422; 51: 8. 456-8; 67: 8. 421, 446; 74: 8. 436; 80: 8. 427, 430; 82: 8. 424; 88: 4. 435; 94: 8. 448-9; 102: 8. 450; 109: 8. 434; 120: 8. 452; 164-6: 8. 427, 433-4; 169: 8. 434; 213: 8. 437; 222: 8. 447; 238: 2. 215; 399: 8. 454; 523: 8. 438

Rinaldo: 1. 420, 510; Canto 1: 31: 1. 188; 53-7: 2. 213, 219; 54: 2. 217; 55, 57: 2. 214-5; 5. 189; 56: 2. 220; Canto 3: 4: 5. 228; Canto 4: 45: 2. 214; 5. 189; 50: 5. 182; 60: 3. 262; Canto 5: 3. 288-90; 13: 2. 217; 14: 8. 505; Canto 6: 15: 5. 188; 46: 4. 175; 52: 4. 215;

5. 262; Canto 7: 62: 1. 305; 83 ff.: 2. 243; Canto 8: 25: 2. 243; 70: 4. 200; Canto 9: 15: 2. 215; 75: 2. 220; Canto 10: 31: 1. 289; 43: 3. 277; 4. 215; 48: 5. 262; Canto 11: 3: 3. 292; 28: 4. 191; 35: 3. 207; 6. 226-7; 48 ff.: 1. 277; 4. 196; 56 ff.: 1. 289; 65: 3. 278; 7. 497; 72: 6. 232; 89-94: 6. 260-2, 264; Canto 12: 23: 3. 205; 55: 1. 299; 4. 191; 6. 207; 56: 3. 277; 6. 217; 75: 5. 188; Canto 16: 34: 6. 232

Tate, Nahum, 8. 497

Tatler, 4. 220, 276

Tattersall, J. F., 7. 313

Tauri, 1. 258

Tauric Chersonese, 1. 258

Tautology, 2. 233; 7. 266

Taylor, A. E., 2. 264; 4. 164-5

Taylor, G. C., 7. 551; 8. 387

Taylor, Hilda, 6. 432

Taylor, Jeremy, 6. 249

Taylor, John, 6. 228-9

Taylor, Stephan, 2. 209

Teach and delight, 1. 311, 315, 340, 348-9; 6. 249

Teares of the Muses, 1. 514; 6. 441-2; 8. 459, 510, 531-42; and *Astrophel*: 7. 484-5; and *Colin Clouts*: 7. 454-5; composition: 8. 529-30, 533-40; criticism: 8. 531-3; date: 8. 320, 531, 533-40; and *Dedicatory Sonnets*: 8. 539-40; and *Doleful Lay of Clorinda*: 7. 501-2; and *The English Poet*: 8. 514; and *F. Q.*: 8. 533; and the *Hymnes*: 7. 660-1, 665; 8. 539, 541-2; influence: 8. 541-2; metre: 8. 537; and *Mother Hubberds Tale*: 8. 534, 536, 539; and *Muiopotmos*: 8. 598, 602; and the "nine Comoedies": 8. 516-7, 534; Platonism in: 7. 665; 8. 539; punctuation: 7. 501-2; and *Ruines of Rome*: 8. 380; and *Ruines of Time*: 8. 326, 525, 528-30, 533, 535-6, 539; and *Shepheardes Calender*: 8. 535, 539; sources: 8. 536-7, 540-1; structure: 8. 530, 539, 542; style: 8. 542; text: 8. 318-9, 712-3; variant readings: 8. 691-2; and *Virgils Gnat*: 8. 539, 679; and *Visions of Bellay*: 8. 326; *Dedication*: 8. 282, 310, 539, 635; 2: 8. 470; 7-12: 8. 311: 19-22: 8. 460; 31: 8. 463; 69-84: 8. 303; 72, 85-90: 1. 514; 75-8: 7. 262; 8. 304; 89-90: 7. 564; 91-6: 6. 337; 93-102: 1. 508-9; 112: 8. 500; 115-68: 1. 280; 5. 181; 8. 346, 394, 404, 437, 609; 164: 8. 343; 179-80: 3. 355; 187-92: 8. 539; 193-204: 7. 608; 198-228: 8. 437; 213: 8. 539; 241-82: 8. 413, 415; 301: 7. 506; 8. 368; 319-34: 8.

539; 361-420: 7. 660-1; 8. 368; 361: 8. 296, 525, 528, 539; 379-84: 7. 392; 393: 6. 217; 398: 4. 216; 421-80: 1. 515; 429-30: 1. 509; 437-8: 1. 509; 7. 608; 451-4: 7. 381; 457-62: 1. 514; 5. 162; 8. 602; 469-72: 8. 303, 559; 499-502: 6. 295; 505-16: 7. 564; 507: 7. 551; 553-8: 8. 538; 559-64: 7. 370; 590: 8. 339

Tears, 1. 209; 6. 232

Tearsheet, Doll, 6. 194

Tebaldeo, Antonio, 8. 434, 442

Tedula, 8. 406-7

Teigue, 2. 373, 446, 448

Teise, 4. 272

Telamon, 8. 345

Tempe, 2. 378-9; 8. 483, 499

Temperament, 7. 527, 529, 533; 8. 387

Temperance, 1. 285, 328-9, 339, 341; 2. 184-5, 381, 403-8, 414-26, 427, 459; 3. 319-20, 322-3, 329, 337, 355, 358, 371; 5. 287; 7. 553; in Ariosto and Spenser: 2. 439-41; Continence contrasted with: 2. 420; medieval and classical: 1. 345, 346; Spenser's differs from Aristotle's: 1. 356; 2. 420; Spenser's more Platonic than Aristotelian: 2. 417. See House of Temperance

Templarius, 4. 316

Temple (London), 8. 502

Temple, William, 1. 314; 8. 306

Temples, 5. 217-8; 8. 306

Ten, 2. 297

Ten Commandments, 5. 345; Second: 2. 276; Fifth: 5. 339; Eighth: 5. 338, 341

Tenantius, 2. 324-5

Tennyson, Alfred, 1. 351; 3. 203; 6. 402; 8. 308, 473, 645, 674; Demeter and Persephone: 2. 353; Idylls of the King: 1. 489; 6. 325, 378; 8. 293; Locksley Hall: 8. 325; The Miller's Daughter: 8. 466; Morte d'Arthur: 6. 277; Oenone: 8. 388; The Princess: 3. 247; Two Voices: 1. 272

Tenses, Mixture of, 1. 211; 5. 187; 8. 718

Terence, 2. 200, 209, 243, 326; 3. 279, 286; 6. 264, 475; 7. 426

Tereus, 8. 343

"teribinth," 7. 330, 337

Termagant, 2. 276; 6. 227-8

Ternate, 5. 248-9

Terpine, 5. 203, 293

Terpsichore, 7. 284; 8. 312, 318, 324-5, 538-40

"Terque quaterque beati," 8. 297

Terra. See Earth

Terry, Roderick, 7. 708, 723

Terwin, 1. 459; 2. 318

Tethys, 1. 209; 2. 364; 4. 240; 8. 386, 413

Tetra, 2. 262-3

Textor (Tixier, Jean), 8. 468

Texture, 3. 393

Thaler, A., 8. 315, 437, 477, 482, 484, 487, 491

Thalia, 4. 274-5; 6. 251, 253; 8. 311-2, 316, 318, 321, 532, 534, 539, 541

Thame, 8. 672

Thames, 4. 242, 316; 6. 246, 398-9; 8. 290-1, 307, 316, 497-8, 500, 505, 664-70, 672-3; marriage with Medway: 1. 363, 371, 441; 3. 243, 269, 386; 4. 239-76, 281, 288, 296, 304, 334; 6. 430-1, 436, 442; 7. 448; 8. 292, 472, 496, 670

Thammuz, 1. 245

"That which (All that) I eate," 7. 307

Thaumantias, 5. 190

Theagenes, 1. 246; 2. 392; 6. 376-7

Theana, 7. 465, 474

Theatre, 8. 316-21, 533-4. See also Drama; Spenser, drama, dramatic power

Theatre for Worldlings. See Van der Noodt.

Theatrum Crudelitatum Hereticorum Nostri Temporis, 5. 321

Thebes, 2. 298; 8. 388

The Longer Thou Livest the More Fool Art Thou, 2. 433-4

Thenot, 7. 253, 256, 258, 276-7, 352, 396, 400, 402, 406, 468, 594, 631, 643

Theobalds, 8. 374, 605

Theocentric contemplation and ascent: 7. 524, 556-7, 564, 674-6; 8. 329-31

Theocritus, 7. 240, 277, 309, 317, 410, 489, 491, 571-4, 576, 579, 581-4, 586, 589, 591-3, 596-7, 599, 615, 622, 625, 631, 637, 642; 8. 657; Epigrams: 7. 337; Idylls: 6. 290; 7. 632; 1: 7. 340, 342, 347, 432, 632; 1. 1 ff.: 7. 310; 1. 3-9: 7. 318; 1. 8: 7. 279; 1. 12-4: 7. 270, 310; 1. 21-3: 7. 310, 345; 1. 23 ff., 37-40, 149: 7. 406; 1. 31 ff.: 7. 350; 1. 35 ff.: 7. 342-3; 1. 52-3: 7. 423; 1. 66: 7. 496; 1. 80 ff.: 7. 499; 1. 100-36: 7. 442; 1. 115-8: 7. 425; 1. 123 ff.: 7. 249; 1. 127: 7. 413; 1. 148: 7. 317; 2: 3. 219, 221; 6. 277; 2. 12-3, 35-6: 1. 233; 2. 17: 2. 295; 3. 1 ff.: 7. 270; schol. 3. 48: 3. 255; 5: 7. 338-40; 5. 31 ff., 45 ff.: 7. 310; 5. 61 ff.: 7. 344; 6. 1 ff.: 7. 310; 6. 39: 3. 222; 6. 43, 129: 7. 406; 7: 7. 340; 7. 52-4: 7. 426; 7. 88 ff., 131 ff.: 7. 310; 7. 97: 7. 288; 7. 117: 4. 232; 8: 7. 340-1, 344; 8. 15-6: 7. 270; 8. 25 ff.: 7. 344; 8. 37: 7. 317; 8. 41 ff., 74 ff.: 7. 249; 8. 49: 6. 239; 9: 7. 338-9, 347; 9. 5: 7. 345, 347; 9. 22: 7. 347, 406; 11. 11 ff.: 7. 249; 13. 25-6: 7. 426; 13. 44: 1. 240; 13. 58-60: 3. 302; 15: 7. 584; 15. 61: 7. 251; 15.

113: 3. 253; 16: 7. 276, 372-3, 384, 391;
8. 297; 18: 8. 471, 652; 19: 2. 273;
8. 456-8; 20. 26-7: 8. 322; 20. 37-9: 8.
490; 27. 50: 2. 217

Theodontius, 7. 289

Theognis, 7. 307

Theology, 7. 560-1, 575, 579; 8. 329; Catholic: 1. 439; of *F. Q.* 1: 1. 439; reformed:
1. 439; Spenser's: 1. 439; 7. 291, 323,
539, 555

Theophilus of Antioch, 7. 559

Theophrastus, 1. 184; 2. 263

Theramenes, 2. 263

Thersites, 2. 226-7

Thersites, 7. 386

Theseus, 1. 236; 2. 269; 4. 223-4, 316; 5.
170; 6. 251

Thessaly, 7. 491

Thestylis, 7. 457, 507; 8. 569

Thetis, 2. 261, 266; 3. 239-43; 6. 253-4,
299; 8. 301, 381, 386, 401, 413, 652

Thetis (river), 4. 254

Thevet, André, 2. 354, 358; 4. 248

" thew," 7. 260

Thieves, 6. 256, 317, 334, 348, 371-7. *See
also* Vagabonds

" Things unattempted yet," 6. 185

Thirty-nine Articles, 5. 337-8

Thisbe, 4. 223

Thoe, 4. 273-5

Thomalin, 7. 267, 292, 323-5, 331, 334-5,
352, 603, 631

Thomas à Kempis, 7. 672

Thomas Aquinas, 1. 275, 282, 310, 448;
2. 294, 423-6; Spenser a better teacher
than: 2. 428; *Commentary on Aristotle's
De Coelo et Mundo*: 8. 493; *De Ordinatione Angelorum*: 7. 540; *Ennarationes* on
Aristotle's *Ethics*: 2. 424; *Summa contra
Gentiles*: 2. 424; 7. 539; *Summa Theologica*: 1. 354-5, 445-6; 2. 424, 426; 7.
554, 675

Thomas the Rhymer, 1. 200

Thomas, William, 7. 322

Thomists, 1. 448

Thompson, Francis (librarian), 8. 706

Thompson, Francis (poet), 1. 206; 7. 618-9

Thompson, Stith, 5. 236

Thompson, William, 8. 467, 474, 482, 485,
659

Thomson, James, 2. 383; 7. 520, 578; 8. 308,
380, 471, 489, 578

Thomson, W. G., 8. 498

Thopas, Sir, 2. 208; 3. 266; 6. 225-6

" thou " and " you," 5. 168

Thrace, 1. 250

Three Proper, and wittie Familiar Letters:

8. 509, 737. *See also*, Harvey, Gabriel;
Letters to Harvey from Spenser

Throckmorton, Elizabeth, 4. 205-7; 6. 205,
350, 363, 384; 7. 450-1, 457-8

Throckmorton, Francis, 5. 320, 324

Throckmorton Plot, 5. 245, 316, 320, 324

Thrones, 1. 310; 7. 553

Θυμός, 1. 446; 2. 198, 227, 230-1, 411, 427

Thyer, Robert, 6. 309; 7. 518, 558

Thyme, 8. 398

Thyrsis, 7. 342

Tiara, 1. 199, 200

Tiber, 8. 278, 284, 291, 384

Tibullus, Albius, Book 1: 2: 3. 213; 3: 1.
235; 3. 256, 239; 4. 222; 5. 160; 6. 280;
4: 7. 407; 5: 3. 241; 5. 252; 6. 299; 10: 2.
247; Book 2: 1: 1. 174; 2: 2. 376; 3:
1. 225; 6: 3. 279; Book 3: 3: 8. 311;
4: 1. 229; 8. 459, 477; 7: 4. 248; Book 4:
1: 3. 214; 2: 6. 193

Tide Tarrieth No Man, 2. 433

Tiepolo, Nicolo, 8. 479

Tiger, 2. 235; 5. 232; 6. 202, 255, 269,
381; 7. 343

Tigris, 4. 271

Tilley, M. P., 2 290-1, 299-300, 339, 387;
7. 382

Tillotson, Kathleen, 7. 473; 8. 287, 291,
399, 673

Tillyard, Eustace M. W., 8. 476, 647

Tilney, Edmund, 7. 467

Tilting, 5. 182-6, 302

Timaeus Locrus, 2. 479

" timber," 7. 423

Time, 1. 480-1; 2. 201, 203, 225-6; 3. 350;
4. 311; 6. 401, 414, 449; 7. 539; 8. 468,
480, 522

Timias, 2. 218, 341; 3. 319, 324-6, 389;
4. 205; 5. 275, 315; 6. 208, 229, 232,
324, 333, 349; and Belphoebe: 2. 218;
3. 312, 315, 319, 325-6, 389; 4. 284,
286; is not Essex: 6. 205-6; and Medoro:
3. 374-5; is Raleigh: 1. 340; 2. 345, 401;
3. 201, 246, 310, 377-9; 4. 205-7, 286;
6. 318, 345, 384; is not Raleigh: 6. 205-6;
and Serena: 6. 328

Timon, 1. 399

Timotheos, 7. 392

Tintoretto, 3. 395

Tipperary, 6. 283-4, 286-7

Tipra Sen-Garmna, 7. 455-6

Tisiphone, 7. 416; 8. 315-6

Titan, 1. 214; 6. 274, 279, 394, 410, 415,
437; 8. 384, 414

Titania, 1. 480

Tithonus, 1. 304

Titian, 2. 270-1, 379; 3. 392-3, 395

Titmouse, 7. 405
Titus, 4. 223-4
Tityrus, 4. 176; 7. 253, 260, 309, 315, 321, 351, 373, 385, 449, 452, 590, 592
Tityus, 1. 297; 8. 342
Tizona, 5. 192
T. M., 8. 575
" to-," 5. 224
Toad, 1. 412; 7. 423
Tobacco, 3. 246
Tolls, 5. 170-1
Tolman, A. H., 7. 608
Tom Piper, 7. 369, 386-7
Tooke, John Horne, 6. 215
Topas, Sir, Tale of (Elizabethan version of Chaucer's *Sir Thopas*), 1. 260
Topothesia, 7. 504
Topsell, Edward, 1. 402
Toscanella, Oratio, 1. 513; 3. 372, 374-5; 5. 348-9
Tottel, Richard, 1. 280, 417, 473; 4. 224, 328; 7. 242, 263, 302, 306, 316, 321, 358, 464, 622, 645; 8. 278, 370, 610
" Totus Mundus," 8. 315
Toulouse, Counts of, 1. 449, 455
Tournaments, 2. 190; 4. 302; 5. 182-6, 201, 302; 6. 263-4
Tove, 4. 257-8
Tower of Babel, 8. 305
Tower of Chastity, 1. 416
Tower of Chivalry, 1. 283, 407, 416; 4. 226
Tower of Doctrine, 1. 283, 415; 5. 239
Tower of Music, 1. 283
Tower of Tristram, 3. 372
Towers, 4. 253; 5. 224, 237
" town," 7. 250
Towry, M. H., 8. 512, 534
Towy, 3. 224-5
Traductio. *See* Polyptoton
Tragedy, 7. 383, 390; 8. 437; Greek: 1. 247; medieval: 4. 167; 7. 440; 8. 394
Trajan: 8. 306
Transformation, 1. 205; 5. 232, 236. *See also* Metamorphosis
Transitions, 1. 248; 2. 197, 339; 4. 188, 192, 196, 203, 239; 5. 163; 8. 304. *See also* Faerie Queene, transitions
Transitoriness. *See* Change, Mutability
Translation, 1. 489; 3. 252; 4. 234; 8. 546-7, 611-24. *See also* Spenser, Edmund, translator
Transmigration. *See* Metempsychosis
Transubstantiation, 7. 609
Trap-door, 5. 210-1, 313-4
Traveiler, The. See Turler
Travers, John, 7. 313
Treason, 4. 222

Tree of Hesperides, 2. 264
Tree of Knowledge, 1. 300-1, 368
Tree of Life, 1. 300-2, 368, 377, 404, 455; 8. 280
Trees, 1. 178-82, 202-4; 2. 264, 266; 7. 261-5; 8. 407-8; carving names on: 4. 209-10
Trembling light, 2. 353
Treneer, Anne, 2. 199, 234, 359, 368; 3. 240, 287
Trent (river), 4. 260, 271
Trent, W. P., 6. 434; 8. 661
Trevisa, John, 2. 458; 8. 437
Trevisan, 1. 277, 459
Trial, 5. 168, 185, 259, 263; 6. 292-3; lovers: 7. 480-1
The Trial of Treasure, 2. 433-4
Triamond, 1. 432; 3. 391; 4. 178, 186, 188, 282, 328
Triangle, 2. 473-84; 5. 215
Trinity, 1. 303; 7. 539, 559-64
Trinity College, Cambridge, 1. 386; 7. 646, 696, 708-9, 719; 8. 681, 697-8, 719
Triptolemus, 8. 339
Trismegistus, 2. 276
Trissino, Gian Giorgio, 1. 248, 332, 348-9, 513; 2. 192, 289, 435, 443-4; 4. 172
Tristram, 3. 236, 372; 6. 194-7, 317, 325-6, 328, 331, 333-4, 340, 342-3, 345, 367-71
Trisyllables, 8. 366, 371
Triton, 4. 242; 7. 461; 8. 402
Triumph, 3. 301, 354-5, 359, 398
Trochilus, 8. 406-7
Troilus, 4. 223; 6. 293; 7. 517
Trompart, 2. 183, 206-7, 216, 219, 234, 425; 3. 246, 314, 328; 5. 273, 278; is Simier: 2. 207, 219, 401-2; 5. 302
Trophies, 5. 226-7, 231; 6. 235
The Troublesome Raigne of King John: 2. 354
Trowis, 6. 426-7
Troy, 1. 490; 3. 283, 285
Troynovant, 3. 283; 4. 253
Trumpets, 1. 226; 5. 183
Truth, 1. 178, 208, 211, 234, 255, 305, 311, 323, 339, 401, 422-4, 433-4, 453, 456, 473-4, 480-2, 495, 501-2; 5. 257; 6. 199; and Beauty: 2. 272; 7. 677; daughter of Horomazes: 3. 244
Truthfulness, 1. 328-9, 342. *See also* Verity
Tryphon, 3. 243
Tuatha De Danaan, 1. 292; 3. 246, 278
Tudor and Stuart Club, 1. 516-8; 6. 458, 472; 7. 709; 8. 681, 697-8, 706-7
Tudors, 1. 266, 352, 450, 482-90, 493, 512; 2. 312, 323, 407, 453-5; 3. 311; 5. 310; 7. 282; 8. 565
Tuell, A. K., 3. 303-4; 8. 599, 602

"tumbling" verse, 7. 292, 635-6, 639
Tundale. *See Vision of Tundale*
Turberville, George, 7. 272, 464-5, 586, 592, 626; 8. 542, 546; *Eclogues of Mantuan*: 8. 600; *Geneura*: 2. 228; 3. 307; *Tragicall Histories*: 4. 197;
Turenne, Viscount, 5. 326
Turinus, 8. 591-2
Turks, 8. 364; are Sansfoy: 1. 449
Turler, Jerome, 7. 361, 612
"turn," 7. 552
Turner, Joseph M. W., 1. 306; 2. 216
Turner, William, 1. 218; 7. 305-6, 361, 443; 8. 398-9, 591-2
Turnus, 3. 268, 282, 336; 5. 222; 8. 395
Turpin, Archbishop, 1. 257; 3. 286; 5. 192
Turpine (in *F. Q.*), 5. 193, 278; 6. 191, 200-1, 203, 210, 215-6, 218, 324, 326, 328, 334, 340, 348
Turtle-dove, 8. 460
Tusser, Thomas, 7. 287, 581, 594, 636-7
Tuve, Rosemond, 1. 254, 290, 292-3; 4. 227; 6. 410; 7. 270, 273, 342-3, 513-4, 564
T. W., 5. 369
Tweed, 4. 261
Twining, Thomas, 2. 386
Twitchett, E. G., 8. 537, 540
"two-handed engine," 5. 210
Two Other . . . Letters (vol. 9, pp. 3-12), 8. 509, 736. *See also* Harvey, Gabriel; Letters to Harvey from Spenser
Twyne, Brian, 4. 259-60
Tybert, 8. 587
Tycho Brahe, 6. 423
Tydeus, 3. 276
Tympany, 1. 220
Tyndall, John, 5. 342-3
Tyne, 4. 261
Tynt, Robert, 8. 649, 651
Typhaon, 5. 250, 257; 6. 188, 213, 270, 341, 388
Typhoeus, 3. 266; 6. 277
Typhon, 3. 279; 5. 215-6; 6. 277, 280
Tyranny, 5. 290-1
Tyrone. *See* O'Neill, Hugh
Tyrwhitt, Thomas, 6. 225
Tzetzes, 4. 245; 6. 312

Ubaldo, 2. 364, 370
"Ubi sunt?" 8. 286-7
ὕβρις, 2. 414
Udall, Nicholas, 7. 379; 8. 471
Uhlemann, Dr., 7. 646
Ulfin, 3. 236
Ulpian, 5. 194
Ulster, 5. 331

Ulysses, 1. 341, 345; 2. 348, 351, 367, 381; 3. 286; 5. 189; 6. 199; 8. 346, 672
Umber, 7. 590
"un-, un-, un-," 4. 195; 6. 309; 7. 496
Una, 1. 178, 196, 199, 201, 206, 211, 234, 250, 254-5, 277, 280-1, 305, 311, 339, 358, 389-93, 397, 399, 406, 416, 419, 459-61; 2. 348, 427; 5. 222; 6. 205, 208, 296; 7. 367, 661; 8. 650; not alive: 1. 284; brave: 1. 497; bride of Man's spirit: 1. 424; character: 1. 444, 465, 496-500; 3. 383-4, 386, 389: 5. 209; compared with other heroines: 1. 284, 305, 496; daughter of classical and Christian philosophy: 1. 466; daughter of God and patriarchal Church: 1. 455; daughter of God and Sapientia: 1. 434; daughter of natural and revealed truth: 1. 466; daughter of Old and New Testament: 1. 457, 466; distinguished from Spenser's other women: 1. 502; is Elizabeth: 1. 465, 473; is the English Church: 1. 466; the false: 8. 364; and Florimell: 4. 288; is heavenly beauty: 1. 502-5; is human: 1. 339, 442-4, 496; maternal: 1. 444, 498; physical beauty not stressed: 1. 502; is Platonic wisdom and truth: 1. 446, 501-5; separation from Red Cross Knight is return to Popery under Mary Tudor: 1. 441, 453; and Song of Songs: 8. 519; is true Religion: 1. 440-1, 453, 456, 458; is Truth: 1. 422-4, 453, 456, 482, 501-5; is Truth gradually revealed: 1. 433-4; union with Red Cross Knight symbol of Reformation: 1. 441, 457; unveiling: 1. 503-4; is Wisdom: 1. 447, 501-5; 7. 665
Uncle Remus, 8. 405
Underdowne, Thomas, 6. 377, 379
"underfong," 7. 321
Understanding, 2. 297, 468, 481
Underworld, 2. 445; 8. 347
Undine, 4. 242
"ungirt, unblest," 4. 195
Unicorn, 1. 398; 2. 235-6, 361
Union of Brussels, 5. 253
University of Chicago Library, 1. 517
University of Washington Library, 1. 516-7; 2. 510; 3. 422; 5. 369; 6. 458
Upham, A. H., 2. 286, 291-3, 297-8, 444
Upton, John, 1. 491-2
Urania, 6. 291, 351; 7. 399, 453, 463, 474; 8. 284, 329-31, 532
Urbino, 7. 676
Urceo, Antonio, 7. 596
Ure (river), 4. 262
Uriel, 5. 175, 180
Usk, Thomas, 3. 219

Uther Pendragon, 1. 264-5; 2. 332, 334, 453; 3. 227-8, 236; 8. 288, 290
Utopia, 1. 344
Ut pictura poesis, 6. 379; 7. 255-6
Utrecht, 5. 319

Vada Boum, 4. 259-60
Vada Saxi, 4. 259-60
Vaenius, Otho, 1. 365; 2. 227
Vagabonds, 8. 354-6, 565, 591. *See also* Thieves
Vain Delight, 1. 406
Vain Glory, 1. 406
Valentine, 1. 293
Valentine, St., 6. 222-3
Valentinian, 2. 331
Valerian, 8. 399
Valerius Flaccus, *Argonautica*: 3. 336; 4. 169; Book 2: 1. 209; Book 3: 1. 193; 3. 302; 7. 266; Book 4: 8. 339; Book 6: 1. 253, 259; 3. 222; 5. 228; Book 7: 2. 274; Book 8: 1. 310; 3. 271; 8. 490
Valerius Maximus, 2. 263; 4. 225; 6. 267; 7. 336; 8. 348
Valla, Laurentius, 7. 237
Vallans, William, *Tale of Two Swans*: 8. 498-9, 502-3, 515, 667-72
Van Clichtove, Josse, 1. 355
Van der Noodt, Jan, 8. 611-3, 616, 619-27; *Theatre for Worldlings*: 2. 226; 6. 378; 7. 353, 416; 8. 273-80, 322, 379, 512, 595, 611-27. See *Epigrams; Sonets;* [*Visions from Revelation*]
Vane, Sir Henry, 7. 290
Vanity, 1. 406; 7. 417; 8. 304
van Kranendonk, A. G., 2. 190
Van Winkle, Cortlandt, 4. 229, 238; 6. 186, 191; 8. 424, 436, 438, 453, 459-94, 637, 652, 656, 673, 720-1
Varius, 1. 176
Varus, 7. 597
Vasari, Giorgio, 7. 238
Vates, 7. 387
Vaughan, William, 5. 327
Veil, 1. 503-4; 6. 294-6, 397-8, 403, 412, 415, 449
Velius, C. Urcinus, 8. 456
Venice, 8. 365
Vennard, Richard, 1. 390, 477-8
Venus, 1. 405-7; 2. 245, 266, 271, 285, 375, 383, 392-3; 3. 208-9, 252-3, 255, 260-1, 295, 342, 344, 346-7, 351-2, 377-9, 393-4, 397; 6. 251, 293; 7. 511, 595, 679; 8. 340, 456-8, 468, 488, 490, 604-7, 652, 667; abode of: 3. 290; 6. 248; and Adonis: 3. 255-6, 260-1; 6. 398; 7. 562; altar of: 4. 229-31; 7. 521; and Amoretta: 3. 377-8; Androgynus: 7. 480; is Beauty: 7. 560; and Belphoebe: 2. 211-2, 219-20; 3. 245-6; cestus of: 4. 193, 286; Concord, source of: 4. 310, 334; Earthly: 2. 431; 4. 318; 6. 411, 413; 7. 559; Evening Star: 6. 255, 310; 8. 481; is Form: 7. 513, 525; Heavenly: 4. 318-21; 6. 411; 7. 559, 563; is Intelligence: 7. 559; and Isis: 5. 213-4; laughter-loving: 4. 236-7; 8. 481-2; and Maia: 8. 483; and Mars: 3. 297; medieval: 7. 282; and Nature: 4. 310, 321, 333; 6. 398, 411-3, 449; and Peristera: 8. 396-7; picture of: 4. 194; 6. 248; 7. 567; power of: 4. 233; priestesses of: 4. 229; Procreatrix: 4. 216, 218, 236; 7. 513; is Sapience: 6. 411; sex double: 6. 412; 7. 480; statue of: 4. 229-32, 238, 310; and swans: 8. 498; temple of: 1. 416; 3. 254, 302, 304, 377, 384; 4. 217-22, 228-38, 287-8, 296, 308; 5. 213, 217-8, 270; 6. 419; veiled: 6. 294, 412, 449; and verdure: 6. 413; and the Virgin Mary: 7. 559. *See also* Aphrodite; Castle, Court, Garden, House, of Venus
Venus la Deesse d'Amor, 5. 242
Verdant, 2. 350, 403, 418, 431, 433
Veres, "the fighting," 8. 540
Verity, 1. 285. *See also* Truthfulness
Verity, A. W., 3. 259; 6. 309; 7. 380, 390, 491, 656; 8. 461
Vermeylen, August, 8. 611
Vernon, Elizabeth, 6. 206, 363
Veronese (Paolo Caliari), 1. 219; 3. 392-3, 395
Verse, 1. 189, 210; 5. 271, 275; 6. 210, 215, 255; blank: 8. 615-6, 618-9, 623. *See also* Metre; Old English Alliterative Verse; Spenserian Stanza; "tumbling" verse
Versor, John, 1. 355
Verstegan, Richard, 4. 180; 5. 321
Vertue, George, 8. 501
Verulam, 8. 284-94, 304, 512, 522-3, 525-6, 528-9
Vervain, 8. 399
Vesta, 5. 243; 6. 300-1
Vestment Controversy, 6. 386; 8. 359, 373
Vicar of Bray, 7. 294
Vicary, Thomas, 2. 469-70, 483
Vice, 1. 323, 513; 2. 365, 418; 4. 306-7
Vices, 1. 364; 2. 183, 230, 256, 284, 286, 338-41; 3. 382; Aristotelian: 1. 333
Vicissitude, 7. 412, 445; 8. 626. *See also* Change; Mutability
Victoria and Albert Museum, 7. 708; 8. 681
Vida, Marco, 1. 187, 350; 3. 250; 7. 240, 587, 596
View of the Present State of Ireland, 2. 186,

208, 229, 280-2; 4. 332; 5. 194, 199, 233, 236, 259, 263, 308-9, 315; 6. 363, 385; 8. 356, 589, 647; Essex in: 5. 332; prose counterpart of *F. Q.* 5: 5. 326; 6. 363; purpose: 5. 332; (the following numbers designate lines in the text as printed in *The Prose Works*, in vol. 9 of the *Variorum*): 8-16: 5. 196; 10-1: 1. 275; 422-5: 2. 285; 6. 285; 452: 7. 278; 538-9: 6. 201, 350; 1152 var.: 1. 482; 1205: 1. 225; 1212-4: 6. 352; 1247-8: 6. 285; 1413, 3642: 5. 161; 1535-1677: 2. 281-2; 1555-7: 5. 235; 1596-1606: 5. 234; 1684: 2. 398; 1687: 7. 475; 1689-91, 1721-2: 4. 174; 1762-80: 2. 281-2; 1804-7: 5. 225; 6. 192; 1937-42: 2. 398; 1997: 8. 463; 2006-9: 6. 204; 2166-9: 7. 392; 2178-82: 2. 208; 6. 225-6; 8. 608; 2216-8: 5. 264; 2268-82: 7. 380; 2688-95: 2. 343; 2865-84: 6. 435-6; 2931: 5. 178; 2944-6: 5. 332; 2956-81: 5. 265; 3061-6: 2. 2. 281; 3062: 1. 275, 493; 3091-3: 4. 267; 3145-50: 1. 275; 2. 284; 3257-64: 1. 261; 2. 285; 6. 291; 3302-92: 5. 265-6, 268; 3552: 8. 447; 3664: 4. 271; 3678: 6. 217; 5092-5: 8. 477; 5099: 7. 607; 5031-5, 5093-101: 6. 266; 5121-4: 6. 256

Vigent, 2. 323

Viglione, F., 8. 279, 321, 333, 391, 409-10, 424, 427, 430, 433, 528, 544, 579, 599, 605, 612, 642

Villiers, George, Duke of Buckingham, 8. 375

Vincent of Beauvais, 2. 364

Violence, 1. 249

Violets, 7. 506

Viper, 8. 421

Virago, 3. 338

Virelay, 7. 405, 442

Virgil, 1. 197, 296, 314-6, 323-4, 327, 362, 421, 514; 3. 250; 4. 235; 5. 181, 311; 6. 185; 7. 253, 268, 314, 373, 385, 415, 426, 428, 432, 448, 571-4, 576, 578-9, 582-8, 594, 620, 642, 679; 8. 564, 594, 637; additions to: 3. 238; Aldine edition: 8. 545; allegory in: 1. 312, 335, 340-1, 345, 357-9, 493, 511, 513; 2. 218, 251, 257; 3. 245-6; 6. 398; 7. 260, 264, 597; and Ariosto: 1. 333; Bembo's text: 8. 334, 545-6, 548-9; Dumaeus text: 7. 415, 426; 8. 312, 316, 334, 336-7, 342, 345, 347, 548-58; Morgan Collection, Princeton: 8. 548; Plantin edition: 8. 547-9; Scaliger's edition: 8. 545; Spenser, compared with: 1. 321, 337, 359; 2. 301; 3. 310; 5. 264, 315; 6. 314; 7. 309, 329, 572-3, 590-8;

8. 334-49, 517, 545-9; Spenser's conception of: 1. 421, 513; 2. 342; 5. 262; Spenser imitates: 7. 371; Spenser's use of Virgil's plot: 2. 202; is Tityrus: 7. 452; *Vita Gudiana*: 7. 242

Aeneid: 7. 622; historical: 1. 359; purpose: 1. 512; Renaissance interpretation: 1. 345, 511, 513; twelve books: 1. 360; Preface: 1. 173; 5. 235; Book 1: 7: 3. 281; 8-10: 1. 307, 510-11; 11: 8. 394; 30: 3. 282; 50-3: 1. 249; 52-9: 4. 215; 85: 4. 215; 148: 4. 174; 150: 6. 202; 159 ff.: 2. 366; 163-4: 2. 392; 167: 2. 194; 192-3: 8. 487; 203: 4. 216; 223-6: 8. 376; 228: 3. 262; 267-77: 3. 281; 282: 8. 391; 294-6: 2. 228; 297: 8. 376; 314-29: 2. 211-12, 217-20; 3. 245-6; 7. 287-8; 394: 2. 347; 403: 2. 214; 3. 253; 415-7: 4. 228-9; 430: 5. 199; 453 ff.: 3. 292; 483: 8. 345; 490: 5. 200; 491-9: 2. 218-9; 493: 2. 243; 535: 4. 244; 548: 6. 254; 592-3: 3. 303; 6. 251; 598: 3. 282; 600-5: 1. 259; 661: 2. 189; 724: 4. 194; 753-6: 2. 202; Book 2: 1-5: 2. 202; 3. 280; 8: 3. 283; 6. 237; 190: 5. 225; 215, 220: 1. 299; 250: 1. 229; 268-9: 8. 410; 296: 6. 301; 305, 496: 2. 342; 8. 384; 413 ff.: 4. 215; 431: 1. 256; 5. 259; 448, 504: 2. 298; 471-5: 4. 185; 496-9: 2. 342; 516: 3. 243; 6. 236; 536: 4. 277; 544-5: 3. 245; 547-8: 1. 227-8; 557-8: 4. 213; 571: 3. 285; 580: 2. 232; 626-31: 1. 259; 7. 265; 632: 4. 236; 644: 3. 242; 707 ff.: 7. 519; 774: 1. 204; Book 3: 19-68: 1. 202-4, 206; 27-42: 1. 203; 48: 1. 277; 57: 5. 262; 64: 2. 194; 72: 2. 339; 73, 77: 2. 357; 87: 3. 282; 192: 7. 460; 208: 2. 357; 245-6: 2. 258; 339: 1. 248; 395: 3. 227; 420: 2. 353; 8. 346; 423: 7. 331; 464: 1. 306; 489: 2. 372; 490: 7. 308; 520: 2. 252; 570-7: 1. 295, 304; 578-80: 3. 279; 594: 1. 279; 668: 2. 357; 687: 5. 262; 690: 3. 281; 705: 1. 252; Book 4: 6. 376, 378; 3: 1. 303; 6-7: 2. 280; 3. 283; 66-7: 3. 212; 68: 1. 201; 69-72: 4. 173; 79: 6. 240; 93-5: 2. 233; 114: 3. 215; 119: 1. 198; 135: 1. 177; 173: 7. 319; 8. 301; 182: 1. 222; 216: 1. 200; 238-46: 1. 223; 2. 370; 4. 186; 8. 376-7; 366: 4. 204; 5. 205-6; 401: 2. 372; 404: 8. 517; 424: 5. 206; 441 ff.: 4. 183; 450: 1. 278; 453: 2. 259; 462-3: 1. 278; 470: 6. 232; 481-2: 7. 303; 487: 7. 394; 511: 1. 230; 585: 8. 466; 620: 3. 282; 657: 4. 214; 660: 2. 191; 684: 2. 388; 688-92: 2. 191-2; 700-1: 8. 396; 705: 4. 184; Book 5: 15: 2. 357; 95: 2. 376; 8. 285, 389; 213:

3. 243; 6. 236; 252-7: 3. 294; 262: 2. 190; 294: 4. 181; 448-9: 1. 259; 457: 1. 227; 525-6, 575-6: 1. 209; 584: 1. 223; 721: 1. 229, 231; 810: 1. 228; 817-26: 3. 240; 4. 274; 837: 8. 487; 854: 1. 190, 223; 864: 2. 365; 869-71: 2. 195; Book 6: 24-6: 3. 220; 80: 7. 239; 95-6: 3. 227; 119-23: 8. 298-9; 126-31: 1. 233; 2. 258; 4. 196; 8. 376; 132, 297, 323: 2. 267; 134: 2. 237; 6. 269; 136 ff.: 2. 264; 138: 6. 293; 179: 1. 181; 190: 4. 210; 237-42: 1. 233; 2. 354; 5. 234; 247: 1. 195, 230, 234; 2. 232; 6. 275; 267: 1. 232; 268: 2. 256, 259; 273-81: 2. 251, 257, 259; 4. 167; 7. 416; 285-9: 2. 251; 295: 1. 234; 323-5: 2. 346; 3. 253; 393: 4. 224; 395: 6. 270; 404: 2. 232; 417-23: 1. 234-5; 425, 439: 8. 385; 426: 2. 267; 454: 2. 224; 469: 6. 208; 517-9: 3. 285; 535: 2. 270; 541: 2. 257; 551 ff.: 1. 234; 2. 232, 248; 576-7: 6. 270; 582-4: 8. 342, 384; 601 ff.: 1. 235; 6. 280; 603: 2. 202; 8. 492; 616-8: 1. 235; 2. 269; 625-7: 4. 240-1; 8. 314; 637-78: 8. 297; 638 ff., 747: 4. 222; 640: 2. 205; 648-9: 1. 234; 679-714: 1. 205; 3. 257; 694: 2. 195; 719-51: 1. 205; 729: 3. 241; 748: 3. 257; 752 ff.: 3. 281; 768: 2. 312; 771, 779, 791: 3. 230; 779-87: 4. 253; 784-7: 8. 382; 848: 3. 201; 853: 3. 203; 881: 2. 342; 893-8: 1. 193-4; Book 7: 9: 2. 353; 15: 2. 370; 19: 7. 426; 25-6: 1. 304; 59-62: 4. 238; 7. 264; 86-91: 5. 218, 220; 104: 7. 319; 8. 301; 136: 2. 376; 8. 285, 389; 281: 2. 342; 295: 5. 202; 318: 3. 282; 324-6: 7. 416; 346: 1. 221; 5. 267; 351: 3. 288; 440-1: 2. 210; 523: 2. 285; 641: 6. 292; 765 ff.: 1. 236, 237; 780: 1. 236; 785-8: 1. 251, 252; 2. 398; 800: 4. 181; 803: 3. 215; Book 8: 22: 2. 353; 116: 7. 285; 184: 2. 202; 193 ff.: 4. 203; 5. 234; 224: 2. 230; 265: 1. 306; 4. 208; 300: 6. 270; 369: 6. 235; 8. 484; 407 ff.: 6. 301; 415: 4. 197; 418: 2. 260; 445: 2. 261; 449-51: 2. 260; 454: 4. 193; 564: 4. 181; 571: 5. 250; 589-91: 8. 504-5; 596: 3. 268; 618-21: 6. 197; 622-3: 5. 241; 628: 3. 281; 630-4: 8. 412; 691: 2. 372; 702: 2. 232; 703: 3. 279; 6. 275; 767: 1. 236; Book 9: 5: 5. 190; 106: 6. 280; 300: 4. 200; 349: 2. 191; 3. 282; 359: 1. 251; 405: 6. 286; 441: 1. 259; 446-7: 3. 272; 481: 6. 199; 486-7: 3. 242; 525-9: 1. 510, 514-5; 565-6: 1. 241; 617: 2. 240; 627: 3. 239; 634-5: 2. 195; 669: 4. 185; 710-6: 1. 305; 6. 213, 277; 742: 5. 222; 792-6: 5. 228; Book 10: 134-5: 6. 251; 180-1:

5. 164; 199: 1. 204; 215-6: 6. 276; 272: 3. 206; 314: 1. 252; 495: 2. 236; 519: 1. 211; 521: 3. 204; 600: 1. 228; 637: 1. 196; 3. 268; 723-8: 6. 259; 736: 2. 236; 745: 6. 239; 764: 8. 413; 803: 4. 185; Book 11: 5: 5. 227; 54: 6. 199; 97: 3. 242; 139: 7. 319; 8. 301; 149: 6. 199; 182-3: 3. 272; 5. 200; 232: 2. 307; 333: 7. 285; 372: 1. 232; 418: 3. 245; 5. 265; 432-3, 498-501, 694-8: 3. 337; 610: 2. 341, 345; 624 ff.: 4. 185; 644: 1. 259; 648-63: 3. 331; 659: 4. 205; 669: 3. 245; 689: 5. 222; 690: 3. 238; 714: 1. 210; 721-4: 1. 277; 743: 3. 266; 748: 1. 200; Book 12: 64-9: 2. 214, 296; 5. 189; 87: 1. 252; 8. 395; 90-1: 2. 274; 94: 3. 204; 101: 6. 207; 260: 5. 218; 284: 2. 345; 309-10: 6. 239; 365-7: 5. 262; 397: 2. 189; 419-20: 3. 242, 247; 451 ff.: 4. 215; 466: 1. 228; 523: 2. 342; 646: 7. 445; 684-9: 1. 305; 715-9: 4. 189; 725-7: 5. 176; 801: 8. 371; 846: 8. 315; 856-8: 4. 173; 845: 2. 200; 879: 1. 233; 3. 241; 896-901: 2. 346; 919: 1. 200; 925: 2. 235; 932: 2. 277; 940-9: 1. 227; 946: 1. 210; 952: 3. 245; 8. 404

Ciris: 3. 219-21; 134: 1. 174; 208-12: 3. 213; 220-376: 3. 334-6; 223, 305: 3. 330; 229-30: 3. 212; 232-3: 3. 219; 344: 3. 221; 411-3: 8. 346; 535: 2. 205

Culex: 8. 312, 334-49, 603; text: 8. 545-58; 2: 8. 404; 8: 6. 291; 15: 8. 397; 27: 5. 220; 44: 5. 251; 95: 8. 312; 110-4: 5. 231; 117: 8. 312, 463; 123-45: 1. 181; 8. 311; 214-17: 8. 301; 218-40: 8. 315, 323, 544; 246: 2. 200; 260: 7. 416; 261: 8. 315-6; 268-96: 7. 381, 446; 328: 5. 212; 410: 8. 399

Eclogues: 6. 372; 7. 242, 266, 466, 572, 589, 591-2, 595-9, 631-2; 1: 7. 252, 312, 351; 1. 2: 7. 380; 1. 4-5: 8. 459; 1. 38-9: 7. 452; 1. 46-58: 7. 311, 315; 1. 54-6: 1. 192; 1. 74: 7. 321; 1. 76: 7. 331; 1. 79 ff.: 7. 365; 1. 83: 7. 251; 2: 7. 278, 572; 2. 5: 7. 249; 2. 33: 7. 299; 2. 40-67: 7. 250; 2. 41, 51: 7. 317, 322; 2. 56: 7. 252; 2. 63-6: 7. 250-1; 3: 7. 338-45, 347, 350, 572; 3. 3-6: 7. 249, 341, 350; 3. 21 ff.: 7. 278, 342; 3. 29-44: 7. 270, 341, 344; 3. 55, 58: 7. 345; 3. 70: 3. 263; 3. 92: 3. 292; 3. 108: 7. 347; 3. 109: 7. 350; 4: 5. 160; 7. 275, 543; 8. 352; 4. 1: 6. 291; 4. 6: 8. 350; 4. 20: 3. 258; 4. 21, 23: 6. 296; 4. 55-60: 7. 318-9; 8. 297; 5: 7. 338-9, 396, 398, 412, 433; 5. 3 ff.: 7. 310; 5. 10-1: 7. 404; 8. 336; 5. 12: 7. 270; 5. 19: 7. 345;

5. 20 ff., 34 ff., 60 ff.: 7. 249; 5. 24-5:
7. 411; 5. 34 ff.: 7. 410; 5. 45-7: 7. 317;
5. 56-7, 64: 7. 412; 5. 60-1: 7. 413; 5.
77: 8. 398; 5. 79: 3. 212; 5. 81: 7. 406;
6: 7. 255; 6. 15-7: 1. 218; 6. 35: 8.
413; 6. 44: 3. 302; 6. 67: 8. 297; 6. 86:
7. 251; 7. 2: 4. 181; 7: 7. 339; 7. 7:
6. 239; 7. 8: 7. 345; 7. 10-3: 7. 310;
7. 25: 7. 390; 7. 52 ff.: 7. 249; 7. 55-
9: 7. 452; 8: 7. 572; 8. 2 ff., 26, 52 ff.:
7. 249; 8. 10: 7. 394; 8. 12-6: 7. 310,
345, 390; 8. 32-3: 7. 250; 8. 55-6: 8.
434; 8. 64: 3. 221; 8. 69: 3. 226; 6.
277; 9. 32-4: 7. 421; 10: 7. 245, 278,
417; 10. 8: 7. 249; 8. 296; 10. 9-12:
7. 496; 8. 498; 10. 13 ff.: 7. 249; 10.
31-69: 7. 442; 10. 42-3: 7. 308; 10. 51:
5. 235; 7. 390; 10. 53: 7. 478; 10. 71-2:
7. 423; 10. 75: 7. 251

Georgics: Book 1: 20: 1. 242-3; 61-3:
5. 157; 215: 2. 275; 218: 8. 406; 221:
3. 213; 224: 2. 342; 278-83: 2. 304; 3.
266; 6. 277; 8. 384; 313-7: 8. 390; 378:
8. 487; 389: 6. 225; 418: 6. 253; 447:
8. 466; 449: 4. 185; 466: 1. 239; 514:
4. 183; Book 2: 42-4: 4. 241, 246;
8. 314; 105: 2. 199; 323 ff.: 4. 235-6;
336: 3. 258; 353: 1. 209; 403-4: 7. 263;
8. 397; 425: 7. 285; 448: 1. 181; 467-
73: 7. 598; 467: 1. 195; 475-502: 8.
331, 367; 490-2: 4. 238; 8. 315; 494:
1. 242; 7. 598; 538-9, 541-2: 4. 199; 5.
193; Book 3: 7. 393; 5: 2. 190; 8: 2. 347;
9: 8. 299; 13 ff.: 8. 427; 16: 4. 231; 34: 3.
201; 35: 2. 307; 84: 4. 204; 92: 3. 296;
219 ff.: 4. 190; 237-40: 8. 385; 242-3: 4.
236; 322-30: 7. 598; 416: 3. 292; Book 4:
7. 393; 30-3, 112: 8. 398; 80: 4. 185;
116: 6. 260; 179: 3. 201; 262: 1. 299;
312: 4. 185; 317: 3. 239; 8. 499; 321:
3. 271; 322: 1. 233; 333, 361: 3. 243;
336: 4. 274; 387: 1. 199; 3. 241; 7. 461;
394: 3. 270; 418: 3. 271; 440: 5. 236;
447: 3. 227; 453-527: 7. 446; 8. 344;
467: 2. 262, 355; 5. 234; 480: 8. 385;
511: 7. 349; 524: 1. 302; 537-53: 4. 181;
6. 212; 363: 3. 242
Virgil (pseudo), Ad Venerem: 3. 297-8;
Aetna: 8. 384; De Musarum Inventis: see
s. v.; Elegiae ad Maecenatum: 7. 426;
epigram: 7. 280, 426
Virgils Gnat, 1. 345; 5. 310; 7. 489, 611;
8. 333-49, 405, 459, 518, 582; composition: 8. 543-4; date: 8. 349, 543-4; metre:
8. 546-7; and Mother Hubberds Tale: 8.
543-4, 547; and Muiopotmos: 8. 599, 601;
publication: 8. 679; quality as translation:

8. 545-50; rhetoric: 8. 595; spelling: 8.
342, 345, 407; and Spenser's other poems:
7. 605; 8. 341, 396, 539, 543-4, 547;
style: 8. 543; and Teares of the Muses:
8. 539, 679; text criticism: 8. 343-4, 692,
713-4; variant readings: 8. 692; Dedication: 8. 539; Prefatory Sonnet: 8. 333,
393, 405, 416, 422, 459, 543, 575, 602,
643; 3: 8. 404; 21-4: 8. 313; 39-40: 5.
220; 41-2: 4. 168; 68: 5. 251; 8. 466; 88:
8. 465; 126-8: 5. 231; 136: 8. 371; 146: 8.
312; 170-6: 5. 231; 179: 8. 463; 197-200:
8. 311; 206-8: 333; 210, 397-400: 4. 169;
229-30: 8. 487; 259: 8. 549; 276: 6. 234;
283: 8. 598; 314: 2. 232; 337-42: 8. 301,
315; 345-52: 8. 544, 546; 369-70: 2.
190; 8. 323; 377-94: 2. 200; 8. 544; 397-
400: 5. 231; 421: 4. 222; 422-4: 8. 315;
423-5, 461-4: 6. 293-4; 433-80: 2. 373; 7.
381, 446; 441-5, 543: 1. 255; 442-3: 3.
302; 443: 2. 285; 449-80: 8. 546; 457-
60: 8. 489; 536: 5. 212; 665-80: 8. 398,
497; 681: 8. 399
Virgin Mary, 1. 251; 7. 558-60, 562, 568;
Byzantine: 7. 565; and Venus: 7. 559
Virginia, 2. 185, 343; 5. 248
Virgo, 5. 158; 6. 305; 8. 350
Virtue, 1. 182, 323, 416, 513; 2. 222-3, 419;
5. 349; 8. 347, 476; and Friendship: 4.
176; and glory: 8. 328. See also Castle
of Virtue
Virtues, 1. 326-30, 340, 513, 515; 3. 371;
Aristotelian: 1. 327-30, 333-4, 337-43,
345, 349, 353-7, 358, 361-2; 2. 183, 197,
256, 286, 338-41, 414-26; 3. 219, 382;
5. 180; angels: 1. 310; 7. 553; four cardi-
nal: 1. 329; 2. 479; heaven, derived from:
6. 185; "politic": 1. 343; Spenser's and
Aristotle's compared: 1. 342; 2. 414-26;
in Tasso: 1. 358; thirteen in Spenser?:
1. 342; why twelve: 1. 329, 342
Visio Pauli, 2. 448
Vision, 8. 304
Vision of Saturnus, 2. 448
Vision of Tundale, 1. 401-4
Vision poems, 7. 416; 8. 598, 611-27; authorship and composition: 8. 611-24; date: 8.
624; and Dreames: 8. 511-2, 613; and
Emblems: 8. 624-7; experiments: 8. 625;
and Muiopotmos: 8. 392-3; and Ruines of
Time: 8. 405, 409, 512, 622, 626; title: 8.
613, 622
Visions, 5. 218, 220; 8. 625
[Visions from Revelation], 8. 273, 279-80,
392, 595, 612-6, 621-2, 627; textual vari-
ants: 8. 678. See also Vision poems

Visions of Bellay, 7. 241, 614; 8. 273, 282; 8. 284-5, 409-14, 507, 509, 512, 611-27; and *Ruines of Rome*: 8. 378-9, 404-5, 529, 626; and *Teares of the Muses*: 8. 326; text: 8. 696-7, 717; and *Visions of the Worlds Vanitie*: 8. 404-5, 414; 1-6: 8. 619; 27-42: 8. 305; sonnets 6, 8, 13, 14: 8. 612-3, 615, 617, 619-20; 92: 8. 493; 116: 3. 297; 127-40: 8. 529; 155-68: 4. 201; 8. 305, 322-3, 415, 615; 169-96: 8. 305, 408; 200: 4. 167; 6. 281. *See also* Vision poems

Visions of Petrarch, 7. 241, 614; 8. 273, 414-6, 438, 507, 509, 512, 611-27; and *Muiopotmos*: 8. 392-3; and *Ruines of Rome*: 8. 378-9, 404-5, 529, 626; text: 8. 697, 718; and *Visions of the Worlds Vanitie*: 8. 404-5, 414; 15-28: 8. 408, 413; 43-56: 7. 279; 8. 413, 626; 85-98: 6. 439; 8. 392-3, 615, 620, 623, 626. *See also Vision* poems

Visions of the Worlds Vanitie, 7. 241; 8. 404-9, 509-12, 611, 620, 624-6, 643; composition: 8. 405-6; date: 8. 404-5; and *F. Q.*: 8. 625; and *Muiopotmos*: 8. 392-3; and *Ruines of Rome*: 8. 378, 404-5, 620; style: 8. 405; text: 8. 696, 717; and *Visions of Bellay* and *Visions of Petrarch*: 8. 404-5, 414; 1-4: 8. 495; 10: 8. 304; 13: 8. 392-3; 43-56: 8. 625; 71-4: 1. 297; 113-26: 8. 624-5. *See also Vision* poems

Vita Gudiana of Virgil: 7. 242
Vitruvius Pollio, 2. 297
Vives, Johannes Lodovicus, 1. 483; 2. 375; 3. 337
Vivian, Percival, 5. 327
Vocabulary, 2. 247; 6. 202, 433, 438, 445-7, 450-1; 7. 614-30; alterations: 7. 624; importations: 7. 238, 624, 628, 630, 647; innovations: 7. 624, 628-9. *See also* Coined Words; Compound Words: Diction; *Faerie Queene*, language; Spenser, language, style
Vocative, 7. 349
Volcano, 5. 220
Voluntas, 1. 446
von Snachenbergh. *See* Snachenbergh
von Wedel, Lupond, 5. 203
Voragine, Jacobus de, 1. 294, 379-80; 2. 448
Vortigern, 1. 265-6; 2. 332-4
Vortimere, 2. 333
Vortipore, 3. 230
Votive offerings, 3. 239
Voyage, 2. 348-51, 446-9; 5. 334
Voyage of Bran, 2. 381, 448
Vulcan, 2. 392-3; 3. 397; 4. 193; 6. 300-1; 8. 411

Wace, 2. 452
Wagner, G., 7. 297
Wagner, Richard, 1. 244; 3. 332
Wagner Book (English), 3. 360, 364
Waibel, Karl, 2. 262, 289, 345; 3. 212, 215, 277-8, 302; 5. 264, 266
Wake, 1. 209
Waldenses, 1. 455
Waldron, F. G., 6. 203; 8. 505, 507-9, 708-10, 736-7
Wales, 1. 489-90; 2. 309, 317-8, 323, 331; 3. 215, 217, 224-6, 236; 7. 354, 439-40; is Fairy Land: 2. 454-5
Walewein, 1. 391
Waley, John, 1. 417
"walk," 8. 489
Walker, George, 8. 418
Walker, J. C., 4. 174; 8. 451, 632
Wall, 3. 342, 345
Wallace, M. W., 6. 354, 356; 7. 492
Waller, Edmund, 2. 390; 8. 331, 397, 429
Wallop, Henry, 7. 475
Walpole, Henry, 7. 675
Walpole, Horace, 7. 472
Walrus, 2. 359, 362, 364
Walsingham, Frances, 6. 350-2, 355, 362; 7. 476, 485, 490, 492-5, 497; 8. 307, 309, 665
Walsingham, Sir Francis, 5. 302, 307, 335; 6. 272, 356; 7. 474; 8. 524-7, 571, 574, 580, 607; is Meliboe: 6. 349-52, 355, 362-3; 7. 472; 8. 302-3, 521
Wandering Islands, 2. 349, 354, 421-2
Wantonness, 1. 406
War, 2. 195; 8. 438, 640
Ward, B. M., 8. 319
Ware, Sir James, 2. 280; 6. 477-8; 8. 270, 431, 510, 710, 737
"Warmonger," 3. 285
Warner, George F., 8. 420
Warner, William, 1. 215-6, 488; 2. 302, 315, 452; 3. 288; 7. 306-7, 464, 481; 8. 530, 536
Warren, Austin, 8. 497
Wars of Alexander, 5. 196
Warton, Joseph, 7. 377, 470
Warton, Thomas, 1. 200, 270, 491; 6. 359; 7. 469, 615; 8. 505, 508, 519
Warwick, Countess of. *See* Russell, Anne
Warwick, Earl of. *See* Dudley, Ambrose
Warwick family, 7. 392
Warwickshire, 7. 312
Washing, 1. 308
Wasp, 8. 408
Wasserman, 2. 362
"watch and ward," 7. 364
Watches, 3. 303

Water, 1. 207, 302-3; 2. 231, 234, 382-3; 3. 243, 251; 4. 239, 242, 276; 6. 231, 247; 8. 311, 415; tumbling: 6. 246
Waterfall, 7. 275, 279-80
Waterhouse, Edward, 5. 318; 6. 442
Waterhouse, George, 8. 418
Watkins, Walter B. C., 8. 508
Watson, Thomas (bishop), 7. 261-2, 362-3, 612
Watson, Thomas (poet), 3. 260; 6. 238, 349; 7. 396, 464, 468-9, 472, 594; 8. 284, 380, 536, 540; Hecatompathia: 8. 430, 456, 458; Meliboeus: 8. 302, 486, 521-2
Watts, Susan, 7. 404
Watts, Thomas, 7. 362, 404
Waves, 2. 231-2; 3. 240
"Way," 4. 175
Way, Albert, 5. 182; 8. 359
Way, G. L., 4. 351
Wayland, John. 1. 417
W. C., 5. 328; 6. 360
The Weald, 7. 329
Wealth. See Gain, Riches
Webb, George, 8. 418
Webbe, William, 1. 513; 4. 216; 7. 276, 280, 283-4, 323, 347, 377, 387, 391, 415, 419, 600, 608, 635, 642-4; 8. 320-1, 510
Webster, John, 8. 497
Wedding, 6. 431; 8. 401, 458-95. See also Marriage
Weever, John, 8. 581-3
Weitzmann, F. W., 7. 484
Well, 2. 196-7; of life: 1. 300-3, 376-7, 403-4, 417, 455
Welland, 4. 259
Wellesley College Library, 7. 708; 8. 681
Wells, Gabriel, 7. 463, 708; 8. 681
Wells, H. W., 2. 244, 259; 7. 259; 8. 499
Wells, Whitney, 1. 401-4
Wellwood, James, 7. 537
Welply, W. H., 7. 235, 313-4, 362, 439, 458, 650, 654; 8. 310, 417, 447, 472, 506, 649, 651, 665
"Welsh words," 1. 517-8, 521; 2. 312, 501, 512; 3. 233
Westmer, 2. 326
Westminster Abbey, 1. 291
Westminster Hall, 5. 239
Westminster Palace, 8. 374
Westminster Review, 8. 501, 615
Westmoreland, Earl of. See Neville, Charles
Wever (river), 4. 240
Weymouth, George, 8. 418
Whale, 2. 359-60; 8. 407
Wharfe, 4. 262
"What for a . . . ?" 7. 278
Wheel, 3. 257; 5. 252; 6. 437, 440

"Where," 3. 240
Whetstone, George, 5. 324; 7. 496, 589, 642-3; 8. 417-8; Account of the Funeral of Sir Philip Sidney: 8. 309; Censure of a Loyal Subject: 5. 323; English Mirror: 1. 474; Promos and Cassandra: 1. 196, 312; A Whip for an Ape: 8. 371
Whipple, E. P., 1. 238
Whirlpool, 2. 359-60
White, Hugh G. E., 8. 541
White, W. A., 8. 697, 699, 706
White lion, 7. 432, 434
White raiment, 1. 285, 308
Whitehall, 5. 238
Whitgift, John, 5. 337-9; 7. 254, 295, 303, 607; 8. 357, 359, 373; is Palmer: 1. 492; 2. 188, 294, 401
Whitman, C. H., 1. 256
Whitman, Walt, 5. 344; 7. 597
Whitney, Geoffrey, 2. 226; 7. 301; 8. 375, 418
Whitney, Geoffrey, Jr., 8. 418
Whitney, J. E., 1. 425-31, 455-8
Whitney, Lois, 2. 185, 344, 356-8, 373-4, 381, 383, 385, 392, 447-9; 4. 203, 248; 6. 226
Whitsunday, 8. 633
The Whole Booke of Psalmes, 8. 477
Wierus, Johann, 1. 205, 294
Wigginton, Giles, 8. 418
Wilcox, Thomas, 6. 387; 7. 295, 324-5, 602, 607; 8. 357-60, 591
Wilde, J. F., 8. 465
Wilkes, Frances, 6. 221; 7. 654; 8. 651
Wilkins, George, 8. 418
Wilkinson, T. T., 7. 269, 297, 306, 313-4, 616
Will, 1. 446-8; 2. 468, 481
William III, 1. 493
William IX, of Poitou, 4. 201
William de la Braunch, Sir, 1. 391, 394
William of Malmesbury, 1. 206; 2. 260, 333
William of Newburgh, 1. 483, 487
William of Orange, 1. 459; 3. 380; 5. 250-1, 253, 318
William of Palerne, 1. 226
Williams, Richard, 5. 327
Williams, Roger, 5. 326
Williamson, G., 6. 423-4
Willimat, W., 1. 275
Willobie his Avisa, 6. 206-7
Willy(e), 7. 267, 338-40, 344-5, 347, 464, 479, 589, 631; 8. 317-21, 533-5, 539, 713
Wilmerding, Lucius, 2. 510; 7. 709; 8. 681, 706
Wilson, E. C., 7. 277, 282
Wilson, George, 8. 418

Wilson, J. Dover, 2. 371, 387

Wilson, John, 1. 244, 260-1, 279-81, 369-74, 496; 7. 290; 8. 599

Wilson, Thomas, 7. 621-2, 626; 8. 319-20; *Art of Rhetorique*: 1. 340, 485; 2. 295; 7. 239, 625; *Rule of Reason*: 2. 408

Wilson, Thomas (actor), 8. 319-20

Wilton, 4. 256; 5. 200

Wily Beguiled, 7. 336

Winbolt, S. E., 7. 483, 656; 8. 661

Winchester Palace, 8. 374

Wind, 3. 277; 4. 215

Windet, John, 8. 507, 736

Window, 4. 209; 5. 205; 8. 352

Windsor, 8. 671

Windsor Castle, 1. 291; 2. 335; 5. 237; 8. 374

Windsor, Lord, 5. 302

Wine, 7. 389-90

Wings, 7. 372, 564; 8. 300-1, 310, 356, 640

Winifred, St., 2. 196

Winstanley, William, 7. 464; 8. 501

Winter, 6. 420; 7. 256

Winter, William, 2. 350; 8. 540

Winwood, Ralph, 5. 171

Wisdom, 1. 416; 2. 279-80, 414, 439; 6. 241; 7. 553; 8. 450; Divine or heavenly: 1. 447, 501-5, 514; 6. 241; 7. 555, 673, 676; literature: 7. 557. *See also* Sapience; Sapientia

Wise, T. J., 6. 434; 7. 708

Wiseman, William, 4. 270

"wished day," 8. 462

Wit and Science, The Play of, 2. 433

Witch, 3. 262-3, 311, 313; her son: 3. 262-3, 327-8, 374, 379; 6. 244

Witches, 1. 204; 3. 262, 268; 8. 486

Wither, George, 7. 594; 8. 659; *Abuses Stript and Whipt*: 1. 272, 276; *Epithalamion*: 8. 466, 468-9, 474, 476, 480; *Mistresse of Philarete*: 6. 290

Wittiness, 1. 342

W. L., 1. 173; 2. 398; 7. 487, 489. *See also* Lisle, William

Wolf, 1. 412; 7. 261-2, 271, 278, 302-4, 350-2, 361-4, 420, 603-4; 8. 351, 375, 562, 592

Wolfe, John, 1. 522, 525, 536; 6. 480

Wolfram von Eschenbach, 6. 369

Wolsey, Thomas, 1. 468, 486, 488; 8. 375, 591

Wolves, 8. 465

Womanhood, 3. 381-91; 4. 237, 276, 287-8

Women, 1. 206, 213, 215; 3. 273, 317-8, 322-9; 5. 274, 304-5; 6. 229; censure of: 3. 267, 273; 6. 270; education of: 3. 337-8; militant: 3. 215, 330-9; 5. 349; place in society: 5. 197-8, 204, 278-9, 297; praise of: 3. 237-8; Spenser's idea of: 1. 499; 3. 216, 310-29, 381-91; 4. 195; 5. 223; 6. 305, 313

Wonders. *See* Seven Wonders

"wont," 7. 341

"wood," 7. 346

Woodberry, G. E., 3. 386-7

Woodcocke, Thomas, 5. 248

Woodcuts, 1. 287, 390

Woode, Anthony à, 1. 417; 4. 259; 6. 267-8, 359; 7. 469-70

Woodes, Nathaniel, 1. 276

Wood-gods, 6. 291

Woodhouse, Peter, 7. 262

Woods. *See* Forest

Woodstock, 6. 298

Worcester, Edward, Earl of. *See* Somerset

Worcester House. *See* Somerset House

Word-coinage. *See* Coined Words

Word-order, 5. 371; 6. 199; 8. 460-1

Words vs. deeds, 4. 188; 6. 229

Wordsworth, William, 1. 281; 2. 389; 4. 287; 7. 282, 417, 489, 615; 8. 489, 674; *The Beggars*: 8. 400; *Ecclesiastical Sonnets*: 1. 497; on *Epithalamion*: 8. 654; *Excursion*: 8. 659; *Lyrical Ballads*: 7. 578; *Miscellaneous Sonnets*: 1. 33: 7. 461; 2. 1: 8. 630; 2. 27: 8. 325; 2. 36: 8. 288; *National Independence and Liberty*: 8. 506; *Ode on Intimations of Immortality*: 8. 659, 677; *Ode to Duty*: 5. 155; *Personal Talk*: 1. 206, 496; *Prelude*: 1. 361; 8. 400, 467; *The Oak and the Briar*: 7. 262; *Recluse*: 8. 659; *River Duddon*: 8. 597

World, 1. 416; 8. 338; decay of: *see* Degeneration; three worlds: 7. 552

Wormius, Olaus, 2. 360-3

Worrall, Walter, 8. 371

Worsthorn Hall, 7. 382, 631

Worthington, John, 7. 313

Wotton, Henry, 2. 188; 6. 290, 351, 358-9, 361-2

Wounds, 5. 189

Wrath, 1. 406, 408, 410-3; 2. 227, 229. *See also* Anger

Wreck, 5. 195

Wrenn Library, 1. 517, 519; 7. 706, 708; 8. 682, 697-8, 706-7

Wrenock, 7. 417, 421

Wrestling, 6. 331-2

Wright, Edward, 2. 252

Wright, Thomas, 2. 464, 469

Wringing of hands, 6. 205

Wriothesley, Henry, Earl of Southampton, 6. 206-7, 363; 7. 367

Wyatt, Sir Thomas, 1. 463-4; 6. 234; 7. 319, 398, 447, 583, 626, 636-7, 640; 8. 369, 423, 445, 562, 637; *Penitential Psalms*: 8. 520; *Satires*: 7. 319; 8. 351, 369, 572; *The Recured Lover*: 7. 636
Wycliffe, John, 1. 216; 5. 174; 6. 265
Wycombe, 4. 254
Wyld, H. C., 7. 626-7; 8. 331
Wylye (river), 4. 256, 271
Wyndham, George, 7. 663
Wynkyn de Worde, 1. 417
Wynne, W., 2. 323; 3. 226, 235. *See also* Llwyd, Humphrey

Xanthus, 2. 342; 3. 281
Xenophon, 1. 214; *Anabasis*: 1. 303; 5. 230; *Cyropaedia*: 1. 313, 346; 5. 230; 8. 367; *Hellenica*: 2. 263; *Memorabilia*: 2. 223, 263, 288; 3. 207; 4. 164; 5. 189; *Symposium*: 7. 252
Xerxes, 1. 214; 8. 335

" y-," 2. 237; 5. 196; 7. 629-30
Yale University Library, 8. 682. *See also* Elizabethan Club
Yardley, E., 3. 295
Yare, 4. 257
Yates, Frances A., 6. 220
Yeats, William B., 5. 315; 7. 557
Yellow, 1. 287
Yet a Course at the Romyshe Foxe. See Turner, William
Yew, 1. 181
Ymner, 2. 320
Yorkshire, 7. 620
Yorkshire Glossary, 7. 305
" you, ye," 5. 194
Youghal, 6. 425; 7. 451, 459: 8. 448, 463, 648-52

Young, Bartholomew, Translation of Boccaccio's *Amorous Fiammetta*: 2. 297; 3. 270; 4. 214; 7. 318; Translation of Montemayor's *Diana*: 8. 485, 492, 494, 652-3
Young, John, 7. 243, 261-2, 278, 296, 310, 328, 330, 336, 354, 361-3, 370, 404, 582, 586, 607-8, 610, 612-3; 8. 418, 568, 576-7. *See also* Roffy
Youth, 1. 176, 415-6; 7. 255-9, 593-4; 8. 599-600
Yseut, 4. 223
Yvor, King, 1. 398

Zambardo, 5. 236
Zander, Friedrich, 5. 213
Zeal, 1. 406, 424; 5. 245
Zedler, Heinrich, 1. 238
Zeebrugge, 8. 537, 540
Zeeland, 5. 249
Zeno, 1. 288
Zenobia, 3. 338
Zenobius, 5. 166
Zephyrus, 8. 495, 675
Zerbino, 4. 188-9
Zeugma, 8. 676
Zeus, 2. 267; 8. 305, 311, 667. *See also* Jove
Zeuxis, 3. 201, 309; 4. 194; 6. 379
Z. I., 8. 507, 708, 736
Ziffius, 2. 362-4
Ziliante, 1. 204
Zodiac, 5. 157-8, 165; 6. 303-8
Zohar, 7. 562, 565-8
Zoroaster, 3. 244; 7. 562-3
Zouch, Thomas, 6. 354; 8. 307
Zouche, Captain John, 5. 173
Zurich Letters, 1. 472-3
Zwingli, Ulrich, 1. 275

DATE DUE

GAYLORD			PRINTED IN U.S.A.